A HISTORY OF THE BORGIAS

A History of

THE BORGIAS

By

FREDERICK BARON CORVO

Introduction by

SHANE LESLIE

GREENWOOD PRESS, PUBLISHERS
WESTPORT, CONNECTICUT

Library of Congress Cataloging in Publication Data

Rolfe, Frederick William, 1860-1913.
  A history of the Borgias.

  First published in 1901 under title: Chronicles
of the House of Borgia.
  Reprint of the 1931 ed. published by Carlton
House, New York.
  1. Francisco de Borja, Saint, 1510-1572.
2. Borgia family. 3. Italy--History--1492-1559.
I. Title.
DG463.8.B7R7 1975   945'.06'0924   75-16857
ISBN 0-8371-8274-3

Originally published in 1931 by Carlton House, New York

Reprinted in 1975 by Greenwood Press,
a division of Williamhouse-Regency Inc.

Library of Congress Catalog Card Number 75-16857

ISBN 0-8371-8274-3

Printed in the United States of America

INTRODUCTION[1]

A BIBLIOGRAPHICAL note has long been due to the rather mysterious and elusive writer who may possibly be known among immortals as "Baron Corvo" as he was to mortals by the equally uncertain "Fr. Rolfe." The prefix stood for Frederick not Father Rolfe, as unwary booksellers have supposed. Rolfe was never more than a tonsured Divinity student or a "spoilt priest" at most. His *floruit* can be placed between the Victorian and Georgian eras, which may account for the complete disregard and disdain he has received from critics. Likewise he fell between the Catholic and anti-Catholic stools and, as none would own and few befriend him in life, death brought oblivion to his works and pseudonyms. He was a master of the ungentle art of raising enemies, none of whom proved more relentless than himself.

Frederick William Serafino Austin Lewis Mary Rolfe (according to the British Museum catalogue) was born in London on July 22, 1860, and died in Venice on October 23, 1913. He became a rather inspiring if eccentric teacher at such schools as the Stationers', Saffron Walden Grammar, and Grantham Grammar, where he came under the friendly influence of Dr. Hardy, later the Vice-Principal of Jesus College, Oxford.—Dr. Hardy appreciated him as a teacher, though on one occasion it was found necessary to collect and destroy a serious reproach which Rolfe dictated to the boys concerning the morals of Martin Luther. Dr. Hardy appeared in *Hadrian VII* as "Dr.

[1] This introduction is reprinted from "In His Own Image," by Frederick Baron Corvo, by and with permission of and special arrangement with Alfred A. Knopf, Inc., authorized publishers.

Strong," a dark, gaunt Titan, and reminded one of the few for whom Rolfe ever found kindness in his heart. From September, 1905, to January, 1907, Rolfe acted as secretary to Dr. Hardy, who has set down his recollection of the friendship which proved Rolfe's only anchor in life:

"I probably know as much as anyone of his career from the time when he became one of my masters at Grantham in 1884 till 1907. I neither saw nor heard anything of him after the beginning of 1907. I much regretted this, as I liked and appreciated his very attractive personality. But his literary work did not appeal to me and I never took it very seriously. It is only fair to say that in spite of his little foibles I always found Rolfe a good and loyal friend, and he was distinctly *persona grata* in my family. I sometimes worked him pretty hard. In the two years when I was Greats examiner he read papers to me for six or seven hours a day for more than two months on end. In the newspaper paragraph, which announced his death, there was a list of his books, and I was amused to see in it *Studies in Roman History* by myself, of which he had helped me to correct the proofs."

When Rolfe was starving, Dr. Hardy invited him to Oxford, where he arrived on foot from Wales with his entire possessions on his shoulders. Rolfe was housed bodily at Jesus and mentally in the Bodleian, where he collected materials for his curious books. With Dr. Hardy's help he wrote a long Ciceronian indictment of the contemporary English Catholics, which was forwarded to Pope Leo XIII and awaits the future historian under the Vatican archives. For fifteen months Dr. Hardy kept and fed him, but Rolfe with the gratitude of Genius insisted on referring to his stay as "those wasted fifteen months!"

In 1886, in a spirit of mingled devotion and revolt, Rolfe had made his peace with the Holy See and left Grantham. He hungered for a time on London and, after joining the staff of a Catholic school founded by the Marquis of Bute at Oban, prevailed on the Bishop of Shrewsbury to send him to study for the awesome office of priesthood at Oscott College, where he entered on October 29, 1887, having on September 10 indited the Latin and English of a hymn to St. William, the boy martyr of Norwich, to whom he felt a deep devotion enough to cover any false quantity.

> Tall pines stand black against the midnight sky.
> The silver moon reigns on her sapphire throne.
> Nailed to his cross the fair boy hangs alone.
> The distant city slumbers silently.
> Magnificat he sang at Evensong,
> And then when music hushed and lamps were low,
> He wandered towards his home, with footsteps slow,
> All in the moonlight sweet, nor dreamed of wrong.
>
> From a dark entry sprang a Jewish horde,
> And, stripped and bound, they bore him to the wood,
> Nailed to a cross his white limbs stained with blood,
> As in the ages dim they nailed his Lord.
> And, while the angels watch his agony,
> To God's sweet Mother breathes his last faint sigh.

SANCTE WILLIELME NORVICIENSIS ORA PRO ME

> Ecce puer gracilis silva jacet ille remota,
>   Purpureus splendor pascitur ore super,
> Occisum iuvenem fulgor cœlestis inaurat,
>   Spissa alibi lucis occubat umbra suis.
>
> Vespere in æde sacra cantus produxerat ; inde
>   Lampades exciderunt, excidit inde melos,
> Tamque vias repetens tardo pede lustrat opacas
>   Inscius à fraudis tectaque solus adit.
>
> Exsilit e latebris Iudaica turba latronum ;
>   Trux illis voltus, mitis at ore puer,
> Qualiter et Dominum vulgus mactaverat olim
>   Huic dabat affingi candida membra cruci :
> At dulcis Genetrix Domini dat robora vires
>   Quo magis æternum mox diadema ferat.

Otherwise there is slight survival of his verse. At Oscott it was written of him that

"He was not of the disposition to be moulded into a serious student of orthodox theology. His abilities were beyond the ordinary, being a good Classical scholar as well as having gifts for painting and

poetry. He received the Tonsure and was delighted at the thought
of being *inter cleros*. In spite of his criticism of those in authority he
clung to the Church and was a devout client of Our Lady. Had he
met with friends such as Francis Thompson met with he might
have attained a wider recognition of his abilities. Unlike the gentle
Thompson his independent character and his pride of birth turned
his would-be friends, amongst whom he counted Bishops and some
notable Catholic laity, against him."

He remained a year at Oscott, where he caused theological *admiratio* by painting a Translation scene of the
body of St. William of Norwich, in which 149 reproduc-
tions of himself in varied vestments performed the ceremony of bearing a *corpo santo* whose only discernible
feature bore a similar resemblance! From Oscott the kind-
hearted Archbishop Smith of Edinburgh sent him to the
Scots College in Rome, where the registers carry the fleet-
ing impress of his name. His amiable eccentricities amused
the College, where he was allowed the privilege of the
black soutane instead of the purple thistle dress of the
raw Scotch Seminarian. He seems to have devoted his
afternoons to fashionable calls in the Apostolic City. Aristocratic converts affect poverty, plebeian proselytes the reverse, and Rolfe endeavoured to signalise aristocratic
blood by developing gout with sundry references to "that
beast of a grandfather!" He became a vegetarian on the
mistaken theory that the College was fed on horse meat.
His unique collection of Anglican stories with Rabe-
laisian endings had a certain vogue, but he tended to be a
nuisance. He astonished the Scots and was reported for
saying that he was like Newman in that he had nothing to
learn when he entered the Catholic Church! He was expelled suddenly and without explanation and his life as an
æsthetic tramp began.

He had to live entirely on his wits and the means of
others, which he always thought right to divert to an
artist's needs. He was fain to take the Duchess Cesarini-
Sforza as his "adopted grandmother," who supported him

awhile and became involved in litigation when her allowance failed. Having failed to become a *sacerdos in æternum* Rolfe took to himself the less exalted style of a temporal Baron and settled at Christchurch in Hants, chiefly at the expense of the Gleeson Whites, who received him as the grandson of a Duchess. He painted the wall painting in the local Catholic Church. Subsequently he indulged alternately in expenditure or asceticism, starved or took tutorships of short duration. After dismissal from the Seaton family it is recorded that he found his way into the Seaton grounds and came to the entrance gate, where the old lady in charge remarked that she might as well let him out though she had strict orders not to let him in! His polished manners stood him in good stead, for in all the superficial he excelled. He affected the triolet, played at photography and at the piano. He was a liturgist to the finger-tips rather than a Christian at heart, which seemed at times to be that of one possessed. He appealed to the Bishop of Aberdeen to finance a scheme for deep-sea photography, apparently with moneys left for the relief of the Catholic poor, and received the humorous answer that "no such sums have been left lately, so that you must have been misinformed. May Our Lord help you out of all your difficulties for I have no faith in submarine photography."

The same appeal fell equally vain on Mr. Astor and Lord Charles Beresford, who accorded him an interview at Chatham, but failed to make the arrangements Rolfe required in order to photograph the hulk of H.M.S. Victoria at the bottom of the Mediterranean!

He was very anxious to offer Queen Victoria a photograph of the Nativity which he had taken from living models by magnesium light. Accordingly Baron Corvo presented his compliments to Sir Henry Ponsonby and "would be very grateful for directions as to the necessary form to be observed on this occasion." The servants' hall at Balmoral would probably be searched in vain for this work of art. At the same time he painted some Saints in the mediæval style, which he offered to the Aberdeen Municipality in quaint terms: "I venture, my Lord Provost, to suggest their appropriateness as a gift in connection with the Royal Wedding, especially as they are the work of an artist who has settled in Aberdeen because of its exquisite suitability for his work." In the end the only work he was able to obtain among the Scots was at a photographic works for 12s. 6d. a week, which reduced him to making application to be certified insane in order that he might enjoy free lodging at least in the Asylum at the cost of the community! He never lost his underlying belief that the Artist should be supported by the unartistic. At another time he was retained to write on the uncongenial subject of South African Irrigation which led to the usual lawsuit. At another he was appealing to the Duke of Norfolk in terms of detailed expostulation: "I cannot think, my Lord Duke, that you have felt the reality of my condition, but when I tell you that I have eaten nothing but four biscuits since Friday last (Sunday 4 a. m.) and that I have no chance of getting any food, it may give you some idea of what I suffer."

For a time he was rescued by the Labour Leader, H. H. Champion, whose secretary he became, and which accounts for his ferocious presentment of Socialism and Socialists in *Hadrian VII*. Then he sank, sank. . . . Debt and difficulty closed and clogged the scholar's path. He changed publishers and pseudonyms. He felt thwarted and pursued. He disguised himself with wig and paint, and walked only at night. How deeply he was reduced appears from a fantastic adventure, which he was fain to publish in the Wide World Magazine for November, 1898, which was then introducing another minor writer of fiction to the British public in M. de Rougemont (R. I. P.). Rolfe's tale was entitled "How I was buried alive by Baron Corvo," and was illustrated with his photograph and "drawings done under his own supervision." He described his own burial in a state of coma after a fit of faintness caused by a lizard slipping up his sleeve. He woke in a sepulchral *loculus,* and not only overheard the Capucins conduct his Requiem, but even his patron, the Duchess, assert that it was a case of murder, since he had been turned out of the Seminary, and all because he would not take the Rector's hints to give him his dressing-bag, the gift of the Duchess to himself! Fortunately, he was able to burst open his coffin and descend by a rope to the floor of the Chapel, whence he was properly fetched home in the Duchess's brougham! The whole tale was indignantly disproved, but was lost sight of in the exposure of de Rougemont.

A contemporary at the Scots College recalls:

"He was wont to condemn the alleged laxity of the Roman Communion in the matter of truthfulness and its subdistinguishing the lie. He himself, brought up as a strict Anglican, had all the Anglican horror of lying, which surprised us as he was universally regarded as about the biggest liar we had ever met. Everything about him suggested one who dabbles. His room was a miniature museum. In innumerable ways he said and did things both in and outside the College, and for a time no doubt it was very interesting. But a certain savage annoyance and scorn towards Rolfe slowly grew up among the students. When we began to hear stories from outside the College, which indicated that his presence among us was making us a subject for gossip and comment, the annoyance became rage and the end was in sight. We put our ideas regarding him before the Rector, and the Rector expelled him. He got a fortnight to look about him, a week was added to that, three days, one day more, then his departure! He seemed to have a keen sense of externalities of all kinds, little or no apprehension of the inward spirit that is in most things. He painted and photoed and wrote about the outsides of things. He tinkered with triolets because they are a manner, a form, nothing else. Nobody with anything to say would say it in triolets. A critical reading of his various books would serve to show that he had a very clear and discerning eye for outside values and superficialities and little else. Forms, manners, colours, sounds, shapes, and beyond a region of vague uninteresting shadows a sort of spiritual and intellectual myopia. There you have the key to all Rolfe. In his tenacious desire for the priesthood was nothing sinister, nothing elevated or fine. He saw himself doing what to him seemed picturesque things in a picturesque way. There was in him little pride in the better sense of the term. He did not disdain to beg. There was a sort of ruthless selfishness about him which led him to exploit others quite regardless of their interests or feelings. Take him all in all he was not very human. He was a sort of sub-species. He must have been very tough and elastic or he would have been utterly crushed and destroyed by the opposition and enmity he met with and did so much to excite. Was there an external element of greatness in him to account for this? Or was it perhaps something more analogous to that appalling saying of Parolles, 'If my heart were great 'twould burst at this. Simply the thing I am shall make me live'? There was little or no warmth or affectionateness in him, probably why he was so selfish and self-centred. His humor was thin and sardonic. I don't know if he could be called revengeful, probably not. He loathed for the same reason that he apparently liked: artistic sense."

And yet many were grateful that Rolfe never received the Catholic priesthood. He had some elements of those Satanic characters who have used their wasted and fallen priesthood to say the Black Mass.

"An Englishman Italianate is a devil incarnate" was a proverb that could be often applied to him. He passed through life forcing men into startled enmity, while he astonished them no less by a certain rare and magnificent impudence. A number of very different types united in describing him as the most striking and upsetting personage they had ever met in their lifetime. A London solicitor was once summoned to give Rolfe professional advice at Christchurch by the telegram, "Come immediately. You will be met by barouche with white livery. Baron Corvo." It was to initiate legal action against Rolfe's Duchess! Even then he was in debt to his hosts, but the solicitor could not refuse such a wire out of the blue, and became so interested in Rolfe's amazing personality that he afterwards introduced him to Mr. Stead of the *Review of Reviews*. Stead, before testing Rolfe's literary talents, handed a penny held by the Baron to his medium Julia, who from another room furnished the oracular reply, "He is a blackguard! He has a hole in his head." Mr. Stead thereupon chased and seized Rolfe until he could feel his cranium, when behold there was a perceptible hole to be found in the skull! He was accordingly dismissed as a blackguard, and for once Rolfe was utterly baffled by powers more sinister than his own! Sinister seems to have been deserved as Rolfe's epithet. He brought amazement, fear and repulsion to men. To none happiness. Women he hated, but not as the Saints have abhorred them. To animals, especially the reptiliar, he could be cruel. He could pierce a live toad with a red-hot poker. But on that score enough!

As a writer Rolfe first swam into notoriety by the stories, which originally appeared in the famous *Yellow Book*. These were reprinted in book form as Number Six in the Bodley Booklets; and by James Douglas were described as "the most amazing, fantastical, whimsical, bizarre, erratic, and hare-brained of books." To these six Rolfe added twenty-six similar tales, and let them be published under the title of "In His Own Image," with the dedication DIVO AMICO DESIDERATISSIMO D. D. D. FRIDERICUS, and the Colophon "From London, in my study, on the eve of Saint George the Martyr, Protector of the Kingdom, MDCCCC." This book was marked by the appearance of the Corvo arms, unsanctified by the College of Heralds, *videlicet,* a Raven for Corvo sable on argent, a lapel of three and a cross potent on a field—argent and sable counter-charged, surmounted by a Hat Priestly sable for crest and surrounded for motto by the Greek—$E\Sigma TAI \; \Pi ANTAKA\Lambda\Omega\Sigma$ (All will be well).

The stories in "In His Own Image" were variously received. To the oldfashioned orthodox they appeared pungently irreverent, but certain converts to Catholicism distributed them under the title of "the fifth Gospel" as the complete reaction from British Pharisaism and Hypocrisy. James Douglas wrote of them as "charged with Corvonian idiosyncrasy, a jumble jargon composed of modern slang, old English, Latin, Italian, Greek," adding that "the Corvo vocabulary is orchidaceous." Another critic summed his language as "classic and colloquial, early Italian and old English, Cockney and Athenian." The *Twentieth Century Review* saw "a beautiful fancy that seduces one into thinking it quite the most delightful thing, which, of course, it isn't, but is very nearly, really." Catholic readers were publicly outraged or delighted surreptitiously. The *Tablet* thought him "unfortunately very amusing." *Church Bells* hoped that "the author's object may be to throw some light upon the superstitious doctrines of modern Rome!"

These tales are unique, and though very uneven, they are very original. They represent a natural comminglement of the Pagan and the Christian tradition in the form of modern Italian folk-lore expressed through the medium of a rather fantastic youth. But at times it is difficult to say whether it is Toto or Corvo who is speaking. The naïveté is always Toto's, but the subtlety is sometimes Rolfe's.

"The Epick of San Georgio" is a Christianisation of the legend of Perseus. Others are based on such incidents as the rebuff given by an English duchess to King Bomba ("About the Holy Duchess and the Wicked King"), or the blessing by Pius IX of an Anglican Bishop ("About Papa Feretti and the Blest Heresiarch"). Others are popular fantasies making furious fun of the Capucins and Jesuits. Most of them are rollicking but exquisite pictures of "the gods" or saints and their emotions in Paradise. One typical sentence describes St. Peter taking off his Tiara, "while he wiped the sweat from his brow, using the Gremial instead of the Fancon provided for such purposes." It requires some liturgical sense to recognise that the Fancon or maniple was originally a handkerchief and the Gremial an episcopal apron. They may be described as anthropomorphic idylls of Italian popular religion and,

being purely artistic, can be regarded as highly religious or insidiously the reverse. The style is only blurred in places by Rolfe's incurable love for fancy coinages and his individualistic spelling. A sentence like "His lampromeirakiodia obeyed each rythmick call" only leaves the reader with an irritated impulse towards the Greek Lexicon.

In politics Rolfe was a mediæval Tory, and *Hadrian VII* contained a violent parody of English Socialism. But he hated factory-owners even more, and the tale *Why the Rose is Red* carried an outburst against "The infamous local Rose of Lancaster dyed red with the Blood of Innocents, victims of minotaur-manufacturers!" He was a fanatical Jacobite, and his eulogy of Cardinal Stefano Borgia was chiefly based on the good turn the last Borgia Cardinal was able to do the last of the Stuarts, Cardinal King Henry IX, who, we learn from a note (and this must be a profound relief to post-war Jacobites), "bequeathed his rights in the English Crown to the descendants of Anna Maria d'Orléans (daughter of Henrietta Stuart and niece of King Charles I), who married Duke Vittoramadeo of Savoja, from whom descends not the Bavarian Princess of the White Rose but King Victor-Emanuele III of Italy." Rolfe worked out an elaborate pedigree to show that Victor Emmanuel was the rightful King of England, to whom, as his rightful sovereign, copies of his books were formally presented.

Rolfe earned no fame and deserved few friends. Even with publishers he carried on acid controversies in green and heliotrope inks as to whether "Sixtus and Sixtine" were only corrupt forms of "Xystus and Xystine." On a point of mediæval spelling or of wilful indentation he would challenge a legion of printers' devils. Artifex rather than artist, he was not a Lord of Language, but a would-be tyrant of words, and words seemed to turn and tyrannise over him. His classical verbalisms amused scholars, but none dared to ask what he meant by "tygendis" **or** "technikrym." Ouche, birth-flare, lickerishly, liripipe, fly-fot, noluntary, solert or talpine, are good English, though rare. But tolutiloquent, contortuplication, fumificables (for tobacco), zaimph, aseity, purrothrixine, banaysically, remain to trouble commentators. The only meaning attachable to "rose-alexanrolith" might occur to a Chinese mind as a portmanteau-word for the London pavements on Alexandra Day. He was very fond of the word *precipitevolissimevolmente,* which would have made his literary epitaph.

As a wordmonger Rolfe describes himself in *Hadrian VII* "and his private dictionary which (as an artificer in verbal expression) he had compiled taking Greek words from Liddell and Scott and Latin words from Andrews, enlarging his English vocabulary with such simple but pregnant formations as the adjective hybrist from ὑβριστης (insulting) or the noun gingilism from gingilismus (loud laughter)." In preserving the correctness of Greek spelling Rolfe outdid the Historian Grote.

This artificial facility found vent in his renderings of the Rubaiyat. "Saprous bones," "somatick atoms" and "aimaterose heart" seem legitimate classicisms; but "methystine lake" requires some explanation as a term for drunkenness. Rolfe brought out the humour and sarcasm which Fitzgerald missed as well as all the coloured epithets such as "tulip-tinctured, xanthine, rubine" necessary to illuminate what he called "diaphotick verse." Rolfe provided an interesting if roundabout way of reaching both the poesy and philosophy of Umar, but as in the case of Fitzgerald the reader unread in Persian can only guess which poet he is reading. The opening Quatrain may be quoted:

"Lo Phosphor! And a voice from the Tavern crieth: enter hilarious Philopots, hybrist youths; enter and fill yet

one more cup of Wine before that Fate shall fill brimful
your Cup of Life."

But his best books disappeared and rarely come into the
market (at least *Hadrian VII* and the *History of the
Borgias*). He failed to be mentioned in any contemporary
save in Fr. Martindale's *Life of Mgr. Benson*—a passage
which gives some substance to an almost mythic personage:

In the winter of 1904-5 Benson met with a book called *Hadrian
VII* and very soon found himself involved in an acquaintanceship
of an absorbing and peculiar sort. So completely was his life for
the next two or three years coloured and interconnected with Frederick Rolfe. . . .

At least then he existed, and Benson embalmed him in
parodic form in *The Sentimentalists*. At least Benson made
a composite picture between Rolfe and another friend, who
supplied most of the outside mannerisms, while Rolfe
supplied the rather unbeautiful character which required
such a drastic cure from the novelist. Mgr. Benson for
some time, like many others, suffered from a fantastic
admiration for Rolfe, and proposed to write a book on
St. Thomas of Canterbury in collaboration, which however was prevented by Benson's friends, thus earning an
undying enmity from Rolfe when he found himself regarded even as a literary outcast. One who read his correspondence with Benson wrote: "I am almost sure he was
possessed by a devil. I have never in my life come near any
one who hated so much and was so virulent an egocentric."

Perhaps a genuine literary memorial to Rolfe occurs in
Henry Harland's novels, for both *The Cardinal's Snuff-
box* and *My Friend Prospero* owe some of their Italian
colour and detail to Rolfe, who certainly claimed both
books as his own children. Harland was always a good
friend to one with whom friendship was a minor experiment in demonology. It remains difficult to place Rolfe in
literature. He possessed a morbid sense of the picturesque

and garish which totally and drug-like undermined his historical sense. When he wrote *A History of the Borgias* he could rejoice in such sentences as the following rocket of racy realism: "So the Senior Branch in the line of the direct descendants of the murdered Duke of Gandia, bastard of the Lord Alexander P. P. VI, withered in sumptuous obscurity!" Savonarola, whom he hated as a Puritan and a Salvationist, he summed up as a "director turned dictator," the subtlety of which epigram he urged in hectic and violent correspondence. Or take his fierce characterisation of the Cardinal Ippolito d'Este: "It is one thing to attempt to blind a bastard brother who is a royal prince. It is another thing to compass the death of a brother who is a reigning sovereign. The robust young Cardinal was equal to the first but above the second." Rolfe used the Borgian era to deck his own imagined character with astonishing fictions, which may generally receive credit for being stranger than fact.

A History of the Borgias is a vivid attempt to rehabilitate Pope Alexander the Sixth from the secular infamy, which "unproved suspicion, kopriematous imagination and ordurous journalists" had combined to heap upon his tiara. In the very remarkable preface Rolfe states that: "No man save One, since Adam, has been wholly good. Not one has been wholly bad. The truth about the Borgia, no doubt, lies between the two extremes. Popes and Kings and lovers and men of intellect and men of war cannot be judged by the narrow code, the stunted standard, of the journalist and the lodging-house keeper or the plumber and the haberdasher." Of this book Henry Harland wrote: "The historic imagination, the big vision, the humour, the irony, the wit, the perverseness, the daring and the tremendously felicitous and effective manner of it! It is like a magnificent series of tapestry pictures of the fifteenth century." Rolfe disclaimed to write in "the Roman

Catholic interest," but he certainly reset Alexander in a magnificent if not a favourable light. "A very strong man guilty of hiding none of his human weaknesses"—would have made a true and a kind epitaph for one of the greatest if not most pious of Popes.

The book is not sustained, and it is difficult to read continuously, for it is a collection of striking monographs loosely fastened together on such subjects as the Ceremonial of Papal Conclaves, Calumny as a fine art, the theory of Cardinal-Nephews or Nepotism, Art under the Borgias, the Science of Poisoning or Venom, Cardinalitial Privileges, the full meaning of Excommunication. In the midst of much that is recondite, interesting and written in stately or striking language, Rolfe can suddenly become personal, and we get a sentence like: "This year also died the twelve-toed, chin-tufted, excommunicated little Christian king, Charles VIII of France, and was succeeded by his cousin, Louis XII, a thin man with a fat neck and lip and an Ethiopic nose and exquisite attire."

Sometimes he shows the touch of Tacitus, which is the same in a modern or classical historian, whether it is a statement of mockery or of truth, or of both. Caesar Borgia, we learn, "hanged all those who betrayed to him, loving the treachery, hating the traitors." Lucretia Borgia "had observed that the lack of money is the root of all evil, and at that root she struck!" Alexander as a Cardinal "gained the reputation of being inaccessible to flattery, incapable of party feeling, impregnable in integrity, *inconspicuous in morals. . . .*"

Sometimes he uses the antithesis of epigram. Of the Borgian and Victorian centuries: "Now we pretend to be immaculate, then they bragged of being vile." In the history of poisons: "The Dark Ages were the ages of Simples. The Age of the Renaissance was the age of Compounds." Or, again, of the American Discovery: "So in return for the Borgia which Spain gave to Italy, Italy and the Borgia gave Messer Cristoforo Columbo and the New World to Spain."

Though the writer states that he "does not write with the simple object of whitewashing the House of Borgia, his present opinion being that all men are too vile for words to tell," he certainly renders the wildest accusations against the Borgia improbable, especially in the matter of poison. Into the details of poisoning he goes at great length, showing that to the sixteen venoms known in the twelfth century only "tri-sulphate of arsenic, orpiment, antimony, corrosive sublimate, aconite or wolfsbane or monkshood, and perhaps white hellebore and black or Christmas rose," were added in the Borgian era, and by his knowledge of mediæval pharmacy he criticises Symonds and Creighton on the supposed transfusion of blood practised by a Hebrew doctor on Innocent VIII. Whether his ambition to write the last word on the Borgian era was fulfilled or not, he was inclined to repudiate the book because he was not allowed to keep all the quaint and meticulous spellings, to say nothing of Appendix III [1] and an appalling extract from Varchi. The Borgia were strong meat, he insisted, and could not be treated in the language of the Religious Tract Society. The only character of the period who might have appealed to the R.T.S. was Savonarola, whom Rolfe terms "mattoid," and criticises fiercely for his minacity and violence compared with the patience and moderation of Alexander VI, "a commander-in-chief dealing with a mutinous mad sergeant."

It is Rolfe's obsession and research for weird detail

---

[1] The suppressed "Appendix III on a suggested Criterion of the Credibility of Historians" was a vivid and virulent impeachment of five historians—Pontano, Infessura, Guicciardini, Varchi, and John Addington Symonds—in the matter of admitting the evidence of moral turpitude. Every copy save one was destroyed by a cautious publisher.

rather than his character-drawing that makes *A History of the Borgias* interesting. Whence did he ferret out his list of practical jokes permissible on ladies in the Borgian era? Could he have invented the recipe for getting rid of unwelcome guests of strewing harp-strings cut small on hot meat so as to writhe like worms?

Hadrian VII with the possible exception of the Book on the Borgias is Rolfe's masterpiece, with all its uneven mixture of news-cuttings, canon law, ecclesiastical scenes, archaic diction and Rolvian propaganda. It might be summed up as "If I were Pope," to take a place beside Richard le Gallienne's "If I were God." There can be little doubt that Rolfe is describing some of his life, and all his likes and dislikes. The sense of a foiled vocation to the priesthood always lay at the back of his own defeated life. His hero is himself, George Arthur Rose, who broods for years over his rejection from Maryvale (Oscott) and St. Andrew's College (Scots College, Rome), wondering "why, O God, have you made me strange, uncommon, such a mystery to my fellow creatures?"

The book was too brilliant not to strike sparks. "Fr. Rolfe can write but hath a devil," the *Daily Mail* suggested. The *Review of Reviews* described it as "a new novel that is unlike all novels and is truly novel in style, in matter and in design." "It appears to be the work of a devout Roman Catholic," said the *Pall Mall Gazette*. On the other hand the *Christian World* felt that "no Protestant could write anything more damaging!"

Hadrian VII saves the necessity of writing Rolfe's life. He was undoubtedly his self-confessor with "reddish-brown hair turning to grey" and "tattooed on the breast with a cross," who wore his grandfather's silver spectacles to write "his wonderful fifteenth-century script"; used spring dumb-bells and slept in glycerined gloves; found "the Roman Machine inexorable in inquiry as in righteousness" and became "a misanthropic altruist." He apologises for his use of pseudonyms:

> In fact, I split up my personality. As Rose (Rolfe) I was a tonsured clerk. As King Clement (Baron Corvo) I wrote and painted and photographed; as Austin White I designed decorations; as Francis Engle I did journalism.

What did he not do for a living?

> I designed furniture and fire irons, I delineated saints and seraphim and sinners, chiefly the former, a series of rather interesting and polyonymous devils in a period of desperate revolt. I slaved as a professional photographer. I did journalism, reported inquests for eighteen pence. I wrote for magazines. I wrote books. I invented a score of things. I was a fool, a sanguine, ignorant, abject fool! I never learned by experience, I still kept on, a haggard, shy, priestly-visaged individual. I made the mistake of appealing to brains rather than to bowels, to reason rather than to sentiment.

He believed all the while that the "salient trait of his character, the desire not to be ungracious, the readiness to be unselfish and self-sacrificing, had done him incalculable injury." *Hadrian VII* is the oddest and perhaps vividest Apologia or Autobiography of present times.

As he grew older and lonelier Rolfe grew fonder of walking only at night and disguised with wig and painted face to avoid meeting his creditors or the sunlight. Finally he withdrew to Venice. He had been a beautiful swimmer and an amateur yachtsman, but as his bodily forces failed he sank into poverty. Rumor said that he had become an amateur gondolier. Certainly his private craft, silken-sailed and fantastically painted, appeared in the canals. Though he had often threatened suicide, there is no reason to believe that he took the celebrated Borgian venom which he believed he had rediscovered. Alone and suddenly he died. And he died fearless and unforgiving, but not necessarily unforgiven unless he refused to forgive himself. He was a self-tortured and self-defeated soul who might have done much had he been born into the proper era or surroundings. The Byronic pose would have suited him even better than the Borgian. That of Oscar Wilde most of all. In the curious game of applying fictitious parentage he might have been placed as a fiery cross between Gilles de Retz and Marie Bashkirtseff. He died quite deserted and there was none to overhear if he muttered the Neronian apothegm *"Qualis artifex pereo!"* As he had written of his own hero Hadrian VII, "Pray for the repose of his soul. He was so tired." After ten years his remains were transferred from the common fosse to a perpetual niche in the presence of a representative of the City of Venice and of one of the Capucin friars whom he had so greatly ridiculed; but the Catholic Church is tolerant to her own children and he had declared himself in *Hadrian VII* to be an obedient son of the Holy Catholic Apostolic Roman See "and therefore I submit myself and all which I have written to Her Judgment." With which submission we leave him.

SHANE LESLIE.

PREFACE

GREAT Houses win and lose undying fame in a century. They shoot, bud, bloom, bear fruit;—from obscurity they rise to dominate their Age, indelibly to write their names in History: and, after a hundred years, giving place to others who in turn shall take the stage, they descend into the crowd, and live on, insignificant, retired, unknown.

Once upon a time, Caesars were masters of the world; and the genius of Divus Julius, of Divus Augustus, was worshipped everywhere on altars. There are Cesarini at this day in Rome, *cosa grande ch' il sole,* masters of wide domains, but not of empires. Once upon a time, Buonaparte held Europe in its grip. Buonapartes at this day keep exile in Muscovy or Flanders. Once upon a time, the Sforza were sovereigns-regnant; and of their daughters were made an empress and a queen. There are Sforza at this day at Santafiora and at Rome; peers of princes only, not of kings. Once upon a time, Borgia was supreme in Christendom. There are Borgia at this day, peers of France; or patricians whose names are written in the Golden Book of Rome.

In little more than a century, from 1455 to 1572, Borgia sprang to the pedestal of fame; leaping at a bound, from little bishoprics and cardinalates, to the terrible altitude of Peter's Throne; producing, in those few years, two Popes, and a Saint and General of Jesuits. It is true that there died, in the nineteenth century, another Borgia of renown, —the Lord Stefano Borgia, Cardinal-Presbyter of the Title of San Clemente—a great and good man, admirable by Englishmen for a certain gracious deed which is not yet written in English History; and who preferred a second place to that giddy pre-eminence on which his kin formerly had played their part.

The history of the House of Borgia is the history of the healing of the Great Schism; of the Renascence of letters and the arts; of the Invention of Printing; of the Muslim Invasion of Europe; of the consolidation of that Pontifical Sovereignty which endured till 1870; the history of the Discovery of a World; the history of the Discovery, by man, of Man.

"To penetrate the abyss of any human personality is impossible. No man truly sees his living neighbour's, brother's, wife's,—nay, even his own soul." (*John Addington Symonds.*) Much more obscure must be his friend's; and darker still, his enemy's;—and these alive. What, then, can be known of personalities, who are but distant, perhaps uninteresting, mere names?

Chronicles there are, and chroniclers; and no more reliance can be placed in those, than in modern morning and evening newspapers. The same defect is common to both, —the personal equation, the human nature of the writer, historian, journalist.

Cardinal Bartolomeo Sacchi (detto Platina) was "a heathen, and a bad one." He had to stand his trial on a charge of worshipping false gods, was acquitted for want of evidence, and departed this life in the Odour of Sanctity. Modern discoveries, in the secret recesses of the catacombs, have proved that he was used to carry on his nefarious practices there, with a handful of other extravagant athenians of like kidney. He wrote a History of the Popes, which fairly deserves to be called veracious: but he had a personal grudge against the Lord Paul P.P. II, Who had put him to trial for paganism and grieved him with the torture called The Question; wherefore, he got even with His Holiness when he wrote His life, and a more singular example of truth untruly told would be hard to find. Platina died in the reign of the Lord Xystus P.P. IV; and

his History of the Popes was continued by Onofrio Panvinii, who, according to Sir Paul Rycaut, gravely states
that, in 1489, the Lord Innocent P.P. VIII permitted mass
to be said without wine, in Norway; because, that country
being cold and the distance far, the wine either was frozen,
or was turned to vinegar, before it could be brought thither.
Obviously, Platina and Panvinii require credible corrob-
oration.

Messer Stefano Infessura lays himself open to suspicion,
as to his bona fides and as to his knowledge, by his remarks on the Lord Xystus P.P. IV.

Monsignor Hans Burchard, whose original Diarium
awaits discovery, is careless, Teutonic, and petty.

The Orators of the Powers compile their state-dispatches from what they have picked up when hanging
about the doors of palaces, or from the observations of
bribed flunkeys.

Messer Paolo Giovio, preconised Bishop of Nocera by
the Lord Clement P.P. VII, Messer Francesco Guicciardini, and Messer Benedetto Varchi, were Florentines, who
wrote in the Florentine manner, of Rome and Roman
affairs, from an antipathetic point of view, and solely on
the gossip and tittle-tattle that filtered through to Florence
after long years. Yet they wrote in sately delicate language,
"Dante's desiderata,—that illustrious cardinal courtly
curial mother-tongue, proper to each Italian state, special
to none, whereby the local idioms of every city are to be
measured, weighed, compared." Only—only—the student
of their work must know that, (in common with all professional manufacturers of squibs, libels, and lampoons, in
every age,) what they liked they praised; and what they
loathed they rhetorically and categorically damned, com-
piling concise catalogues of all the worst crimes known
to casuistry, to lay at their foe's door. Therefore, the student of history must learn the personal sympathies and
antipathies of these historians; he must find their personal

equation: and, when he has deducted that, he may arrive at least in juxtaposition with truth. This method has been attempted in the present work—in the absence of impersonal authorities.

Mi sembra che la storia si sia servita della famiglia Borgia come di tela sopra la quale abbia voluto dipingere le sfenatezze dei secoli XV, XVI. "It appears to me that history has made the House of Borgia to serve as a canvas whereon to depict the unbridled licence of the Fifteenth and Sixteenth Centuries." (*Ragguali, sulla vita di Marino Sanuto, 207. note.*) By some historians, the Borgia women are delineated as "poison-bearing maenads," or "veneficous bacchantes"; the Borgia men as monsters utterly flagitious: both men and women of a wickedness perfectly impossible to human nature, perfectly improbable even in nature kakodaimoniacal. By other historians, chiefly, strange to say, of the French School, and afflicted with the modern itch for rehabilitation, the identical Borgia are displayed in the character of stainless innocents who shine in the light of inconceivable virtue.

No man, save One, since Adam, has been wholly good. Not one has been wholly bad. The truth about the Borgia, no doubt, lies between the two extremes. They are accused of loose morals, and of having been addicted to improper practices and amusements.

Well; what then? Does anybody want to judge them? Popes, and kings, and lovers, and men of intellect, and men of war cannot be judged by the narrow code, the stunted standard, of the journalist and the lodging-house keeper, or the plumber and the haberdasher. So indecently unjust a suggestion only could emanate from persons who expect to gain in comparison.

Why should good hours of sunlight be wasted on the judgment seat, by those who, presently, will have to take their turn in the dock? Why not leave the affairs of Borgia to the Recording Angel?

All about the Borgia quite truly will be known, some day; and, in the interim, more profitable entertainment may be gained by frankly and openly studying that swift vivid violent age, when "the Pope was an Italian Despot with sundry sacerdotal additions;" when "what Mill, in his Essay on Liberty, desired,—what seems every day more unattainable in modern life,—was enjoyed by the Italians; *there was no check to the growth of personality, no grinding of men down to match the average."*

"Amorist, agonist, man, that, incessantly toiling and striving,
"Snatches the glory of life only from love and from war—

that is the formula in which the Borgia best may find expression. For they, also, were human beings, who were born, struggled through life, and died.

.   .   .

In this Ideal Content of the House of Borgia, there is matter for a score of specialists. The present writer lays no claim to any special knowledge whatever; although his studies obviously have led him more in one direction than in another. Curbed by his limitations, he makes no pretensions to the discovery of new or striking facts: but he humbly trusts that he has been enabled to throw new and natural light on myths and legends, and to re-arrange causes and events in a humanly probable sequence.

In dealing with circumstantial calumny, he has adopted an unworn system; *e.g.,* in the case of persons said to have been raised to the purple in reward for criminal services. Here, he furnishes complete lists of the persons raised to the purple; and, when the names of those accused of crime do not appear therein, he takes the fact as direct and positive refutation of the calumny.

Touching the matter of names and styles, he has made an attempt to correct the slipshod and corrupt translations of the same, which, at present, are the vogue. To allude to Personages in terms which are appropriate enough for one's terrier, or for one's slave; to speak of sovereigns as mere John, or of pontiffs as plain Paul; are breaches of etiquette of unpardonable grossness. The present writer has tried, at least, to accord to his characters the use of the names, and the courtesy of the styles that they actually bore.

In this manner of writing, he has endeavoured to rush from mood to mood, in consonance with the subject under consideration, with something of the flippant breathless masterful versatility which Nature uses. For men were very natural in the Borgian Era.

It is said that the style of a history should be grave and stately; and so it should be, when History is written in epic form. But to write of men and women,—human men and women,—on those inhuman lines, is nothing but an unnatural crime; and, also, as ridiculously incongruous and inconsistent, as it would be to sing the *Miserere mei Deus* to the tune of the *Marseillaise*. For human nature is not at all times grave and stately; but has its dressing-gown-and-slipper periods,—the human nature. The aim of this work is to display the Borgia alive and picturesque and unconventional, as indeed they were; not monumentally to freeze them into ideally heroic moulds, or to chisel them into conventionally unrecognisable effigies.

The writer does not write with the simple object of "white-washing" the House of Borgia; his present opinion being that all men are too vile for words to tell.

Further, he does not write in the Roman Catholic interest; nor in the Jesuit interest; nor in the interest of any creed, or corporation, or even human being: but solely as one who has scratched together some shreds of knowledge, which he perforce must sell, to live.

It should be unnecessary to say that no persuasion of, and no offence to, any man, or any school of thought, is intended in these pages; and that the writer, in the absence of desired advice, has written what he has written under correction.

He returns thanks to the officers of the Oxford University Galleries, of the Bodleian Library, and of the British Museum, for courteous and valuable assistance.

FREDERICK BARON CORVO.

ROME

CONTENTS

BOOK I

BOOK II

BOOK III

BOOK IV

A HISTORY OF THE BORGIAS

"A fire, that is kindled, begins with smoke and hissing, while it lays hold on the faggots; bursts into a roaring blaze, with raging tongues of flame, devouring all in reach, spangled with sparks that die; settles into the steady genial glare, the brilliant light, that men call fire; burns away to slowly expiring ashes; save where smouldering embers flicker, and nurse the glow, until propitious breezes blow it into life again."

BOOK THE FIRST

THE KINDLING OF THE FIRE

"A fire, that is kindled, begins with smoke and hissing, while it lays hold on the faggots"

In the year 1455 of Restored Salvation, Christendom was in a parlous way. The Muslim Infidel swarmed from the dark Orient, sworn to plant the Crescent on the ruin of the Cross. In resisting encroachment, King Wladislaw of Hungary and the Apostolic Legate, the Most Illustrious[1] Lord Giuliano Cesarini, Cardinal-Bishop of Tusculum, a Roman of Rome, and scion of a most splendid family,[2] had laid down life at the Battle of Varna. After three and fifty days of siege, Constantinople fell to the Great Turk, the Sultan Muhammed II. Ioannes Palaiologos, "King and Autocrat of the Romans," was dead; and his successor Konstantinos Dragases XIII, the last Christian Emperor of the East, was slain in defence of his capital. By the fall of the great Byzantine Empire, the bulwarks of Christendom were broken down; the Infidel was raiding on her borders. Alone, with no ally, Jan Hunniades desperately defended Hungary's frontier. The Powers of Europe occupied themselves with less important matters.

At this time, Rome was the eye, and the brain, of the

---

[1] The epithet *Most Eminent* (Eminentissimo) was granted to cardinals by the Lord Urban P.P. VIII, 1630. Prior to that, they were styled *Most Illustrious* (Illustrissimo) ; or, in the case of the Cardinal-Dean and Cardinal Nephews, *Most Honourable* and *Most Worshipful* (Osservantissimo, Colendissimo).

[2] They claim descent from the Gens Julia. Their armorials show the Bear (Orsini) chained to the Column (Colonna) with the Imperial Eagle displayed in chief.

world; and Rome had seen and realised all that was portended.

During many years, since the first signs of Muslim activity, fugitives from Byzantium descended upon Italian shores. The glory of Greece had gone to Imperial Rome. The grandeur of Imperial Rome had returned to Byzantium. And now the glory and grandeur of Byzantium was going to Christian Rome. When danger menaced, when the days of stress began to dawn, scholars and cunning artificers, experts skilful in all knowledge, fled westward to the open arms of Italy with their treasures of work. Italy welcomed all who could enlarge, illuminate, her transcendent genius; learning and culture and skill found with her not exile but a home, and a market for wares. Scholarship became the fashion. "Literary taste was the regulative principle." It was the Age of Acquisition. "Tuscan is hardly known to all Italians, but Latin is spread far and wide throughout the world"; said Filelfo. But to know Greek was the real test of a gentleman of that day; and Greek scholars were Italy's most honoured guests. Not content with the codices and classics of antiquity that these brought with them, Italian princes and patricians sent embassies to falling Byzantium, to search for manuscripts, inscriptions, or carven gems, and bronze, and marble. Greek intaglii and camei graced the finger-rings, the ouches, collars, caps, of Venetian senators, of the lords of Florence, of the sovereigns of the Regno,[1] of the barons and cardinals and popes of Rome. "They had made the discovery that the body of a man is a miracle of beauty, each limb a divine wonder, each muscle a joy as great as sight of stars or flowers." Messer Filippo Brunelleschi, who truly said that his figure of Christ was a crucified contadino, erected the marvellous dome of Florence. For the Lord Eugenius P.P. IV, Messer Antonio Filarete carved the Rapes of Leda

[1] The kingdoms of Aragon, Naples, the two Sicilies, and Jerusalem.

and Ganumedes on the great bronze gates of St. Peter's. Messer Lorenzo Ghiberti modelled the marvellous doors of the Baptistry. Messer Simone Fiorentino (detto Donatello) placed, on the north wall of Orsanmichele, his superb St. George in marble; and cast in bronze for Duke Cosmo the nitid David of the Bargello. Tommasco di Ser Giovanni degli Scheggia, called Masaccio (great hulking Tom), painted St. Peter and St. Paul raising the dead, with the skill which he learned from Tommaso di Cristoforo Fini, called Masolino (pretty little Tom). Paolo Doni, nicknamed Uccello (Bird), put birds into his pictures according to his wont. The Blessed Giovangelico da Fiesole filled triptychs with his visions of the angelic hierarchy. Fra Filippo Lippi painted the St. Gabriel Archangel with the argus-eyed wings in an admirable Annunciation. Petrarch and Boccaccio hunted convents, abbeys, and museums of Byzantium for codices. Messer Poggio Bracciolini discovered manuscripts of Lucretius Carus, of Vitruvius, of Quinctillian, and Cicero's Oration *For Caecina.* "No severity of winter cold, no snow, no length of journey, no roughness of road, prevented him from bringing the monuments of antiquity to light," says Francesco Barbaro. Nor did he hesitate to steal, when theft seemed necessary to secure a precious codex. Three pupils of Manuel Chrysoloras won renown beyond all competitors in the distinguished race: Giovanni Aurispa collected no fewer than two hundred and thirty-eight valuable manuscripts of antiquity; Guarino da Verona and Francesco Filelfo came back laden from Byzantium.

Drunk with the joy of the new learning, Italy failed to perceive the true inwardness of her acquisitions. She was blind to the peril which they most surely portended.

But Rome saw. And, during many years, Rome had lifted up her voice and cried aloud that Italy enjoyed these accessions to her treasure only because Byzantium was no longer a safe repository for them. During many decades, Rome proclaimed the danger implied by the advance of the Muslim Infidel. But Christendom lent deaf ears, and compared Rome to Kassandra. Then Immortal Rome was lulled into a kind of apathy: her voice was heard less frequently, speaking in feebler, in less insistent tone. And, gradually, the potent spell of the Renascence mastered Rome; and, in the reign of the Lord Nicholas P. P. V,[1] she fell a victim to the fashionable delirium. Churches and palaces were planned, and builded, and decorated. Manuscripts were collected, collated, copied. Libraries and colleges were formed. Culture, at last, and for once, was supreme; and the phenomenon of needy genius was unknown. It was an age when the demand for learning, and for the fine arts, exceeded the supply.

Then, Rome knew that the beautiful may be purchased at too dear a price; that its essential evanescence needs the safeguard of virtue and of heroism, of honour and of arms; precisely as woman needs the protection of man. Rome perceived that the irruption of the Muslim Infidel was a menace to civilisation, and she cried on Christendom to resist the flood of barbarism now outpoured.

Hungary, alone of all the Occidental Powers, responded; but then Hungary was actually in the Muslim clutch.

England, lately torn by Jack Cade's rebellion, was entering upon a conflict bloodier than any American Civil War or Boer Revolt. The reign of King Henry VI. Plantagenet, gentlest saint that ever wore an earthly diadem, drew near its close: from those pale prayer-raised hands—holy hands that had lifted to Christ's Vicar a petition for the canonisation of England's Hero, King Ælfred the Great [2]—the sceptre was about to fall. Trumpets were sounding from Northumberland to Kent. The clean air of Yorkshire

---

[1] *Pater Patrum;* the official style of the Roman Pontiff.

[2] The process of canonisation of King Ælfred, though initiated by a Majesty of England (himself a saint *by acclamation*), has not yet been completed by the Court of Rome after four hundred and fifty years.

wolds sang with the hissing of cloth-yard shafts, with the clang of steel of lance on shield. England was an armed camp; and the War of the Roses was begun.

Germany and Austria, under the rule of the Holy Roman Emperor, "Caesar Semper Augustus" Friedrich IV (The Pacific), seethed with politico-religious discontent. Under the guise of a desire for reform, political and personal ambitions strove. Caesar Friedrich IV held the reins of government but loosely. Excellent as a figure-head, ornamental as an emperor, he had not his empire in the grip of a *mailed fist*. The symbol A.E.I.O.U. (AUSTRIAE EST IMPERATOR ORBIS UNIVERSI—ALLE ERDE IST OESTERREICHS UNTERTHAN), which he had invented for his motto, represented his desire, but not his potentiality. Personal aggrandisement employed the feudal sovereigns of the empire: their suzerain's influence was no check upon them.

Italy, then, deserved the designation given to it in modern times by Metternich; it was not a nation, but a geographical expression. In the north were the Republics of Venice, Genoa, Florence, and their smaller imitators; with the royal duchies of Savoja, Milan, and Ferrara. Across the country, from Rome and the Mediterranean, to the Mark of Ancona and the Adriatic, in a north-easterly direction, stretched the Papal States. The east and south, with Sicily, Sardinia, and the Islands, were called The Regno; and were ruled from Naples by kings of the House of Aragon. And dotted all over the land were small semi-independent cities and territories, held as feudal fiefs by local noble houses, whose barons bore the harmless title of Tyrant, and exercised absolute lordship within their little states, *e.g.,* the Manfredi, Tyrants of Faenza; the Malatesta, Tyrants of Rimini; the Sforza, Tyrants of Pesaro, Chotignuola, Santafiora, Imola and Forli; etc.

France, having burned her greatest glory, The Maid of Orleans, was recovering from victories by which, from 1434 to 1450, she had deprived England of all French territory save Calais. Her feeble dastard King Charles VII. was dead; and Louis XI., a gentleman of pleasure and piety, occupied her throne.

Spain, united, after centuries of strife among her divers kingdoms and antagonistic races, by the marriage of King Don Hernando of Aragon to Queen Doña Isabella of Castile, was preparing for an era of colonial expansion.

Portugal was consolidating African discoveries and acquisitions.

Norway and Sweden, after brief separation, once more were united under the sceptre of Denmark; and were learning the lessons of peace.

And then, in Rome, in 1455, on the 24th of March, being Monday in Passion-week, the Lord Nicholas P.P. V was dead: and, with His death, the tide of the Italian Renascence stayed.

The College of Cardinals assumed the government of Rome and of the Universal Church, while the Conclave for the election of the Successor of St. Peter was assembling. During nine days the Novendialia, the quaint ceremonies connected with the obsequies of a Pope, were celebrated. On Good Friday, the 4th of April, after the Adoration of the Cross, the Mass of the Presanctified, and the Exposition of the Vernicle (or True Image of our Divine Redeemer, vulgarly known as The Veronica), had been performed in the Vatican Basilica, the cardinals were immured; the doors and windows of the Vatican were bricked up; Pandolfo, Prince Savelli, Hereditary Marshal of the Holy Roman Church, entered upon the guardianship of the Conclave; and the election was begun.

The College of Cardinals consisted then of twenty members. Of these, only fifteen assisted at the Conclave of 1455. In the fifteenth century, a journey across Europe, from some distant see, occupied a longer time than the eleven days which should elapse between a Pope's death and the enclosure of the Conclave. Of these fifteen cardinals present, seven were Italians, four Spaniards, two Frenchmen, two Byzantines. As usual they were divided into factions; but, strange to say, the division was not one of nationality. The ancient and interminable feud between the great Roman baronial houses of Colonna and Orsini, penetrated even here. Not temporal policy of the Holy See, not differences of pious opinions, but simply rivalry of clan, governed this election.

The Most Illustrious Lord Prospero Colonna, Cardinal-Archdeacon of San Giorgio *in Velum Aureum,* creature (*creatura*) of the Lord Martin P.P. III, undoubtedly would have been elected had the Lord Nicholas P.P. V died at the beginning instead of at the end of a long illness: for, according to the dispatch of Nicholas of Pontremoli, Orator of Duke Francesco Sforza-Visconti of Milan, dated the first of April, 1455, he was then the favourite. Herr Ludwig Pastor, whose valuable history of the Popes is also the latest, most unaccountably urges that the great age of Cardinal Colonna prevented his election. But the accurate Ciacconi raises him to the purple with Cardinal Capranica at the Lord Martin P.P. III's fourth creation in 1426, he being then still a youth (*"adhuc iuvenis"*) ; the publication of his elevation being delayed till the fifth consistory of the 8th of November 1430. Supposing him to have been of the age of twenty-one years in 1426—a very liberal assumption in an age when boys became cardinals at thirteen, benedicks at puberty, and fathers at fifteen—he only would have reached the age of fifty in 1455. The disability of senility may therefore be dismissed. In default of Cardinal Prospero, the Most Illustrious Lord Domenico Capranca, Cardinal-Presbyter of the Title of Santa Croce *in Gerusa·lemme,* Cardinal-Penitentiary, Bishop of Fermo, and him· self a Roman noble of the Ghibelline party, was put for· ward by the House of Colonna as their second candidate.

On the other side, the wealthy business-like Roman

Guelf, the Lord Latino Orsini di Bari, Cardinal-Presbyter of the Title of San Giovanni e San Paolo *in Monte Celio,* represented the interests of the House of Orsini : who offered, as an alternative for the suffrages of the Sacred College, the Venetian Lord Pietro Barbo, Cardinal-Presbyter of the Title of San Marco, and Bishop of Vicenza.

The first three scrutinies produced no result; and the cardinals conferred regarding the merits of the candidates, and of the causes that they represented. Much was said on behalf of Cardinal Capranica. He was "Romano di Roma," his character stood above reproach, his breeding was polite and high. But Cardinal Orsini and his faction, though unable to bring in their own nominee the Cardinal of Venice, were strong enough to out-manœuvre the candidate of Colonna: and the electors found themselves at a deadlock.

In this emergency, the College, sought, and found, a neutral; a partizan neither of Colonna nor of Orsini. There were two Byzantine cardinals; the one, the Lord Ioannes Bessarione, Cardinal-Bishop of Tusculum, Monk of the Religion [1] of St. Basil, Archbishop of Trebizond; the other, the Lord Isidoro of Thessalonika, Cardinal-Bishop of Sabina, Monk of the Religion of St. Basil, Archbishop of Ruthenia. Of these two, Cardinal Bessarione had many recommendations. He was a convert from the Greek Schism; he had been a pupil of Gemisthos Plethon at Constantinople; no one was of higher repute in Christian piety, more admirable in doctrine, more ornate in generous manners. (Ciacconi II. 906.) He had no enemy in the Conclave. At a juncture, like the present, the election of a Byzantine Pontiff, who naturally sympathised with the hapless Byzantines, would have secured for Christendom a champion against the triumphant Muslim Infidel. When night closed the Conclave's deliberations, it appeared certain that Cardinal Bessarione would ascend the Throne of St. Peter on

---

[1] Religion—a gathering together for a pious purpose. It was the fifteenth century equivalent for Order or Society.

the morrow; indeed his brother-cardinals asked favours of him, as though he were already in possession of the Keys. Had he condescended to canvass the other fourteen electors, or to make the slightest exertion on his own behalf, his election would have been secure.

But, in the morning of that Easter Monday, the French Archbishop of Avignon, the Lord Alain Coëtivy Britto, Cardinal-Presbyter of the Title of Santa Prassede, created a diversion against Cardinal Bessarione. "Shall we Latins," he protested, "shall we Latins go to Greece for the Head of the Latin Church? My Lord of Trebizond has not been among us long enough to shave off his beard [1]; he is a mere neophyte, a newcomer to Italy and to the Holy Roman Church, and shall we set him over us?" All day long the cardinals debated; but no election was achieved. Night came, bringing no solution of the difficulty.

On the 8th of April a compromise was suggested. It was resolved to postpone the contest, by electing an old man whose life was almost at an end. Therefore a cardinal was chosen, whose age, in the course of nature, would cause a new election in the near future; whose colourless character neither would alter nor interfere with the traditional policy of the papacy; who during a long life had eschewed pomp and vain glory; whose profound learning, wisdom,

[1] The Lord Clement P.P. VII (Giulio de Medici) 1523-34, appears on Cellini's lovely medals in a full beard. Probably, in His case, there was no choice; for, during the Sack of Rome in 1527 by the Lutheran Goths and Catholic Catalans of the Elect-Emperor, Carlos V., His Holiness was holding the Mola of Hadrian, or Castle of Santangelo, and enduring the hard privations of a siege. Afterwards He did not shave; and full beards became the fashion for the clergy. Later, the Lord Alexander P.P. VII (Flavio Chigi), made the Vandyke beard and upturned mustachio the clerical mode; and, later still, the whole face was shaved according to the present rule. But, at the time when the Cardinal of Avignon reflected upon the Cardinal of Trebizond's beard, there appears to have been a distinct prejudice in favour of a shaven, indeed of a shorn, pope. This may be seen in the medals of popes and cardinals of the fifteenth century (when cleanliness was a mark of gentility), where the large tonsure and shaven faces are very noticeable.

and moderation had won for him his high place; whose reputation was blameless; whose political capacity was high; who was the intimate of the friend and neighbour of Holy Church, Don Alonso de Aragona, King of Naples; lastly, one who, being of the Spanish race, was the hereditary foe of Islam, and pre-eminently qualified to defend Christendom from the Muslim Infidel. The aforesaid Cardinal of Avignon, and the Lord Ludovico Scarampi dell' Arena Mezzaruota, Cardinal-Presbyter of the Title of San Lorenzo *in Damaso,* exerted all their influence to this end; and, after a new scrutiny, the Cardinal-Dean, the Lord Giorgio Flisco de Savignana, Cardinal-Bishop of Ostia and Velletri, made proclamation of election,

"I announce to you great joy. We have for a Pope the Lord Alonso de Borja, Bishop of Valencia, Cardinal-Presbyter of the Title of Santi Quattro Coronati, Who wills to be called Calixtus the Third." [1]

.   .   .

The Spanish House of Borja claims to originate in King Don Ramiro Sanchez de Aragona, A.D. 1035.

Until the time of Don Pedro, Count of Aybar and Lord of Borja, who died in 1152, the family was confined to Spain. Then, according to valid authorities, the Junior Branch, in the person of Don Ricardo de Borja, migrated to the kingdom of Naples and the Two Sicilies, and took service there. This Don Ricardo is named in a document of donation in the reign of the Lord Lucius P.P. III, 1181-1185 (Ricchi); which should go to prove that the Junior Branch was naturalised in Italy. Its lineal descendants un-

[1] In the Acta Consistorialia of the Vatican Secret Archives, this Pope is called Calixtus the Fourth, evidently by the stupidity of some Apostolic Scribe, who happened to know that one John, Abbot of Struma, called himself Calixtus III (having got himself schismatically and uncanonically elected in the reign of the Lord Alexander P.P. III) ; and who had not the sense to know that the Holy Roman Church has the habit of ignoring pseudopontiffs and other pretenders.

doubtedly are living there at the beginning of the twentieth century; the latest recorded being Don Alessandro Borgia, who was born at Milan in 1897. For purposes of clear arrangement, the history of this Junior Branch may be relegated to later pages; the main interest lies in descendants of Don Ximenes Garcia de Borja, the eldest son of the aforesaid Don Pedro, and founder of the Senior Branch; which, though transplanted to Italy in the middle of the fifteenth century, and flourishing there for some generations, must always be regarded as Spanish and not Italian.

There is a record of a son of Don Ximenes Garcia de Borja in 1244, called Gonzales Gil: his son, Don Raymon de Borja was the father of Don Juan Domingo de Borja, Lord of La Torre de Canals in the city of Xativa in Valencia. By his wife, Doña Francisca, this Don Juan Domingo had at least two daughters and a son—Juana, Caterina, and Alonso.

Doña Juana married Don Jofre de Lançol; Doña Caterina married Don Juan de Mila, Baron of Mazalanes; a third daughter, whose name is missing, also married; and the offspring of these three became later of extreme importance.

The son, Alonso, was born on St. Sylvester's Eve, 1378, the year of the opening of the Great Schism, at Xativa, and baptized in the church of St. Mary in that city. He himself has told us this, in two Bulls dated 1457.[1] His youth was spent at the University of Lerida, where he specialised in jurisprudence for the degree of Doctor in Civil and Canon Law, and obtained a professorship and

[1] Villanueva (I. 18, 181) quotes two Bulls of the Lord Calixtus P.P. III, giving relics to the church at Xativa. On p. 51, Villanueva alludes to him as *"Don Alonso de Borja, natural de la Torre de Canals, bautizado en la Iglesia Collegial de Xativa, hoy S. Felipe, electo en 20 de Agosto de 1429 por el Legado de Martin V. Conservo el gobierno de esta Iglesia hasta el año en que murió, sienda yu Papa Calixto III. En 1457 concedió á esta Iglesia un jubileo en el dia de la Asuncion de nuestra Señora, imponiendo para la fabrica la contribucion de diez sueldos."*

Holy Order. While he was a young priest (1398-1408) he chanced to assist at a sermon preached by the great Dominican Vincent Ferrer in a mission at Valencia. At the close of his discourse, the friar singled out from the crowd Don Alonso de Borja, to whom he addressed this remarkable prediction: "My son, you one day will be called to be the ornament of your house and of your country. You will be invested with the highest dignity that can fall to the lot of man. After my death, I shall be the object of your special honour. Endeavour to persevere in a life of virtue." Don Alonso was impressed by this saying, for he repeated it to St. John Capistran in 1449, and he tenaciously waited for the fulfilment. After His election to the papacy, He performed the solemn canonisation of St. Vincent Ferrer on the twenty-ninth of June, 1455.

Don Alonso proceeded from his University professorship to a canonry in the cathedral of Lerida, which was conferred upon him by his countryman Don Pedro de Luna, the Pseudopontiff Benedict XIII. Later, he entered the arena of politics as secretary to King Don Alonso I (The Magnanimous) of Naples and the Two Sicilies; and, here, his diplomatic skill and legal training raised him to the unofficial but important post of confidential counsellor to the Majesty of the Regno. Now that he was domiciled in Italy his fortunes moved swiftly. In 1429 he won the gratitude of the Lord Martin P.P. III (or V) by winning for His Holiness the support of Spain, and by negotiating the renunciation of the Spanish Pseudopontiff, Don Gil Muñoz, who called himself Clement VIII.

These days of the Great Schism, when the Roman Pontiffs had much ado to hold Their Own against irregularly elected pseudopontiffs, must have been utterly horrible. A reigning sovereign is uneasy when pretenders to, or usurpers of, his crown appear. Republican France farcically banishes men whose nobler forefathers represented other forms of government. England sometimes wakes prodigally to spend blood and treasure in support of her suzerainty. If secular powers, then, strive, struggle for their life; and, in the struggle, cause distress, how many times more distressing must have been the rivalry of the Great Schism, when the price at stake was the Headship of Christendom. This consideration will make it easy to understand how great an obligation the Lord Martin P.P. III lay under to the skilful canon, who actually persuaded His rival peaceably to renounce his claim to the triple crown, terminating the thirty-eighth schism of the Holy Roman Church. As a reward, Canon Alonso de Borja received the bishopric of Valencia, his native diocese; and, after his consecration, he continued to be useful to King Don Alonso de Aragona, by re-organising the government of the Regno, and by supervising the education of the King's Bastard and subsequent successor, Don Ferrando.

.   .   .

The fifteenth and sixteenth centuries were not more filled with improbable situations than the twentieth. The situations were different, that is all. The situation of bastards was quite curious, and must be realised by any one who desires intelligently to understand the time. To this intelligent understanding Ludovico Romano's theories will lend aid. He argues that it is false to say that bastards are infamous and incapable of honours. To the infamous is denied the dignity of Decurion (command of ten men). But bastards may become Decuriones. Therefore bastards are neither infamous nor incapable of honour. Giampietro de' Crescenzi Romani, in *Il Nobile Romano,* states the case thus: Plebeians are not eligible to the Decurionate. Bastards are eligible to the Decurionate. Therefore, bastards are not plebeians, but nobles if born of noble stock. Bastards are capable of nobility, of secular and civil dignity; for Ishmael was not hunted from his father's house on account of his bastardy, but on account of his insolence. It is not necessary to quote Crescenzi's argument as to the bastards of King David, from whom descends the Son of David, son cf Abraham, according to the Scripture, and Whom the Fathers of the Church acclaim as One of royal generation; nor to give more of his catalogue of noble bastards than Theodoric, King of the Goths of Italy and of Spain, the Emperor Charlemagne, Roberto and Pandolfo Malatesta, Tyrants of Rimini, Giovanni Sforza, Tyrant of Pesaro, William (called The Conqueror), Duke of Normandy and King of England. He continues to say that nature does not distinguish between bastards and legitimates; that the former are called natural children because they are true children of nature. Neither does grace distinguish; and, as bastards are capable of temporal nobility, so also they are capable of spiritual, as witness St. Bridget of Ireland, and other natural children of signal grace and distinguished virtue. Further, he holds that the sons, of bastards who lose nobility by rebellion, are not infamous; and recover nobility on their father's death; that infamy of any kind is washed-out by baptism; and that the Pope can free from subsequently contracted infamy by His dispensation. He distinguishes between bastards only legitimated by princes or the emperor, who are ineligible to ecclesiastical benefices; and bastards legitimated only by the Pope, who cannot succeed to the fiefs of other princes. He concludes that bastardy purges itself at the latest in the fourth generation.

In the twentieth century, an inheritance devolves from the holder to "the heirs male of his body lawfully begotten"; in the fifteenth, the proviso "lawfully begotten" did not invariably obtain. A bastard, legitimated and recognised by his father, was as valid and capable as the son of a lawful marriage. The sin of the father and mother was a sin personal to them, and none the less a Sin: but it was not allowed to affect their innocent children. The Lord Pius P.P. II, on his way to the Congress of Mantua in 1459, was met on the frontier of Ferrara by eight bastards of the royal House of Este, including the delicious Borso, reigning duke, and two bastards of his highness's bastard brother and predecessor Duke Leonello. These matters should be understood; for a large proportion of the personages in this history were of illegitimate birth, and under no disability of any kind thereby.

.   .   .

King Don Alonso I de Aragona did not feel safe with the crown of the Regno which he wore. The House of Anjou claimed it. Madame Marguerite d'Anjou, daughter of the poet-king Réné, had ceded or sold her rights to the Christian King Louis XI of France, whose claim was supported by the Lord Martin P.P. III. The Magnanimous King Don Alonso I threatened to espouse the cause and benefit by the aid of the Pseudopontiff (called Clement VIII); and so the materials for a devastating conflagration were brought together. But the diplomacy of Bishop Alonso de Borja was repeated here. Once again, by negotiating the peaceful disappearance of a pseudopontiff, he earned the gratitude of the Pope; and the Lord Martin P.P. III, Who owed so much to Bishop Alonso, was easily persuaded to look favourably also upon Bishop Alonso's royal master. Unfortunately the Pope died, and His Successor, the Lord Eugenius P.P. IV had a prejudice for the French claim, which resulted in a renewal of the quarrel in 1439. But a third time the difficulties of the Roman Pontiff were turned to account by Bishop Alonso. When the schismatic Synod of Basilea, to gain some private ends, futilely pronounced a sentence of excommunication and deposition upon the Lord Eugenius P.P. IV, and elected the ambitious Duke Amadeo of Savoja as Pseudopontiff with the name Felix V, all Christendom expected that King Don Alonso, who was a very crafty potentate, would be only too happy to make common cause with the rival of that Pope who would not confirm his crown to him. But all Christendom was disappointed. King Don Alonso's secretary ably manœuvred in his accustomed manner. First, Bishop Alonso de Borja in his proper person refused to attend that schismatic Synod of Basilea; and, by this act, became persona gratissima at the Vatican. Second, the King of Naples instructed his Orators (ambassadors) to play with Pontiff and pseudopontiff, to find out which would meet him with a satisfactory concession. Third, Don Francesco Sforza-Visconti, Duke of Milan, began to harass the Lord Eugenius P.P. IV. And, then, the Pope agreed to receive an embassage from the King of Naples, and to hear his cause pleaded by Bishop Alonso de Borja.

This was the cause of King Don Alonso. A bastard of the House of Aragon, he had been adopted by Queen Doña Juana of Naples, who lacked a lineal heir, in 1420. He was acknowledged by the people as sovereign of the Regno, and was actually in possession of the crown.

The Christian King Louis XI. also claimed to have been adopted by Queen Doña Juana: but he never had been acknowledged, nor ever had possessed the crown.

Then there was the matter of King Don Alonso's bastard, Don Ferrando. The childless Queen believed him to be the son of Doña Margarita de Hijar, one of her ladies; and, in jealous rage, she smothered her. Whereupon the King banished his wife to Aragon, and legitimated Don Ferrando as his heir.

Let it be recognised that, in the fifteenth century, Popes acted, and were expected to act, in the letter, as well as in the spirit, of the momentous words which are said by the cardinal-archdeacon to all of Them at Their coronation, *Receive this tiara adorned with three crowns, and know Thyself to be the Ruler of the World, the Father of princes and of kings, and the Earthly Vicar of Jesus Christ our Saviour.* The twentieth century is apt to conceive of the Pope as an uninteresting, far-away, semi-diplomatic species of clergyman, nourishing pretensions of utter insignificance. It will be well to remember that once upon a time the Pope was a Power, Who saw nothing figurative, metaphorical, or extravagant in the exordium just quoted, Who was not by any means a négligeable quantity in the world's affairs, and Who literally had the unquestioned right of making or unmaking princes and kings or even emperors.

Here was a case in point. King Don Alonso was a crowned king; but he perfectly was aware that he was powerless to keep his crown, much less to secure the succession for the offspring of his illicit love, unless he could gain the confirmation, the licence, of the Roman Pontiff—in technical phrase, a sovereign found it to be indispensable that he should be able to add to his style of King By The Grace Of God, *And By The Favour Of The Apostolic See.*

Hence the embassage to the Lord Eugenius P.P. IV, headed by Bishop Alonso de Borja, to whose incessant labour and exquisite mastery of affairs was due the treaty, ratified in 1444, by which the Pope's Holiness of the one part confirmed the crown of Naples, the Two Sicilies, and Jerusalem, to King Don Alonso I. de Aragona, and licensed the legitimation of Don Ferrando; while the King's Majesty of the other part agreed to defend the Lord Eugenius P.P. IV against His enemies, and especially against Duke Francesco Sforza-Visconti of Milan.

As a reward for his skill in the rôle of peacemaker, Bishop Alonso de Borja was raised to the purple on the second of May 1444, as Cardinal-Presbyter of the Title of Santi Quattro Coronati with curial rank; and so King Don Alonso, the Magnanimous, lost his most trusted counsellor. The Bishop's bastard, Don Francisco de Borja, who will appear later in this history, had been born at Savina, in Valencia, in 1441.

.   .   .

The Cardinal of Valencia at the Court of Rome gained

the reputation of being inaccessible to flattery, incapable of party-feeling, impregnable in integrity, inconspicuous in morals, inexhaustible in capacity for business and in knowledge of canon-law. In 1446, the Lord Eugenius P.P. IV restored the Hospital of the Confraternity of Santo Spirito, in the Region of Borgo, to something of its pristine glory; and He undertook to contribute a yearly sum whereby its usefulness among the poor and needy might be maintained. The pontifical example of practical Christian charity set a fashion for the cardinals of the curia. The quaint Bull containing the subscribers' names is signed by

I, Eugenius, The Bishop of the Catholic Church,

and by nine cardinals, of whom the last is

I, the Cardinal of Valencia, Presbyter of the Title of
Santi Quattro Coronati.

Cardinal de Borja assisted at the election of the succeeding Pontiff, the Lord Nicholas P.P. V; at Whose death, in 1455, the prediction of St. Vincent Ferrer was fulfilled.

.   .   .

At the time of His elevation to the Supreme Pontificate, the Lord Calixtus P.P. III was a feeble old man of the age of seventy-seven years. His duties, as Governor of the Bastard of Naples, as Bishop of Valencia, as Orator of King to Pope, as Plenipotentiary between Pope and King, as Counsellor of King, as Cardinal-Counsellor of Pope, and his ceaseless studies in jurisprudence and canon-law, had worn away the bodily strength of him—the perishable thin scabbard that hid steel indomitable and keen.

Outside the Vatican very diverse opinions were entertained of Him. His long connection with King Don Alonso I. caused anxiety, suspicion, and jealousy, among the powers of Italy. They were always disgusted, those Powers, to find the Pope on easy terms with a temporal sovereign, with one of themselves; and the Magnanimous

King Don Alonso was the next-door neighbour, so to speak, of the Lord Calixtus P.P. III. Such a combination inevitably inspired distrust. The fear was expressed that Naples, through his former secretary, would rule the Holy See—and Christendom. The official despatches of the Orators of Florence, Genoa, and Venice, hypocritically displayed the greatest satisfaction: but their private letters were in a diametrically opposing strain. A great grievance was made of the fact that the new Pope was a Spaniard and a foreigner. Some thought that a handful of discontented cardinals should leave Rome, set up a pseudopontiff in another city, and inaugurate a Fortieth Schism. Oh, people knew one another to be properly cantankerous in the fifteenth century! But Rome considered the Lord Calixtus P.P. III a just and right-minded man. The Procurator-General of the Order of Teutonic Knights wrote to the Grand Master on the third of May 1455: "The new Pope is an old man, of honourable and virtuous life, and of excellent repute." Messer Bartolomeo Michele, a Sienese, wrote to his native city, exhorting the Sienesi to send the most splendid possible embassage to congratulate the Pope, selecting for the same only eminent and worthy men, inasmuch as that the Lord Calixtus P.P. III was excessively learned and clear-sighted: "He is a man of great sanctity and learning, a friend and adherent of King Don Alonso. He has always shown Himself well-disposed to our city, and by nature He is peaceable and kindly." But the best appreciation of all is given by St. Antonino, that gentle, brave Archbishop of Florence, whose quality all the world admires and loves. He wrote to Messer Giovanni of Orvieto, the 24th of April 1455.

"The election of the Lord Calixtus P.P. III at first gave little satisfaction to the Italians. Inprimis, he was Valencian or Catalan; and they feared lest He should transfer the Papal Court to another country. Also, they feared lest He should entrust to Catalans the fortresses of Holy Church, which, only after many difficulties, could be recovered. But now they are reassured by more mature reflection, and by the reputation that He bears for goodness, penetration, and impartiality. And, also, I have seen His solemn promise that He will devote all His powers against the Turks and for the conquest of Constantinople. It is not to be believed or said that He is attached to one nation more than another, but rather that, as a just and prudent man, He will give to every one his due. Meanwhile, let us always think well of the Holy Father, and judge His actions more favourably than those of any other human being. And let us not be frightened by every little shock. Christ guides the Barque of Peter, which, therefore, can never sink."

That letter contains a concise summary of the situation, written with the benevolent simplicity of a dignified fine gentleman, and with the unerring sapience of a saint.

.   .   .

The Pope is the Bishop of Rome. The insignia of His office are the Fisherman's Ring, the Triple Crown, the Triple Cross, and the Keys. At His election by the Conclave, He receives the Ring. Afterwards the insignia are conferred, with the Pallium that He wears at all times in sign of universal jurisdiction, at His coronation by the Cardinal-Archdeacon in the Collegiate-Basilica of St. Peter-by-the-Vatican. But yet another ceremony awaits performance. As Bishop of Rome, He must take formal possession of, and be enthroned in, the cathedral of His diocese, either in person or by proxy. That cathedral is not St. Peter's: but St. John's *in Laterano,* which, consequently, bears on its façade the magniloquent title

MOTHER AND MISTRESS OF ALL CHURCHES IN THE CITY
AND IN THE WORLD

It is the most important church in Christendom.

The Lord Calixtus P.P. III was elected on the eighth of April 1455. On the twentieth He was crowned as "Ruler of the World, Father of princes and of kings, and Earthly Vicar of Jesus Christ our Saviour"; and the same day He made a triumphal progress through the city to take possession of the Lateran. In the porch of that cathedral there is a low marble throne, called Sedes Stercoraria, on which the Pope sits to receive the homage of the Lateran Chapter while cantors chant the anthem

> "He raiseth-up the poor out of the dust:
> "and lifteth the needy out of the dung-hill.
>
> "That He may set him with princes:
> "even with the princes of His people.
> (Ps. cxiii. 7, 8).
>
> *"Suscitans a terra inopem:*
> *"et de stercore erigens pauperem.*
>
> *"Ut collocet eum cum principibus:*
> *"cum principibus populi Sui.*
> (Vulgate, Ps. cxii. 6, 7).

It has been seen that the Lord Calixtus P.P. III was not unnaturally popular. It will be readily admitted that the Roman baronial houses of Colonna and Orsini would have been more than human had they not felt some mortification at the failure of their conclavial manœuvres to secure the Papacy for one of themselves. Still, the thing was done. A Catalan—the Romans of the fifteenth century called all Spaniards Catalans—a Catalan indubitably had been elected; but He was old, He was feeble, He might be influenced, He might be amenable to intimidation, to a show of force. It is so easy for the twentieth century, with its jaded physique and sophisticated brain, and the magnificent perspective of half a thousand years, to read the motives which actuated the physically strong and intellectually simple fifteenth, when the world—the dust which makes man's flesh—was five centuries younger and fresher; when colour was vivid; light, a blaze; virtue and vice, extreme; passion, primitive and ardent; life, violent; youth, intense, supreme; and sententious pettifogging respectable mediocrity, senile and debile, of no importance whatever.

So, while the Lord Calixtus P.P. III was at the Lateran, the barons of Rome took action. A slight quarrel arising in the crowd between one of the Orsini and a retainer of Anguillara (hereditary foes of Orsini) provided a pretext. Instantly shouts ascended, and men of arms coursed through the city roaring *Orso, Orso* (Bear, Bear—war-cry of Orsini, alluding to their badge). From every dark and narrow alley of the Regions of Campo Marzo and Ponte, from the Albergo dell' Orso (Bear Inn) by the Torre di Nona, from the castellated fortress which Orsini had made of Pompey's Theatre, came the clang of arms, with the rush of hurrying feet of desperate brigands, adherents and mercenaries of Orsini; and Don Napoleone Orsini was at the head of three thousand men. Outside the cathedral, the hum of a maddened mob swelled into a raucous roar as of bears hungry for hot blood, when Count Averso of Anguillara fled into the Lateran Basilica, seeking sanctuary in the very presence of Christ's Vicar; and, above the roar, the voice of Orsini pierced the holy portals of the Prince of Peace, penetrated to the ears of Pope Calixtus throned as Bishop of Rome among His canons in the centre of the apse, launching a hideous threat to storm and sack the Lateran unless the body of Anguillara were given to him as meat for his three thousand bears. There was a movement in the ermine and scarlet college that stood near the papal throne, and Cardinal Latino Orsini di Bari hurried down the nave to confer with his turbulent brother, Don Napoleone. Though disappointed that he had failed to win the Triregno [1] for himself, this cardinal appears to have had some feeling of decency as to what was due to Holy Church. As a churchman he felt bound to stand by his order; although as an Orsini he would have preferred a different state of affairs. Still, the object of the riot had been attained, the Lord Calixtus P.P. III had re-

[1] The pontifical diadem, consisting of a conical cap woven of the plumage of white peacocks and encircled by three crowns of gold. It is sometimes called the Tiara, and must be distinguished from the Mitre.

ceived an object-lesson poignant and pregnant to an ultimate degree, concerning the kind of kakodaimons that He
would have to quell, the species of subject that He was
called to rule. No doubt these were the arguments used to
his brother by the cardinal. It was not the writhing
mangled body of the Eel (Anguillara) that the Bear
(Orsini) craved. That was the merest subterfuge. But to
humiliate the Holiness of the Pope at the very moment of
His exaltation from Sedes Stercoraria to Lateran Throne,
to terrify Him into malleability, into subjugation to Orsini's
will—that—that had been done and well done. Surely an
aged man, so near His grave as was the Lord Calixtus
P.P. III, would wish to purchase peace with any sacrifice,
now that once it had been shown to Him what kind of
devildom environed His very throne-steps. Don Napoleone
Orsini allowed himself to take this view. He withdrew his
myrmidons. The riot was over. Presently the Pope was
riding on His crimson-caparisoned palfrey towards the
Vatican, through a peaceful city kneeling at the roadside
for Apostolic Benediction.

The fashion which foreigners affect in writing of Italy
makes one laugh—and weep.

They drawl of a dreamland of subtle sweetness and
softest light, of delicate fantasy, of neutral hue; peopled by
shades from faded frescoes æsthetically tinctured, academic,
conventional, conformant to the canons of that unspeak-
ably abominable dilution which the twentieth century calls
Art; and mitigated only by a leavening of organ-grinders
and fortune-telling paroquets.

They must be blind, these foreigners—blind, physically
and mentally—blind, as those who will not see.

Italy is, and always has been, a land of raw reality, of
glittering light, of pure primary colour, of nature naked
and not ashamed, of perfectly transparent souls, of rapid-
est versatility, cleared mystery, ultimate simplicity, steel,
and brains, and blood.

Else she had made no mark, no singular distinguished mark in history.

Has she made no mark?

Ah—what a mark she has made!

The greatest historian of this period, perhaps the most alert and agile writer of any period, Enea Silvio Bartolomeo de' Piccolhuomini (who afterwards became Pope with the title of the Lord Pius P.P. II), says of the Lord Calixtus P.P. III, that His attention to the duties of His office was amazing; that His patience at audiences was astounding; that He Himself dictated the Apostolic Briefs and Bulls written to kings and princes, nor trusted them to the official scribes; that jurisprudence was His recreation; that He was as familiar with canon-law as though He were still professor at the University of Lerida.

Two problems confronted Him at the beginning of His reign: the Renascence of Learning, and the Infidel in Christendom. His predecessor had been a man of words. The Lord Calixtus P.P. III was a man of strenuous deeds. His attitude to Letters and Art was in strong contrast to that of the Lord Nicholas P.P. V. This "withered canonist," as a wit styled Him, was not in sympathy with Culture. Wholly occupied in matters ecclesiastical and political, He had nor time nor means nor inclination to patronise the fashionable scholarship of His day. His vogue was strictly practical.

One of the secrets of the success of the Holy Catholic Apostolic and Roman Church is her catholicity. All sorts and conditions of men can, and do, live within her boundaries. The Lord Nicholas P.P. V had been a Maecenas of Letters and the Arts. In His reign scholars, scribes, and artificers had found their golden age. The Lord Calixtus P.P. III entirely employed Himself in the defence of Christendom, and the clients of His predecessor were conscious of the change. Literature and the fine arts have one very sorry effect upon their professors. Intellectual nature is violently fascinated by the bogey; has singularly well informed itself of the nature, colour, shape, condition, and location, of the forbidden fruit; has minutely investigated every inch of ground and every blade of grass, and every bird and bush in the strictly preserved covert, simply and solely in order that it may avoid poaching, sampling the forbidden fruit, or becoming a prey for the bogey. When one has the duty of avoiding a thing, it is well to know what the thing is which one must avoid; but it is quite easy to know more than enough. All this intimate realisation of the hideousness of sin, this systematic cataloguing of its divisions and sub-divisions, with elaborate excursions along its divers ramifications, certainly inspires a loathing of the intensest kind. It also has another effect. It induces an exaggerated consciousness of virtue. When human nature knows, and is able to describe, with a wealth of detail ordinarily inaccessible, the horrible things which it does not do, it becomes "puffed up," in the words of St. Paul. This condition of "unctuous rectitude," inspired entirely by a horror of sin, is a proximate occasion of the sin of calumny. Roman Catholic human nature, not unconscious of its own integrity, when confronted by an antipathetic personality, instantly conceives of the latter as a sinner. I am right—you disagree with me—therefore you are wrong—is the absurd syllogism or logical process which it uses. And, drawing upon its copious catalogues of sins, on the principle that he who offends in the least is guilty of all, Roman Catholic human nature will proceed to shew how exceedingly sinful it is possible for an enemy to be. The said enemy, or perhaps a mere opponent, incontinently finds himself accused of breaking the Ten Commandments of God, the various Precepts of the Church; of committing the Seven Deadly Sins—Pride, Covetousness, Lust, Anger, Gluttony, Envy, Sloth; the Six Sins against the Holy Ghost—Presumption of God's Mercy, Despair, Impugning the Known Truth, Envy at another's Spiritual Good, Ob-

stinacy in Sin, Final Impenitence; the Four Sins Crying
to Heaven for Vengeance—Wilful Murder, Sin of the
Cities of the Plain, Oppression of the Poor, Defrauding
Labourers of their Wages; or, if he has not achieved the
guilt of these in his proper person, at least he has been
an accomplice of some other sinner, in the Nine Ways by
which a Man may be Accessory to Another's Sin—*i.e.,* by
counsel, command, consent, provocation, by praise or flattery, by concealment, by partaking, by silence, by defence
of the ill which is done. That is, (in the twentieth century
when Catholics are ruled by a Press ostentatiously Fenian
and Anglophobe, and was, in the fifteenth century when
Catholics were also human, but not vulgar or sophisticated), the predicament of anybody, Pope or peasant, who
incurs or incurred, the disesteem of, or who makes, or
made, himself unpleasant to a brother in the Faith. By
hints, inferences, insinuations, ill-motives assigned, and a
hundred ingenious methods, rarely by defined accusations,
the sin of calumny is, and was, committed, absolutely and
utterly because the calumniator so hates sin as to have no
difficulty in persuading himself that the man who flouts
him must be a sinner. For be it noted, that all the calumnies
that bespatter the House of Borgia, all the "liability to disesteem," which through five centuries has been their portion, and has made their very name a synonym of Turpitude, all these have a Roman Catholic origin. Roman
Catholics are the primal calumniators who have muddied,
and do muddy, God's Vicegerents, the Lord Calixtus P.P.
III, and His nephew the Lord Alexander P.P. VI, with
every species of ordure, with ascriptions of every crime
known to casuistry (the science of cases of conscience),
including those which are unspeakable except in an appendix veiled in a learned language *quo minus erubescamus.*
Bishop Vespasiano da Bisticci of Vicenza was a Roman
Catholic; Messers Stefano Infessura, Monsignor Hans
Burchard, Messer Francesco Guicciardini, Bishop Paolo

Giovio of Nocera, Messer Giangiovio Pontano, Sannazar "The Christian Vergil," Messer Benedetto Varchi:—they were all Roman Catholics who inaugurated the campaign of calumny against the Supreme Pontiffs of the House of Borgia. In dealing with calumny, the difficulty is to obtain definite evidence of a definite charge which is intrinsically false and, at the same time, derogatory to the person against whom it is laid. This difficulty is one that continually confronts the investigator. Prelates, priests, princes, penmen, sometimes because they had a grievance, sometimes confessedly wilfully, sometimes by way of wanton babble, habitually launched against their enemies or superiors accusations of depravity the most loathsome, of crime the most odious. What they said by word of mouth cannot surely be known Until The Books Are Opened. What they wrote in pasquinades, in diaries, in official despatches, in official chronicles, or for the mere æsthetic pleasure of recording a salacious gibe in curial Tuscan or in golden Latin—these remain. A few of the more important icily will be discussed here. The student of history knows no more refreshing recreation than that of nailing liars, like vermin, to the wall.

The statement of Bishop Vespasiano da Bisticci of Vicenza, quoted above, is a fair example of the less fœtid species of calumny: it only amounts to an accusation of "philistinism." However, it at once may be described as being both stupid and improbable. With regard to the naif surprize, said to have been shown by the Lord Calixtus P.P. III, on seeing "so many excellent books," is it likely that, as Bishop Alonso de Borja, Ambassador Plenipotentiary and Confidential Counsellor of the Majesty of Naples, he never had seen fine things before? Is it likely that Cardinal Alonso de Borja, eleven years cardinal of the curia residing in the Court of Rome, had never seen splendid books before? Of what kind then were the missals and pontificals which, as bishop, he would have used in his

daily mass? Is it likely that Cardinal Alonso de Borja—
one of the actual electors of the Lord Nicholas P.P. V,
constantly at His side from beginning to end of His reign,
if not assistant to, at least cognizant of, His every action—
had never seen, had never touched, handled, tasted, those
identical five hundred books, bound in crimson velvet with
clasps of silver, with which that august Pontiff enriched
the Vatican library. The assumption is ridiculous, absurd.

The calumny that the Lord Calixtus P.P. III gave books
to the Bishop of Vich in the manner of a Vandal arose in
this way. The Lord Cosimo de Monserrato, Bishop of
Vich from 1460 to 1471, was ordered by His Holiness to
compile a catalogue of the books in the Vatican library,
on the sixteenth of April 1455, four days before His coronation. A copy of this catalogue was brought to Vich by
this same Lord Cosimo on his appointment to the bishopric
five years later. It was most likely made by one of the
Vatican scribes,[1] and it contains numerous marginal notes
in the bishop's handwriting. From these notes, a precise
list of the number of books actually given away by the
Lord Calixtus P.P. III may be obtained. They were five—
not "several hundred"—of no great value, and—duplicates.
Two of these, a copy of the Epistles of St. Augustine,
annotated by Nicholas of Lira, and a Book on the Truth
of the Catholic Faith, were presented to the Pope's late
patron, King Don Alonso de Aragona of Naples, the Two
Sicilies, and Jerusalem. The note against them in the catalogue is *S.D.N. dedit hunc domino regi Arag.* ("Our Holy
Lord gave this to the lord king of Aragon.") Now, if He
only gave two books to His old friend and former em-
ployer who (as may be judged from the fact that he employed the renowned Messeri Lorenzo Valla and Giangiovio
Pontano as his secretaries) had a very pretty taste for
letters, who was a reigning sovereign, and an extremely

---

[1] The first printing press in Italy did not arrive till October 1465
at Subjaco in the Sabine Hills.

serviceable and powerful ally of the Holy See, is He likely to have given "several hundred" to the Cardinal of Ruthenia and Catalan nobles? Finally, the heathen Cardinal Platina, who wrote his History of the Popes in the reign of the Lord Xystus [1] P.P. IV (the third in succession from the Lord Calixtus P.P. III,) expressly mentions the magnificence of the library of the Lord Nicholas P.P. V, which, certainly, he could not have known if it had been destroyed in the manner described by the lying Bishop Vespasiano da Bisticci of Vicenza.

One "philistine" act may be admitted on behalf of the Lord Calixtus P.P. III. He sold the silver from the bindings of those books. He sacrificed them for the crusade in defence of Christendom. He also sold all the Vatican plate. He insisted that the salt-cellar of His Own table should be of earthenware, not gold; and, indeed, He even offered His tiara in pledge for the same admirable object. He was blamed.

The Lord Calixtus P.P. III was by no means the enemy of letters. He made havoc among the decadents, the affected literary poseurs who infested the Borgian as well as the Victorian Era; but He cherished genius, and to scholars of distinction He was a generous patron. The diverting case of Messer Lorenzo Valla will serve for an example. This notable, being one of the secretaries of King Don Alonso I, was well-known to the Holiness of the Pope. He was erudite beyond most of his contemporaries, of a daring temperament, and impatient of bad scholarship, falsehood, and superstition. In 1440 he indited a merciless exposure of the monstrous fiction now known as the

---

[1] The first Pontiff of this name, fifth in succession from the Lord St. Peter P.P., is named in the Canon of the Mass as XYSTUS [Ξυστός cf. Xanthus (Ξάνθος)]. The same form XYSTUS occurs in the Kalendarium, and, in fact, in all officially issued liturgies; and is adopted also in the authorised English version of the Liturgy. The word SIXTUS does not appear to be a Latin word at all, and is not in Andrew's Latin-English Lexicon. It most likely is a debased corruption from XYSTUS, when Latin liquefied into the Italian SISTO.

Forged Decretals and Donation of Constantine, upon which, in perfect good faith, the temporal dominions of the Papacy then were held. Also, he attacked the leaden Latin of the Vulgate, and lauded the Golden Latin of Vergil and Cicero, or the Silver Latin of Tacitus. The twentieth century—which knows the Latin of the Roman Mass to be the low Latin of Roman plebeians of the first five centuries, from the age of the Lord St. Peter P.P. to that of His successor the Lord St. Gelasius P.P., Whose "Prayer for Peace" is the latest known addition to the canon—will not find Messer Lorenzo Valla to have been guilty of any very shocking crime herein. But the clergy of Naples considered him in the light of a menace to the Christian Palladium, and mentioned him to the Inquisition. When he was brought before them, the Inquisitors invited him formally to assent to a profession of faith, which was neither the Apostles' nor the Nicene Creed, nor the Creed of St. Athanasius, but one which they had drawn up to suit the fancied needs of his case. The situation was the historical parallel of one which sullied the dying years of the last century. Messer Lorenzo knew too much; took an impish delight in saying what he knew; he was a nuisance, a disturbing influence. To the proposition of the Inquisition he opposed a firm refusal; he would not sign their specimen of a creed. The circumstances now were becoming strained. But the Inquisitors of the fifteenth century had more serpentine wisdom than those of the nineteenth. They did not proceed at once to an abrupt and tactless excommunication, exacerbating to all parties. They tried another line. Would Messer Lorenzo Valla have the courtesy, then, to propound his own creed, that his judges might examine whether it were heretical or no? The reply of Messer Lorenzo was delicious. "I believe," he said, "I believe what Holy Mother Church believes. She *knows* nothing. But—I *believe* what she *believes*." Just at this stage the king sent a mandate to the Inquisitors of Naples, bidding them to had been retrieved by a treaty, known as the Concordat of the Lord Eugenius P.P. IV.

At the beginning of His reign, while waiting for the formal homage of The Pacific Caesar Friedrich IV, the Lord Calixtus P.P. III observed the terms of this Concordat. When the news of His election in April reached Germany, a Diet of the Empire was held at Neustadt to appoint Orators,[1] and to consider the chances of squeezing fresh concessions. "Now is the time to vindicate our liberty, for hitherto we have only been the handmaid of Holy Church," said Jacob of Trier; and Caesar Friedrich IV privately grieved that the Papacy gave him little support in his difficulties with turbulent sub-sovereigns and subjects. The celebrated Lord Enea Silvio Bartolomeo de' Piccolhuomini, Bishop of Siena, poured oil upon the troubled waters of the Diet. He had lived many years in Germany, as poet-laureate, orator to Utter Britain [2] (Scotland), novelist, historian, and confidential secretary to Caesar; and he knew his Germany. He deservedly was trusted both by Church and State. He soothed Caesar, saying that the mob was always inconstant, dangerous, and that a ruler did a vain thing when he tried to please. He soothed the Diet, saying that the interests of Papacy and Empire were identical, and that from a new Pope new favours might be gained. The Diet named Bishop Enea Silvio, with the jurist Hans Hagenbach, as orators who were to offer to the Lord Calixtus P.P. III the obedience of the Holy Roman Empire, and to lay before Him the grievances of Caesar.

The Lord Calixtus P.P. III was more independent of Germany than His two predecessors had been; and in a position to command, not compromise. The Lord Eugenius

[1] The business of these Orators (ambassadors) was conducted more by means of florid eloquence than by the writing of despatches; though, of course, the last was not neglected.
[2] "...horribilesque ultimosque Britannos." C. Valerius Catullus XI.

P.P. IV, being in need of temporal support, had purchased Germany's obedience by secret concessions and promises of money. The Lord Nicholas P.P. V was privy to these arrangements, and, feeling bound by them, had paid His share ; but there was a matter of twenty-five thousand ducats yet unpaid. The Lord Calixtus P.P. III had taken no part in these negotiations. During His cardinalate, He had had ample opportunities of reckoning up Caesar Friedrich IV as a feeble, feckless old simpleton, devoid of moral backbone, whom no concessions ever could stiffen into any semblance of imperial capacity. The Pope's Holiness felt that He could do quite well without the Emperor's Augustitude.

Therefore, when Caesar's Orators arrived in Rome, on the tenth of August 1455, and prayed for a private audience, (at which, as the custom was, they would try to squeeze the Holy Father, making the proffer of their sovereign's homage dependent upon the Pope's willingness to oblige), the Lord Calixtus P.P. III refused to entertain requests until after the obedience of Germany should have been received.

The Orators were confounded, so they said, by this demand ; but, as loyal sons of Holy Mother Church, (Bishop Enea Silvio was the spokesman), and that scandal might be avoided, they would give way. Before a public consistory of cardinals, they presented to the Pope the homage of Caesar, in an elaborate oration containing no mention of unpleasant topics, such as the imperial demands and the Concordat of the Lord Eugenius P.P. IV, but mainly consisting of a string of formal compliments to the Supreme Pontiff, and declamations against the Muslim Infidel. (Pii II. Orationes I, 336.)

After this the Orators could not insist upon the Rights of Caesar. On his behalf, they might only approach the strenuous Pope as suppliants appealing to His clemency, as children begging a father's favour. They had cut the ground from under their own feet; and, as Bishop Enea Silvio knew quite well, that was precisely what had been intended. The Lord Calixtus P.P. II disclaimed any obligation of paying His predecessor's debts, having other uses for five-and-twenty thousand ducats; and the question of Caesar's rights to nominate to bishoprics, and to have a share of the tithe about to be raised for the Crusade, should be considered in due season, said the Pope to the Orators.

.   .   .

Meanwhile the Eternal City was engaged in making ready for war. Immediately after His coronation, the Lord Calixtus P.P. III privately proclaimed the Crusade. In August, He made the same proclamation in public consistory, and read the following vow: "We, Calixtus the Pontiff, swear to God Almighty, the Holy and Undivided Trinity, that We relentlessly will follow the Turks, the enemies of the Name of Christ, with war, with maledictions, with interdicts, with execrations, and indeed with every means in Our power." (Ciacconi II., 981.) This oath in holograph, was constantly before the Pope's eyes during His pontificate, and was found hanging on the wall by His bedside as an ornament of His chamber when at length He died.

The infirmities of age chained the Pontiff to His room: recreation was to Him a thing unknown, for the business of the Crusade consumed His energies. His firm and unrelenting will, set upon this single aim, would brook no control, no influence. He knew Himself to be the "Ruler of the World," and He shut His mouth down fast against all opposition. To the quarrelsome sovereigns of Christendom He envoyed ablegates charged to reconcile all differences, to urge the setting aside of private squabbles, of petty ambitions, in favour of the greater necessity, resistance to and annihilation of the Muslim Infidel. Through every Christian country He sent Apostolic Missionaries, curial bishops and prelates, friars and monks renowned for eloquence, to preach the sacred duty of fighting against the enemies of the Christian Faith. On every Christian country He imposed tax of a tithe to meet the cost of the Crusade. Archbishop St. Antonino of Florence nobly seconded His efforts, raising the standard of St. George's rose-red cross, and preaching like a new St. Bernard. The buildings, with which the preceding Pontiff had begun to adorn the city, were stopped, and the swarms of workmen dismissed. The revenues of the Papal States were applied to the construction of a fleet of swift galleys for the harrying of the Turk. Daily the Holy Father descended to St. Peter's with His Own hands to fix the cross on the breasts of recruits enlisting. The papal jewels were pawned, and their price added to the war-chest. The Pope's Holiness trusted much in Duke Philip of Burgundy: He tried to persuade the Magnanimous King Don Alonso de Aragona to take the cross.

In the east of Europe, the black cloud of the Muslim Infidel advanced continually. Skanderbeg, a chieftain of romantic past, renowned for military deeds, opposed them. The fame of his achievements is the one brightness in the holy war. His army, composed of divers races naturally antagonistic, only was welded together by the magic of success or of his personal influence. Such a bond is but a weak one. A cause, that rests upon a single man, will stand no strain. Presently his Albanians revolted, at a moment when the Infidel pressed him hard. Defeated, he withdrew to mountain fastnesses; and sent couriers to Rome with an appeal for reinforcement. The Lord Calixtus P.P. III replied with money, wherewith Skanderbeg bought the allegiance of his disaffected troops and retrieved his position. But on the heels of triumph came fresh disaster. To avenge some slight, his own nephew made cause against him, persuaded the Albanians to fresh revolt, and deserted with them to the Infidel.

.   .   .

In the nature of human things, every man, in every rank of life, must submit to some affliction of mind or body. Has any one ever troubled to inquire what may be the special affliction proper to the Pope? It is loneliness—utter loneliness—loneliness in a crowd. The Pope cannot have a friend; for friendship postulates equality: and who is the equal of the Pope? The cardinals who surround Him are of the faction that opposed His election, or of the faction that claims favour in return for support. He, Who sits upon the Throne of Peter, looks down from that pinnacle upon the peoples, the nations, and the tongues, in His heart knowing them to be enemies or suitors. What wonder then that, though His spirit indeed be willing, His humanity shall crave human sympathy!

This consideration is offered to explain the nepotism of the Popes of the Renascence. They surrounded Themselves with men of Their own families; men bound to Them by ties of blood and kinship. Being generally of mature age themselves, They chose Their young relations; and upon these They conferred the rank which qualified them to enter the inner circle of the curia. This action appears to have been dictated by the natural desire of human man for offspring. Certainly a Pope can always create cardinals, who are to Him as spiritual sons; but to create cardinals of those who already are of one's own family is a thing nearer, a more intimate relation. So the human heart of the Pope would become rejuvenated, would renew its strength, would gratify its natural longing for an entourage of creatures in which it might place confidence and trust. For the cardinal-nephews, loathed by all other cardinals, owing everything to the Pope, would be bound to Him and to His interest as by chains of iron. The system is proved to be liable to abuse. That is the corollary of all human systems. It is indefensible; but it is explicable; and the foregoing is an attempt only in the direction of explanation.

On the twentieth of February 1456, at the beginning of

the second year of His reign, the Lord Calixtus P.P. III proclaimed to a stormy consistory the creation of three cardinals, two being His Own nephews, and one the son of the heir to the crown of Portugal. Let it be remarked that He did nothing for His son, Don Francisco de Borja, now a charming and eligible young man of fifteen years.

The Sacred College murmured and objected: but, in this matter the will of the Pope is law. The new creatures were:—

(α) Don Luis Juan de Mila y Borja, of the age of twenty years, celebrated for vigorous physical beauty. He was the son of Doña Caterina de Borja (sister of the Pope's Holiness) by her husband Don Juan de Mila, Baron of Mazalanes. To him the Pontiff gave the scarlet hat, which He had relinquished on His election to the papacy, that of Cardinal-Presbyter of the Title of San Quattro Coronati.

(β) Don Rodrigo de Lançol y Borja, of the age of twenty-five years, distinguished by that marvellous Spanish courtliness and magnificence of person which was the theme of admiration until he died. He was son of Doña Juana de Borja, (sister of the Pope's Holiness,) by her husband Don Jofre de Lançol. To him the Pontiff gave the scarlet hat of Cardinal-Deacon of San Niccolo in *Carcere Tulliano*.

(γ) Don Jayme de Portugal, Archbishop of Lisbon and son of the Infante Don Pedro de Portugal. To him the Pontiff gave the scarlet hat of Cardinal-Deacon of Sant' Eustachio. There appear to have been reasons of state for the elevation of this young man; and it was usual for the reigning Houses of Europe to have one of their junior scions in the Sacred College. The Cardinal of Portugal lived a retired and saint-like life, distinguished for his modesty and maiden purity. He died in 1459 at the age of five and twenty years; and his tomb, by Messer Antonio Rossellino, in Samminiato al Monte at Florence, one of the most exquisite monuments of the Renascence, bears the touching epitaph:

> "Regia stirps Jacobus nomen Lusitana propago,
> "Insignis forma, summa pudicitia,
> "Cardineus titulus, morum nitor, optima vita,
> "Iste fuere mihi: mors iuuenem rapuit;
> "Ne se pollueret, maluit iste mori.

Bishop Enea Silvio Bartolomeo de' Piccolhuomini says of these creatures in his commentaries, "All are young, but of an excellent nature." The only concession that the Pope would make to the objecting cardinals, was the postponement of the ceremonial conferring of insignia until the ensuing September; when many of the malcontents vented vain spleen by quitting Rome.

.   .   .

This was a year of strife. The peace of central Italy was disturbed by the bandit Niccolo Piccinino, a bastard of Visconti; who, believing the country to be about to be denuded of armed men, saw an opportunity for self aggrandisement. He collected mercenaries, and marched against Siena, a small republic, very loyal to the Holy See, which, in this age of culture, had destroyed the lovely Aphrodite of Lusippos in its dread of paganism, and consecrated itself to Madonna under the title "Sena Ciuitas Virginis." Meeting the Papal and Milanese forces which were concentrating for the Crusade, but quite ready for a little incidental fighting on the way, Piccinino withdrew to the mountains. King Don Alonso of the Regno, as usual, was playing a double part. It did not suit him to show conspicuous friendship for the Pope's allies, lest the Lord Calixtus P.P. III should become independent. Stipulations were made favourable to Piccinino; and, their appeal to Naples having failed, the Sienesi were forced into a disgraceful peace with the brigand.

Sultàn Muhammed extended his conquests to Servia, and prepared to devour Hungary, launching one hundred and fifty thousand infidels against Belgrade. Fra Jan Capistran's eloquence and pious zeal roused the Magyars to consciousness of the imminent peril; Cardinal Bernardino Caravajal, the ablegate, inspired their patriotism with his wisdom and devotion; and Jan Hunniades, the Vaivod of Hungary, resolved to resist invasion. Confidence in princes was, as always, vain. The terror-stricken King Wladislaw fled with his court and his guardian, Count de Cilly, from Buda to Venice; and along the valley of the Danube poured the locust-swarms of Infidels to invest Belgrade. The Vaivod Jan Hunniades raised an army at his own expense; whence came the means, the men, is still unknown, for most important documents connected with the siege of Belgrade yet attend discovery: but there was a Magyar army, commanded by Jan Hunniades, ministered to by Fra Jan Capistran, which advanced to relieve Belgrade; and the ablegate, Fra Bernardino Caravajal, remained behind at Buda, by the Vaivod's request, to collect and forward reinforcements. On the fourteenth day of siege the Magyars collided with the Infidels. Already the walls of Belgrade sorely were shaken: but the arrival of the Vaivod, breaking the Muslim line and winning a complete victory, put courage into the hearts of the beleaguered. In three months time, once more the Muslim concentrated, and on the twenty-first of July the city suffered a second storm. Jan Hunniades and Fra Jan Capistran, from one of the towers, directed the defence. At a crisis in the fray, the heroic friar rushed, like a second Joshua, through the Christian host, waving the crucifix and a banner with the sacred monogram invented by San Bernardino of Siena. Behind him came the Vaivod with aid. Through breaches in the walls many times the Infidels streamed in, and always the stream was dammed and driven back. Fra Jan Capistran himself led a squadron of Magyar huszars [1] who put

---

[1] *Huszar*, derived by a roundabout route from Italian *cossaro*, corsair, reelance (v. Murray).

Suspecting his bonafides, they mentioned their suspicions to their August Uncle, with the result that he was forbidden to approach the Vatican. Not to be beaten, Cardinal Scarampi discovered a fervent zeal for the Crusade. There could be no surer way into the Pope's favour. His Holiness considered that this prelate might devote his enormous fortune to the war-fund; and He lost no time in receiving him in audience, and naming him Pontifical Admiral. The Cardinal-Nephews urged the advisability of flying him with a string; and therefore his authority was restricted. A man of his fashion and quality could have put in a fine dignified time ashore. But that would not have suited the Cardinal-Nephews; and the Lord Calixtus P.P. III perceived no signs of the unbuckling of the Cardinal-Admiral's pouches. So they gave him banquets, and his sailing-orders. A fleet of transports left the Tiber with five thousand troops aboard: but the Cardinal-Admiral stayed in Rome to assure the Pope's Holiness that these were insufficient for any practical purpose; and that a fleet of thirty galleys was absolutely necessary.

Then the strenuous Pontiff remembered that King Don Alonso had promised to provide Him with such a fleet; and it gently and firmly was intimated to the Cardinal-Admiral that he might go to Naples and collect the same: if he failed to go, he had the alternative of facing a judicial inquiry into his doings as generalissimo under the Lord Eugenius P.P. IV. Thereon the Cardinal-Admiral scoured away hotfoot for Naples; where he found that King Don Alonso the Magnanimous had belied his promises, having sent the ships to settle a little private dispute in which his Majesty was engaged with the Republic of Genoa. This was bad news for the Pope: but it did not alter His determination by the breadth of a single hair. He was quite well-used to the vagaries and magnanimities of the King of Naples, whom He had known for more than forty years. He was equally well-resolved to use the services which the Cardinal-

Admiral had volunteered. Men had thought Him to be a feeble old man who could be influenced with ease. They found out their mistake. We are accustomed to think of youth as fiery and headstrong : but what can bend the will of fiery headstrong age? His Holiness sent imperative commands to the Cardinal-Admiral that he must make the best of the ships in hand, and sail for the Ægean Sea, where at least he could help the Crusade by creating a diversion among the islands that the Infidels owned there.

.   .   .

Fresh troubles were at hand in Hungary. Round Belgrade, the putrefying carcases of the Muslim thousands envenomed the air. The rudiments of antiseptic sanitation were unknown. Those who have had to do with Boers, or Cubans, or Filipinos will know the unspeakable horror that this implies. Pest decimated the Christian army. Plague swept away the Magyar host, that Infidels in vain had tried to overcome. When they told him that his end was near, that Viaticum was approaching to be his strength on that dark road which man must tread alone, the noble Vaivod Jan Hunniades, said : "It is not fitting that our Lord should visit his servant" ; and, rising from his death-bed, he dragged himself to the nearest altar, where, after confession and communion, in the priest's hands he fell and yielded up his great and splendid soul, the eleventh of August 1456. On the twenty-third of October Fra Jan Capistrano also died.

From Rome came the voice of the Pope strenuously appealing to the Powers. His ablegates preached in every country. The common people heard Him gladly, and responded to His Call : but the nobles lent deaf ears. Upper Germany and Nürnberg equipped battalions of crusaders, which were increased by contingents from England and France.

In November the faineant young King Wladislaw returned to Hungary, and visited the field of Belgrade. Since the death of Jan Hunniades the Count de Cilly had made himself of supreme authority over his royal ward. Belgrade still was mourning the mighty Vaivod; and the nobles under Wladislaw Corvinus, Hunniades's son, resenting the insolent assumptions and cowardice of De Cilly, slew him there. The young king concealed his wrath, and persuaded the sons of Jan Hunniades to follow him to Buda. All unsuspicious of that treachery of which cowards are capable they obeyed, and, on arrival in the capital, the Majesty of Hungary had them seized, and Wladislaw Corvinus Hunniades publicly beheaded as a traitor. Hungary was now in woeful plight. Deprived by axe and pest of those strong leaders who had merited her trust, her king a venomous child, her throne with no legitimate heir, she waited, in fear and trembling, to hear again the Infidel thundering at her gate. All discipline was at an end; the Magyar Huszars were disbanded, and returned to their homes.

.   .   .

In Germany, the question of the Magyar Succession was regarded as confusion worse confounded; and the Electors of the Empire considered the time a suitable one for re-applying the screw to feeble needy Caesar Friedrich IV, their suzerain.

They invited him to preside at a Diet at Nürnberg, on St. Andrew's Day, 1456; and, indeed, their conduct throughout was thoroughly Caledonian. Their ostensible object was the projection of a new crusade; and they announced an intention of acting independently if Caesar should refuse to come. In reality they meant to pit Pope against Emperor, and Emperor against Pope; so that, in the confusion, they might gratify their private ambitions by snatching concessions from one or other of those Powers. By pretending to desire a new crusade they would gain pontifical favour. By taking independent action they would arouse imperial ire. The Pope might be trusted to grant them what they called Ecclesiastical Reform in return for their alliance to His plans against the Infidel. Caesar might be trusted to concede extension of their political power, in return for their allegiance to him as suzerain. In either case they stood to win something.

Caesar promptly forbade the assembling of the Diet at Nürnberg. His command was slighted; the Diet sat, and was attended by a Papal Ablegate. Purely political discussions ensued; and the Diet adjourned before reaching any conclusion. Then the Elector Albrecht of Brandenberg found it worth his while to form a strong Caesarian party; and the Electors of the papal faction were left in a minority. The cry for Church Reform was raised. The Papacy was threatened with what it was supposed to dread more than a General Council—viz., a Pragmatic Sanction,[1] *i.e.,* a definite assertion of Imperial Supremacy. The Electors kept their proceedings secret, and little news was allowed to reach Rome, where the curia was determined to resist in any case.

The cry for Church Reform is a popular one. The expression of desire for the cultivation and consummation of the Christian Ideal invariably wins sympathy. It is, perhaps, a little unfortunate that the soi-disant reformers of the fifteenth century attached to the word Reform a baser meaning than that which it bears in the twentieth.

Rome had her champion ready in the Lord Enea Silvio Bartolomeo de Piccolhuomini, Bishop of Siena, to whom she entrusted the task of her defence; and that he might be well-armed with all authority, the Pope's Holiness created him Cardinal-Presbyter of the Title of Santa Sa-

[1] Pragmatic Sanction, term of Byzantine origin, was applied to Imperial Edicts (Τὸ Πραγματικόν) containing decrees issued as Fundamental Laws. The Decrees of the Council of Basilea were embodied in a Pragmatic Sanction by the Diet of Mainz, 1434; but at the Council of Vienna, 1448, most of the advantages which it intended to secure for the Church in Germany were abandoned.

bino. "No cardinal ever entered the college with greater difficulty than I; rust had so spread over the hinges (*cardines*, specimen of fifteenth-century pun) that the door could not turn and open. Calixtus used battering rams and every kind of instrument to force it," said the new Cardinal of Siena to the Lord Giovanni Castelleone, Bishop and Cardinal of Pavia. (Pii II. Ep. 195.) The Sacred College had not forgiven the Lord Calixtus P.P. III for the creation of the Cardinal-Nephews; and its policy was to oppose God's Vicegerent and all His works. This new creature, too, was credited with liberal proclivities; and the conservatism of the Italian cardinals was up in arms. The Cardinal of Siena had been so long a resident in Germany that he was looked upon as more a German than Italian, more of a friend to Caesar than to Peter. Above all, his transcendent talents and versatility were excessively distasteful to mere mediocrity.

The adjourned Diet of Nürnberg resumed its session at Frankfort-on-the-Main. Here it became definitely hostile to Caesar; and, by announcing its intention to resist the collection of tithe, to the Pope also. It committed the strategical error of uniting its two enemies by the bond of a single interest. The Lord Calixtus P.P. III instantly appealed to Caesar Friedrich IV on behalf of the Crusade; and so ended the year of grace 1456.

Let it be conceded that Germany was aggrieved; that there were engagements unfulfilled by Rome. What then? Rome, and all the world, knew Germany's habit of clamouring for Reform, wherever she saw a chance of being paid for silence. Rome, and all the world, knew that these clamours only originated with insincere and venal prelates and Electors, who would become obsequiously dumb on a sop being thrown to their personal interests.

The leader of the Electors was the Lord Hans of Baden, Prince Archbishop of Mainz. His chancellor, Martin Mayr, in writing congratulations to the Cardinal of Siena on his

elevation, took occasion to be very bellicose about Papal
treatment of Germany. "His Holiness observes neither
the decrees of the Council of Constance, nor of Basilea,
nor the agreements of His predecessors, but sets the German nation at naught," he said. "Our elections of bishops
arbitrarily are annulled. Reservations are made in favour
of cardinals and papal secretaries. You yourself have a
general reservation of benefices in the provinces of Mainz,
Trier, and Köln, to the value of two thousand ducats per
annum—an unprecedented and unheard-of grant. Annates
rigorously are exacted, grants of expectancies habitually
are given, and his Holiness is not content with His due.
Bishoprics are not given to the most worthy, but to the
highest bidder. Fresh tithes are imposed without the consent of our bishops, and are paid to the Pope. In every way
Germany, once so glorious, is used as a handmaid. For
years she has groaned in slavery. Now her nobles think
that the time has come to make her free."

This letter reads like a genuine cry of distress. The Cardinal of Siena was an adept at dealing with such dishonesty
as this, which would deceive one less expert. He could read
between the lines; and he knew this Chancellor Mayr. He
began by asserting Papal Supremacy, and rejecting the
decrees of the schismatic Council of Basilea. He agreed that
the Concordat of the Lord Eugenius P.P. IV should be
observed. He said that the Lord Calixtus P.P. III was willing to redress grievances, if the Electors would send envoys
to lay them before Him in proper form. So far, nothing
could be more satisfactory; and then the Cardinal of Siena
got to work. Papal interference with elections, he said, was
purely judicial intervention, due to the ambition and greed
of claimants, not to papal rapacity. If any payments had
been made by would-be bishops to bribe officials of the
curia, the said would-be bishops just could not blame His
Holiness, but their own ambition, which would do anything
for its own aggrandisement. Men were not more angelic

in Rome than in Germany : when money was offered they
naturally took it. But the Holy Father must not be blamed
for that. He wished to stop the extortions of his officials.
He Himself received nothing but His due. Every one thinks
it a grievance to part with money, and will think so always.
Bohemia made the same complaint against Germany as
Germany made against Rome, that money was drained
from the land : yet Germany, owing to her connection with
the papacy, steadily had grown in wealth and importance,
and was richer now than at any previous time, despite of
her complaints. To descend to personal matters, the Cardinal of Siena thought it very hard that Chancellor Mayr
should object to the provisions which had been made in his
favour. As poet-laureate of the Empire and orator of
Caesar he had lived and laboured in Germany so long, that
he now found it hard to be classed as a stranger. In conclusion, *he thanked the Chancellor for his personal offer of
help to realise the said provisions; and would be glad to
know of any eligible benefices which should fall vacant.*

The sting was in the tail of this letter. It is evident that,
while Martin Mayr was writing for publication his precious
list of grievances, he also was sending to the cardinal in
private a second letter offering his own services as rent-
collector. In theory, he pretended to treat his connection
with the Lord Enea Silvio as having no existence. In practice, he was very anxious to be employed as agent on commission. To such a venal Janus only one reply was possible ;
and the Cardinal of Siena exposed the worthless insincerity
of Germany's spokesman by answering his private and his
public letters together on the same sheet.

This device, as was intended, provoked a proposition
from Chancellor Mayr's superior, the Prince Archbishop of
Mainz; who sent his secretary to Rome on the tenth of
September, 1456, with plenary powers to negotiate with the
Cardinal of Siena towards an alliance with the Pope against
the Electors. This renegade prelate's terms were, that he

was prepared to desert the German party of reform, if he were conceded the right of confirming episcopal elections throughout Germany as the price of his treachery; a right which would enable him to tax candidates for bishoprics at his will.

The Cardinal of Siena lashed the Prince Archbishop with courteous but stinging pen. He rejoiced to hear that his High Mightiness no longer cared to be allied with those malignants who attacked the Holy Father; but regretted that he should ask for that which was a right inherent in the Papacy, and which none of his predecessors had enjoyed. No bribe, no secret understanding, was necessary between God's Vicegerent and His subjects. All were bound to obey. He was sure that the modesty of the Archbishop had been misrepresented by this improper request, which he, for his part, could not dare to lay before a Pope so blameless and so upright as was the Lord Calixtus. (Pii II. Ep. 338.)

Now that the venal nature of the cry for reform had been made clear to all the world, the Cardinal of Siena wrote eloquently and reasonably to Caesar Friedrich IV, to the King of Hungary, to the Princes and Prelates of Germany, pointing out the futility of quarrelling with the Pope, from Whom they derived so many benefits. (Pii II. Ep. 320, 344, 349.) He also expanded his letter to the discomfited Chancellor Martin Mayr into a pamphlet called *De ritu, situ, conditione, et moribus Germaniae,* in which he shewed that Germany had received from Rome far more than she ever had given. His wise and irrefragable reasoning, with the diplomatic skill of the papal envoy Lorenzo Rovarella, made Germany pause. To pause was to weaken. Then came the death of King Wladislaw of Hungary on the eve of his marriage with Madame Marguerite de France. His dominions in Austria, Hungary, Bohemia, were claimed by several pretenders. The German Powers became intensely interested. Their attention was diverted from their attempts to blackmail Christ's Vicar. And so the end of the Lord Calixtus P.P. III was attained; the crisis was averted without issue of a Pragmatic Sanction.

.   .   .

Meanwhile the Cardinal Admiral was in the Ægean. Being neither hero nor enthusiast he merely cruised from place to place, making a show of activity, capturing a few unimportant islands from the Muslim Infidel, relieving the necessities of the Knights of Rhodes. His sole object was to avoid that judicial inquiry with which the Cardinal-Nephews had threatened him; and hence he showed himself as but a perfunctory crusader. In fact, his influence was bad; for by giving the Ægean islanders the notion that Rome was their defender, he lulled them into false security and destroyed their self-reliance.

The plight of Eastern Christendom became more hopeless. Only the Holiness of the Pope, of all the Western powers, took any practical measures. France promised, but failed to keep her word, and would not pay the tithe. The Duke of Burgundy collected the tithe, and kept it. Norway, Denmark, and Portugal sat still. The Duke of Milan and the Republic of Venice disregarded the Pope's entreaties. The Signoria of Florence refused to help Him. A few of the Italian barons, tyrants of petty fiefs, provided him with money and men. The Republic of Genoa was loyal; and, in return, the strenuous Lord Calixtus P.P. III protected Genoese colonies on the Black Sea littoral, and conferred honours on her nobles. The dark outlook momentarily was lightened by a victory over the Muslim fleet, in which five and twenty galleys became a Christian spoil. It must be recorded that it was solely the determination, foresight, and energy, with which the aged Pontiff in Rome personally directed naval movements, which inspired His sailors to achieve this triumph. Had the Cardinal-Admiral Scarampi been endowed with the plenary authority which he had desired, very much less enterprising and successful would have been the policy of the papal fleet.

There can be no doubt but that German captiousness prevented the accomplishment of the Pope's designs for the protection of the Oriental Christians. Skanderbeg had but a handful of huszars wherewith to oppose the Muslim Infidel. And there was no encouragement for him; for the apathy of Caesar and the Powers prevented him from following up his victories. The King of Naples was as a thorn in the Pope's eye. He had hoped for better things of His old patron who had brought Him to Italy; and He was bitterly enraged by King Don Alonso's treachery in sending the fleet, which, though constructed in the port of Naples, had been paid for with papal gold, to carry on a private quarrel with a Christian Power, the Republic of Genoa, at the very moment when Christendom was in the direst peril from the Infidel.

The forbearance of the Lord Calixtus P.P. III ended there, as far as Naples was concerned. Henceforward He relentlessly opposed the policy of King Don Alonso, especially his scheme for an alliance with Milan by which he hoped to make doubly sure the succession of the Bastard Ferrando, whose legitimation had been recognised by two preceding Pontiffs.

At the beginning of 1458, György Podiebrad renounced the Hussite heresy on his election to the throne of Bohemia. King György made no difficulty about swearing allegiance to the Holy See; and he also promised to take the cross of the Crusade. Considering that his dominions immediately were menaced by the Infidel, his policy would appear to have been dictated by reasons of state rather than by religious zeal.

The Holiness of the Pope was consoled by this accession to the thinned ranks of His allies. He hoped that the example of King György would be of good effect to the Bohemian heretics; for spiritual matters are not uninteresting to a Roman Pontiff. It seemed that the occasion might be used to bring the powers into line; and He summoned a congress to meet in Rome, whose object was the Unity of Christendom. Pious men have pursued that object ever since—the religious unity. In the days of the Lord Calixtus P.P. III, political unity was the aim desired, and striven-for again, in vain.

. . .

After the Crusade, the work nearest to the Pope's heart was the promotion of His nephews' interests. Why He should never have done anything for His own most charming son remains a historical mystery. The elevation to the cardinalate of Don Luis Juan de Mila y Borja, and of Don Rodrigo de Lançol y Borja, already has been recorded. There was a younger brother of Cardinal Rodrigo, younger by a year and a half, Don Pedro Luis de Lançol y Borja, a gorgeously beautiful sneak and coward, to whom the Pope extended the envious admiration that feeble age must feel for youth and strength; and for whom nothing had been done. The Lord Calixtus P.P. III, though quite independent of the good opinion of the Sacred College, did not cause a second storm by raising this young man, also, to the purple. He himself preferred a secular career, and it was thought that the hot blood of Borja suited him to cut a military figure. On that account, his Uncle, in the capacity of an Italian despot, named him Duke of Spoleto, Gonfaloniere of the Holy Roman Church, Castellan of all pontifical fortresses, and Governor of the cities of Terni, Narni, Todi, Rieti, Orvieto, Spoleto, Foligno, Nocera, Assisi, Amelia, Civita Castellana, Nepi, and of the Patrimony of St. Peter in Tuscany,—an extravagance of generosity which is justifiable solely on the score of good-will towards His family, which, after long years, an octogenarian was able to put into effect. Of course there arose the usual uproar of protest from the Sacred College, led by the

Lord Domenico Capranica, Cardinal-Presbyter of the Title
of Santa Croce *in Gerusalemme;* and something akin to a
riot among the citizens of Rome, who always hated foreigners, and especially Catalans. For the idea had got abroad
in Spain that in Rome preferment awaited Spaniards, and
thither they flocked to receive the good gifts which, they
imagined, a Spanish Pope would have in store. Rome was
furious at this immigration; but Borgia made overtures of
friendship to Colonna, and treated the Romans to a display of Spanish arrogance. As for the strenuous Lord
Calixtus P.P. III, He announced His defiance of public
opinion by installing Don Pedro Luis de Lançol y Borja
in the Prefecture of the City, an act which involved the
surrender into Borja hands of the Mola of Hadrian, or
Castle of Santangelo, the impregnable fortress on Tiber
which dominates Rome. Don Pedro Luis was looked upon
by Orsini as a mortal foe, on account of his displacing Don
Giovantonio Orsini in this Prefecture. Thus the inimical
relations of Borja with Orsini very naturally qualified them
for an alliance with Colonna, in a simple age when a man's
friends were his friend's friends, and his enemies his
friend's enemies; and Colonna was the most powerful
house in Rome. A nursery ditty of the period will show in
what esteem Colonna was held:

> "Che possa avere cinque figli maschi,
> "E tutti quanti di Casa Colonna,
> "Uno Papa, l'altro cardinale,
> "Ed uno arcivescovo di Colonia,
> "Ed uno possa aver tanta possanza
>   "Da levar la corona al re di Franza
> "E l'altro possa aver tanto valore
>   "Da levar la corona all' imperatore.

So, for a brief space, the Eternal City became absolutely
an appanage of the House of Borja. Catalans pervaded the
streets, engaged in robbery and murder. The intimidated
Conservators (equivalent to a modern municipal council)

servilely thanked the Pope for the appointment of His nephew, and even suggested that Don Pedro Luis should be made King of Rome.

.   .   .

On the twenty-seventh of June, 1458, died King Don de Alonso Aragona, The Magnanimous, of Naples, the Two Sicilies, and Jerusalem. The Lord Calixtus P.P. III at once refused to acknowledge His quondam pupil, the Bastard Ferrando, as successor; and impetuously threatened to plunge Italy into war, by declaring on His Own account a claim to the Regno as a fief of the Holy See.

A favourite policy of ecclesiastical persons of all ranks, and in all ages, appears correctly to be summarised by Patrizzi in this formula:—*Advance pretensions and presently they will become realities.* The Pope's Holiness desired to benefit Don Pedro Luis. If His claim, as suzerain of the Regno, could be substantiated, then He would be able to crown Don Pedro Luis as its King. It was an extensive and important domain, including the whole of Southern Italy, the Abruzzi, Apulia, and Calabria, with the Three-Tongued [1] Island of Sicily. From a commercial standpoint, the Pope's action was distinctly smart and businesslike. And there was this further consideration:—Supposing that the Bastard Ferrando were strong enough to make resistance, at least some part of the Regno would have to be sacrificed as a concession for the sake of peace; and so a fief could be created for Don Pedro Luis, who, in any case, stood to win. Failing the Regno, it was the Pope's intention strenuously to press the reconquest of Constantinople, and to crown His nephew King of Cyprus and Emperor of Byzantium. As an earnest of His good-will He lost no time in naming him Lieutenant of Benevento and Tarracina

[1] Sikelian—Greek—Latin.

within the Neapolitan boundary, confirming him in this post by Brief of the thirty-first of July, 1458.

In Rome indignation knew no bounds. It was plain that these strong young men, the pontifical nephews, were, after the Crusade, all-powerful with the Ruler of the World. The city seethed with jealousy and revolt, attacking anything in the shape of a Catalan on sight. Spaniards, rash enough to show themselves in the streets, courted assassination. As for the Pope, age and mortal sickness seemed to fan the flame, to white heat, of His inflexible imperious will. The Cardinal of Santa Croce *in Gerusalemme* was banished to distant embassages, and threatened with imprisonment if he again broke silence, on account of the protest which he made. The Apostolic Prothonotary, Fra Bernardino Caravajal was sent to Germany. The Cardinal-Admiral Scarampi was kept at sea. Cardinal Latino Orsini and his faction fled into exile. Only four of the Most Illustrious preserved their loyalty to the Pope and the Cardinal-Nephews; these were:—The Roman Lord Prospero Colonna, Cardinal-Deacon of San Giorgio *in Velum Aureum;* the Venetian Lord Pietro Barbo, Cardinal-Deacon of Santa Maria Nuova; the French Lord Guillaume d'Estouteville, Cardinal-Bishop of Porto; and the Sienese Lord Enea Silvio Bartolomeo de' Piccolhuomini, Cardinal-Presbyter of the Title of Santa Sabino. Profiting by the temporary absence of opposition, the Holiness of the Pope gave the Bishopric of Lerida to His nephew, Cardinal Luis Juan of Santi Quattro Coronati; and to Cardinal Rodrigo of San Niccolo *in Carcere Tulliano* he gave the Vice-chancellorship of the Holy Roman Church.

At last, the Bastard of Naples decided on his course of action; and summoned the Neapolitan nobles, demanding their acceptance of him as their king. He made no claim upon the kingdoms of Aragon, Valencia, and Catalonia, in Spain; nor upon Sardinia, the Balearic Islands, and Sicily, which King Don Alonso had left by will to his own brother, King Don Juan of Navarre: but for the crown of Naples and the Sovereignty of the Order of the Stola, which his father had founded, he was prepared to fight. Further, in defence of his right, he appealed from the Pope to a General Council—a stupid enough proceeding, but one of the customs peculiar to aggrieved personages of the Borgian Era. Incidentally, it may be mentioned that the Lord Calixtus P.P. III, was not the only disputant of Don Ferrando's claim. Even supposing that the right of King Réné of Anjou were set aside, he had a third rival in the shape of his cousin Don Carlos of Biana, son of King Don Juan of Navarre.

The Pope knew well that, though He might disturb the peace of Italy, He, single-handed, could not hope to triumph in a war with Naples; and He, therefore, tried to win over Don Francesco Sforza-Visconti, Duke of Milan, who, after the Cardinal of Siena, was the greatest and most far-seeing statesman of his time. Duke Francesco answered shortly and sharply, that the Neapolitan Succession had been settled by the Lord Nicholas P.P. V to the satisfaction of all Italian princes, and that he intended to fight for King Don Ferrando I sooner than see his country devastated by civil war.

This last bitter disappointment caused the collapse of the Pope's health. With the summer heat plague appeared in Rome. The Lord Calixtus P.P. III lay in the throes of fever; and Orsini took up arms against all Catalans in open war. Of the Pontifical Nephews the layman showed the white feather; the stalwart cardinals were staunch. Don Pedro Luis de Lançol y Borja, as Prefect of Rome, sold the Mola of Hadrian to the Sacred College for two and twenty thousand ducats; and fled from the city, escorted by his Catalans. The Cardinal of Venice helped him to a boat on Tiber, by which means, owing to the darkness of the night, he reached Civita Vecchia in safety, having avoided

Orsini who watched for him at the gates of Rome. On the
26th of September, says Lo Spondano, suddenly he died.

.   .   .

One of the claims of the church is that of a Divine
Promise of Her Maintenance until the end of the world. It
is interesting to the student of history to notice that, from
time to time, Her responsible authorities comport themselves as though they had no faith in the validity of that
prediction. They seem to think that its fulfilment solely
depends upon their own exertions. The strange conviction
of the necessity of his present existence, which is innate in
the ordinary man, is perhaps the explanation of the extraordinary expenditure of energy to avert death, to invalidate
the most fervent and frequent professions of belief in The
Life Of The World To Come, to consolidate human insti-
tutions and human plans, which obtains on such occasions
as the close of a prelacy or the end of a pontificate. If it
be true that actions speak louder than words, then the
confusion attendant on a Pope's death must tell a sorry tale.

On the sixth of August, 1458, the Lord Calixtus P.P. III
lay dying in the Vatican. Rome was in a turmoil. Colonna
and Orsini were sharpening their swords. The banished
cardinals were hurrying back for the ensuing Conclave.
The four loyal cardinals were fortified in their palaces.
Only the Cardinal-Nephews attended at the Pope's bedside.

The curious privilege which was accorded to these last,
at this period, could not be exercised in the present case.
By the very conditions of their juniority in the Sacred College, added to the powerful influence which they were
supposed to hold over the reigning Pontiff, the Cardinal-
Nephews were the objects of intense dislike (to put it
mildly) on the part of their colleagues. Their elevation was
an offence; their enrichment, a matter for envy; their indifference to opinion, a matter for positive hatred. The only

consolation to the other cardinals, creatures of previous Pontiffs, which their situation held, was that it must end with the demise of their creator. When their Pontifical Uncle ceased to live in this world, the Cardinal-Nephews sank at once to their proper place in the Sacred College. Under these circumstances, the said Cardinal-Nephews were used to make their hay while yet the sun was shining, to avail themselves of their opportunities for securing a satisfactory future, as junior cardinals, by the acquisition of property, real estate, benefices, jewels, or money, at the pleasure of the Pope. And when their time was drawing near its close, when their August Uncle was entering His last agony, it was the custom for the Cardinal-Nephews to plunder the apostolic palace of any valuables which already had not passed into their hands. This privilege was their last chance; for, at the instant of the Pontiff's death, the Cardinal-Chamberlain assumes possession as representative of the curia; and, in an age when self-aggrandisement was not less a ruling passion than at the present hour, the practice was at least connived at, on the principle that every dog should be allowed to have its day.

But, on the present occasion, there was no plundering by the Cardinal-Nephews. The fury of the Romans against all Spaniards made it expedient for them to avoid the risk of a journey across the City, to their palace encumbered by the mules which bore their spoils. This would seem to be the human explanation of their presence in the Vatican, while the Orsini faction made havoc of the Catalans, and despoiled all who bore arms in the Borgo or pontifical Region of Rome.

.   .   .

The learned Dr. Creighton has well said that men of decided opinions and eminent ability who come to their power late in life, spend the accumulated passion of a lifetime in the accomplishment of long cherished desires. The Lord Calixtus P.P. III would come into that category.

Though He was unenthusiastic regarding the Renascence of Letters and the Arts, and checked the tremendous schemes of His predecessor, yet He was by no means inattentive to the duties involved by His position. He restored the palace and church of Santi Quattro Coronati, because He had occupied them during His cardinalate. He improved the church of San Sabastiano *extra muros* above the Catacomb of San Calixto, in honour of the saint from whom He took His papal name. He repaired the church of Santa Prisca, and began the new roof of the Liberian Basilica on the Esquiline. He employed the painters, who did not leave Rome on His election, in painting banners for the Crusade. The Vatican school of arras-weavers, founded by the Lord Nicholas P.P. V, was continued, and flourished exceedingly under His benevolence. He created nine cardinals in the course of His short pontificate. The Porporati of the Consistory of the twentieth of February, 1456, were named on p. 40. At the Consistory at Christmas the same year, He elevated to the purple :—

(a) The lord Rainaldo Pisciscello, the virtuous and learned Archbishop of Naples, as Cardinal-Presbyter of the Title of Santa Cecilia :

(β) Don Juan de Mella, brother of the celebrated Franciscan Frat' Alonso de Mella, and a noble of Spain, Auditor of the Ruota to the Lord Martin P.P. III, as Cardinal-Presbyter of the Title of Sant' Aquila e Santa Prisca :

(γ) The Lord Giovanni Castelleone, patrician of Milan, Legate to Caesar Friedrich IV, and Bishop of Pavia, as Cardinal-Presbyter of the Title of San Clemente :

(δ) The Lord Giacomo di Collescipoli Teobaldi, a Roman citizen, as Cardinal-Presbyter of the Title of Santa Anastasia : [1]

(ε) The Lord Richart de Longueil Olivier, Bishop of Constance, Archpriest of the Vatican Basilica, one of the judges at the Rehabilitation of Madame Jehanne de Lis, the Maid of Orleans, as Cardinal-Presbyter of the Title of Sant' Eusebio :

(ζ) The Lord Enea Silvio Bartolomeo de' Piccolhuomini, as Cardinal-Presbyter of the Title of Santa Sabina.

The Lord Calixtus P.P. III has no share in the evil reputation which has been cast upon His House. The worst that has been said of Him is, that He was obstinate, irritable, and inspired no affection. They were disappointed suitors who so spoke. The Pope's Holiness used Himself ever gently to the poor and needy, who found in Him a good samaritan. His benefactions to the hospital of Santo Spirito have been recorded. In His will He left five thousand ducats to found a hospital in His cardinalitial palace of Santo Quattro Coronati. His private life was one of rigid piety, simplest habits, apostolic fervour. He left one hundred and fifty thousand ducats in the Pontifical Treasury, which He had collected for the Holy War.

But the whole force of His resourceful and masterful character was concentrated upon the Crusade, and the settlement in life of His beloved nephews. On those two points He would brook no opposition. With the violent impetuosity of age, of Spanish blood, He was inflexible, overbearing, inconsiderate, on all matters connected with

---

[1] Note his epitaph in the Church of Santa Maria *sopra* Minerva, recorded by Ciacconi.

"Cardineo Divus Honore Decoravit Calixtus."

Obviously the fifteenth century used "Divus" as Tacitus also used it of Julius and Augustus; and as the twentieth century would say "the late ——."

these projects. All the ardour, and all the zeal, which He devoted to the delivery of Christendom from the Muslim Infidel, was doomed to fail. The Muslim Infidel defiles Constantinople now. But His dealings with His nephews produced more permanent results.

Yet "it must always be an honour to the Papacy that, in a great crisis of European affairs, it asserted the importance of a policy which was for the interest of Europe as a whole. Calixtus and his successor [1] deserve, as statesmen, credit which can be given to no other politicians of the time. The Papacy, by summoning Christendom to defend the limits of Christian civilisation against the assaults of heathenism, was worthily discharging the chief secular duty of the office." (Creighton.)

The Lord Calixtus P.P. III died on the sixth of August 1458, in the fourth year of His reign; and was buried by four priests in the crypt of the old Basilica of St. Peter-by-the-Vatican.

.   .   .

.   .   .

[1] The Lord Pius P.P. II (Enea Silvio).

KINDLING

I⊤ has been said that the junior branch of the House of Borja (which originated in Don Ricardo de Borja, second son of Don Pedro, Count of Aybar, Lord of Borja, who died in 1152), emigrated to the kingdom of Naples, where it became naturalised, and softened its name to the Italian Borgia. From Don Fortunio, the son of the aforesaid Don Ricardo, descends Don Rodrigo who had two sons :—

- (α) Don Romano Borgia, Monk of Vall' Ombrosa and Bishop of Venafri, A.D. 1300. (*Ricchi.*)
- (β) Don Ximenes Borgia, Captain in the Army of Naples, whose son, Don Antonio Borgia, married Madonna Girolama Ruffola of Naples, and had issue :—
  - (α) Don Niccolo Borgia, familiar of King Don Alonso I, The Magnanimous, Regent of Velletri, 1417, married the Noble Madonna Giovanna Lamberti of Naples, and had issue ....
  - (β) Don Girolamo Borgia (detto Seniore)....

Reverting to the Senior Branch:—

The career of Don Francisco de Borja, bastard of Bishop Alonso de Borja of Valencia (afterwards the Lord Calixtus P.P. III), is an unsolved mystery from his birth in 1441 until 1497. ....

Of the five children of Doña Juana de Borja by her husband Don Jofre de Lançol :—

- (α) Doña Francisca married Don Ximenez Perez de Arenas ;

(β) Doña Tecla married Don Vitale de Villanueva;
(γ) Doña Juana married her cousin Don Guillelmo de
Lançol, and had issue:—
  Girolama,
  Angela,
  Pedro Luis (Pierludovico) ....
  Juan (Giovanni seniore) ....
(δ) Don Rodrigo, Vicechancellor-Cardinal-Deacon
of San Niccolo *in Carcere Tulliano* ....
(ε) Don Pedro Luis, Duke of Spoleto, Castellan of
Santangelo, Prefect of Rome, died on the twenty-
sixth of September, 1458, leaving two bas-
tards:—
  Juan (Giovanni giuniore) ....
  Silvia, married Don Alonzo Gomiel.

Of the two children of Doña Caterina de Borja by her
husband Don Juan de Mila, Baron of Mazalanes:—

(α) Don Luis Juan, Cardinal-Presbyter of Santi
Quattro Coronati, Bishop of Lerida, retired to
his diocese on the death of his August Uncle
and Creator, and lived there secluded till his
death in 1507. (The career and character of this
prince of the church, cardinal at twenty, bishop
at twenty-three, and during those three years
living in the very arcana of the pontifical court;
who then thought fit to bury himself in a remote
university city during half a century, while his
nearest kin were ruling Europe and Christendom, awaits, and should repay, investigation.)
(β) Doña Adriana came to Italy, married Don Luigi
Orsini, and had issue Don Orso Orsini. ....

.   .   .

The chief personage of the House of Borja, on the death
of the Lord Calixtus P.P. III, was Cardinal Rodrigo, of
the age of twenty-seven years.

His position was a precarious one; and it is perfectly amazing that he was not forced to follow his cousin, the Cardinal de Mila, into permanent retirement. That he was able, not only to remain in Rome but to carve out for himself a unique career there, undoubtedly is due to those superb talents and alert vigor of character which have made him such a prominent figure in history.

He had only two friends in Rome, the Cardinal Enea Silvio of Siena. and the Cardinal-Archdeacon Prospero Colonna. Quite unmoved by the hatred of the other Purpled Ones, he entered the Conclave of 1458 for the election of the new Pope, with no such stupid thing as a plan of action; but with a determination to comport himself so, according as opportunities arose, as to improve his position and his prospects. It was impossible to know beforehand what steps he would have to take: he could be guided only by circumstances. To a young man of such temper the gods send opportunities. There arrived a deadlock in the Conclave; and of that deadlock Cardinal Rodrigo seized the key.

There are five ways by which a Pope may be elected:—

(*a*) By Compromise—*i.e.,* when the cardinals appoint a committee of themselves with power to name the Pope:

(*β*) By Inspiration—*i.e.,* when a number of cardinals put themselves to shout the name of some cardinal, as "The Cardinal-Prior-Presbyter is Pope," or "The Cardinal-Archdeacon is Pope;" by which method of shouting other voices are attracted, and the minimum majority (of two-thirds plus one) attained:

(*γ*) By Adoration—*i.e.,* when the minimum majority (of two-thirds plus one) of the cardinals go and adore a certain cardinal:

(δ) By Scrutiny—*i.e.,* when each cardinal secretly records a vote:

(ε) By Accession—*i.e.,* when, the scrutiny having failed to give the minimum majority (of two-thirds plus one) to any cardinal, the opponents of that cardinal, whose tally is the highest, shall accede to him.

In the Conclave of 1458 the method of Compromise was not used, and no cardinals were moved to proceed by Inspiration or to Adoration. Votes were taken by the Scrutiny, which revealed an extraordinary state of things. The French Cardinal d'Estouteville had a certain number of votes; the Cardinal Enea Silvio of Siena had a higher number; but neither had the minimum majority. The cardinals sat upon their green or purple thrones, beneath their green or purple canopies, watching and waiting for a sign.

Then the young Cardinal-Vicechancellor Rodrigo de Lançol y Borja rose up and proclaimed: "I accede to the Lord Cardinal of Siena." His friend and ally, the Cardinal Archdeacon Prospero Colonna, followed him: "I accede to the Lord Cardinal of Siena." Cardinal Teobaldi, who, as a Roman citizen, followed Colonna, said also: "I accede to the Lord Cardinal of Siena." The three lowered their green and purple canopies. They were in the presence of the Pope, in Whom all authority resides, before Whom none may remain covered. The minimum majority had been attained. The Lord Enea Silvio Bartolomeo de' Piccolhuomini, sometime Caesar's ambassador in "the horrible and ultimate Britains" (Scotland), sometime poet-laureate, novelist, historian, bishop, and cardinal, had become the Lord Pius P.P. II.

By this act, which practically gave the proud triregno to his friend, the Cardinal-Vicechancellor put himself into high favour with the new Pontiff, Whose enchanting temperament delighted in the brilliance and aptitude of the Borgia, and made his future the object of especial interest.

.   .   .

Materials for the history of Cardinal Rodrigo during this reign are but scanty, in the absence of opportunities for original research. In 1459, he went a-holiday-making with the Lord Pius P.P. II, on a triumphal progress through Florence; where the Holy Father chatted with a lovely boy of seven years, called Leonardo da Vinci, bastard of a Florentine notary and a contadina. They visited Siena; and Corsignano, where the Pope's Holiness was born, which He was pleased to rename Pienza, in honour of His papal name, and to build there a cathedral, an episcopal palace, and the Piccolhuomini palace for His Own family on the three sides of the public square. By way of showing His confidence in the Vicechancellor-Cardinal-Archdeacon (Archdeacon *vice* Cardinal Prospero Colonna), perhaps, also, to curb, with useful employment, the exuberance of manlihood which had been giving evidence of revolt against the convenances, the Lord Pius P.P. II left the superintendence of these buildings in the hands of Cardinal Rodrigo, who has not scrupled to adorn their façades with the armorials of the House of Borgia. *Or, a bull passant gules on a field flory vert, within a bordure gules semée of flammels, or.*

Vicechancellor-Cardinal-Archdeacon Rodrigo had lived the life of a gallant handsome prince and man of the world of the fifteenth century, in no wise differing from his antitype of the twentieth. The Renascence had brought about an age when sensuousness degenerating into sensualism was found in prominent places. It is difficult to see what else was to be expected. "Ye can not serve God and Mammon." Learning and art, essentially, radically, and necessarily are antagonistic to Christianity, hard though that saying may be found. Towards them the Church's policy always has been a policy of compromise. "You may learn the wisdom of the world, but you may not learn all," She says; trying to serve God, paltering the while with Mammon; "Nudus, Nudum Christum sequens" went Beato

Fra Francesco when he renounced the world; and the Church compromises with St. Sebastian for Phoibos Apollon. Therefore, as long as Grace and Nature are served up on the same dish, it is stupidly unreasonable to hold up holy hands in horror when high ecclesiastical dignitaries happen to comport themselves like human beings.

The twentieth century is no whit more chaste than the fifteenth, and can ill afford to cast a stone. Nor was the fifteenth century the stew of universal depravity which some would have us believe it to have been. It was unmoral as the twentieth is immoral. But there were pure and maid-white souls then, as there are now; and the difference between the fifteenth century and the twentieth is a mere difference of fashion. Now, we pretend to be immaculate; then, they bragged of being vile. Much of the literature of the fifteenth century is most suitably presented in the original. Poets and historians, especially historians, allowed little scope for exercise of the imagination. The convention of concealment, of suggestion, had not been invented. Messeri Stefano Infessura and Benedetto Varchi rank among the most eminent Chroniclers of their day; certainly the Latin of the one, and the Tuscan of the other, would serve for models: but a complete unbowdlerised translation of the former's Journal of Roman Affairs (*Diarium Rerum Romanum*), or of the latter's Florentine History (*Storia Fiorentina*), incontinently would be suppressed by the police. Yet it would be absurd to conclude that these writers, or others of their kidney, have given a just account of the morals of their age. "The divorce court and the police news do not reflect the state of morality in England. No more do Juvenal's Satires give us a complete or impartial picture of Roman society. We must read side by side with them the contemporary letters of Pliny, which give a very different picture, and also weigh the evidence offered by inscriptions." (E. G. Hardy. Satires of Juvenal, p. xliv.) That is the spirit in which the student of the fifteenth century should approach his task. He will read all, and hear all sides, and form his own conclusion, which, at best, must be a faulty one, until the secrets of all hearts are known.

The Vicechancellor-Cardinal-Archdeacon was a human being. If he were, as Gaspar Veronensis describes him at a later date, "a comely man, of cheerful countenance and honeyed discourse, who gains the affections of all the women he admires, and attracts them as the loadstone attracts iron," what must he have been in the glow of his superb youth? This is not by any means a suitable reputation for a churchman; and only its non-singularity prevents it from being a disgraceful one. Viewed from a theological stand-point, Cardinal Rodrigo's carnal lusts are, of course, wholly indefensible: but this work is an attempt at the study of certain human beings prominent in history; and not a theological treatise nor an act of the *advocatus diaboli*. The Lord Pius P.P. II has said, "If there are good reasons for enjoining celibacy of the clergy, there are better and stronger arguments for insisting on their marriage"; and that Supreme Pontiff was far and away the wisest and most observing man of His Own (or perhaps of any) time.

Therefore, it is suggested that, knowing of the proclivities of Cardinal Rodrigo, being in truth his firm friend, desirous that he should live up to the obligations of his rank, and, above all, actuated by a sense of duty as Christ's Vicar, the Pope's Holiness set him to supervise the buildings at Pienza—to keep him out of mischief.

In 1460 was born Don Pedro Luis de Borja, bastard of the said Cardinal-Archdeacon and a spinster (soluta). The child was openly acknowledged and honourably reared.

About this time the Lord Pius P.P. II wrote a letter, to remonstrate with Cardinal Rodrigo and with the Lord Giacopo Ammanati, Cardinal-Presbyter of the Title of San Crisogono, concerning their divergences from ecclesiastical discipline. It is a genial and paternal letter, in which frank hatred of Sin is displayed with affection for the sinners. Cardinal Rodrigo replied, correcting some mis-statements of fact: but, that the Pope's Holiness was not satisfied, appears from a second letter of a firmer and more admonitory nature. Much has been made of this correspondence by some writers, whose pose is to think ungenerously of ecclesiastics. It should be noted, however, that the Lord Pius P.P. II took exception to certain long visits which those cardinals paid to ladies of their acquaintance, and to nothing more. Apparently there was nothing more of which to complain; and the fact that the Pope's Holiness should deem these visits to be indiscretions on the part of ecclesiastics, goes to prove rather the extreme and strict solicitude of the Holy Father for the spiritual welfare of his flock, than any dissolute conduct of the two cardinals. But the defamers of Cardinal Rodrigo misrepresent the said visits in the worst possible light, as nocturnal orgies and debaucheries; and long night visits obviously would constitute a grave and serious scandal. The misrepresentation very likely is due to careless ignorance. The fact is, that the Italian method of computing time in the fifteenth century is deceptive to the superficial student. Something is known of the dials of Italy which count the hours up to 24 o'clock; and when it is said that Cardinal Rodrigo paid visits to ladies in their gardens "from the 17th to the 22nd hour," instantly cynical carelessness predicates nocturnal orgies. But when it is understood that, in the fifteenth century, the first hour began at half an hour after sunset, and that the visits took place in time of summer, it will be realised that Cardinal Rodrigo simply went to the mid-day dinner, and left his friends an hour and a half before sunset: which may have been indiscreet, but certainly was not essentially criminal, as some would have us believe. But when the careless or wilful calumniator sets out to ruin a reputation, he finds it an easy thing to twist a fault into a crime.

The Vicechancellor-Cardinal-Archdeacon is recorded to

have astonished Rome with the splendour of the array adorning the outside of his palace on the Festival of Corpus Domini, 1461. The buildings at Pienza occupied him through 1462. Of 1463 there is no history with which he is connected.

In 1464 "an aged man, with head of snow and trembling limbs," took the rose-red cross in the Basilica of St. Peter at Rome. This was no other than the Sovereign Pontiff, the Lord Pius P.P. II, unique in all history, Who, as an example to the apathetic potentates of Christendom, went, dying as He was, a crusader against the Muslim Infidel. Cardinal Rodrigo was in attendance upon His Holiness in that terrible journey in parching summer heat across Italy to the Adriatic; where, while waiting for the fleet, at Ancona, in August, the Lord Pius P.P. II died. Cardinal Rodrigo, stricken by fever there, unable to return to Rome for the Conclave, was obliged to forego his official privilege as Cardinal-Archdeacon, the crowning of the Lord Paul P.P. II on the sixteenth of September.

This Pontiff (lately the Lord Pietro Barbo, Cardinal of Venice) wished, on His election, to take the name Formosus, in allusion to His handsome person. It was a naïve age, when men hid neither their vices nor their virtues; and the story possibly may be true: but it is very likely to be one of the spiteful little distortions of motive, which ecclesiastics of all ages are wont to ascribe to each other. The Popes, after the first six centuries, have never shown much originality in choosing Their pontifical names, and generally fall back upon the name of one of Their immediate predecessors. At present the changes are rung upon Pius, Leo, and Gregory; the fifteenth century had a wider range: but many of the lovely old names, such as Anacletus, Fabian, Felix, Silvester, Hadrian, Victor, Evaristus, were buried in oblivion. It is far more kind to suppose that the Lord Cardinal of Venice had the idea of reviving the beautiful name of the Lord Formosus P.P., Who reigned from

891 to 896, and was the hundred and twelfth Pope from the Lord St. Peter P.P. Persuaded against this course by the cardinals, He spent two hundred thousand fiorini d'oro on a triregno set with sapphires; built St. Mark's Palace (Palazzo Venezia) at the end of the Corso in Rome; and instituted carnival races of riderless horses (called Bárberi, as a pun upon his name), and of Jews heavily clothed in garments of thick wool and stuffed to the throat with cake. In 1467 was born Madonna Girolama de Borja, bastard of the Vicechancellor-Cardinal-Archdeacon, by an unknown mother. The child was openly acknowledged and honourably reared. During this reign Cardinal Rodrigo remained in favour; and, on account of his fine presence and habitude to curial manners, he was chosen to receive, at Viterbo, Caesar Friedrich IV, The Pacific, coming on a state-visit to the Pope in 1469.

At the death of the Lord Paul P.P. II, Cardinal Rodrigo de Lançol y Borja, Cardinal Guillaume d'Estouteville, and Cardinal Ioannes Bessarione were the only foreigners in the Conclave of 1471. Once more the Vicechancellor-Cardinal-Archdeacon was clever enough to put a Pope under an obligation, by leading an accession to Cardinal Francesco della Rovere, who thereby was elected, and chose to be called the Lord Xystus P.P. IV. All the chroniclers save one allege that this Pope owed His election to the accession of Cardinals de Borja, Orsini, and Gonzaga of Mantua, who reaped rich rewards in the shape of benefices and preferments. The Pope's Holiness gave to Cardinal Rodrigo the wealthy Abbey of Subjaco *in commendam;* who left a memorial of his abbatial tenure in the tower which he added to the castle of Subjaco, where the armorials of the House of Borgia still remain. The last official act of Cardinal Rodrigo, as Archdeacon of the Holy Roman Church, appears to have been the coronation of the Lord Xystus P.P. IV on the twenty-fifth of August, 1471. After that he was ordained priest, and consecrated bishop, and elevated to the rank of Cardinal-Bishop of Albano, one of the seven sub-urban sees. He continued to hold the Vicechancellor-ship; and, in this capacity, he built for himself in Rome a palace on Banchi Vecchi, which, even in that sumptuous epoch, excited extravagant admiration. A little less than a third of it is now the huge Palazzo Sforza-Cesarini on Piazza Sforza-Cesarina, nearly opposite to the Oratory, called Chiesa Nuova. Since the unification of Italy in 1870, a new wide street (Corso Vittoremanuele) has been driven through the city, necessitating the demolition of more than two-thirds of Cardinal Rodrigo's building, and the con-struction of an undistinguished modern façade on the mod-ern street: but the remaining courts, whose frontage is still on Banchi Vecchi, are more or less *in statu quo*. The history of the passing of this palace into the hands of Sforza-Cesarini belongs to a later page.

On the twenty-third of December, 1471, Cardinal Ro-drigo was sent as Legate *a latere* to Spain, to preach a new Crusade against the Muslim Infidel. It is a curious thing that while he was unpopular in Italy on account of his Spanish origin, he was unpopular also in Spain where they considered him an Italian; a most ridiculous confusion, for Don Rodrigo de Lançol y Borja was a pure Spaniard by birth, descent, aspect, character, tastes, and habit, and so continued until his life's end, in no way influenced or modi-fied by his long residence in Italy. During his absence, the Lord Xystus P.P. IV built the Xystine Chapel of the Vati-can; and called to Rome, from the gardens at Florence of Lorenzo de' Medici his patron, the vivacious and bizarre Messer Alessandro Filipepi (nicknamed Botticelli), won-drous pupil of Fra Lippo Lippi, of Masaccio, of Beato Gio-vangelico da Fiesole, to decorate its walls with frescoes *in tempera,* the colours of which are mixed with the yelks of country-laid eggs for the deeper tints, and of town-laid eggs for the paler tints, according to the rules of Messer Cennino Cennini who wrote in 1437. In 1471 the bronze antique, known as *Il Spinario*, was found on the Capitol.

About this time the Lord Rodrigo de Lançol y Borja, now Cardinal-Bishop of Porto, Vicechancellor of the Holy Roman Church, and of the age of three and forty years, maintained irregular relations with Madonna Giovanna de' Catanei, a Roman lady, born the thirteenth of July, 1442, and of the age of thirty-two years, wife to one Don Giorgio della Croce. Whether her husband was used to trade in his wife's favours (like the criminal who, as late as 1780, was marched through Rome wearing a pasteboard mitre labelled *cornuto voluntario contento*), is a matter for conjecture. But, in 1474, Madonna Giovanna gave birth to a son, Don Cesare, who is called Borgia; and it is claimed that Cardinal Rodrigo was his father. As far as historical research has gone, no evidence has been found to prove that Cardinal Rodrigo ever directly denied paternity; and, as he was undoubtedly deeply in love with Madonna Giovanna, and intimate with her during ten subsequent years, it is probable that his reticence was actuated by kindly feelings. But there is a very strong suspicion that another cardinal, in every way the notorious and life-long rival of Cardinal Rodrigo, was the father of this child; and many mysterious historical inconsistencies would be explained by the establishment of the truth of this suspicion. However, for the present, merely the birth in 1474 of Don Cesare (detto Borgia) is recorded, and the question of his paternity will be examined at a proper place.

In 1475 Madonna Giovanna de' Cataneri bore, to Cardinal Rodrigo, Don Juan Francisco de Borja, to whom (after the death in 1481 of Don Pedro Luis de Borja) his father ever gave the honours and the affection which are due to an eldest son and heir. This is the most important circumstantial evidence against Don Cesare's right to the name of Borgia.

In January of the same year, Cardinal Rodrigo was

deputed, with a nephew of the Lord Xystus P.P. IV, one Cardinal Giuliano della Rovere, who, as a lad, had peddled onions in a boat between Arbisola and Genoa, to welcome King Don Ferrando I of Naples at Terracina, on the occasion of his state-visit to the Holy See. Three days later, Cardinal Rodrigo said mass for his Majesty at San Paolo *extra muros* when the king was leaving for Colonna's fief at Marino, where English envoys from King Edward IV Plantagenet, who had just conferred the Most Noble Order of the Garter upon Duke Francesco Sforza-Visconti of Milan, were waiting with a similar attention for the King of Naples.

On the tenth of June, 1476, the plague appeared in Rome, and the Lord Xystus P.P. IV, attended by Cardinal Rodrigo, removed His court to Viterbo, where cooler air lessened the danger of contagion.

In 1478 was the hideous Conspiracy of the Pazzi at Florence, which created no small stir in all Italy. Also in this year Madonna Giovanna de' Catanei bore, to Cardinal Rodrigo, Madonna Lucrezia Borgia.

On the first of October, 1480, "Xystus, Bishop, Servant of the servants of God, to His beloved son Cesare (de Borja), a scholar of the age of six years," sent "greeting and the Apostolic Benediction," and dispensed him from the necessity of proving the legitimacy of his birth; a rule which must be observed (in the absence of a dispensation) by whoever shall wish to become eligible for ecclesiastical benefices.

In 1481 died Don Pedro Luis de Borja, the eldest bastard of the Vicechancellor-Cardinal Rodrigo. He was of the age of twenty-one years, and betrothed to a mere child, the Princess Doña Maria de Aragona. Also, in 1481, Madonna Giovanna de' Catanei bore, to Cardinal Rodrigo, Don Gioffredo Borgia.

On the twenty-fourth of January, 1482, Madonna Giro-lama Borgia, bastard of the Vicechancellor-Cardinal by an unknown mother, was married, at the age of fifteen years, to Don Giovandrea Cesarini, scion of a Roman Baronial house of Imperial origin. The same year, on the sixteenth of August, the Lord Xystus P.P. IV named Cardinal Rodrigo administrator of all benefices that should be conferred upon Don Cesare (detto Borgia) until the latter reached the age of fourteen years. There is a second brief of this date from "Xystus, Bishop, Servant of the servants of God, to His beloved son Master Cesare (de Borgia)," naming the child Canon of Valencia and "Our Notary"; little bits of preferment producing sufficient revenues for his education. These three briefs relating to Don Cesare, are found in the Secret Archives of the Dukes of Osuña and Infantado, whose line was extinguished in 1882 at the death of Don Mariano (v. suggested genealogical tree).

In 1484 died the Lord Xystus P.P. IV, and the Genoese Cardinal Cibo ascended the papal throne under the title of the Lord Innocent P.P. VIII.

.   .   .

During the six and twenty years that had elapsed between the death of the Lord Calixtus P.P. III and the accession of the Lord Innocent P.P. VIII, the position of the Vicechancellor-Cardinal Rodrigo considerably was changed. Then, he was a young man with only two friends; a junior Cardinal-Deacon surrounded by a host of enemies. Now he was in his ripe maturity, senior member of the Sacred College, Dean of the Cardinal-Bishops, Vicechancellor of the Church, powerful enough to be able to command as many friends as he might choose to have—and rich enough to buy; rich beyond the richest of that rich age, from the revenues of his numerous benefices; and in rank second only to the Pope Himself. To such a man, with the paramount ambition and magnificence of Cardinal

Rodrigo, only one thing in all the world remained for him to do. He deliberately set himself to capture the triregno.

There is no chronicle of his history during the eight years' reign of the Lord Innocent P.P. VIII. Evidently he withdrew himself from the public life of the curia, from the splendour of legations, to nurse his revenues, to ingratiate himself with those who, in the next Conclave, would have the crowning or the crushing of his hopes. With the wisdom of the serpent and the harmlessness of the dove he was to build his house : but, first, like the prudent man, he counted the cost. Cardinal Rodrigo was far too polished a diplomatist, far too keen a man of business, to neglect long and meticulous preparation. He perfectly knew his century—indeed, as an organiser, he would have been illustrious in any century—; and, with wisest generalship, he made ready his forces against the striking of the hour for action. The smoothness with which the machinery ran in the Conclave of 1492, makes it plain, to the least experienced student of human affairs, that a master-mind had designed the gear, to ensure a minimum of friction and an exact performance.

.   .   .

In September 1484 the Lord Innocent P.P. VIII named Don Cesare (detto Borgia), who was now of the age of ten years, Treasurer of the Cathedral of Cartagena (Carthago Nova).

In 1485, the year of the supposed murder in England of King Edward V Plantagenet and of his brother Duke Richard of York, there died in Rome Don Giorgio della Croce, husband of Madonna Giovanna de' Catanei. On the seventh of June 1486 she married Don Carlo de Canale, a noble of Mantua, and from this time her irregular relations with Cardinal Rodrigo ceased. In an age when trade was not considered disgraceful, except for patricians, when even the greatest artists kept shops (not studios by way of compromise, but regular shops, *botteghe,* like the blacksmiths or the cobblers), it is not shocking to know that Madonna Giovanna owned an inn in the Region of Ponte. This does not mean that she performed the duties of a female boniface. She was a very great lady, bien-vue in Roman society, with a lovely villa near San Pietro *ad Vincula;* but she certainly drew a comfortable income from the Lion Inn (Albergo di Leone), opposite the Tordinona, in the Via del Orso, which was then a street of inns for foreigners. The Tordinona, from whose upper window dangled a permanent and generally tenanted noose for evildoers, has now disappeared: but the cavernous cellars of the Lion Inn, formerly filled with wine on which, by pontifical favour, no tax was levied, remain exactly as they were when the Spanish cardinal's mistress was their owner.

Deprived of the society of Madonna Giovanna de' Catanei, Cardinal Rodrigo, in the fifty-fifth year of his age, amused himself with the high-born maiden Madonna Giulia Farnese, nicknamed in Rome *La Bella,* who was betrothed and afterwards married to Don Orso Orsini, himself of Borgian descent. A faded representment of her marvellously brilliant beauty may be seen in the mannered fresco by Messer Bernardo Betti (detto Pinturicchio) in the Borgia Tower of the Vatican, where she was painted as Madonna; or on the tomb of her brother Alessandro (afterwards the Lord Paul P.P. III) in the Basilica of St. Peter, where she was sculptured in marble by Messer Guglielmo della Porta as a naked Truth (clumsily draped, after an erotomaniac Spanish student of theology had taken the statue for Lucian's goddess Kuthereia). The fruit of her early intrigue with Cardinal Rodrigo was Madonna Laura, detto Orsini, born in 1489, and adopted by Don Orso Orsini, the husband of Madonna Giulia.

The reign of the Lord Innocent P.P. VIII is notable for the extreme of lawlessness into which lax government had let Rome fall. The Sovereign Pontiff was a family man, who openly acknowledged the paternity of seven bastards, and Whose chief concern appears to have been their settlement in life. A son, Don Franciotto Cibo, a silly avaricious weakling, He married to Madonna Maddalena, daughter of Lorenzo de' Medici; His daughter He married to Messer Gheraldo Usodimare, a rich merchant of Genoa; the wedding-feast took place at the Vatican, the Pope's Holiness presiding; and so the world was made to lose sight of the high ideals of the Papacy, as exemplified by the Lord Pius P.P. II, and to regard the Supreme Pontiff in the light of a mere monarch, a mere man. Cardinal Piero Riaro, in 1473, had bargained with Duke Galeazzo Maria Sforza-Visconti of Milan to create him King of Lombardy, in return for money and troops, by the aid of which he himself might ascend the papal throne, his uncle, the Lord Xystus P.P. IV being willing to abdicate in his favour: and, but for the sudden death of Cardinal Piero, this abominable scheme would not have lacked completion.

Nicholas had been a scholar and a gentleman; Calixtus, a zealous strenuous champion of an impractical cause; Pius, a gentle saintly genius and skilful statesman; Paul, a noble figure-head; Xystus, a plebeian nepotist; and Innocent was a lethargic paterfamilias. Naturally the condition of a kingdom, under such a series of sovereigns (considering the Popes in their temporal, and not in their spiritual capacity), would go from bad to worse.

Yet Letters and the Arts were flourishing, as in the golden reign of the Lord Nicholas P.P. V. Canon Angelo Ambrogini (detto Poliziano) was showing, in his fine hymn, *In Divam Virginem,* that it is possible to write Christian verse in Latin good as Golden; and in his Ἐρωτικὸν Δωριστί and Ἐρωτικὸν περι του χρυσοκομου that a clergyman of the fifteenth century, whose Greek was not learned at school or college, could indite as dainty verses as Theokritos. Can the twentieth century visualise the fifteenth? Can the twentieth century realise how poor the fifteenth was in material which every board-school boy may have to-day for the asking? The title of the book "De Omnibus Rebus et Quibusdam Aliis," provokes a guffaw now. Then it was used in sober earnest; for, then, it was possible for one man to know all that was known—so little was there known in the fifteenth century. Dante Alighieri knew all, at the beginning of the fourteenth. Lionardo da Vinci knew all at the beginning of the sixteenth—literally all. Go and look at his manuscript note-books, and see what divers things he knew, to what depth of knowledge he had delved, how ingenious an application he made of the wisdom that he had gained; his inventions of conical bullets, of boats with paddle-wheels, of flying machines, of a cork-apparatus for walking on water. Consider that he was machinist, engineer, architect, and mathematician, constructor of artillery, fortifications, canals, and drains; and that, incidentally, he painted pictures, the lost "Cenacolo" at Milan, which the whole world knows—lost, because Messer Lionardo made the experiment of painting fresco in oil. Mark, too, in the note-books, how artfully and easily he wrote from right to left, to keep his knowledge from vulgar superficial eyes that pried. Mark his fluent gesture, his decisive master-strokes, and the little illuminating diagrams with which he illustrated every page. Can the twentieth century understand that the Italian mind of the fifteenth, in the absence of material, was concentrated on workmanship? Hence the marvels of handicraft which we use for models now, carving, metal-work, and textile design. The workmanship was everything then in Art and in Letters also. "So long as the form was elegant, according to their standard of taste, the latinity copious and sound, the subject-matter of a book raised no scruples. Students of eminent sobriety, like Guarino da Verona, thought it no harm to welcome Boccadelli's *Hermaphroditus* with admiration; while the excellent Nicholas V. spent nine days perusing the filthy satires of Filelfo." (*Symonds' Renascence* II. 574.) The workmanship was everything. The civilisation of the fifteenth century was as high as that of the twentieth, in conception and production of the beautiful. But clearly let it be realised that "civilisation has nothing to do with morality or immorality"; that "great reformers generally destroy the beautiful"; that "high civilisation is generally immoral." The age of the Renascence, which found nothing shameful in the profession of the ἑταίρα (if we may judge from the epitaph of one, *Imperia, Cortisana Romana, quae digna tanto nomine, rarae inter homines formae specimen dedit. Vixit a. XXVI. d. XII. Objit MDXL. die XV. Aug.*), though free from the hypocrisy engendered by the German Reformation of a later date (which the maxim "Si non caste tamen caute" so admirably describes), was frankly and unblushingly unmoral, as far as a proportion of its leaders was concerned. Yet its unmorality was kept within certain bounds, and circumscribed by a force which, now, is no restraint. Printing was in its infancy. Written books were few, and very costly. In Milan, a city of two hundred thousand inhabitants, there were only fifty copyists. Not till 1465, in the reign of the Lord Paul P.P. II, was there a printing-press in Italy, at Subjaco in the Sabine Hills; while Florence had no press till 1471. And, at first, printed books were regarded with disfavour by reason of their cheapness. One rich man said that he would be ashamed to have them in his library, as now a rich man would be ashamed to have Brummagem electro instead of hall-marked silver. Yet, by means of ambulant printers, who printed only one page at a time on a hand-press in a mule-cart (and who were the pioneers of that curse to real civilisation, the printed book), before 1500 no fewer than 4987 works had been printed in Italy alone. Here again the fifteenth-century passion for perfect workmanship came into play. Look at an Aldine Classic, and mark its exquisite form. Messer Aldo Manuzio of Venice set a great artist, Messer Francesco Raibolini (detto Il Francia), who painted the dulcet Pietá in the National Gallery, to cut a fount of type after the lovely handwriting of the poet Petrarch. That is the Aldine, or original Italic type; the script of a fourteenth-century singer. Can the twentieth century, with its manifold appliances, its labour-saving machinery, better that handiwork, or approach that design; or would a Royal Academician condescend to cut types for a printer! Look at the portrait-medals and pictures of the day to see of what fashion were these elaborately simple men of the fifteenth century:— The English type, sturdy, recondite, and simple; the French type, simple and light and vain; the Italian, subtle and simple and strong—an English Hospitaller, a French cardinal, an Italian scholar called, The Phoenix of Genius; John Kendal, Grand Prior of the Knights of St. John of Jerusalem in England; Cardinal-Archbishop Georges d'Amboise; and Messer Giovanni Pico della Mirandola; on their medals in the British, and Victoria and Albert, Museums. The painters of this era, after Giotto, had emancipated themselves from the domination of the Church. They refused any longer to be bound by that decree of the Council of Nicaea (A.D. 787), which calmly, inexorably, and altogether justifiably ordained:—*It is not the invention of the painter which creates the picture; but an inviolable law, a tradition of the Church. It is not the painter, but the holy fathers, who have to invent and dictate. To them, manifestly, belongs the composition; to the painter, only the execution.* The fifteenth century was the century of broken bonds—bonds of discipline, bonds of morality. Men tasted liberty, had discovered Man; and, like schoolboys breaking bounds, playing truant, dazed in some rich orchard, they revelled and rollicked among fruits hitherto forbidden, potentialities long-dormant now alive. Unaccustomed sight had yet but imperfect impressions. Men saw "men as trees walking"; but as far as they went

the impressions were vivid, life-like, true. Study the mercilessly precise drawings of Cavaliere Andrea Mantegna, the
Lombard, pupil of Squarcione, who painted for the Lord
Innocent P.P. VIII that chapel on the Belvedere which
was destroyed by the Lord Pius P.P. VI, and who won his
knighthood by painting for the Marquess Don Francesco
de Gonzaga of Mantua. Study the works of Messer Luca
Signorelli, "the first and last painter except Michelangelo
to use the body without sentiment, without voluptuousness,
without any secondary intention whatsoever, as the supreme decorative principle" (*Symonds' Renascence*) ; who,
having had killed at Cortona his young and splendid son,
stripped the body naked, and, with iron nerve, painted from
it during a day and a night, "that he might be able, through
the work of his own hand, to contemplate that which nature
had given him, but which an adverse fortune had taken
away." (*Vasari.*) Above all, study Messer Alessandro
Filipepi (detto Botticelli), who, having finished the chapel
of the Lord Xystus P.P. IV, was back again in Florence,
painting for Lorenzo de' Medici. How many of the Medici
he put into his pictures we never shall know ; but if ever a
painter painted from the life Alessandro Filipepi was that
painter ; and, with a little sympathetic ingenuity, one can
trace at least a single precious portrait through his pictures, and into the pictures of another and more conventional painter ; and, in this way, learn what like was one
very prominent personality of the Borgian Era, as παίς,
μειράκιον, σιδεύνης, ἐφήβος, ανδρός. Study the angel-boys
and San Giambattista in the round Madonna of the National Gallery and the round Coronation of Madonna at
the Uffizi. Study the Hermes Ptenopedilos in the Prima-
vera that Botticelli painted on the verses of Lucretius Carus
(737-740) as a setting for a portrait of an unknown lady
of the House of Medici. And study the limber San Sebastiano at Berlin. Then study murdered Giuliano's bastard,
the Lord Giulio de' Medici, Archbishop of Florence, Knight

of St. John of Jerusalem, and Cardinal-Deacon of Santa Maria *in Domnica,* in the portrait of the myopic Lord Leo P.P. X by Messer Rafaele Sanzio da Urbino. So shall a lean, muscular, vivid, thoughtful, pious, unmoral, voluptuous yet hardy, typical, young Italian of the Borgian Era be clearly, intimately, seen and known. And the medals:—Note how that the medallists have not learned to flatter or idealise; that, what they saw in their model, that they chiselled in perennial bronze. Note the character, the distinguished individuality, here preserved; the Sforza medals, for example, with their clean, compelling, vigorous, venomous, Greek profiles, which that illustrious House got (and preserves to this day in Prince Guido Sforza and his sister Princess Carolina Corsini) from Countess Polissena Russa of Montalto, who married Duke Francesco. Observe, from their manner of clothing him, how these people worshipped Man. Not for them was the concealment of his grace in dented fractured cylinders. Every natural line must be preserved, every contour displayed, in that age of unconventional realism. The frescoes of Messer Bernardo Betti (detto Pinturicchio), in the cathedral library of Siena, are said to be the fashion-plates of the day and month (1503-1507), done by an eminent artist. And the fabrics of which they made their clothes were fine and simple; for the uses of shoddy were not known. Sumptuous brocades, fairest linen of flax, furs from the East, and delicate enduring leather, adorned those men and women who had not learned to change their garments as often as they changed their minds; and who went to bed at night simply as nature made them. That they were meticulously clean, is witnessed by the embossed basins and ewers for frequent washings, the hanging lavabo on the wall of every room (when washing was a ceremonial habit), the elaborate supplies of water, the baths of macerated sweet herbs, glasswort, white lily, marsh-mallow, and lupin-meal, alkaline, mucilaginous, emollient, demulcent, which were the substitute for soap.

Care for the personal appearance was extreme. Little signs show this. For example, the twentieth-century man, confection of his hosier and his tailor, plays with watch-chain, stick, or card-case; the writer, hesitating over the turning of a phrase or waiting for the just word, rolls a cigarette; the painter, considering an effect, dabbles in a tobacco-jar and lights a pipe. Man has a natural craving to employ his hands. In similar situations, Messer Lionardo da Vinci's model and studio-boy, the curly-headed Salaino, would bring rosewater and towel to refresh his master's fingers; Canon Angelo Ambrogini (detto Poliziano) would take out an ivory comb and comb his long stranght hair; and a dandy anxiously would study his image in polished metal mirrors set like bosses on his dagger sheath, or chew comfits of coriander-seeds, steeped in marjoram vinegar and crusted with sugar, to bring a special commodity to the memory. In an age when personal and private functions were pursued after the methods of cats or dogs according to the temperament of the pursuer, when that which is now called sanitaton was unknown, great and incessant efforts in the way of cleanliness were imperative; and he who insistently displayed, who publicly exhibited, his cleanly habits, naturally enjoyed the consideration and approval of his equally modish contemporaries. And they were practically pious too, these hardy ardent exquisites, who shed an enemy's blood as remorselessly as though murder were a natural function. They would weep real tears of devotion over the drama of the Passion of our Divine Redeemer enacted in the ruined Colosseo of Rome; and, afterwards, zealously adjourn with knives to the houses of known Jews, or perfervidly hunt the dark lanes of the city for any of the accursed race who was so misguided as to show his yellow-patched jerkin on the street. The Venetians had a penchant for holy relics, and deemed no sacrifice too great for increasing their collection. In 1455, the republic made a bid of ten thousand ducats for the Seamless Coat, now at Treves, and ordained days of humiliation when the offer was refused. The Doge of Venice was obliged officially to assist at twelve public processions in each year. To please the piety and vanity of Florence, Lorenzo de' Medici personally applied to the city of Spoleto for the corpse of the painter Fra Lippo Lippi; but Spoleto answered that it had none too many ornaments as a city, especially in the shape of the cadavers of distinguished people, and begged to be excused. "The men of the Renascence were so constituted that, to turn, from vice and cruelty and crime, from the deliberate corruption and enslavement of a people by licentious pleasures, from the persecution of an enemy in secret, with a fervid and impassioned movement of the soul to God, was nowise impossible. Their temper admitted of this anomaly, as we may plainly see from Cellini's autobiography." (*Symonds' Renascence.*)

. . .

The Lord Innocent P.P. VIII made no impression on His age; as a despot, He was an accented failure. "The Patrimony of St. Peter would be the most delightful country in the world if it were not for Colonna and Orsini," said the Sieur Philippe de Comines, Orator of the Christian King Louis XI of France. The States of the Church became a seething cauldron of lawlessness and licence. Rome herself, "where everything that is shameful or horrible collects and is practised" (*Tacitus*), swarmed with assassins, professional and amateur. Every man who valued his personal safety put on a mail-shirt when he left his naked bed, and set no foot in the streets till he had buckled a sword, or at least a dagger, by his side. The very perfection of these fifteenth-century mail-shirts, which could be hidden in two hands, and yet were proof against a thrust or cut at closest quarters, tells its own tale. The trade of an armourer became an honourable art and mystery, when men staked their lives at every turn as men callously stake money now on their convictions or opinions. A whole embassage from Maximilian, King of the Romans, as the heir of Caesar Friedrich IV was styled, was assailed by brigands and stripped to the shirts in sight of Rome.

In July 1492 Lord Innocent P.P. VIII showed signs of decay, the feebleness of age increased, and He was only kept alive by women's milk. Modern chroniclers of His last hours have fallen into serious error, in relating that the operation for transfusion of blood was performed by a Hebrew chirurgeon upon the Holiness of the Pope without accomplishing its end. The error arises from forgetfulness of the facts: (a) that the idea of the operation for transfusion could not occur to any one to whom the circulation of the blood was unknown; (β) that the phenomenon of the circulation of the blood was not discovered by Harvey until the seventeenth century. Before the circulation of the blood was known, the visible veins were taken for sinews. Verrochio thought them to be sinews when he carved them on the lean young arms of his alert David. The blood was conceived of as stagnant in the flesh; the heartbeats as a pulsing of the bowels. If the idea of transferring blood from a healthy to a feeble body had occurred to any one of them, the ordinary fifteenth-century chirurgeons would not have been contented with a single incision, but would have filled up the weak body through numerous apertures, to be closed with the red hot cautery as usual; and the patient most certainly would have died under the operation, of syncope, caused, not by loss, but by acquisition of blood. Modern historians have misunderstood the words with which Infessura and Raynaldus describe the death of this Pope: and their misunderstanding further is caused by a casual and superficial knowledge of the pharmacy of the fifteenth century. Infessura and Raynaldus say that a certain Jewish physician promised to the Pope's Holiness the restoration of His health; that he took three boys of the age of ten years, giving to them a ducat a-piece, saying that he wished to restore the Pope's health, and that he required for that purpose a certain quantity of human blood, which must be young; that he drew all the blood out of those three boys; that the said boys incontinently died; that, when the Lord Innocent P.P. VIII knew, He execrated the crime of the Jew and gave order for his arrest; that the Jew had taken himself by flight out of the reach of the torturers; and that the Pope received no cure. This, Dr. Mandell Creighton and Mr. John Addington Symonds call transfusion of blood. They appear to be unaware of the fifteenth-century passion for sublimation and distillation : and they appear to have missed this sentence of Raynaldus, *ut ex eo* (the young blood) *pharmacum stillicidium chimica arte paratum propinandum Pontifici conficeret;* which plainly shows that it was a draught, a drink,[1] the quintessence of the boys' blood, prepared by his alchymical art, with which the Hebrew physician was going to fail to save the life of the Pope.

.   .   .

These were the times, and the men, which the Vice-chancellor-Cardinal Rodrigo de Lançol y Borja had to deal.

.   .   .

.   .   .

[1] The saving virtue of a drink of human blood was no new idea. Compare Tertullian Apol. IX. *"Item illi qui munere in arena noxiorum iugulatorum sanguinem receptem (de iugulo decurrentem exceptum) avida siti comitiali morbo medentes hauserunt, ubi sunt?"*

BOOK THE SECOND

THE ROARING BLAZE

"A fire that is kindled begins with smoke and hissing, while
"it lays hold upon the faggots; bursts into a roaring blaze
"with raging tongues of flame, devouring all in reach;

THE subject of this book has furnished occasion for liars of all ages—reckless liars, venal liars, raving liars, careless liars, clever liars, and futile liars, to perform their functions.

The Lord Innocent P.P. VIII died on the twenty-fifth of July 1492. The Lord Rafaele Galeotti Sansoni-Riarjo, Cardinal-Deacon of San Giorgio *in Velum Aureum,* Cardinal-Chamberlain of the Holy Roman Church, sent guards to seize and hold the gates of Rome. *Caporioni,* priors of the fourteen Regions, patrolled the city to deal with seditions and disorders. Patarina, the great bell on Capitol, that only tolls when the Pope is dead, knelled unceasingly.

At this time the Sacred College consisted of seven and twenty cardinals. Four of these were absent in distant sees, and were unable to reach the Eternal City in the nine days at their disposal. They were:—

 (*a*) The Lord Luis Juan de Mila y Borja, Cardinal-Prior-Presbyter of the Title of Santi Quattro Coronati;

 (*β*) The Lord Pedro Gonsalvo de Mendoza, Cardinal-Presbyter of the Title of Santa Croce *in Gerusalemme;*

 (*γ*) The Lord André Spinay, Cardinal-Presbyter of the Title of San Martino *in Monte t.t. Equitii;*

(δ) Frère Pierre d'Aubusson, Grand Master of the Knights of Rhodes, Cardinal-Deacon of Sant' Adriano.

Twenty-one cardinals entered the Conclave. They were :—

(α) The Lord Rodrigo de Lançol y Borja, Cardinal-Bishop of Porto and Santa Rufina, Dean of the Sacred College, Vicechancellor of the Holy Roman Church, etc. ;

(β) The Lord Giovanni Michele, Cardinal-Bishop of Praeneste, Bishop of Verona ;

(γ) The Lord Oliviero Carafa, Cardinal-Bishop of Sabina, Archbishop of Naples ;

(δ) The Lord Giorgio Costa, Cardinal-Bishop of Albano ;

(ε) The Lord Antoniotto Pallavicini, Cardinal-Presbyter of the Title of Sant' Anastasia ;

(ζ) The Lord Girolamo Basso della Rovere, Cardinal-Presbyter of the Title of San Crisogono, Bishop of Recanata ;

(η) The Lord Domenico della Rovere, Cardinal-Presbyter of the Title of San Clemente, Archbishop of Taranto ;

(θ) The Lord Giuliano della Rovere, Cardinal-Presbyter of the Title of San Pietro *ad Vincula;*

(ι) The Lord Palo Fregosio, Cardinal-Presbyter of the Title of San Sisto, Archbishop of Genoa ;

(κ) The Lord Giovanni de' Conti, Cardinal-Presbyter of the Title of San Vitale, Archbishop of Consano ;

(λ) The Lord Giangiacomo Sclafenati, Cardinal-Presbyter of the Title of San Stefano *in Monte Celio,* Bishop of Parma ;

(μ) The Lord Ardicino della Porta, Cardinal-Presbyter of the Title of San Giovanni e San Paolo, Bishop of Alba ;

(ν) The Lord Lorenzo Cibo, Cardinal-Presbyter of the Title of Santa Cecilia, Archbishop of Benevento;

(ζ) The Lord Francesco de' Piccolhuomini, Cardinal-Archdeacon of Sant' Eustachio, Archbishop of Siena;

(o) The Lord Rafaele Galeotti Sansoni-Riarjo, Cardinal-Deacon of San Giorgio *in Velum Aureum*, Cardinal-Chamberlain of the Holy Roman Church;

(π) The Lord Giovanni Colonna, Cardinal-Deacon of Santa Maria *in Aquiro;*

(ϱ) The Lord Giambattista Orsini, Cardinal-Deacon of Santa Maria *Nuova;*

(σ) The Lord Giovanni de' Medici, Cardinal-Deacon of Santa Maria *in Domnica;*

(τ) The Lord Giovanni Savelli, Cardinal-Deacon of San Niccolo *in Carcere Tulliano;*

(v) The Lord Giambattista Zeno, Cardinal-Deacon of Santa Maria *in Portico;*

(ϕ) The Lord Ascanio Maria Sforza-Visconti, Cardinal-Deacon of San Vito e San Modesto *in Macello,* Martiri.

At the last moment, before the Conclave finally was immured, there came:—

(χ) Fra Mafeo Gheraldo, Cardinal-Presbyter of the Title of San Nereo e Sant' Achilleo, Patriarch of Venice;

(ψ) The Lord Friderico Sanseverini, Cardinal-Deacon of San Teodoro.

On the sixth of August 1492, this Conclave of twenty-three cardinals listened to the preliminary exhortations of Fra Bernardino Lopez de Caravajal, and the business of election was begun.

.   .   .

Man mercifully has been left unable to foresee the effect which his actions will have upon the future. Many of these cardinals had assisted before at the election of a Pope; it was a routine with which they were acquainted. But by no means could they know what a mark upon the world's history they would make with this election. Subsequent events, however, have shown that the seed of tremendous issues here was sown, issues as great as the consolidation of a European kingdom under a sovereign dynasty that endured until 1870. As such, the Conclave of 1492 must be regarded as one of the most pregnant that ever have occurred; and its details, as worthy of intent consideration.

There was a faction and a shadow of a faction among the cardinals. The candidate of the first was the Dean and Vicechancellor-Cardinal Rodrigo de Lançol y Borja, nephew of the Lord Calixtus P.P. III. He actively was supported by the very influential cardinals Sforza-Visconti, Colonna, and Riarjo, whose friendship he is said to have cultivated during the reign of the late Pope, by promises of preferment and by gifts. He also is said to have won the alliance of fourteen other cardinals by similar inducements, and so to have placed himself at the head of a faction of eighteen. His supporters were led to believe that his Spanish nationality would make him neutral to the political parties of Italy; and much stress was laid upon the fact that Spain was now the rising power in Europe, with whom the Church would do well to be allied. The standard of morality of the day prevented objections to the character of Cardinal Rodrigo; and it was made clear to all that he was by far the richest cardinal, holding all the most lucrative appointments, which last would have to be vacated, and would be his to give away, in the event of his election.

The candidate of the second faction was Cardinal Giuliano della Rovere, a nephew of the Lord Xystus P.P. IV. He was the life-long disappointed rival, in more senses than one, of Cardinal Rodrigo. His candidature was an attempt on the part of the Christian King Charles VIII of France to set up a Pontiff devoted to French, and not to Spanish, interests; to which end the King's Majesty deposited two hundred thousand ducats with a Roman bank for the purchase of cardinalitial votes.

There was an independent candidate, Cardinal Lorenzo Cibo, a nephew of the Lord Innocent P.P. VIII, to whom Cardinal Pallavicini was bound by ties of gratitude: but he had no other supporter, and became submerged in the majority.

Of the two contestants, Cardinal Giuliano della Rovere had the poorer chance. His own cousin, Cardinal Girolamo and Domenico della Rovere, would not support him. His personality was universally antipathetic; his opponent's was universally sympathetic. The French money which he had taken, was but as a drop in the ocean compared with the enormous wealth and desperate determination of the Spaniard. Also, there were no votes for sale. Four cardinals —the Lords Oliviero Carafa, Giorgio Costa, Francesco de' Piccolhuomini, and Giambattista Zeno—announced that they would vote independently and under no influence; while the remnant of the Sacred College, consisting of seventeen cardinals, having been fiercely canvassed by Cardinal Ascanio Maria Sforza-Visconti, representative of the reigning House of Milan and hereditary foe of France, were already in the pocket of the Vicechancellor-Cardinal-Dean.

The third night of the Conclave concluded the preliminary discussions; and at dawn, on the eleventh of August 1492, Cardinal Rodrigo was elected Pope, by the large majority of twenty-two out of twenty-three, consisting of his own vote with those of the Cardinal-Bishops Giovanni Michele, Oliviero Carafa, Giorgio Costa, the Cardinal-Presbyters Antoniotto Pallavicini, Lorenzo Cibo, Mafeo Gheraldo, Girolamo Basso della Rovere, Domenico della Rovere, Paola Fregosio, Giovanni de' Conti, Giangiacomo

Sclafenati, Ardicino della Porta, the Cardinal-Archdeacon Francesco de' Piccolhuomini, the Cardinal-Deacons Rafaele Galeotti Sansoni-Riarjo, Giovanni Colonna, Giambattista Orsini, Giovanni de' Medici, Giovanni Savelli, Friderico Sanseverini, Giambattista Zeno, and Ascanio Maria Sforza-Visconti.

Rome was exciting herself about this election. Four mule loads of silver had been taken from the palace of Cardinal Rodrigo to the house of Cardinal Sforza-Visconti before the immuring of the Conclave, most conceivably to be guarded there more safely. Rome guessed that the Spaniard was so certain of his own election as to be preparing for the pleasant custom, which the citizens used, of pillaging the palace of the cardinal who was elected Pope. Some of the silver perhaps may have passed into Sforza's possession; but there is no direct evidence to prove the absurd statement of Monsignor Burchard that it was the price of his vote. In the first instance, the security of the silver was most probably the motive for its transference. After the election the Pope would naturally wish to reward his most useful supporter; and no doubt left the silver [1] with Cardinal Sforza-Visconti while bestowing on him other and more proportionate acknowledgments.

In the Conclave, if one can believe reports, there was no less excitement. All the sombre dignity of Spain left Cardinal Rodrigo at the supreme moment of his life. He

---

[1] Only one piece of antique silver, a salt-cellar, was possessed by the House of Sforza in the latter years of the last century. All the rest was not recov red from that Don Marino Torlonia, who usurped the Sforza-Cesarini titles and esta'es from 1832 to 1836, when he was deprived of them by the Ruota, the Supreme Tribunal of the Holy See, in favour of Don Lorenzo Sforza-Cesarini, grandfather of the present duke. The line of the great Francesco Sforza-Visconti, Duke of Milan, to which Cardinal Ascanio Maria belonged, is now extinct. The present House of Sforza-Cesarini descends from Don Bosio Sforza, Count of Santafiora, 1441-1476, brother of the great Francesco, and second son of Don Giovanni Muzio Attendolo, detto Sforza.

showed himself as just a human man, successful in the most daring, most immense, of all ambitions, when his quondam colleagues lowered their green or purple canopies to his, as he joyfully cried: "We are Pope and Vicar of Christ!"

The cardinals knelt at His feet, and Cardinal Sforza-Visconti said that undoubtedly the election was the work of God. Then the new Pope recovered at least decorum of speech, replying that He was conscious of His Own weakness, and relied entirely upon Divine Guidance; but His order to Monsignor Burchard, the Caerimonarius, to write His name on little slips of paper, and fling them from a window for the satisfaction of the citizens who swarmed impatiently outside the Vatican; and His haste to retire behind the altar for the purpose of changing His cardinal-itial scarlet for the papal habit of white taffetas with cinc-ture, rochet of fair linen, embroidered crimson stola, house-cap, almuce, and shoes of ermine and crimson velvet (of which vestments three sizes are prepared, to suit the stature of any Pope); this order and this haste show that the Pope's Holiness was most deeply moved, as any human being well might be.

Outside, Rome rejoiced. Inside, the cardinals asked what name the Pope would choose, suggesting Calixtus as a compliment to His dead Uncle and Creator, Who had brought Him first to Rome. But now, the Pontiff had regained His magnificent composure, and He answered mightily: "We desire the name of the Invincible Alexander." Cardinal Giovanni de' Medici, a clever, serious boy of the age of seventeen years, whispered to Cardinal Cibo: "Now we are in the jaws of a ravening wolf, and if we do not flee he will devour us." But the gigantic Cardinal San-severini lifted the Lord Alexander P.P. VI in his strong arms and throned Him on the altar; and the Sacred College paid Him the first adoration, kissing the cross embroidered on His shoe and on the ends of the stola at His knee, and the Ring of the Fisherman on His right forefinger, while

Cardinal-Archdeacon Francesco de' Piccolhuomini and the
second Cardinal-Deacon made proclamation to the crowd
at the re-opened door of the Conclave.

"I announce to you great joy. We have for a Pope the
Vicechancellor-Cardinal-Dean Rodrigo de Lançol y Borja,
Who wills to be called Alexander the Sixth."

[1] And, incontinent, says Monsignor Hans Burchard the
vulgar tittle-tattling Caerimonarius, (wilfully misquoting
the Vulgate Psalm cxi. 9) having assumed the papal power,
dispersit et dedit pauperibus bona sua, He hath dispersed,
He hath given to the poor, his goods. (*Authorised Version,
Psalm* cxii. 9.) To Cardinal Orsini He gave the Vicechancellor's palace of San Lorenzo *in Damaso,* the fortalices
of Soria and Monticelli, the revenues of the cathedral of
Cartagena in Spain, worth five thousand ducats (which He
had been administering for Don Cesare (detto Borgia) in
accordance with the Breves of the Lords Xystus P.P. IV
and Innocent P.P. VIII), and the legation of the Mark of
Ancona. To Cardinal Ascanio Maria Sforza-Visconti He
gave His new palace on Banchi Vechi (*v.* p. 74), the town
of Nepi, the revenues of the cathedral of Agria in Hungary, worth ten thousand ducats, and named him, at the age
of thirty-seven years, Vicechancellor of the Holy Roman
Church. To Cardinal Colonna He gave the Abbacy of
Subjaco with all its fortresses and rights of patronage, confirming the same to his house for ever. To Cardinal Riarjo
He gave the huge palace in Trastevere (now Corsini)
vacated by Cardinal Sforza-Visconti, benefices in Spain
producing four thousand ducats yearly revenue, and confirmed him in his office of Cardinal-Chamberlain. To Cardinal Savelli He gave the legations of Perugia and Civita
Castellana, including twenty towns and a revenue of three

[1] This paragraph rests entirely upon the gossip and conjectures
of Manfredi, Orator of Ferrara at Florence; Stefano Infessura
(Ed. Tommasini) Hans Burchard (Ed. Thuasne); Bernardino
Corio (Storia di Milano).

thousand ducats; and to other cardinals the remainder of the preferments which He now vacated.

If these gifts were given and taken as the price of votes, then an enormous act of Simony technically was committed, the buying and selling of ecclesiastical power. Afterwards, His enemies continually were charging Him with Simony; but, at the time, no serious accusation was made. Even the four cardinals, who had announced that they did not intend to be bribed, voted for the Lord Alexander P.P. VI. And here it may be noticed, that though Simony, by the Bull of the Lord Julius P.U. II *De Simoniaca Electione,* is held to invalidate an ecclesiastical election; yet the said Bull was not issued until after the death of the Lord Alexander P.P. VI, and was not retrospective in effect, although the vehement personal hatred of Julius for Alexander, hatred worthy rather of Carthaginian Hannibal than of the Vicar of the Prince of Peace, leaves no doubt whatever of the intention to defile the memory of the preceding Pontiff with an insinuation which never has been made valid. Under these circumstances, it perhaps may be permitted to those irrational persons who habitually usurp the functions of the Eternal Judge, and who already have condemned the Borgia Pontiff, to remember that, if this election was invalidated and annulled by Simony, He never was a Pope at all, and therefore cannot be blamed, attacked, condemned, in a papal capacity. Much satisfaction of a kind may be derived from that reflection. At the same time, though the theory might be allowed for private consumption, as a "pious opinion," distinguished from a "dogma," it would be highly injudicious to court collision with another Bull—the Bull *Execrabilis* of the Lord Pius P.P. II—which provides all proclaimed aspersions of the Popes with pains and penalties. But when all has been considered, no evidence is forthcoming to prove that a single cardinal sold—*sold*—his vote to Cardinal Rodrigo buying. None but a purchased or unpurchased cardinal can testify that he sold, or did not sell; and none of these have testified. That the new Pope gave great gifts is not denied. Popes always do. They cannot help Themselves. The Lord Alexander P.P. VI vacated so much preferment, that He had much to give. To give that preferment was one of the duties of His office; and, naturally, He gave it to His friends, and not to His single enemy and envious rival, Cardinal Giuliano della Rovere, who, in revenge, alleged Simony.

.   .   .

The Lord Innocent P.P. VIII died on the twenty-fifth of July 1492. The Lord Alexander P.P. VI began to reign on the eleventh of August. During the seventeen days that intervened, while the city was under the rigid rule of the white-faced Cardinal-Chamberlain Riarjo, a matter of some two hundred and twenty assassinations took place: in such order had the deceased Pope left His capital that more than nine murders were committed every day among a population of a mere five and eighty thousand. The Lord Alexander P.P. VI acted with decision to end this abominable state of lawlessness. An assassin was caught red-handed—there was no difficulty about that—he and his brother were forced to look on while their house was rased to the ground (the worst disgrace possible to a Roman); and then they were ceremoniously hanged among the ruins. A commission was established to decide all quarrels, which, formerly, had been settled by cold steel. Official inspectors of prisons were appointed; arrears of official salaries paid up to date; and a bench of four judges established for dealing with capital crimes. So the first act of this pontificate was the restoration, at least provisionally, of public order. The admiring Romans said that this vigorous administration of justice was due to the direct disposing of the Almighty.

The coronation, on the steps before the Basilica of St. Peter in the Vatican, of the Lord Alexander P.P. VI by the Cardinal-Archdeacon on the twenty-sixth of August was a scene of unlimited magnificence, attended by the Orators of the Powers who hailed the Pope with the most laudatory congratulations. Canon Angelo Ambrogini (detto Poliziano), who spoke for Siena, said:—

"Præstans animi magnitudo quae mortales crederes omnes ante-"cellere—Magna quaedam de te, rara, ardua, singularia, incredibilia, "inaudita, pollicentur.[1]

The Orator of Lucca said:—

"Quid iste tuns divinus, et maiestate plenus, aspectus?

The Orator of Genoa said:—

"Adeo irtutum gloria et disciplinarum laude, et vitae sanctimonia "decoraris, et adeo singularum ac omnium rerum ornamento dotaris, "quae talem summam ac venerandam dignitatem praebeant ut valde "ab omnibus ambigendum sit, tu ne magis pontificatui, an illa tibi "sacratissima et gloriosissima Papatus dignitas offerenda fuerit.

The Venetian Senate rejoiced:—

"propter divinas virtutes ac does quibus Ipsum insignitum et or-"natum conspiciebamus, videbatur a Divina Providentia talem "Pastorem gregi, dominio et sacrosancto Romanae Ecclesiae Vica-"rium Suum fuisse delectum et praeordinatum.

Manfredi, the Ferrarese Orator at Florence, wrote to his Duchess:—

"Dicesi che sara plorioso pontifice!

Those words were re-echoed from Milan, from Naples, even from far Germany. "They say that this will be a glorious Pontiff!" All who were permitted to approach Him were enchanted by His magnificent presence and His honeyed tongue; every one praised His talents, His notable mastery of affairs, His active benevolence and beneficence. He was admired because His habits were of the simplest kind, and His magnificence free from prodigal ostentation:

---

[1] For an English parallel of riotous superlatives, compare the inscription on a picture of Elizabeth in the Hall of the Post-Reformation Jesus College, Oxford.

"Diva Elizabetha Virgo Invictissima Semper Augusta Plus Quam Caesarea Angliae Franciae et Hiberniae Potentissima Imperatrix Fidei Christianae Fortissima Propugnatrix Literarum Omnium Scientissima Fautrix Immenso Oceani Felicissima Triumphatrix Collegii Jesu Oxon Fundatrix."

though it must be added that the Ferrarese Orator said that people disliked dining with the Lord Alexander P.P. VI because His meals consisted of a single dish. But Rome and Italy generally were very proud of Him, because, at sixty-one years of age, He combined the vigour of manhood's prime with the wisdom of experience of life. If peace could be maintained, while a strong hand guided politics, the auspices were all propitious.

On the thirty-first of August, at the First Consistory, the Lord Alexander P.P. VI named his nephew, Don Juan de Borja y Lançol (Giovanni Borgia, detto Seniore) Cardinal-Presbyter of the Title of Santa Susanna. This Most Worshipful Purpled One was the son of the Pope's sister, Doña Juana. He had been Apostolic Prothonotary, Corrector of Pontifical Breves, and Archbishop of Monreale, under the Lord Xystus P.P. IV; and powerless Governor of Rome under the Lord Innocent P.P. VIII. He was a great man of business, dexterous and capable with plenary powers, and competent to deal with grave matters. The Lord Alexander P.P. VI, like His August Uncle, lost no time in securing the services of blood relation near to His Own person.

The chorus of flattery was not altogether free from discords. The sinister Cardinal Giuliano della Rovere, every day becoming more and more aggrieved by the success of his abhorred rival, called for a General Council (according to the ridiculous custom of his age) to adjudge the Lord Alexander P.P. VI guilty of Simony. In Florence the eccentric Fra Girolamo Savonarola, a friar of the Religion of St. Dominic, was prophesying evil days. Lorenzo de' Medici, "that monster of genius," was dead; and he, literally, had been the Keeper of the Peace. His sons, Don Piero and Don Lorenzo Secondo, brothers to Cardinal Giovanni, were no fit successors to their renowned father. Fra Girolamo really ruled in Florence; and his rule was baneful, because he let his personality over-ride his principles. Starting, a few years before, to convert the sinners of Florence, he had preached naked Christianity. When he had smitten many souls to penitence, his converts (in the manner of converts) leaned upon him. He allowed himself to become a director. From director it naturally was but a step to dictator: and there is the human error of Fra Girolamo Savonarola. That is the point from which he went astray. As dictator, he brought not peace but a sword —privilege of not a human man. He ordained what the world calls eccentricities; he became impatient of opinion, of resistance, of control; his penitents were the Salvation Army of the fifteenth century, making singular exhibitions of frenetic benevolence. He had made himself, by perfectly legal means, independent of his local Dominican superiors; the Archbishop of the province had no jurisdiction over him; he was subject only to the General of Dominicans and to the Pope in Rome. He was absolutely sincere; he was a fervent Catholic; of his bonafides there can be no doubt whatever. He had no attraction of manner; his personal aspect was vulgar, terrible, appalling. Yet there must have been some charm in his teaching, for great and holy men left all to follow him; Messer Alessandro Filipepi (detto Botticelli) joined him. And now he claimed to be the prophet of the Most High, prophesying of evils at the door.

. . .

Milan menaced the peace of Italy. By the assassination of Duke Galeazzo Maria Sforza-Visconti in 1476, the duchy passed to his infant son Duke Giangaleazzo; whose widowed mother, the Duchess Bona of Savoja, ruled as Regent. Four brothers of her dead husband conspired against her; and in 1479, the eldest, Don Ludovico Maria Sforza-Visconti (detto Il Moro), took possession of her child and deprived her of the regency. Cardinal Ascanio Maria, brother of Il Moro, exerted himself in Rome to obtain confirmation of this heartless deed. Duchess Bona, distracted when she found her young son torn from her arms, knowing his infant life to be the only bar between his uncle Don Ludovico Maria and the throne of Milan, made frantic appeals for the intervention of France. But the Christian King Louis XI died before he could reply to that poor mother: and Don Ludovico Maria, as Regent, thrived, keeping the boy-duke at Pavia in a palace that was, in fact, a prison, in conditions not cruel nor fatal but assuredly not ducal, nor suited to the enjoyment and maintenance of life. In 1489 Duke Giangaleazzo reached the age of twenty years; and then it was remembered that his mother, the Duchess Bona, had affianced him in his infancy to Madonna Isabella, daughter of the heir of Naples, Duke Don Alonso de Aragona of Calabria. There appeared to be no reason why Don Ludovico Maria should exacerbate the royal House of Naples by interference with the keeping of this contract; the boy was eager, the girl was marriageable; and the wedding was celebrated with appropriate pomp. The usurping Regent insisted, however, that, as the young Duke was a minor, he should still remain in the condition of a ward; and the newly-wedded children retired to try conjugal life at Pavia. A year later, 1492, a son was born; and then Duke Giangaleazzo, by paternity emboldened into manlihood, became restive against his uncle's yoke, protesting that he no longer would submit to the treatment of a boy. But Don Ludovico was well aware that long confinement shortens life; and he had kept his nephew a prisoner for ten years. He was not precisely of the stuff of which murderers are made; or a knife-blade delicately pushed between the youngster's neck and spine long ago would have made the sceptre of Milan his. As Regent he had absolute power; and he was well content to wait. So he took no notice of Duke Giangaleazzo's remonstrances; and, to pass the time, he practised marriage in his proper person, wedding the lovely Madonna Beatrice d'Este of Ferrara in 1491. (Don Francesco Sforza, son of Don Bosio Sforza and Madonna Cecilia Aldobrandeschi, heiress of Santafiora, the kinsman of Don Ludovico Maria, who arranged this marriage, was the Orator of Milan at the coronation of the Lord Alexander P.P. VI in 1492.) After the nuptials of the usurping Regent, the young Duke Giangaleazzo resigned himself to bear his lot. But his wife was furious, and thought of the interests of her baby son. "In real truth," cried Madonna Isabella to her feeble spouse, "thou art Duke of Milan, and I thy Duchess. But thou art content to abide in Pavia while that Black, Don Ludovico, ruleth in thy duchy, and seateth Madonna Beatrice near him in my place on thy throne. I will have that girl to know that she is no duchess, and that I, I Isabella, am Duchess of Milan." And the lady wrote to her father, Don Alonso de Aragona, Duke of Calabria, who was heir to the crown of the Regno, inciting him to resent the insult put upon her, his daughter, to end the usurpation of Don Ludovico Maria, and to restore Duke Giangaleazzo to his duchy.

Duke Don Alonso was not unwilling. War was imminent between Naples and Milan. Then the Pope died; the Lord Alexander P.P. VI succeeded Him; and, it being an age when the Pope frankly was admitted to be Ruler of the World, Father of princes and of kings, etc., all Italy and Christendom waited to know the new Pope's pleasure.

This was the first of a series of extremely delicate positions in which the Lord Alexander P.P. VI found Himself involved. On the one hand, the Papacy was at peace with Naples. On the other, the Pope's Holiness found His brilliant young Vicechancellor-Cardinal Ascanio Maria Sforza-Visconti to be exceedingly valuable; and he was own brother to that Don Ludovico Maria (detto Il Moro) against whom Naples was invoked. Momentous consequences waited on His action.

·   ·   ·

On the eleventh of December 1492, there arrived in Rome Don Federigo de Aragona, Prince of Altamura, second son of King Don Ferrando I, ostensibly to offer to the Pope's Holiness the obedience of Naples, with congratulations on His coronation. The royal envoy sumptuously was entertained by Cardinal Giuliano della Rovere, whose chief occupations at this period appear to have been the feeling of the pulses of the Powers, and the search for a potentate willing to be used against the Borgia.

Manifestations of goodwill between Papacy and Regno pleased the Romans. The frontier of Naples was but a day's ride from Rome; and the Romans liked to feel that beyond that frontier flourished a friend, not lurked a foe. In private audience, however, Don Federigo said that the assistance of the Pope's Holiness was required in a family affair; and he made it clear that the attitude of Regno to Papacy would be determined by the extent to which the Lord Alexander P.P. VI would go on behalf of Naples.

This was the case in question. King Matthias Corvinus of Hungary had married Madonna Beatrice, a bastard of King Don Ferrando I. On the death of King Matthias Corvinus, his childless widow Queen Beatrice had intrigued to get the Hungarian crown settled upon King Wladislaw of Bohemia, who, in return for her Majesty's services, had promised to marry her. Such a promise of marriage was equivalent to a betrothal, and a betrothal was only less binding than an actual marriage in that it was capable of being dissolved; whereas a marriage was, and is, indissoluble. King Wladislaw of Bohemia had been crowned King of Hungary through the exertions of Queen Beatrice. She, preferring the situation of Queen Regnant to that of Queen Dowager, had performed her part of the contract; and now King Wladislaw had changed his mind, and was about to ask the Pope for a dispensation from the obligation of fulfilling his promise of marriage. This was a grievous insult to the bastard of the King of Naples, whose counter-petition to the Lord Alexander P.P. VI was that no such dispensation should be granted to King Wladislaw, and that he should be compelled to perform his part of the bargain. Nothing was said at this time regarding the affair of the Duchess Isabella of Milan in which the Regno also was interested. The cases of queens take precedence of those of duchesses.

The Lord Alexander P.P. VI, with the experience of seven and thirty years of curial diplomacy behind Him, required time in which to reflect upon His answer ; and would enter into no immediate engagement with the Neapolitan prince. Don Federigo, who imagined that the Regno had but to ask and have, was much aggrieved ; and his host, Cardinal Guiliano della Rovere, inflamed him with sardonic sympathy, and eyed the Regno, for a purpose, from that day forward. An uncouth pugnacious schemer was this Most Illustrious Lord Cardinal. As a captain of condottieri he might have captured a kingdom: but as an ecclesiastic he was at all times utterly disedifying. The Lord Alexander P.P. VI seems to have treated him with admirable forbearance, with contemptuous indifference, than which no attitude is more calculated to sting and irritate an angry mediocrity. He had been allowed to proceed in his turn to the cardinal-bishopric of Ostia without let or hindrance: he had rank, riches, and power. But he was discontented, jealous, filled with envy, hatred, malice, and all uncharitableness.

.   .   .

It is imperatively important to be able to distinguish between the Office and the Man; and to avoid the excessively vulgar error of confounding the general with the particular. The pontifical acts of Rodrigo, Who is called Alexander P.P. VI, will compare favourably with those of any Supreme Pontiff, from Simon, Who is called Peter P.P., to Gioacchino Vincenzo Rafaele Luigi, Who is called

Leo P.P. XIII. His comportment as man, and Italian despot, is another matter. The just necessity of the distinction insistently is laid upon the student of His history.

Man does not yearn to please a person who is playing ugly tricks upon him. The Lord Alexander P.P. VI particularly did not yearn to please the King of Naples. While the envoy of the Regno was displaying his royal father's petition at the feet of the Father of princes and of kings, the Pope's Holiness was digesting news of a trick which has been played upon Him by the intrigues of King Don Ferrando I.

Don Franciotto Cibo, bastard of the Lord Innocent P.P. VIII, had been enriched by his Father with the lordships of Cervetri and Anguillara. These were pontifical fiefs, held by feudal tenure from the Pope. Being a silly avaricious weakling, rather frightened of the responsibility of baronage, Don Franciotto Cibo sold the said lordships to Don Virginio Orsini for forty thousand ducats; and went to live at Florence under the protection of his brother-in-law Don Piero de' Medici. Now Don Virginio Orsini had borrowed those forty thousand ducats from the King of Naples, who was his firm friend, and perfectly qualified to understand the loan to be a super-excellent investment. The lordships of Cervetri and Anguillara lay between the Regno and the territories of the Republic of Florence; and their transference into the hands of Orsini, Naples' friend, signified the opening of a road from Naples into Tuscany, along which a Neapolitan army easily might travel, should King Don Ferrando be pleased to campaign in a northerly direction.

It was Don Ludovico Maria Sforza-Visconti (detto Il Morro), the usurping Regent of Milan, who first saw the serious portent of this move: but, though he communicated his discovery to the Holiness of the Pope, he laboured under a slight misapprehension; for usurpers are the most touchy of mankind, and see an enemy in everything which they do not understand. The northern frontier of Tuscany impinged upon the southern frontier of Milan. Now that the southern frontier of Tuscany was connected, by Cervetri and Anguillara, with the Regno, Don Ludovico Maria suspected an alliance between Don Piero de' Medici and King Don Ferrando I, between Tuscany and Naples, an alliance which most possibly implied designs detrimental to the Duchy of Milan—after all the real Duchess Isabella was Naples' bastard, thought Don Ludovico Maria, the Usurper—; and he envoyed swift couriers to his brother the Vicechancellor-Cardinal in Rome, with instructions to advise the Pope's Holiness of the imbroglio.

That was the news of which the Lord Alexander P.P. VI chewed the cud at the time when He gave audience to the Prince of Altamura. With His magnificent talent for resolving diplomatic problems into their elements, from which He could discard those that He deemed useless while reserving those possessing salient features, the Pope's Holiness concluded that the politics of Milan, of Tuscany, of the Regno, and the affairs of their respective rulers, were of secondary importance and altogether negligble; but that the secret unauthorised transfer of papal fiefs into the hands of dangerous malcontents of the very powerful House of Orsini, required prompt decisive assertion of the rights of the Pontifical Suzerain.

At the beginning of 1493, Cardinal Ascanio Maria Sforza-Visconti was found to be urging the Supreme Pontiff to act against the illegal transfer of Cervetri and Anguillara. Loyalty to his brother, the usurping Regent of Milan, and his duty as Vicechancellor bound to maintain the paramountcy of the Holy Roman Church—these make clear his point of view.

A clashing of interests between Papacy and Regno was an opportunity which Cardinal Giuliano della Rovere greatly relished. He did not hesitate to take the part of

Naples. If he had one enemy whom he hated as perfervidly as he hated the Pope, that enemy was Cardinal Ascanio Maria Sforza-Visconti whose exertions on behalf of his rival had deprived him of the tiara or triregno; and, having sworn that either he or Sforza-Visconti should quit the Sacred College, he avidly seized the present chance of belabouring the cardinal as well as the Pope. He had the support of Orsini, naturally. Colonna, always more Ghibelline than Guelf, was not unwilling to espouse the cause of a man who went about saying that the Pope's Holiness was plotting to ruin his reputation—his reputation!—and to deprive him of his dignities: and hence arose a very singular and unusual combination.

The Papacy generally has been allied with Colonna or with Orsini. Such was the importance of these houses, that during many hundred years all European treaties and concordats contained their names on one side or the other. But here, for once in their mysterious and interminable feud, these mighty barons of Rome, with all their collateral branches and their myriads of armed retainers, were found united in a common cause. The phenomenon may be explained by the rise of other baronial houses, who were becoming quite as numerous and quite as potent as Colonna or Orsini; and who were equally desirable as allies. The most prominent of these, in 1493, were the Sforza and the Cesarini. The Sforza descended from Don Giovanni Muzio Attendolo (detto Sforza); and included the Sovereign-Duchy of Milan, by the marriage of the great Francesco with the heiress of Duke Giangaleazzo Visconti; the Sovereign-County of Santafiora, by the marriage of Francesco's brother Bosio with the heiress of Aldobrandeschi; and the Tyrannies of Pesaro, Chotignuola, Imola and Forli. The Sforza blazon the lion rampant with the holy flower of the quince for Santafiora, and the salvage boy couped at the thighs issuant from a serpent statant for Milan. The Cesarini were a Roman house of enormous wealth and dis-

tinction, claiming a Cesarian origin. It was already allied
with the Lord Alexander P.P. VI by the marriage in 1482
of His bastard Madonna Girolama Borgia with Don Giovandrea Cesarini. Its representative, Don Gabriele Cesarini, was the Gonfaloniere of Rome, who fought the Prior
of the Caporioni for precedence at the coronation of the
Lord Alexander P.P. VI, Who, in person, accorded the
first place to Cesarini. Don Giangiorgio Cesarini, the heir,
was allied with Sforza by marriage with Madonna Maria
Sforza di Guido di Santafiora; and Don Giuliano Cesarini
held office in the Apostolic Chamber. It was a house which,
during centuries, had been content with secondary rank,
while accumulating immense reserves of power, now to be
brought into action. These were the two patrician Houses
which the Pope's Holiness found ready to His hand when
Colonna leagued with Orsini against His peace. In fact,
Sforza and Cesarini were the right and left hands of the
Lord Alexander P.P. VI, as Colonna or Orsini were of
His predecessors and successors.

Cardinal Giuliano della Rovere, after relieving himself
of some treasonable speeches, considered Rome to be un-
safe; and fled down Tiber to his bishopric of Ostia, where
he fortified himself and advertised for mercenaries.

The word war, to the bloody men of valour of the end
of the fifteenth century, signified a game like that of chess.
The sole object of war was profit. It was undertaken simply
to deprive an enemy of his goods. Prisoners were captured,
and held to ransom. Cities and fortresses were reduced by
starvation, or by a display of overwhelming force. But
bloodshed—and this is noteworthy—was avoided as far as
possible; and the game chiefly was played by strategic
marches, counter-marches, and manœuvres. It was a business, a profession, "not more hazardous than that of a
professional football-player." The superfluous men of
Europe, and the temperamental fighters, served as hired
mercenaries under the captains and the princes who could

pay their price and afford them a roystering life. Patriotism, the honour of the fatherland, were unknown. Except in the case of England, there was no national army. When a position had been won, a city captured, the conquerors satisfied themselves with the ransoms and the richest spoils. If the citizens wished to avoid the inconvenience of a sack, they collected a sum sufficient to pay off the rank and file. Otherwise the mercenaries took the women, and had licence to recoup themselves by pillage. Resistance meant torture and death: but bloodshed was an accident, not an essential of war.

The action of Cardinal Giuliano della Rovere was an invitation to the Lord Alexander P.P. VI to engage in war. He had thrown down the gauntlet. He had made the first move in the game; and his gambit was a very fine one, for the fortress of Ostia dominated Tiber mouth, and enabled him to paralyse Rome by stopping sea-borne supplies.

Like all important characters, the Pope's Holiness was neurotic; not by any means a coward, but quick to scent danger, susceptible of momentary fright. Early in the spring of 1493 He was going to a picnic, at the villa which the Lord Innocent P.P. VIII had built for pontifical refreshment at La Magliana, outside the walls; and when a cannon saluted His approach He was stricken with a sudden panic, and galloped back to the Vatican amid the frank execrations of His escort disappointed of their dinner.

Here was the situation. The Pope was comfortably embroiled with Cardinal Giuliano della Rovere and his allies of Naples, of Colonna, of Orsini. To some extent His interests tied Him to Sforza and Milan. Tuscany was undecided between the Pope and Naples. The other Powers looked on.

While Don Ludovico Maria Sforza-Visconti was suggesting an alliance between the Pope, the duchy of Milan, and the Republic of Venice, to overawe the Neapolitan Bond, King Don Ferrando was intriguing with a view to discover whether he could make a better bargain with the Sovereign-Pontiff than with Colonna + Orsini + della Rovere. This was not treachery. It was merely the Neapolitan method, of which all Italy was fully cognizant. The King's Majesty sent envoys to Rome, to Milan, and to Tuscany, to try to settle the Cervetri-Anguillara affair by pacific means.

The Lord Alexander P.P. VI was well aware that no confidence could be placed in King Don Ferrando I: but by way of giving him a chance He proposed a marriage between His bastard, Don Gioffredo Borgia, now of the age of twelve years, and Madonna Lucrezia, a granddaughter of the Majesty of Naples. At the same time He gathered troops and fortified the Vatican and the Mola of Hadrian, with the gallery-passage, called Lo Andare, which connects them, enabling Pope and cardinals to run, in time of danger, from the Apostolic Palace to the impregnable fortress tomb by Tiber.

The Republic of Venice flung itself into the arms of Don Ludovico Maria Sforza-Visconti; for the Doge and Senate were dreadfully afraid lest the impassioned appeals of the Duchess Isabella on behalf of her husband, the pathetic Duke Giangaleazzo, should receive the attention of Naples. If the said Duke Giangaleazzo should come to owe his throne to King Don Ferrando I, then Milan would be, to all intents and purposes, a fief of the Regno; and to have Naples lording it in Northern Italy would by no means satisfy Venice, which, on this account, preferred alliance with the usurping Regent, even at the cost of winking at his usurpation of the Regency of Milan. Now Milan and Venice in alliance were a menace to their own neighbours; and, acting on the principle that made those two Powers one, the duchies of Mantua and Ferrara, and the Republic of Siena, hastened to fall into line with them. This concatenation, being superior to anything that Naples could exhibit, also caused the Lord Alexander P.P. VI to arrive at a decision: and, on the twenty-fifth of April 1493, accompanied by an armed cavalcade of Sforza and Cesarini for the ocular instruction of Colonna and Orsini, the Holiness of the Pope proceeded through Rome to the Venetian church of San Marco, on Piazza Venezia, where He ceremonially published the Bull of League between the Papacy, the duchies of Milan, Mantua, and Ferrara, and the Republics of Venice and Siena; after which, the river-port of Rome at Ostia being in His enemies' hands, He began to fortify the land-port of Rome at Civita Vecchia, by way of giving effect to His warlike proclamation.

At this call of check, Cardinal Giuliano della Rovere howled aloud for a General Council to depose the Lord Alexander P.P. VI; and Don Alonso de Aragona, Duke of Calabria, wanted immediately to unite with Don Piero de' Medici and the Signoria of Florence, and, aided by the Colonna of Paliano and Marino and the Orsini of Gravina and Bracciano, to assault Rome from the outer side, while Colonna + Orsini, who were in the city, engaged in similar diversions. But King Don Ferrando was too sly. He had yet another piece to play. He knew, and none knew better, that the territories of the Holy See during a long course of centuries had been distributed among pontifical relatives and favourites; that, at present, the States of the Church were smaller than an ordinary duchy; and he had heard of the Lord Alexander P.P. VI as a singularly affectionate father, devoted to His children's interests. Wherefore the Majesty of Naples conceived, and with absolute correctness, that the Pope's Holiness intended, by hook or by crook, by diplomacy, by marriages, or by war, to recover the possessions of the Papacy, and to use them to promote the fortunes of His family. Secondly, King Don Ferrando I knew France to be Milan's northern neighbour; and he saw the exceeding possibility of an alliance between the usurping Regent, Don Ludovico Maria Sforza-Visconti, and the Christian King Charles VIII of France; a combination which, with the Papacy, the duchies, and republics, already joined in league, would be absolutely and permanently overwhelming and disintegrating to the very Regno itself. To turn the flank, as it were, to give France occupation in another direction, he resolved on courting an alliance with Spain.

To this end he indited an invective against the Lord Alexander P.P. VI, adopting all the gratuitous insults and lying babble foamed out of the malignant Cardinal-Bishop Giuliano delle Rovere. "He leads a life that is abhorred by all, without respect to the seat He holds." [Compare the speeches of the Orators and contemporary dispatches.] "He cares for nothing save to aggrandise His children by fair means or by foul." [So far He had done nothing at all, by foul means or by fair, for His children; except to deprive His reputed bastard Don Cesare (detto Borgia) of the revenue of the cathedral of Cartagena in favour of that very Cardinal Giambattista Orsini who now deserted Him.] "From the beginning of His pontificate He has done nothing but disturb the peace." [This is partly true. The Pope's Holiness wonderfully had done more than any preceding Pontiff to restore good government and order and security to Rome. But He had behaved, in a certain instance, in a way that was extremely offensive to the Spanish ideal of peace. According to the notions of King Don Ferrando I de Aragona, himself a Spaniard—according to Spanish notions, and the Majesty of Naples was a Spaniard writing to Spaniards—the Lord Alexander P.P. VI was indeed a disturber of the peace. But the facts are these. In 1492, the horrible Spanish Inquisition—that frightful and diabolical atrocity constantly condemned by Rome—under the guidance of the Grand Inquisitor Torquemada, had procured the expulsion of the Jews from Spain. The Spaniards have much of the Moor, a touch of the oriental, the element of the human devil, in their blood. Throughout Christendom the Jews were looked upon with horror, by no means undeserved. Many long years before, England had cast them out; and now they were forced from Spain. The sufferings, with which the fiendish Spaniard visited them, were so fearful as to excite pity even in Papal Italy, whose loathing of Jews was a habit of mind, an article of faith, not an inhuman vice. Messer Giovanni Pico della Mirandola (detto Fenice degli Ingegni) said:—

"The sufferings of the Jews, in which the glory of Divine Justice "delights, were so extreme as to fill us Christians with commisera-"tion.

Senarega said:—

"The matter (*i.e.,* the expulsion of the Jews) at first sight seemed "praiseworthy as regarding the honour done to our religion; yet it "involved some amount of cruelty, if we look upon them (the Jews) "not as beasts but as men, the handiwork of God.

Many of this miserable race came to Rome, where, under the expressed order of the Lord Alexander P.P. VI, they were protected, and allowed to share in that security of life and limb which He, at the beginning of His pontificate, had ordained. The Romans did not like these Marañas, as the Moorish Jews were called, any more than they liked, or like, Catalans, or Franks, or Goths, or any other foreigners save the English-speaking race; and, following hereditary instinct, there were occasional attempts at persecution, the rigorous stamping out of which, by the justice of the Pope, caused intermittent rioting and disaffection of the citizens who only could look upon the Jews as fair game. That was the only disturbance of the peace with which King Don Ferrando could charge the Holy Father; and it was an act of justice and humanity. But the fifteenth century, in common with the nineteenth (the twentieth is too young yet to be judged), was very wont to give a bad name to the dog that it had failed to hang.]

.   .   .

Any success that might have attended the rabid calumnies of the Majesty of Naples was prevented by an occurrence of the most startling species.

A mariner of Genoa, called Messer Cristoforo Colombi, announced to the Spanish Court, in March 1493, the astounding news of his discovery of a continent. An explorer's ardour, combined with religious zeal, had made him seek to extend the boundaries of Christendom. He had set out in the hope of finding a few islands. He returned to Europe solemnly asserting that he had found a world. Universal curiosity was awakened, and a fresh expedition planned, with which the intrepid mariner set forth on a second voyage to prove, and to secure, his prize. Meanwhile, Don Hernando and Doña Isabella, the Catholic King and Queen of Spain, thought it would be prudent to bind this new world to their domain by a bond that easily could not be broken. The Pope, as Ruler of the World and Earthly Vicar of Jesus Christ, was held to have authority over all heathen lands, and to His Holiness an envoy went from Spain commissioned to announce the discovery, and to pray Him graciously to confirm it to the Catholic King and Queen.

Precipitevolissimevolmente (no other word describes the act) was issued a Bull, dated "At Rome by St. Peter's, the year of our Lord's Incarnation, 1493, the fourth day of the nones of May, and the first year of Our pontificate," giving to Don Hernando and to Doña Isabella, and to their heirs and successors, all islands and continents discovered or yet to be discovered, in the western ocean, west and south of a line to be drawn from the North Pole to the South Pole, one hundred leagues west of the Açores and Cape Verde Islands. The language of this Bull is exquisitely touching; strong, pregnant, earnest, and majestic, as the Authorised Version of the Epistles of St. Paul. The motive undoubtedly is the motive of an Apostle to convert a world to Christ. The grant is made to the Majesty of Spain, with commands to send honest God-fearing learned and expert men to teach the Christian Faith; and the penalty of excommunication *latae sententiae* is imposed upon anyone, even royal or imperial, who shall interfere. This supremely beautiful Pontifical Act, the Bull *Inter caetera* of the Lord Alexander P.P. VI, is given verbatim in Raynaldus, sub anno, 1493. So in return for the Borgia, which Spain gave to Italy, Italy and the Borgia gave Messer Cristoforo Colombi and the New World to Spain.

Don Hernando and Doña Isabella, the Catholic King and Queen, were Spaniards. And when that is said all is said; and all the hideous history of the New World under Spanish domination is explained. Those sovereigns bore no good-will for the Lord Alexander P.P. VI although He was a Spaniard. They, like every other sovereign of Europe, were quite prepared to harass and to flout an unobliging Pope up to the verge of excommunications and interdicts; when they, of course, would cringe and cower like the villainous usurper John Plantagenet: but the quick granting of their petition in this matter of the New World, the immense distinction which the Bull *Inter caetera* conferred on them and on Spain, turned them, from suitors prepared with impertinence, into the abjectly devoted adherents of the Lord Alexander P.P. VI, at least for the time; and absolutely prevented King Don Ferrando's application for an anti-pontifical alliance from meeting with success. This, no doubt, is that on which the Pope's Holiness counted. Very seldom in life does a man so clearly see his duty with the certainty of reward for its prompt performance. And very rarely, in the pontificate of the Lord Alexander P.P. VI, did He deign, so immediately and so unreservedly, to grant a favour. He must have perceived, with that marvellous instinct of His, which led Him inevitably to the very roots of matters, that for once the paths of duty and of pleasure coincided. Certainly He unhesitatingly walked therein.

.   .   .

On the twelfth of June the Lord Alexander P.P. VI married His bastard, Madonna Lucrezia Borgia, of the age of fifteen years, to the Tyrant of Pesaro, Don Giovanni Sforza, of the age of twenty-six years, with all the magnificence due to His secular rank as an Italian despot; and thereby set wagging the tongues of those who lamented the decay of ecclesiastical discipline, and who could not distinguish between the dual and contradictory offices which the Pope was expected to reconcile; as well as the pens of professional manufacturers of squibs and lampoons. The wedding-banquet took place at the Vatican, in the presence of the Pope, ten cardinals, and fifteen Roman patricians with their wives. The Holy Father presented to the ladies silver cups filled with sweetmeats, throwing them into their bosoms *ad honorem et laudem Omnipotentis Dei et Ecclesiae Romanae,* says the golden-mouthed, venomous, untrustworthy historian, Messer Stefano Infessura. In the evening there was dancing, with comedies of the conventional coarse but common type. This event is one of the bases from which disgusting charges have been levelled against the Lord Alexander P.P. VI. It summarily may be stated that those charges consist entirely of the unprintable gossip of enemies or inferiors, and that not one of them satisfactorily can be proved. That the Vicar of Christ should have condescended so far is impossible; that a temporal sovereign should have condescended so far is probable, and, perhaps, regrettable; but the status of the guests, the ten cardinals, and the fifteen Roman patricians with their wives, guarantees the utter respectability of the Despot's little private party from a contemporary point of view.

.　　.　　.

In June, also, arrived in Rome Don Diego Lopez de Haro to offer to the Holiness of the Pope the homage and obedience of Spain. These having been accepted, the Orator proceeded to remonstrate with the Pope, in the name of the Catholic King and Queen, regarding the asylum extended to the Marañas who were fled from the Spanish Inquisition to Rome. Thousands of these unfortunates were encamped among the tombs on the Appian Way, and had brought the plague with them. Spain execrated the Papal tolerance, and wondered that the Holy Father, as the Head of Christianity, should protect those whom Spain had driven away as being enemies of the Christian Faith. Further, the Spanish Orator said that the Christian King Charles VIII of France was threatening to invade Italy and to take advantage of the quarrels of the Italian Powers; wherefore he urged the necessity of peace, and an agreement among the sovereigns of whom the Pope was chief. By way of showing that concessions would ensure the unanimity of Italy, he set forth a list of ecclesiastical grievances that needed remedies; grievances "which, since the days of the Council of Constance, had been standing complaints against the Papacy, to be urged in all negotiations for other purposes." (*Creighton* iv. 199.)

.   .   .

Publicly Don Ludovico Maria Sforza-Visconti harped upon the league between Venice, Milan, and the Papacy. Privately he entered into a secret treaty with the Christian King Charles VIII through Belgioso, Orator of Milan. Being an usurper he trusted not even his allies: preferring to have two strings to his bow, he believed that he could consolidate his position only by disturbing the peace of Italy.

Publicly, from his fortress of Ostia, that psychic epileptic, Cardinal Giuliano della Rovere, continued to shout for a General Council to depose his Rival. The abominable character of this cardinal well may be exposed by stating that he was endeavouring to rend the Church and Christendom with a Fortieth Schism, in order to satiate his personal revenge.

And, like Gallio, the Pope's Holiness cared for none of these things—for Spain, for Milan, for the contemptible cardinal. He believed in Himself, and in His Own power to rule. At least, He officially had been saluted as Ruler of the World.

The intrigues and invectives of the King of Naples deservedly having failed, his Majesty made the experiment of a hostile demonstration. His second son, Prince Don Federigo of Altamura appeared with eleven galleys at Ostia on Tiber mouth; and rapturously was hailed by that traitor-cardinal-bishop, with the Colonna and Don Virginio Orsini.

The Lord Alexander P.P. VI was willing to negotiate. Borgian negotiations invariably meant that Borgia would give its opponents something, but not the something that they wanted, and always in such a way that it could not be refused. The Naples + Colonna + Orsini + Cardinal Giuliano della Rovere conspiracy had demanded Cervetri and Anguillara for Orsini (and Naples) and the disgrace of the Vicechancellor-Cardinal Ascanio Maria Sforza-Visconti to satisfy the spleen of him of Ostia. On the twenty-fourth of July the cardinal, the Neapolitan prince, and Don Virginio Orsini came to Rome to hear the pontifical terms, which were :—

(α) That the Pope's Holiness would confirm Cervetri and Anguillara to Don Virginio for life; at his death they would revert to the Holy See : but he must pay into the pontifical treasury their price of forty thousand ducats, which he previously had paid to Don Franciotto Cibo :

(β) That the Pope's Holiness was willing to forgive and to show favour to Cardinal Giuliano della

Rovere: but He refused to disgrace the Vice-chancellor-Cardinal Ascanio Maria Sforza-Visconti:

(γ) That the Pope's Holiness would consent to ally Himself with the Royal House of Naples by the marriage of His bastard, Don Gioffredo Borgia, to Madonna Sancia, bastard of Don Alonso de Aragona, Duke of Calabria and heir of King Don Ferrando I. This agreement was ratified by betrothal; and Don Gioffredo set out for Naples to see the girl, and to receive her dowry with the title Prince of Squillace. The marriage was postponed for the present, because neither bride nor bridegroom had completed their thirteenth year.

No sooner was the treaty of peace signed, than the Sieur Perron de Basche, Orator of the Christian King Charles VIII of France, arrived in Rome, armed with instructions to prevent an alliance between Papacy and Regno, and to obtain pontifical confirmation of the election, by the Rouen chapter, of Messire Georges d'Amboise as Archbishop. The Supreme Pontiff, by way of emphasising His independent attitude to France, refused to receive the Orator in audience, annulled the election of Messire Georges d'Amboise, and named one of His Own court to the Archbishopric of Rouen. This was what the twentieth century timidly calls an "unfriendly act"; and the Christian King forthwith began to sympathise with Cardinal Giuliano della Rovere's recent clamour for a General Council to depose the Lord Alexander P.P. VI, and to meditate thereon day and night.[1]

. . .

[1] Sdegnati di questa collazione contro del Papa, il Re tenne il dì medesimo gran consiglio, dove furono proposte e trattate piu cose contro del Papa in riformatione della chiesa. (Dispatch of 31 Aug. 1493, Canestrini, Négociations avec la Toscane, I. 249.)

To strengthen His influence in the Sacred College by adding creatures of His Own, at the Second Consistory of the twentieth of September 1493, the Lord Alexander P.P. VI named twelve new cardinals.

These were :—

(α) The Lord John Morton, Archbishop of Canterbury, Lord High Chancellor of England, whose virtues have been praised by another English Chancellor, the Blessed Sir Thomas More;—Cardinal-Presbyter of the Title of Santa Anastasia;

(β) The Lord Giovantonio di Sangiorgio;—Cardinal-Presbyter of the Title of San Nereo e Sant' Achilleo;

(γ) Frère Jean Villiers de la Grolaye, Lord Abbot of Saint Denys by Paris;—Cardinal-Presbyter of the Title of Santa Sabina;

(δ) The Lord Bernardino Lopez de Caravajal, Apostolic Legate to Caesar Friedrich IV, the eloquent preacher at the Conclave of 1492;—Cardinal-Presbyter of the Title of San Marcellino e San Pietro:

(ε) The Lord Raymond Perauld,[1] a Frenchman, Apostolic Nuncio in Germany;—Cardinal-Presbyter of the Title of San Giovanni e San Paolo:

(ζ) The Lord Cesare (detto Borgia), reputed bastard of the Lord Alexander P.P. VI, and of the

---

[1] There is a tale about this personage, that, having allowed himself to be frightened by one of the calumnies of Cardinal Giuliano della Rovere, to the effect that the Pope expected to be paid for the red hat (in addition to the six hundred ducats which every cardinal offers in return for the cardinalitial sapphire ring), he became so nervous on Ash Wednesday, when it was his office to scatter ashes on the head of the Sovereign Pontiff, as to substitute for the formula of administration, "Memento, homo, quia pulvis es, et in pulverem reverteris," the words "Memento, homo, quia Papa es, et ego pecunias non habeo."

age of eighteen years;—Cardinal-Deacon of
Santa Maria *Nuova:*

(η) The Lord Ippolito d'Este, of the age of fifteen
years, a great athlete and fighter from boyhood
to youth, and a prince of the Royal House of
Ferrara; "tall he was of frame, brawny of
sinew, mighty of limb, strengthening his robusti-
tude with exercises, archery, and hurling jave-
lins; grace and charm bloomed on the face of
him; his bright eyes beamed with grave tranquillity, worthy of all praise; most royal was his
whole aspect; he was an expert swimmer; and
with whatsoever weapons he adroitly strove he
inured himself to heat and cold and night-long
vigils";—Cardinal-Deacon of Santa Lucia *in
Silice, alias in Orfea:*

(θ) The Lord Fryderyk Kasimierz Jagelone di Po-
lonia, son of King Kasimierz of Poland, Bishop
of Cracow;—Cardinal-Deacon of Santa Lucia
in Septisolio, alias in Septizonio:

(ι) The Lord Giuliano Cesarini (detto Giuniore),
Apostolic Prothonotary, Canon of the Vatican
Basilica;—Cardinal-Deacon of San Sergio e San
Bacco:

(κ) The Lord Domenico Grimani, Apostolic Prothonotary;—Cardinal-Deacon of San Niccolo *Inter
Imagines:*

(λ) The Lord Alessandro Farnese, Apostolic Prothonotary (nicknamed "Cardinal Petticoat," on
account of the Pope's partiality for his sister,
Madonna Giulia Orsini nata Farnese);—Cardinal-Deacon of San Cosma e San Damiano:

(μ) The Lord Bernardino de' Lunati, Apostolic Prothonotary, friend of the Cardinal-Vicechancel-

lor :—Cardinal-Deacon of San Ciriaco *alle Terme Diocleziane.*[1]

The vigour of this deed struck Cardinal Giuliano della Rovere and his friend King Don Ferrando into frantic silence. By a mere act of His Sovereign Will the Holiness of the Pope immensely had increased His Own potentiality. Two of the new creatures were scions of reigning dynasties, whose loyalty thereby was secured. The virtue and eloquence of the English cardinal were as twin towers of strength. The two French creatures were as a sop to France. The minor diaconate conferred on Don Cesare (detto Borgia) gave him a standing, from which the splendour of his youth might do great things. And the other cardinals were proved adherents, who, by being made to owe their promotion to the Lord Alexander P.P. VI, became bound (in so far as human foresight went) to His interests by the bond of gratitude. It was a most paralysing and disheartening stroke for the enemies of the Sovereign Pontiff; and the year 1493 ended amid renewed demands for a General Council from Cardinal Giuliano della Rovere, and renewed invectives from the Majesty of Naples.

.   .   .

On the twenty-fifth of January 1494, King Don Ferrando I died, in the seventieth year of his age and the thirty-fifth of his reign. He was a cautious and experienced politician; and, since the Lord Pius P.P. II, Lorenzo de' Medici, and the great Duke Francesco Sforza-Visconti, the greatest secular statesman of his century. His policy was directed to the preservation of Italy from French invasion, and to the destructon of the Papal States. He was

[1] Infessura, in Eccard II. 2015. Alberi, Rel. Ven. Sen. III. 314. Rivista Cristiana II. 261. Ugolini, Storia . . . d'Urbino II. Doc. 13. Ciacconi, Vitae Pontificum, sub anno. Gregorovius, Geschichts de Stadt VII. 340. Matarazzo, Cron. di Perugia in Archivio Storico xvi. See I. pt. ij. 3.

not harsh in his dealings with his subjects; but to his barons and to his opponents he behaved with cruelty and treachery. He liked to have his enemies always near him, either alive in the dungeons of his palace, or dead, and embalmed, and clothed in their habits as they lived. Yet he died regretted; for his heir, the thick-haired, thin-lipped, narrow-eyed, fat-jowled, asymmetrically-featured Don Alonso de Aragona, Duke of Calabria, enjoyed a reputation for violence and brutality the bare idea of which created universal terror.

The game of politics entered on a new phase. The Christian King Charles VIII of France was burning for an opportunity of asserting himself; and had collected an army, ostensibly for a Crusade against the Great Turk, the Sultán Bajazet, really for purposes of French aggrandisement—purposes yet undefined. He was a self-conceited little abortion, this Christian King, of the loosest morals even for a king, of gross semitic type, with a fiery, birth-flare round his left eye, and twelve toes on his feet hidden in splayed shoes, which set the fashion in foot-gear for the end of the fifteenth century in Italy; and, like all vain little men, he was anxious to cut a romantic and considerable figure. He announced a claim to the crown of Naples.

This made it necessary for the Lord Alexander P.P. VI to compare the advantages of France as an ally with the Regno; and, in the meantime, that He might lead the Christian King to declare himself with more particularity, the Pope's Holiness addressed a Brief to him in which the subject of Naples was not named: but which assured him of pontifical favour, and gave him leave to pass through Rome with his army on the way to his contemplated Crusade. There was dissatisfaction in the Sacred College about the matter of the Archbishopric of Rouen; and some of the cardinals were beginning to think that the time was come for turning coats, especially as it was known that the Orator of France had made overtures of friendship on the part of his sovereign to Cardinal Giuliano della Rovere.

The Supreme Pontiff finally concluded that He would rather have an ally on His frontier, than an ally whose territories were separated from His by the domains of other princes. He decided to leave France out of the question; and to recognize the heir of the late King Don Ferrando I. Accordingly He conveyed this news to Don Alonso de Aragona, Duke of Calabria, adding that He would envoy a Legate to Naples to concede investiture and to perform the ceremony of coronation. At the same time, the Pope's Holiness sent the Golden Rose to the Christian King; and it is hard to know whether this gift symbolized consolation or contempt. If the former, then the gift should have been a sword; for the Sword is the pontifical gift to kings. If the latter, then it was bitterly appropriate, for the Golden Rose is the pontifical gift to queens. Yet only with difficulty one can conceive of the Pope as deliberately setting himself to provoke a reigning sovereign who heads a mobilized army; and the act may have been merely one of those slipshod performances which the greatest geniuses, from time to time, provide to remind mankind of the maxim *non semper arcum tendit Apollo*. But all the same the Lord Alexander P.P. VI was a very strong man, guilty of hiding none of His human weaknesses.

When the Pope issued His Bull on this matter of the Investiture in Public Consistory, storms ensued. Cardinal Giuliano della Rovere, again diplomatically deprived of his Neapolitan friends, flitted from Rome to Ostia with the pontifical condottieri at his heels. From Ostia, he shipped to Genoa, and made haste to present himself to the pink-eyed Majesty of France. The French Orators in Rome shrieked "We are betrayed" in the consecrated formula; and hurried to safe places. And the fortress of Ostia capitulated to the Pope.

In May, the Lord Giovanni Borgia, Archbishop of

Monreale and Cardinal-Priest of the Title of Santa Susanna, received his Brief as Apostolic Ablegate, and went to Naples to crown the new king. The fourteen-year-old Don Gioffredo Borgia accompanied his Most Worshipful cousin; and was married on the coronation-day, the seventh of May.

Madonna Sancia, bastard of King Don Alonso II, who confirmed to him the title of Prince of Squillace with a revenue of forty thousand ducats. Also, as an earnest of his gratitude to the Pope, the King of Naples conferred the Principalities of Teano and Tricarico on Don Juan Francisco de Lançol y Borja, eldest surviving bastard of the Lord Alexander P.P. VI (who already had procured for him the Spanish duchy of Gandia;) and enriched Cardinal Cesare (detto Borgia) with Neapolitan benefices. The Papacy and the Regno now were a Dual Alliance.

.　　.　　.

In Italy of the fifteenth century, men's minds chiefly were occupied with the accumulation and disposition of matters connected with the intellect and the tastes. The Elect-Emperor Maximilian, who in 1493 succeeded the Pacific Caesar Friedrich IV on the throne of Central Europe (called the Holy Roman Empire) was adding outlying territories to the possessions of his dynasty, the Habsburg House of Austria. Spain was freeing herself, by means of steel and faggot, from her brain, *i.e.,* the Moors and Jews; and in exploiting her New World. England was enjoying peace and a new dynasty, since the close of the War of the Roses in 1485. France had made peace, at a price, with King Henry VII Tudor in 1492; and with Spain, at the cost of her frontier provinces of Cerdogne and Rouissillion, in 1493. Lastly, the Christian King Charles VIII of France had pacified the rage of the Elect-Emperor Maximilian, whom he had robbed of his betrothed the Duchess Anne of Bretagne, by ceding to him the greater part of Burgundy. For the rest, nearly all the kingdoms, duchies, and fiefs of France had fallen into the hands of the vaunting Charles, by conquest, inheritance, lapse or marriage. Finding himself at the head of a great army experienced in the art of war, and with a domain smiling with prosperity, he looked for fresh fields to conquer. The chivalric glamour of the Crusade had by no means faded: it dazzled the pink eye of France; and, at one time, undoubtedly the Christian King intended to march on the Muslim Infidel, now settled in Europe and unmolested. But, with the death of King Don Ferrando I, the fickle Frenchman revived an old claim of the House of Anjou to the crown of Naples, intrigued with Cardinal Giuliano della Rovere, and brought his veteran army south to Lyons; where he spent his time in lubricity, until he should have felt the pulses of the Italian Powers with reference to his undertaking. French envoys reported to him that the Papacy was allied with Naples, and Naples with Don Piero de' Medici of Tuscany; that Don Filiberto the Fair, (the boy-duke of Savoja, married to the Elect Emperor's daughter Anne,) with Duke Ercole d'Este of Ferrara, the Marquesses of Monserrat and Saluzzo, and the Republic of Venice, were neutral. The auguries were not propitious for France; but the Christian King, emboldened by the presence, and attentive to the rhodomontades of, Cardinal Giuliano della Rovere, and stupidly believing it possible to reduce a Pope by fear, joined in the duet and cried for a General Council. Indeed, he placed more confidence in the virtue of this threat than in his army; for he definitely threatened the Lord Alexander P.P. VI with deposition and deprivation of the Apostolic dignity, not by force of arms, but by canonical proof of His simoniacal election—unless He would concede to France the crown of Naples. (Corio, Storie di Milano. III 525.)

It is very difficult to understand these shouters for a General Council. They were so clever, so logical, in other matters, that it is perfectly impossible for them to have been unaware of the extreme futility of their cry. They could not have been ignorant: then they must have been malignant. Suppose that an assemblage calling itself a General Council had been convened by the Cardinal-Bishop of Ostia and the Majesty of France, and had proved to its own satisfaction that Cardinal Rodrigo de Lançol y Borja had bought, by bribery, the votes of his brother-cardinals, raising himself by these means to the throne of God's Vicegerent; what end would have been served? There was a moral but no legal prohibition then, as already has been shown, to prevent a cardinal from buying votes, if he could find cardinals criminal enough to sell. The money-changers were, as now, in possession of the Temple; and the whip of small cords still on the Knees of God.

Suppose that a self-called General Council had decreed the deposition of the Pope on the ground of simony; the decrees of a General Council are ineffective until they have been promulgated with the expressed sanction of the Roman Pontiff. Is it probable that the Lord Alexander P.P. VI, that the sanctimonious Cardinal Giuliano della Rovere, that any human man, would sanction the promulgation of the decree that ordained his own deposition? If he did so declare himself to be no Pope, what would be the value of such a declaration? If he were Pope, he would not; if he were not Pope he could not, depose himself. Then what would have been the good, (if the Socratic method be so far permitted,) of a self-called General Council which only could compile ineffectual decrees?

We are dealing with this matter in its human aspect only. Humanity was master of the mighty then, as now; Morality of the humble and meek. Suppose that a self-called General Council had decreed the deposition of the Pope: what would have happened? This—the Sacred

College would have split into two or more factions; let us say two, to keep the argument in reasonable bounds. The Lord Alexander P.P. VI would have headed one faction; the envious Cardinal Giuliano della Rovere the other. Both would have gone into Conclave; the one in Rome, the other in France. The Roman Conclave would have affirmed the Lord Alexander P.P. VI to be the Pontiff-Regnant. The French conclave would have elected Cardinal Giuliano della Rovere, who incontinently would have blossomed forth as Pseudopontiff Julius II. Each would have created cardinals. Each would have administered as much of the Church and Christendom as he could have persuaded to submit to his administration. There would have been a Pontiff in Rome, a pseudopontiff in France. The sheep of Christ's Flock would have been neglected, while the shepherds exchanged anathemas. It all had happened before—many times before. It would have been the Fortieth Schism. In course of time, death would claim the Pontiff or the pseudopontiff. His party would replace him. In course of time subdivision would take place, a schism in a schism. A section of cardinals would secede from Pontiff, or from pseudopontiff; call themselves the Sacred College in Conclave, and elect a second pseudopontiff, Christendom would have been torn asunder. The crime would have been capable of infinite development. All had been seen before, many times before—last, in this identical Fifteenth Century—the century of the Thirty-ninth Schism of the Holy Roman Church, the Thirty-ninth Rending of the Seamless Robe of Christ.

And that was the atrocious turpitude to which Revenge was leading Cardinal Giuliano della Rovere, and Vanity was leading the Christian King Charles VIII, all light-heartedly.

. . .

Being now in amity with Colonna and Orsini through

Duke Louis d'Orleans. On the eighth of September, the Admiral of Naples took Rapallo, a little city six leagues from Genoa, and landed troops. The French commander made an accipitrine swoop from Genoa, cut up the squadrons of Naples, and put Rapallo to sack and pillage for entertaining them. All Italy was amazed, paralyzed with horror, at war conducted on these bloodthirsty lines. The idea of being killed, except perhaps accidentally by being trampled underfoot in a rout, or in a simple personal quarrel, was terrible to people accustomed to battles which were processions, and sieges which were decorative occupations for gentlemen of leisure. Admiral Don Federigo led the remnant of his fleet to Naples without an hour's delay.

Vicechancellor-Cardinal Ascanio Maria Sforza-Visconti now became aggressive, and successfully detached from the Pope the Houses of Colonna and Savelli; (the last, until their dynasty became extinct, held the office of Hereditary Marshal of the Holy Roman Church). Colonna and Savelli then collected their retainers and menaced the Eternal City. On the eighteenth of September Don Fabrizio Colonna recaptured Ostia, and held it in the name of its renegade Cardinal-Bishop. French galleys transporting troops anchored in the mouth of Tiber. Crippled Naples dared not to advance on Milan leaving Rome unprotected. Then Madonna Caterina Sforza-Riario, countess and witch, (daughter of the great Francesco, and widow of the infamous Count Girolamo Riario of the Pazzi Conspiracy,) declared for France in her citadel of Imola, and made things worse for Naples and the Papacy by showing them that an enemy was in their midst. In this strait, and having no sovereign friend in Europe save the Majesty of Naples, the Lord Alexander P.P. VI applied to the Great Turk, the Sultán Bajazet. That wily oriental agreed to help, on condition that his brother and rival, the Sultán Djim, long years held hostage by the Papacy, should be delivered to his tender mercies. This the Pope's Holiness refused, not caring to connive at fratricide; and so completed the isolation of Himself and King Don Alonso II.

On the sixth of October, the Supreme Pontiff thundered from the Vatican a demand for the restitution of Ostia, (held by Don Pierfrancesco Colonna [?]) on pain of the Greater Excommunication. He "fills a great place in history because he so blended his spiritual and temporal authority as to apply the resources of the one to the purposes of the other." (*North British Review.*) At the same time having intelligence of a Colonna plot to capture the Sultán Djim on behalf of France, He moved His mysterious ward from the Vatican by way of Lo Andare to the Mola of Hadrian on Tiber; and sent the Lord Francesco de' Piccolhuomini, Cardinal of Siena, as Apostolic Envoy to the Majesty of France. But the Christian King would not receive him, saying that he was coming to Rome to see the Pope Himself.[1]

.   .   .

The Sultán Djim was a Mystery—the Fifteenth-Century equivalent for the Man in the Iron Mask. The brother and rival of the Great Turk, the Sultán Bajazet, who reigned at Constantinople, he was given as a hostage to the Knights of Rhodes at a time when Bajazet wished to win the good graces of the Christian Powers, and to rid himself of a dangerous menace to his throne's security. The Great Turk offered to pay forty thousand ducats every year, so long as the Sultán Djim was kept away from Byzantium; and he sent also the celebrated emerald, on which is carved an Image of our Divine Redeemer, to the Lord Innocent P.P. VIII. After a long detention, Frère Pierre d'Aubusson, Grand-Master of the Knights of Rhodes and Cardinal-Deacon of Sant' Adriano, transferred this valuable hostage

---

[1] "Aiunt etiam multo vulgo inter illos iactari, regem Roman venturum et statum Romanae Ecclesiae reformaturum. (Letter from Cardinal of Siena to Pope, from Lucca, IIII. Nos. 1494.)

to the Pope for greater security. The Sultán Djim was accorded apartments in the Vatican Palace, and kept a court of his own there in oriental luxury. The crumpled roseleaf of his existence was his constant fear lest his brother should envenom him; and envoys from the Great Turk were only allowed to enter his presence when rigorous and ceremonial precautions had been taken;—for example, an envoy bringing a letter from Bajazet was compelled to lick it all over, outside and inside, under Djim's own eyes, before the last would touch it. The Lord Innocent P.P. VIII and His successor the Lord Alexander P.P. VI, regarded the Sultán Djim as a precious guarantee for the good conduct of the Great Turk. "As long as Djim is in Our hands, Bajazet continually will be uneasy, and neither raise armies, nor molest the Christians;" wrote the Lord Innocent P.P. VIII. Later, the Great Turk conceived an alarm lest his discontented mamelukes should depose him in favour of his brother; and he proposed to pay a hundred and twenty thousand ducats to the Pope for the restoration of the Sultán Djim: undoubtedly intending to put him out of the way according to the methods observed by oriental potentates in reference to their rivals. But the Lord Innocent P.P. VIII refused to have art or part in crime, though He would have been very glad of the money for His family; and the Sultán Djim continued to remain in Rome. The same policy was pursued by the Lord Alexander P.P. VI, notwithstanding that the Great Turk had ceased to send the yearly forty thousand ducats, thus making his brother the pensioner, as well as the ward, of the Papacy. Then in October 1494, when the Eternal City was about to be the scene of war and tumult, the Pope's Holiness placed His ward for safety in the Mola of Hadrian, the fortress-tomb which also was His own refuge.

     •   •   •

On the same day when Admiral Don Federigo de Aragona fled with the Neapolitan fleet from Rapallo to Naples, the Christian King followed his army across the Alps. Being but a shallow-pated Frenchman, enervated with the most horrible of all diseases, he already was in a quandary: he had no money wherewith to pay his troops; his march for some weeks would lie through friendly territory, and, until he reached the pontifical states, he could find no cities to sack for the appeasing and encouragement of his mercenaries. To meet him, hurried Don Ludovico Maria Sforza-Visconti, also in a quandary: he was an usurping regent, with his legitimate sovereign under lock and key; and he was going to meet a legitimate sovereign-regnant. Whether Don Ludovico Maria would complete a little loan, was the question agitating the mind of the Christian King. Whether the Majesty of France would want to champion his Order, to release his brother sovereign and place him on his throne, and to behave severely and unpleasantly to an usurping regent, was the difficulty of Don Ludovico Maria. The two met at Asti. The Christian King at once broached his trouble; and Don Ludovico Maria, with his capacious Sforza brain-pan and his determined Sforza jaw, instantly perceived that he could recommend himself by being useful. He advised France rapidly to advance southward through the Romagna where rich spoils awaited him. And he found the means. Of the man who will lend money at the very moment when it is urgently required, none but the very best opinion can be formed. The Christian King was quite prepared to accept Don Ludovico Maria's own estimation of himself, now. It was even safe to let him see the pathetic sovereign of Milan in his prison.

After being detained a few weeks by that which Italians call the French disease, because it was introduced into Italy by this Christian King, Charles VIII dawdled on to Pavia; and visited Duke Giangaleazzo Sforza-Visconti. The condition of that luckless prince was scandalous in the extreme. He was of the age of five and twenty years. He had been a prisoner during fifteen years. He was decrepit of body, helpless and dull of mind. His only joy in life was in his Duchess Isabella and in his four-year-old son, for whose protection he piteously entreated the Christian King. France put on a sympathetic aspect—it was perhaps the most gracious moment in the little creature's life—; the nostrils of his ham-shaped nose wore an air of disgust at Duke Giangaleazzo's suffering; the glare of his boiled eyes in their congenital flush, and the severe fat line of his mouth, horrified the usurping Regent. Had the money of Don Ludovico Maria been in the coffers of any one just then except the Christian King's, undoubtedly right would have been done by the might of France. But, with promises to return, with excellent intentions to attend to the affairs of Milan when Naples should have been reduced with Milan's money, the Christian King was persuaded to hasten on to Piacenza.

There, on the twenty-first of October, news came to him that the prince whom he had left in his prison, Duke Giangaleazzo Sforza-Visconti, was dead; and that Don Ludovico Maria had proclaimed himself, and had been accepted as, Duke of Milan. It was also said that the uncle had envenomed the nephew, having observed him to have gained the sympathy of France, and fearing lest that sympathy should restore him to his throne. It may have been so: but there is no evidence whatever on the subject beyond the mere assertion. But it equally might have been the effect of concentrated despair, at seeing deliverance come and pass away, acting on a body, naturally weak, worn by passion and imprisonment, which killed Duke Giangaleazzo Sforza-Visconti of Milan. The Fifteenth Century (and also the first decades of the Sixteenth) was so radically ignorant of the art and science, as well of venoms, as of their practical exhibition, that, unless direct in addition to circumstantial evidence be forthcoming, mere unproved charges based on "on dit," "aiunt," "fertur," or "dicant," may be disregarded and a natural cause of death assigned.

.   .   .

Florence, capital city of Tuscany and ancient friend of France, was in a critical condition. Lorenzo de' Medici was just dead. His son, Don Piero, had succeeded him. Don Piero's brother Messer Giovanni, raised to the purple at the age of thirteen years, red-hatted at seventeen, was a Cardinal of Rome. The genius of the great Lorenzo had made him disguise his power. He had married at his own mother's bidding Madonna Clarice Orsini, a patrician of Rome. His sons, educated by Canon Angelo Ambrogini (detto Poliziano), had grown up intellectual, grand, and gay, with an overweening sense of their own consequence; and, when the sceptre fell into his young inexperienced hands, Don Piero forgot his father's advice, "Remember that thou art but a citizen of Florence, even as am I;" and he behaved autocratically, despotically, independently, to the immense antipathy of the Lily-City.

When the Majesty of France began his interference with Italian politics, Don Piero de' Medici and Florence, being contracted to the Regno, declined the offer of a French alliance. The Christian King retorted by banishing Florentine merchants from France. This gave occasion for the enemies (which, in common with all great Houses, Medici had) to blaspheme, muttering of the evils of a tyranny, of the advantages of a republic: and Don Piero's cousins, Don Giovanni and Don Lorenzino, fled to the Christian King at Piacenza; saying that not Florence, but Don Piero only, was the foe of France.

Fra Girolamo Savonarola, friar of the Religion of St. Dominic, became a prominent and responsible figure in this

imbroglio. Ecclesiastically he was a subject of the Domini‑
can Congregation of Lombardy, who was led to desire
independence and a pied à terre in Florence. Don Piero
de' Medici, seeing naught amiss, supported his application
to Rome for the separation of the Tuscan Dominicans
from allegiance to the Lombard Congregation; for, it was
urged, the erection of a separate Congregation for Lombardy would add to the dignity of Florence, and would be
a slight to Milan. The Lord Alexander P.P. VI, when the
case was laid before Him in 1493, was inclined to favour
Milan on account of the Vicechancellor-Cardinal who was
brother to the usurping Regent; but, on the advice of Cardinal Oliviero Carafa, who officially had examined the
matter on its merits, and who reported in favour of Don
Piero de' Medici and the weird friar, the Pope's Holiness
issued the Bull of Separation on the twenty-second of May
that same year. Fra Girolamo Savonarola then transferred
himself to the new Tuscan Congregation, was elected Prior
of San Marco and Vicar-General; and so became the absolute ruler of the Dominicans in Florence, and subject only
to the General of the Religion of St. Dominic, and to the
Pope, in Rome.

He was a truly pious man, of the hard ascetic type, and
very masterful. He used his independence rigorously to
reform his Convent of San Marco, with, for a wonder, the
complete concurrence of his friars; and so he formed a
centre of the exclusively religious life. He would make no
compromise whatever. He would have God entirely served;
and countenance no paltering with Mammon. He utterly
spat upon and defied the World. He burned every pretty
worldly thing. Lewd lovely Florence executed a quick
change, and followed him in sackcloth and ashes. The
alluring melody of Lorenzo de' Medici's Canti Carnaleschi
was drowned in the chaunting of the *Miserere mei Deus*
and the Seven Penitential Psalms with Litanies; while dis-
ciplines and scourges in the public streets fell like flails

on youth's white flesh. Fra Girolamo preached penance in the Advent of 1493. In the Lent of 1494, he preached from the book of Genesis. When he arrived at Noah's Ark, he dwelled upon it; his subject fascinated him; each plank, each nail, became a symbol: but the moral of his allegory was, "Enter the Ark of Salvation that ye may escape the wrath to come."

Florence was disturbed by expectation of the French invasion; which, said Fra Girolamo, (mixing his metaphors in the only way that the vulgar really understand) was the Scourge of God for the Purification of the Church. In September, he preached again. Visions came to him; and he preached of them in parables. His success, his ever-growing power, produced in him an effect like inebriation. Not yet having lost his self-control, he was able to see his danger. He made an effort, and ceased to preach. His brain was in a ferment; sleeplessness gnawed the remnant of his physical strength. Again he mounted the pulpit of San Marco, and thundered like a prophet, like a seer, not his own words now, but "Thus saith The Lord." He claimed εἰσπνοη—Divine Afflatus—Inspiration. Humanly speaking, he had gone out of his mind—was mad.

The excitement of Florence became a frenzy. "Behold," Fra Girolamo Savonarola tremendously declaimed, "Behold I bring a flood of waters on the earth!" And the French army entered Italy.

Florence was half-dead with terror, terror of the French, terror of the Wrath to Come. She had exasperated the Christian King, was disunited in herself, and she had no troops. Yet—she might resist. On her frontier were the strong fortresses of Sarzanella and Pietrasanta. A few resolute patriots might hold the mountain-passes on the road through Lunigiana; and an initial check which ruined French prestige would restore self-confidence to Florence. This was the time of the trial of the stuff of Don Piero de' Medici; who, being in three minds, failed to stand.

First, he sent his brother-in-law, Don Paolo Orsini, to garrison Sarzanella. Secondly, he quavered, because the Florentines appeared sulkily to him. Thirdly, he dallied with the notion of submission to the Christian King. From the fortress of Pietrasanta he whined for a safe-conduct. Arrived in the French camp he collapsed: lying prostrate at the twelve-toed feet of the Majesty of France, he implored pardon for his impertinence in thinking to defend his fatherland; and he offered reparation. He assented to the French demand for the withdrawal of the Tuscan army from the Romagna; for the castles of Sarzana, Sarzanella, Pietrasanta, Pisa, and Livorno, to be held as pledges until Naples should capitulate; for a forced-loan of two hundred thousand ducats; the pledges immediately to be delivered and a treaty signed at Florence. The French had never dreamed that the road should open to them as though by miracle; and by simplest Induction they said that God was on their side.

Florence was dismayed. Don Piero de' Medici stayed with the French: his brothers were in the vast Medici Palace (now Palazzo Riccardi) at the corner of Via Larga, which Michellozzo built for mighty Cosmo. "It is time to make an end of this government by children and to recover our liberty," said the grave and sterling Don Piero Capponi; and the Signoria sent out an embassage to undo the mischief. There were five ambassadors, including Fra Girolama Savonarola whom Florence loved, and Don Piero Capponi whom she admired. They left the city on the sixth of November with plenary powers to modify the disgraceful conditions of surrender. On the seventh, they found the Christian King at Lucca; and followed him to Pisa. He received them very coldly, saying that he would arrrange no terms except in Florence. To diseased France the degenerate Fra Girolamo forthwith prophesied, "Know "thyself for an instrument in the hands of the Lord, "Who hath sent thee to heal the woes of Italy and to "reform the prostrate Church. But if thou dost not show "thyself just and pitiful, if thou respectest not Florence "and her people, if thou forgettest the work for which "the Lord hath sent thee, then He will choose another "in Thy place, and in His Wrath engulph thee. I speak "in the name of the Lord." (*Savonarola's Compendium Revelationum.*)

On the eighth of November, Don Piero de' Medici reappeared in Florence. The City of Lilies knew that Don Paolo Orcini held the Porta di San Gallo for him, with troops disposed about the district; and suspected that he would summon her citizens and force himself upon them as Dictator. On the ninth, suspicion redoubled, because he went with an imposing retinue to the Palace of the Signoria where the magistrates were in conclave. The door was shut: a voice bade him enter by the postern, but alone. Don Piero de' Medici turned away. A partisan of Medici in the Signoria followed him, and brought him back. In attempting the little gate, there was some scuffle, some dispute; and the gate was slammed upon him in a gathering crowd which cried "Away—away—and leave the Signoria in peace." In a storm of hissing where stones were flying Don Piero de' Medici flashed out his sword, —and—irresolutely—let it fall. His escort closed him in, and hurried him to old Cosmo's palace, where all of the few Medici were arming. Cardinal Giovanni de' Medici, not nineteen years of age, risked his sacred person—risked, because a Florentine mob had flung an archbishop in pontificals (Archbishop Salviati of Pisa) at a rope's end from a window; and bleached with mortal terror the visage of a boy-cardinal (the Lord Rafaele Galeotto Sanzoni-Riario Cardinal-Deacon of San Giorgio *in Velum Aureum,* æt 16), not sixteen years before,—his sacred person, because he who *suadente diabolo* lifts hand against the person of one tonsured *ipso facto* incurs the Greater Excommunication,—he risked his sacred person among a Florentine mob, endeavouring to rouse them as of old to follow Medici with the war-cry "Palle—Palle—Palle." [1] All was in vain.

The well-worn cry had lost magnetic virtue; and none in Florence now dared to own himself a friend of Medici. Don Piero rushed to the Porta di San Gallo, where Medici had never cried in vain. None answered him. His courage left him there. He infected with fear Don Paolo Orsini and his bands; and all fled to Bologna. At night Cardinal Giovanni and his sixteen-year-old cousin, Messer Giuliano Knight of St. John of Jerusalem of Malta, escaped in the frocks of Friars Minor; and from Bologna these three Medici journeyed on to Venice where Italian exiles always found a home: while Florence sacked the Medici Palace, plundered the priceless Medici Library of Manuscripts, and set a price upon the head of Lorenzo's son Don Piero.

This revolt was the work of Fra Girolamo Savonarola. For sixty years Florence had enjoyed prosperity under Medici. She was the centre of learning, the mediating power of Italy with influence in every state; in fact, as the Lord Boniface P.P. VIII said on receiving the Orators of the Powers in Rome at the Jubilee of 1300, *"i fiorentini sono il quinto elemento."* But the Dominican Friar had roused in Her those moral aspirations which Medici had lulled to atrophy; and the contemptible blunders of Don Piero had proved a final exasperation. The newly-formed republic set up Donatello's statue of Judith with the Head of Holofernes on a pedestal before Palazzo Vecchio, with this inscription for the benefit of budding despots, Exemplum Salutis Publicae Cives Posuere MCCCCXCV. And on the day of the expulsion of the Medici, little Pisa revolted also, and threw off the yoke of Florence.

· · ·

[1] Allusion to the five red balls and the lilied bezant in the Medici armorials.

The fortune of the Lord Alexander P.P. VI appeared to be in serious danger. The French unhindered were advancing, and sedition was sown in Rome. One more overture the Supreme Pontiff made, sending Cardinal Raymond Perrauld, a creature of His Own, to treat with the Christian King, who with no difficulty persuaded the French Cardinal to turn traitor to the Pope. A Brief, appealing to the Elect-Emperor Maximilian for help proved ineffectual. The forces of Colonna beleaguered the Eternal City. Within the walls, three disaffected cardinals, the Lords Ascanio Mario Sforza-Visconti, Friderico Sanseverini, and Bernardino de' Lunati, were interned with the Pope in the Mola for the sake of safety. When the pontifical citadel of Civita Vecchia fell, the loyalists became yet more disheartened. Orsini turned its coats and joined the French. Cesarini alone of all the patricians of Rome continued to be staunch and true. Resistance was useless, things being as they were; and the Lord Alexander P.P. VI gave leave to the Christian King to enter Rome. He came. He humanly was master of the City and of the situation, face to face with the Holiness of the Pope, practically having His person in his power. The Majesty of France demanded the calling of a General Council; and God's Vicegerent opposed him with a blunt and unconditional *Non Possumus*. Whenever the World has driven the Church against the wall, She has become inexorably invincible.

The year 1495 opened with Rome in panic and disorder, in the clutch of a foreign army bringing desolation and a new disease. The Christian King, who had come to accomplish the conquest of the Regno by means of the deposition of the Pope, found the way completely blocked. He had strutted on his twelve-toed feet to Rome, prepared to crow so very gallically. The decree of deposition actually was prepared, and only required confirmation by a competent authority. Inflated with gigantic megalomaniacal illusions, he had believed that an evil conscience would have made

the Lord Alexander P.P. VI obedient to him. He thought
by the threat of a General Council (which he intended to
convoke at Ferrara,) to blackmail the Pope into conceding
the investiture of Naples. He ineffectually had battered the
defences of the Pope with cannon. And now his Frenchmen would fight no longer, as some say; but others, like
Briçonnet and de Commines, assert that it was the king
who blenched. At last, with his shallow mind congested
with half-thought thoughts and uncompleted facts like
these, he became aware that a General Council was not a
General Council unless it had the Pope's authority, which
last he was not likely to obtain; and that, without some
means of bending the pontifical will, he could not hope to
win the crown of Naples. Evidently, he could not depose
the Pope. He might, however, conquer Naples by force of
arms; and, perhaps, the question of investiture by the Ruler
of the World, the Father of princes and of kings, the
Earthly Vicar of Jesus Christ our Saviour, which he
realized to be imperative, would wear a different aspect
when he should ask for it as a conqueror with the Regno in
his hand.

While the Christian King was stumbling to these con-
clusions, the invincible Lord Alexander P.P. VI remained
with His little court in the Mola of Hadrian where He
had His hostages secure, viz., the Sultán Djim, earnestly
desired by France as a weapon against the Great Turk,
and the renegade cardinals, friends of Colonna and the
French. Here, He was practically impregnable. The Papal
States might go to wrack and ruin: Rome Herself might
be crushed by an alien heel, but from the Mola of Hadrian
a Pope, surrounded by His faithful few, could, and often
did, defy blockade as long as provisions held out; could,
and often did, launch the lightnings of the Church, censures, excommunications, interdicts; and force acknowledgment, and reluctant obedience, from rebellious sovereigns who, after all, believed and admitted Him to be Ruler

of the World, Father of princes and of kings, Earthly
Vicar of Jesus Christ our Saviour, titles, in defence of
which (so very glorious are they) Pontiffs of these clear
ages did not hesitate to court the death, admitting of no
compromise of no rebate. Our potency, said they, if worth
having, is worth fighting for, is worth dying for. And, as
so often is the case, when a man shows that he wishes
nothing better than to lose his life for a cause, he saves
both cause, and life.

From the Mola of Hadrian then, the Lord Alexander
P.P. VI deigned to make these terms with the Christian
King:—The French army was to be withdrawn from
Rome. The Pope's Holiness would not interfere; and
would lend to France as hostages for six months, the
Sultán Djim with whom to menace the Great Turk
Bajazet, and Cardinal Cesare (detto Borgia). The question
of the investiture of Naples was not even named. Having
secured Himself by this agreement, in which He had con-
ceded neither of the two French claims, the Supreme
Pontiff received in formal audience the Christian King,
who shortly after marched his troops southward along the
Appian Way, by Albano, Arricia, and Genzano, toward
the Neapolitan frontier.

.   .   .

At the Third Consistory of the sixteenth of January
1495, the Lord Alexander P.P. VI named one cardinal,
who was

the Lord Guillaume Briçonnet, Overseer of the Treasury
to the Christian King Charles
VIII, editor of a book of
prayers dedicated to the said
king (Encheiridion precum);
Cardinal - Presbyter of the
Title of Santa Pudentiana.

.   .   .

At Velletri there lived a certain Don Pietro Gregorio Borgia, son of that Don Niccolo Borgia of the Junior Branch, Regent of Velletri and Familiar of King Don Alonso V, by his marriage with the Noble Giovanna Lamberti. In 1495 this Don Pietrogorio was about the age of twenty-one years (the age in fact of Cardinal Cesare;) and, when the French king halted for the night at Velletri, he found means to exchange habits with the said Cardinal Cesare (detto Borgia) and to help him to disappear, remaining as hostage in his place. It was a daring act, and soon discovered: but the cardinal was safe in Rome concerting new schemes with the Pope. The Majesty of France gave instant orders for the hanging of Don Pietrogorio and for the firing of the city; and hurried on to Naples. But the king's first secretary, who had been commissioned to execute his master's vengeance, out of sheer admiration for the courage of Velletri's Regent's son, gave him a swift horse and leave to reclaim his own clothes from Cardinal Cesare (detto Borgia) in Rome; nor did he give Velletri to the flames.

Immediately on hearing of the French approach, King Don Alonso II abdicated in favour of his son Don Ferrandino de Aragona. Envoys from the Catholic King Don Hernando of Spain embarrassed the Christian King Charles VIII of France with remonstrances on his invasion of the territories of the House of Aragon: but the latter was not to be rebuffed. The fortress of Monte San Giovanni capitulated to him. His march through the Regno was a series of victories; and, in the capital, he announced his intention altogether to relinquish the Crusade, and to add Naples as a fief to France.

But three causes prevented this from becoming more than a French boast:—the action of the Pope, the action of the Powers, the action of Providence. Directly after the French had quitted Rome, the Lord Alexander P.P. VI retired to the pontifical castle of Viterbo, a mighty fortress in a cool air, and pleasant as a summer residence; where He was joined by Cardinal Cesare (detto Borgia) with Don Piero Gregario Borgia (now the last Most Worshipful Lord's lieutenant and standard-bearer); and whence He commenced vigorous diplomatic negotiations directed against the French.

The Powers of Italy had taken alarm. It had never been contemplated that France would meet submission all along the line, and actually become arbiter of the whole country. Milan, Florence, the Papal States, and now the Regno, had fallen: with the French in France in the north, and the French in Naples in the south, these intermediate duchies, states and republics found themselves in the position of an uncracked nut in a monkey's jaw: wherefore Italy gave way to fear. Also, Spain was the enemy of France, so was the Holy Roman Empire; and the Elect-Emperor Maximilian and the Catholic King realized the arrival of a unique opportunity for invading France by south and east, seeing that the French army was in Naples, cut off from its base by the Italian states. All these circumstances and considerations, skilfully perceived and engineered by the Pope's Holiness from His eyrie at Viterbo, quite naturally resulted in the conclusion of a Holy League, consisting of the Papacy, the Empire, Spain, and the Italian Powers, against France.

His position having become untenable, the Christian King resolved upon retreat. Half his army he left in Naples; and marched northward with the rest. His coming had been a triumphal procession. His going was a flight through hostile territory. A second time he entered Rome with the hope of retrieving his lost prestige: but the Pope again retired, this time to Orvieto, and refused to meet him. Enraged by the slight, the polite chivalry of France to pain the Pope avenged itself on women, pillaging the house of Madonna Giovanna de' Catanei, and making Madonna Giulia Orsini (nata Farnese) a prisoner. Onward, northward, went the Christian King, conferring with the mattoid Fra Girolamo Savonarola at Poggibonzi; fighting a desperate battle at Fornuovo, where he lost his army stores; reaching France, with his forces disgraced and in disorder; and he himself disabled by the sentence of the Greater Excommunication which the thoroughly angry and triumphant Pontiff fulminated after him.

.   .   .

In Florence, Fra Girolamo ceased not to labour on behalf of the Christian King, sowing seeds of political discord, and preparing the germs of certain calumnies which, in later years, were used by Florentine friends of France. His sermons were French manifestoes, and denunciations of Medici. He had stepped from the pulpit of the pastor to the platform of the politician. His power was admirable and admired, his sincerity unquestionable; and earnest efforts were made to reclaim him from the doubtful practices in which he was embarked. The Lord Alexander P.P. VI summoned him by a kindly and paternal Brief to Rome; saying that He wished to hear him personally, and to confer with him as to the methods which he advocated. How revoltingly inconsistent are the writers who rail against the Pope for His treatment of this degenerate friar! Leaving out of the question matters of dogma, articles of Faith, in reference to which the Founder of Christianity definitely promised to permit no error, it must be admitted that, regarding ordinary affairs of government and discipline, a Pope well advised is superior to a Pope ill advised. Well, here is the Pope having heard many hard things of Savonarola, definitely and gently offering to hear that madman's own defence, definitely trying every means, every most intimate and stringent means, to render Himself well-advised before proceeding to judgment. If the subsequent actions of the Lord Alexander P.P. VI deserve to be called ill advised, it is not He Who should be blamed, but Fra Girolamo Savonarola, who with inconsequent evasion, excused himself and continued his traitorous machinations against the peace of his country, in defiance of the law, and in contempt of the powers that be. Order issued from Rome, inhibiting him from public preaching, and placing his Convent of San Marco again under the rule of the Lombard Congregation. Then, Fra Girolamo professed ready obedience to the Pope; but begged for the independence of his convent, a prayer which he supported with such arguments as to obtain a favouring response, though the inhibition was repeated. Before the formal Brief arrived Don Piero de Medici attempted to return to Florence from Venetian exile; being foiled solely by a violent diatribe in which Fra Girolamo denounced him. As time passed, the friar intrigued with Ferrara, gained over and cultivated many influential Florentines; and then the Signoria took up his cause and formally appealed to Rome for the removal of his inhibition.

.　　.　　.

The passage of the French through the Papal States, like a blight of caterpillars, brought famine into the country districts. In the Fifteenth Century, armies were not encumbered by a commissariat. They robbed right and left, living on the produce of the land in which they were, paying for nothing, and invariably leaving utter desolation and destitution in their rear. Distress and discontent ravaged Rome. Winter storms brought Tiber down in flood and the City was under water. So the year 1495 ended.

At the beginning of the new year, Don Virginio Orsini joined the French in Naples, against the King Don Ferrandino II, the Pope and Venice. At Atella the French were defeated, and the Holy League grew powerful. England joined it. The Lord Alexander P.P. VI, who, with His magnificent ability for doing many things, had been superintending the decoration of the quire of Santa Maria *del Populo* by the Flaminian Gate which opens on the great north road, (the nearest gate to England), went, with a solemn cavalcade, to hold a papal chapel for publishing the Bull of Alliance with King Henry VII Tudor. France had no friend save Florence, where the Signoria had taken upon itself to remove the inhibition from Fra Girolamo Savonarola. That incontinent friar preached a course of Lenten sermons defending himself, violently denouncing Rome, particularizing certain vices which everywhere were general. His incorrigible attitude appears like "the rage of a man who knows that he has chosen the lower when he might have chosen the higher." He was in open revolt, not against the Catholic Faith, but against the laws of the land, and the Rule of the Religion of St. Dominic to which, voluntarily, under no compulsion whatever, he had chosen to swear allegiance on the Sacrament of the Lord's Body. To make things easy for him, the Pope's Holiness proposed to erect a new Dominican Congregation which he might be willing to obey, under Cardinal Carafa who already had given evidence of his sympathy with the friar. But Fra Girolamo intractably refused to hear: and it must be said that the minacity and violence, with which he attacked his superiors, form a bitter contrast to the patience and moderation which the Lord Alexander P.P. VI extended to him, in this—and let this be noted—the third year of his disgraceful extravagance and disloyalty.

.   .   .

At the Fourth Consistory of the twenty-first of January 1496, the Lord Alexander P.P. VI named one cardinal, who was

The Lord Philippe de Luxembourg; Cardinal-Presbyter of the Title of San Marcellino e San Pietro.

.   .   .

The condition of the country improved as the year 1496 expanded. An ill-advised attempt of the Elect-Emperor Maximilian to revive the waning Imperial power by a progress through the Italian realms, was averted by the opposition of Venice and the remonstrances of the Sovereign Pontiff. The Elect-Emperor having withdrawn into the Tyrol, the Lord Alexander P.P. VI was free to deal with the Pontifical States. The Regno flourished under the young King Don Ferrandino II, and the French occupation was becoming a thing of the past. Only the rebellious vassals of the Holy See remained; and, of these, Colonna and Savelli appear to have made their submission; but the Orsini were still in arms, and Malatesta, Riario, Manfredi, and Sforza, were fortified at Cesena, Imola and Forli, Faenza and Pesaro.

.   .   .

At the Fifth Consistory of the nineteenth of February 1496, the Lord Alexander P.P. VI named four Spanish cardinals, who were

- (*a*) The Lord Don Bartolomeo Martino, Bishop of Segovia; Cardinal-Presbyter of the Title of Saint' Agata *in Suburra:*
- (*β*) The Lord Don Juan de Castro, Prefect of Santangelo, Bishop of Girgenti, ('Ακραγαντῖνος) in Sicily; Cardinal-Presbyter of the Title of Santa Prisca:
- (*γ*) The Lord Don Juan Lopez, Canon of the Vatican Basilica, Apostolic Datary; Cardinal-Presbyter of the Title of Santa Maria *in Trastevere, tit. Callisto:*

(δ) The Lord Giovanni Borgia (detto Giuniore,) a
Pontifical Nephew, Bishop of Melfi; Cardinal-
Presbyter of the Title of Santa Maria *in Via
Lata.*

.   .   .

Appointing His bastard, Don Juan Francisco de Lançol
y Borja, as Captain-General of the pontifical army, and
assisted by the Majesty of Naples, the Lord Alexander
P.P. VI proceeded to reduce Orsini. At the opening of
the campaign, Don Virginio Orsini was captured by the
Neapolitans; but when Orsini's stronghold of Bracciano
was relieved by Don Vitellozzo Vitelli of Città di Castello,
the papal condottieri were forced to raise the siege. And
before the end of the year the Pope lost His ally King Don
Ferrandino II, who died at the age of twenty-eight "worn
out with fatigue and with the pleasures of his marriage to
his aunt Joanna whom he loved too passionately." (Symonds, Renascence, I. 513.) The year 1497 began with the
defeat of the papal troops by Orsini at the battle of
Soviano, a reverse which was counterbalanced by the success of Don Gonsalvo de Cordova. This captain was at the
head of a band of mercenaries sent by Spain in aid of the
Papacy; he took the fortress of Ostia from Cardinal
Giuliano della Rovere, whose five years of treachery and
recalcitrancy were now punished by the Holiness of the
Pope, with deprivation of his benefices (which took from
him the "sinews of war") and the deposition of his brother,
Don Giovanni della Rovere, from the Prefecture of Rome.
As for the French Orators who made protest at this
unaccountably long-delayed act of precautionary justice,—
unaccountably long-delayed, except on the hypothesis of
this Pope's singular patience, long-suffering, and dislike
of proceeding to extremities,—the Supreme Pontiff contemptuously remarked that they were come from an Ex-

communicated King; and that it was well for them that Cardinal Cesare (detto Borgia) did not hear them. This, by the bye, is the first instance of the amazing influence which that young Porporato was beginning to attain, an influence which within the next few years increased by leaps and bounds until the name of Cesare (detto Borgia) stood among the most important names in Europe.

Further to emphasize the slight to France by shewing His appreciation of Spain's support, the Lord Alexander P.P. VI decorated His bastard, Don Juan Francisco de Lançol y Borja Duke of Gandia and Prince of Teano and Tricarico, as representing the Spanish branch of His House, with the titles of Count of Chiaramonte, Lauria, and Cerignuola, Tyrant of Benevento and Tarracina, and Grand Constable of Naples.

. . .

In honour of her son's good fortune, Madonna Giovanna de' Catanei gave a supper at her villa by San Pietro *ad Vincula,* where were present the young Duke of Gandia of the age of twenty-two years, and Cardinal Cesare (detto Borgia) his senior by a year. Their sister Madonna Lucrezia, who had had much unpleasantness with her husband, Don Giovanni Sforza the Tyrant of Pesaro, had left him; and was living in the Convent of San Sisto in Rome, as noble ladies do who wish to guard their reputations in delicate circumstances.

When supper was over, and the night advancing, the Cardinal advised Don Juan that it was time to return to the Vatican where they lodged. In view of the popular delusions concerning this occurrence, it may be advisable to refer to the fact that sunset was taken to end a twenty-four hour day; that "one hour of the night," *i.e.,* one hour after sunset, was the fashionable supper-time, which at this time of the year (the fourteenth of June) would be about 9 P.M. Before midnight then, at a generous computation, the Cardinal and the Duke of Gandia mounted their horses and rode through Rome together as far as the palace of the Vicechancellor attended by a small escort. It is worth noting that the palace of the Vicechancellor was not the Cancelleria, the palace of the Chancery at San Lorenzo *in Damaso,* perhaps the most beautiful palace in the world, which Messer Bramante Lazzari built for the white-faced Cardinal Rafaele Galeotto Sanzoni-Riari: but the new palace built by Cardinal Rodrigo de Lançol y Borja, and given by him after His election to the Supreme Pontificate, to the Vicechancellor-Cardinal Ascanio Maria Sforza-Visconti; (now Palazzo Sforza-Cesarini on Banchi Vecchi).

There, the ardent Duke (he already was married to a princess of Spain, and the father of two children,) said to the Cardinal that, before going home, he wanted to amuse himself somewhere; and, taking leave of the said Most Worshipful Lord, and dismissing his suite with the exception of a certain bully whom he kept, took on his crupper an unknown man in a mask who waited there, and who daily during a month had come to see him at the Vatican, as well as on this very night during the supper in the garden of his mother. Then he turned his horse in the direction of the Jew's Quarter, (there was no Ghetto till 1556), and disappeared in the twilight of a midsummer night. He never again was seen alive.

When the City awoke in the morning, (Romans always were early risers,) the Duke of Gandia's bully was found on Piazza Guidei, wounded by the steel of an assassin; and all efforts to obtain information from him proved futile. He died without having spoken.

The news trickled into the Vatican, and was mentioned to the Pope; who thought that perhaps Don Juan was staying with some courtesan, wishing out of consideration for his Father to avoid the scandal of being seen to issue from such a house in open day. But when night came again, and the Duke did not appear, the Pope's Holiness took alarm; and ordered an inquisition and the usual dragging of Tiber. The wags of Rome instantly said that notwithstanding all that Cardinal Giuliano della Rovere had alleged concerning the election of the Lord Alexander P.P. VI as being simoniacal, it was now certain that He was a true Successor of St. Peter as a Fisher of men.

Among other bearers of news, there came to the inquisitors a certain Giorgio, of the Schiavoni, a waterman, asserting that, while guarding his boat on Tiber during the night, he had seen two men, who came to the shore to look whether any one was there; behind them came two others making the same inspection. He, the speaker, being in the shadow of his beached boat escaped all notice. When these four had assured themselves that the place was empty, there came on a white horse, conveying behind him a dead man, whose feet and arms hung down, held by two foot-men. Having come to the water's edge, they turned the crupper of the horse to the river; and, lifting the corpse, swung it into the stream. The rider looked on: but seeing a dark object which floated,—it was the dead man's cloak, —he ordered the others to throw stones at it until it sank.

After hearing this tale, the Pope groaned, and reproached the waterman in that he did not give immediate notice to the bargelli (police) of the crime which he had witnessed. The man impudently answered that he had seen such sights a thousand times: but never had he known of any one who cared to hear about them.

The Vicechancellor-Cardinal Ascanio Maria Sforza-Visconti wrote to his brother the Duke of Milan, relating the deposition of Giorgio the waterman, and the disquietude of the Pope.

Later, the corpse was found in Tiber, completely clothed in the sumptuous garments of the Duke of Gandia, the dagger in its sheath, the pouch intact adorned with jewels of great value. Eleven—some say fourteen—wounds, of which an enormous one was in the throat, were the cause of death. The unfortunate young Duke was buried at Santa Maria del Popolo. (*Maricont.*) That, actually, is all that is known of the murder of the Duke of Gandia.

The only person, except the murderer or murderers, who could give any salient information, was the bully; and he expired without uttering a word. The mystery of the unknown man in a mask has never been solved (nor the archives of a Roman patrician House published); and, for a time, the matter rested there.

.   .   .

The effect upon the Lord Alexander P.P. VI was terrible. He had loved Don Juan Francisco with a very great love. Notwithstanding the fact that Cardinal Cesare (detto Borgia) was a year older than the Duke of Gandia, the Pope had always treated the latter as His heir;[1] and had foreseen in his vigorous manlihood the foundation of a dynasty of Grandees of Spain who would render more illustrious the House of Borja. The founding of a family has always been an object very near to the hearts of great men.

And now the irruption of hideous and ruthless Death turned the Pope's Holiness, for a moment, from a spiritual and temporal sovereign and despot into a very human man. At such a moment, when man most poignantly is reminded of the Inevitable Universal waiting in the background, he feels his utter helplessness, his entire unworthiness, and would appease, make satisfacton. Broken-hearted, the Lord Alexander P.P. VI spoke of abdication, and a change of life; as other famous men have done, whom trouble, or fear, have driven to La Trappe. He made good resolutions. He gave munificent gifts to churches; for His revived

[1] A most important inference may be drawn from this, as to the paternity of Cardinal Cesare.

piety manifested itself in practical form. He appointed a Commission of six cardinals, including Cardinals Carafa and Costa, to reform ecclesiastical abuses. He named Cardinal Cesare (detto Borgia) as Apostolic Legate for the pacification of Umbria. By way of restoring unity to Italy, He endeavoured to persuade Florence to annul her alliance with excommunicate France: in which admirable intent He was thwarted solely by the indescribable efforts of Fra Girolamo Savonarola, who, during the Lent of this year, had preached in favour of unswerving subservience to the Christian King. The Powers of Europe, especially England, the Holy Roman Empire, Venice, Naples, and Spain, who formed the Holy League with the Papacy, on receiving official intimation of the Pope's bereavement and His bitter sorrow, sent Orators with suitable expressions of condolence.

During summer and autumn, which should have been occupied in drafting the Bull of Reform (a task subsequently performed by the Council of Trent,) the Reform Commission had to study, and deal with, and advise the Pontiff in, the more urgent case of the friar of Florence. Riots and affrays between the partisans and opponents of Fra Girolamo Savonarola disgraced the Lily-City of Tuscany: and, at last, after more than four years' forbearance, all gentler measures having failed, he was placed under sentence of excommunication.

Meanwhile, Cardinal Cesare (detto Borgia) proceeded to Naples as Apostolic Ablegate for the coronation of King Don Federigo de Aragona. (The Sword of State which was borne before His Worship on this occasion is in possession of Caïetani Duke of Sermoneta: but the scabbard of embossed leather is in the Victoria and Albert Museum.)

.   .   .

In September 1497 the Lord Alexander P.P. VI published the creation of one cardinal, whose name, for

political reasons, He had reserved *in petto* since the Second
Consistory of September 1493, who was

> The Lord Don Luis de Aragona, son of King Don
> Ferrando I; Cardinal-Presbyter of the Title of
> Santa Maria *in Cosmediv*. (He was commonly
> called "The Cardinal of Aragon.")

.   .   .

At the incoming of winter arrived an opportunity for
the enemies of the Lord Alexander P.P. VI to blaspheme.

Madonna Lucrezia Borgia was living in the Convent of
San Sisto, separated from her husband, Don Giovanni
Sforza the Tyrant of Pesaro; and seeking a decree of
nullity of marriage, alleging a canonical impediment. This
young man was cousin to the Duke of Milan, very handsome in person, and intelligent. He already had been married to Madonna Maddalena Gonzaga, who in 1490 had
died *di cattivo parto* (Gregorovius). In 1493, being then
in his twenty-sixth year, he had married Madonna Lucrezia, from whose Father he held his Tyranny of Pesaro
by way of fief, consolidating the alliance of Sforza and
Borgia. He had most of the advantages of life, illustrious
birth, rank, youth, health, a splendid position, intimate
relationship with his feudal lord, and a wife acknowledged
by all contemporaries as the most beautiful woman of her
time : and now, after little more than three years, he was to
be held up to the derision of all by the annulment of his
marriage on the score of ἀδῆνᾱμία.

Nothing, at any time, is more certain to enrage a man
than this; and, in the Fifteenth Century, the Century of the
Discovery of Man, when ἀνδρεία was prized and worshipped, a charge which made him look ridiculous in the
estimation of his species, which struck at the very root of
his manlihood, was sure to be furiously resented. When
his wife left him to enter her petition, Don Giovanni Sforza

sped to Milan invoking the support of his kin, the Vice-chancellor-Cardinal Ascanio Maria Sforza-Visconti and the Duke Ludovico Maria (detto Il Moro). On news reaching them to the effect that evidence had been given before the legal tribunal in Rome, which proved the marriage to lack consummation and Madonna Lucrezia to be παρθένος ἀδμήτη, he violently protested, and with unrestrained rancour. Don Beltrando Costabili, the Orator of Ferrara, writing from Milan to his government, asserted that Don Giovanni said to Duke Ludovico Maria, "Anzi haverla conosciuta infinite volte, ma chel Papa non gliela tolta per altro se non per usare con lei." It is most improbable that a reigning sovereign would admit a foreign ambassador to a discussion of his family affairs; and unless Costabili actually heard those words, they can only be accepted as a piece of gossip reported, not as legal evidence. Duke Ludovico Maria ingenuously proposed to Don Giovanni an ordeal which, in that naive age, was usual in similar cases, of submitting formally and publicly to the judgment of a jury of men of bonafides and the papal legate: and, on his refusal, his own relations, the Duke and the thin-faced clear-witted Vicechancellor-Cardinal, obtained from him a written confession that Madonna Lucrezia was justified in her petition, and advised him to let the law take its course. The case of a man temporarily ἀδύνατος at the age of Don Giovanni physiologically is no uncommon one. Much has been made of the circumstances under which his first wife died, and of the fact that his third, Madonna Ginevra de' Tiepoli, bore him a son, Don Costanzo Sforza, eight years later (1505). As for the infernal calumny against the Pope's Holiness, Don Giovanni Sforza was its inventor, says the Orator of Ferrara, and the mortifying humiliation of a libidinous laughing-stock its proximate occasion. On the twentieth of December 1497, the decree of nullity of the marriage was published in Rome, the Tyrant of Pesaro refunded the lady's

ples with their overhanging brows pointed in the middle, struck the note of ideality, and conquered the animalism of the man. It was this cataclysmal violence of difference, this trenchant contrast, that made him what he was. In him there were two inimical characters, the character of the saint, the character of the ram. That of the saint vanquished that of the ram: but the poignant struggle overthrew the mental balance of the saint. His proper place was not the Convent of San Marco in Florence: but the Hospital of Santo Spirito in Rome.[1]

So in sorrow, in anger, in horrid uncertainty, the year 1497 ended.

.　　　.　　　.

After the coronation of Don Federigo de Aragona as King of Naples, Cardinal Cesare (detto Borgia) announced a determination which he had nourished since the murder of the Duke of Gandia. Whether he was the Pope's bastard or another's, it was his pose to aggrandise the House of Borgia; moreover he was young, only twenty-four years of age, and of an ardent and forceful habit of mind and body. Don Gioffredo Borgia was occupied with his wife Madonna Sancia de Aragona and his principality of Squillace; and his age of seventeen years did not render him a capable representative of his illustrious House. Cardinal Cesare felt that his scarlet hat debarred him from the pursuits for which Nature had devised him. The foes of Borgia were active on all sides: the territories of the Holy See were a hot-bed of revolt. Sforza sulked in Milan; Orsini, never forgetful of injury, entrenched themselves in their strongholds; their fierce brigands ravaged the country far and wide: and there was no Borgia to hold them in check. Wherefore Cardinal Cesare requested leave to renounce his cardinalate, to receive secular rank, to marry a royal princess, that he might be free to adopt a

---

[1] The Roman phrase "to go to Santo Spirito" means "to go mad."

military career, and to perpetuate the Borgia dynasty. It was an extraordinary plan: but, though it presented advantages of high political value, it was opposed and shelved by the Lord Alexander P.P. VI, whose behaviour to Cardinal Cesare was never that of a father, but of a patron and benefactor who patronized, and benefited, him for the sake of another than himself. Yet, though the attitude of the Pope to the Cardinal was one of lifelong distinct antipathy, He set immense value on his advancement, and incurred peril and made sacrifices to promote it. What was the motive of conduct which presents such contradictory features? Is it possible that Cardinal Cesare was the son of Madonna Giovanna de' Catanei, not by Cardinal Rodrigo de Lançol y Borja, but by the eternal rival of the last, Cardinal Giuliano della Rovere? It is extremely possible and extremely probable. Cardinal Rodrigo undoubtedly had loved Madonna Giovanna very greatly since 1474. She undoubtedly was the mother of Cardinal Cesare, who was born in 1474. She had had relations with Cardinal Giuliano before that. And Cardinal Rodrigo never acknowledged the paternity of Cardinal Cesare, although he never denied it. The theory, which lacks not some proof (to be given in a proper place), would explain the unconquerable malice of Cardinal Giuliano della Rovere towards the Lord Alexander P.P. VI, Who had deprived him of his mistress as well as of the triregno, the object of his ultimate ambition; and the loathing of the Pope's Holiness for His enemy's bastard, whom He, at the same time held as a hostage to be used against Cardinal Giuliano in an extremity, feared for his incorrigible and antipathetic disposition, and advanced and enriched for the love which He had borne to his mother. That is the only rational explanation of certain mysteries which, otherwise, remain inexplicable.

The proposal of Cardinal Cesare (detto Borgia) had many recommendations. The lax and feeble government of the late Pope, the Lord Innocent P.P. VIII, had played havoc with order in the vast domain of Umbria, of the Mark of Ancona, of the Romagna, that splendid realm in north-eastern Italy verging on the Adriatic Sea. A few strong men, tyrants of petty fiefs, threw off allegiance to the Pope as their Over-Lord. Don Oliverotto da Fermo, a brigand of the worst kind, made himself Tyrant of Fermo by the simple process of assassinating his uncle, Don Giovanni Fogliani, and all the chief citizens, at a banquet. Don Vitellozzo Vitelli garrisoned Citta di Castello, Don Paolo Orsini was fortified at Sinigaglia, Madonna Caterina Sforza-Riario at Imola and Forli, the Oddi and Baglioni at Perugia, the Manfredi at Faezna, the Varani at Camerino, the Bentivogli at Bologna. Safe in their strongholds these Tyrants paid no dues, no feudal tribute to their Lord Paramount. From time to time they sallied forth with armed condottieri to replenish their stores from the pillage of towns and villages. The province was ravaged from end to end by their excesses. In the Library of San Marco at Venice may be read letters (Lat. Cl. x. 176) which report on the condition of Umbria when the Lord Alexander P.P. VI began His reign; a condition of horror unspeakable, which He was determined to abolish.

To this end, He had sent Cardinal Cesare (detto Borgia) as Apostolic Legate into Umbria, in the summer of 1497, just a month after the murder of the Duke of Gandia. The Legate went unarmed save by his sacred office, and with too small an escort for offence. The idea was to test the moral authority of the Suzerain of Umbria, the Roman Pontiff, in a place where the civil power practically was helpless, and where a man's life depended only on the fear which he inspired.

On the day of his arrival at Narni, the sixteenth of July, 1497, Cardinal Cesare already had formed an opinion which he communicated to the Pope's Holiness in these words: "It is very necessary to provide me with an army against "these kakodaimones; for they go not out by holy-water." [1]

The brigand Don Bartolomeo d'Alviano seized a town belonging to the Pope in despite of the Legate, and sacked it before his face. Cardinal Cesare summoned him to keep the peace: he refused; and matters went from bad to worse.

"They offend as they did at first, and will not hearken "unto my commandments"; [2]
he wrote to the Pope eleven days later.

The inhabitants of Todi fled from their town to save their lives. Brigandage was in its hey-dey. "Your Holiness "can well understand that the only remedy for these evils "lies in the coming of men of arms, whose delay has caused "Todi to be desolated and the city, from my departure till "now, totally derelict and left empty." [3]

At Perugia, the Legate took the bull by the horns in a singularly daring manner and with singular success; putting the more uproarious of the ringleaders under the ban of expulsion, "which thing was done with such obedience "and calm that nothing better could be desired." [4]

But he did better than that. He caught a murderer in flagrante delicto. "I captured two robbers and murderers; "and with no tumult, but to the delight of the people, they "were put in gaol—a thing long unknown in this city— "and this morning I hanged one." [5]

---

[1] "E molto necessaria la provisione de le genti d' arme contro questi demonii che non fugono per acqua santa." xvi. ful. 1497.

[2] "Commensano nel primo modo offenderse et non dare loco ad mei commandamenti." xxvii, ful. 1497.

[3] "La Sᵃ Vᵃ po ben comprendere che tucto lo remedio di questi male in la venuta de la gente d'arme, le quali tardando piu forniscere el paese de Todi da desolare, essendo da la partita miu la cita totalmente derelicta et lassata vacua." xxx. ful. 1497.

[4] "Procedono le cose qui con tanta obedientia et quieta che meglio non si potriano desiderare." xxx. ful. 1497.

[5] "Du becharini homicidi ho facti piglia, et son stati senza tumulto et piacer del populo menati in presione—cosa da bon tempo in qua insolita in questa cita, et questi matina ne è stato appichiato uno." II Aug. 1497.

'Twas immense. There was no tumult, and the people were pleased. That a murderer should pay a penalty for his crime was a charming and fantastic novelty to Perugia. The strong arm of the law struck the city with consternation, and deeds of violence ceased as though by magic. In this manner Cardinal Cesare (detto Borgia) gave a taste of his quality; and came before the world, for the first time, in the rôle which Nature intended him to fill, with his splendid personality, and swift unerring pitiless masterfulness of action.

The prosecution of this work was prevented by the condition of affairs in Rome. It was impossible for the Holiness of the Pope to gather an army while the marriage of Madonna Lucrezia was before the courts, and the frenzy of Fra Girolamo Savonarola before the Reform Commission. Cardinal Cesare, also, was required for other service.

But now, at the beginning of 1498, after the coronation of King Don Federigo, at the close of his legation to Naples, Cardinal Cesare reverted to the work begun the year before; and preferred his petition for leave to doff the scarlet of an ecclesiastic, and to embark on a secular career. The news was bruited about Rome on the eighth of February. Four days later, on the twelfth, the Ferrarese Orator at Venice heard it said that Cardinal Cesare was the murderer of the Duke of Gandia, and that His Worship and Madonna Lucrezia Borgia were seeking matrimonial alliances with the Royal House of Naples. Four days would be exceedingly quick travelling for a piece of gossip from Rome to Venice, when news was carried by mounted couriers, or a-foot, and would have to pass through the Romagna hell: and it is also most important to note that this suspicion was not published till eight months after the murder; and, then, in Venice. No evidence was offered to support it. It emanated from the numerous Orsini whom Venice sheltered, and who said that Cardinal Cesare had killed the Duke in order that he might take his place as the Pope's soldier-son. Once started, the accusation was repeated by Cappello the twenty-eighth of September, 1500; and by Don Silvio Savelli in November 1501; three and four years after the event: nor does it lack repetition by cheap and showy panderers to a guileless public fond of having its flesh made to creep at the present day. All that is known of the murder already has been set down here. But one vital consideration remains to be stated, one new point of view to be described; and it is due to the rumour of Orsini invention mentioned above.

According to Monsignor Hans Burchard the Caerimonarius, Cardinal Cesare and the Duke of Gandia parted, on the night of the fourteenth of June, 1497, by the Vicechancellor's palace (Palazzo Sforza-Cesarini) on Banchi Vecchi; whence the latter, saying that he was going to amuse himself, etc., went in the direction of the Jews' Quarter with his two attendants, the bully, and the unknown mask who undeniably had come by appointment.

Rome of 1497 was divided for purposes of government into fourteen Regions (Rioni) ruled by captains (caporioni) under a prior. The Vicechancellor's palace on Banchi Vecchi is in the Region called Ponte, which extends from the church of San Giovanni de' Fiorentini to the Region called Santangelo after the church of that dedication in the Fishmarket (Pescheria). Now this Region of Ponte was inhabited chiefly by the Orsini faction; as the region of Trevi and the Region of Ripa were inhabited by the Colonna and Savelli factions respectively. In this Region of Ponte lived also Jews: it was the quarter of the bankers and the money-changers, as well as of the prisons, public and private torture-chambers, (no evidence was taken from commoners except under torture,) all under the official protection of the House of Orsini. Here is Cord Lane (Vicolo della Corda), where the ordinary Question or

Torture of the Cord [1] was applied. Here is Old Pillory Square, (Piazza della Berlèna Vecchi.) Here is Executioner Lane, (Vicolo dello Mastro.) And here were four Orsini fortresses, Monte Giordano, Tor Millina, Tor Sanguigna, and Torre di Nona. The Region of Santangelo, also, almost exclusively was inhabited by Jews under the protection of Orsini who held yet another palace-fortress here in the Theatre of Marcellus, (formerly the stronghold of the great mediaeval Jewish House of Pierleoni,) near by the site on which the Ghetto was built in 1556 under the Lord Paul P.P. IV, and abolished in 1890 under the Lord Leo P.P. XIII.

These topographical facts appear to point in one direction. A conclusion may be reached by the following degrees.

(a) The Duke of Gandia took eleven (or fourteen) wounds.

[1] This was quite a common torture. Every patrician had the right to inflict it on his plebeians; and every inventory of palaces begins with "Ropes for the Cord." In many palaces and castles, iron rings through which the Cord was passed remain to be seen. The witness had his hands tied, hanging loosely behind him. One end of the long Cord was attached to his wrists; the other end was flung over a beam or through a ring and held by the official torturer. Then the witness delicately was drawn up as high as possible. He hung there by his wrists which were strained backward and upward, with his shoulders generally dislocated. Then, with a frightful jerk he was dropped to within a braccia (2 feet 7 inches) of the floor, completing the dislocation with a shock. At this moment, the Question was put; his answer distinguished from his shrieks, and written down. Any stubbornness, or insolence, or reticence, was met by attaching weights to his feet, and subjecting him to fresh elevations and fresh drops, till his arms were torn from the sockets and his sinews strained to the uttermost. Or, as a variant, he was left to hang until his questioner had obtained the information required. Evidence of commoners, without the Question, appears to have been considered by the Fifteenth Century as valueless as evidence unsupported by oath or affidavit and untested by cross-examination at the present day. The nearest modern equivalent to the Torture of the Cord would be the smelling of a greasy testament *plus* the stratagems of a cross-examining counsel. It was merely a legal form.

(β) His pouch with its precious jewels was intact.

(γ) He had parted from Cardinal Cesare before witnesses in Banchi Vecchi.

(δ) He said that he was going to amuse himself.

(ε) He went towards the Jews' Quarter.

(ζ) Cardinal Cesare returned to the Vatican.

(η) Banchi Vecchi is in Ponte, the Region of Jews and of Orsini.

(θ) The Jews' Quarter *stricte dicte* was in Santangelo, a Region also dominated by Orsini.

(ι) The Orsini were in mortal strife with the Lord Alexander P.P. VI, Who had visited them with appalling disaster, Who was likely to cause them infinite loss of life and spoil in the near future, Whose favourite son, heir, *and military right hand,* was the Duke of Gandia.

(κ) It was Orsini who started the rumour, eight months later, that Cardinal Cesare (of whom Orsini went in horrid fear by reason of his exploits in the Romagna) had murdered the Duke of Gandia.

The human and natural conclusion would seem to be that Don Juan Francisco de Lançol y Borja, Duke of Gandia, Prince of Teano and of Tricarico, Count of Chiaramonte of Lauria of Cerignuola, Tyrant of Benevento of Tarracina, Grand Constable of Naples, *and Captain-General of the pontifical army against Orsini,* living apart from his wife Doña Maria de Aragona who was with his two children at his duchy in Spain, being a handsome pleasure-loving youth of twenty-two years, went to keep an assignation on that night of the fourteenth of June, 1497; and fell by the furious dagger of one of Orsini's Jews, a rival? a father? an outraged husband?—or by the vengeful poignards of his own and his Father's deadly foes, the Orsini.

The great number of his wounds, the safety of his valuables, may be thus accounted for. The unknown mask would be the decoy, disguised as pandar. The murder of the bully speaks of more assassins than one.

Then, did not Orsini strike at the heart of the Pope in the slaughter of His eldest son?

At all events, no formal accusation of the guilt of this most foul and treacherous crime has ever been laid against Cardinal Cesare (detto Borgia). There is absolutely no evidence against him—only suspicion, rumour and conjecture. And the three spring from a tainted source—the lair of the Bear—Orsini.

.   .   .

Plans for the settlement of the Romagna had to be set aside. The affair of Fra Girolamo Savonarola monopolized the attention of the moment.

That Friar began the year 1498 by preaching a fierce defence of his disobedience to the inhibition and to the sentence of excommunication; and by a frenetic onslaught on the Roman as distinguished from the Tuscan clergy. The Lord Alexander P.P. VI, the acknowledged Head of the Christian Church, (indeed He was the *only* representative of Christianity in Authority at that time) found Himself in the position of a commander-in-chief dealing with a mutinous mad sergeant whom captains, colonels, and generals have failed to reduce to order. The Pope's moderation and long-suffering, prior to his allowing the law to take its course, are perfectly marvellous. Fra Girolamo had been in a state of mutiny for more than four years. Preaching the duty of obedience, he would not practise it. He was totally insensible to the many graces with which he had been indulged; and he met all overtures for peace with evasion or with insolence. After all, he was "a man under authority," under authority to which voluntarily he had vowed, and refused, submission while admitting the right of that authority to claim it:—an anomalous position, illogical, scandalous,—the position of a mad man. To the Signoria of Florence, then, the Lord Alexander P.P. VI issued a Brief commanding the withdrawal of support from the excommunicated friar; threatening Florence with an Interdict (a hideous lash that invariably brought curs to heel) if His commandment were disobeyed: but, at the same time, offering to absolve the rebellious son of St. Dominic, upon submission. The Signoria replied, defending Savonarola; and the Pope's Holiness replied that, either he must be imprisoned, or be sent to Rome: a decision which was explained at greater length to the Signoria by the Florentine Orator in Rome, who also described the Pope's natural feelings of embitterment at finding His reasonable demands so spurned and set aside. Half measures only were taken. The Lord Alexander P.P. VI justly was dissatisfied when the Signoria simply forbade the friar to preach. His Holiness commanded, then, the entire vindication of His supreme authority.

Here, Fra Girolamo Savonarola committed his final sin. He joined in the stale howl appealing to the Powers of Europe for the convocation of a General Council; and he redoubled his treacherous intrigues with the Christian King Charles VIII: completing the exasperation of the Lord Alexander P.P. VI.

Events moved swiftly then. Defying the commands of his acknowledged superior, the Pope, as well as the injunctions of the Signoria, he fell on disrepute. His influence in Florence waned and withered; his prophecies fell thick and fast on no believers: and then the Signoria insisted on his submission to the Pope.

He replied by demanding the Ordeal Of Fire; offering to walk through a blazing furnace with one of the many who opposed him, the person who should take no hurt from that Ordeal to be adjudged innocent and under the special protection of God.

Fra Francesco of Apulia a Friar Minor (a Religion always bitterly antipathetic to the Religion of St. Dominic) accepted the challenge thus thrown down. He said that he knew that both parties to the Ordeal would be burned to death: but it would be better so, than that one heresiarch should be left free to carry on his treasons to Christ's Church and State.

Again Fra Girolamo Savonarola put forth an evasion. He refused, after challenging—he refused the Ordeal in his proper person: but he offered one of his friars of San Marco, one Fra Domenico, as his representative.

From Rome the practical common sense of the Pope's Holiness fulminated disapproval: but the Ordeal went on. Faggots were piled in the great square of Florence, and set in flame. The skin of the faces of the crowd grew hot and scarlet and crackled in the glare. The Friar Minor came forward in readiness to die for the good of the people. Fra Girolamo made delays—delays—he said that Fra Domenico must bear our Lord-in-the-Sacrament, the Sacred Host, Gesù Sagramentato, in an ostensorium through the raging flames. The pious simple souls of the Signoria knew this for irreverence, for sacrilege; retired to discuss the point; returned; refused permission. Fra Girolamo persisted while the fire burned lower. The long slow day was passing. Already his dictatorship, the day when he ruled Florence with a word, had passed. The fire was dying, and then, finally, except upon his own mad terms, Fra Girolamo refused the Ordeal which he had challenged, evaded, delayed, denied.

All faith in him was gone. Objurgated by a thousand raucous throats, torn at by a thousand furious hands, the people's broken idol sought refuge in his Convent of San Marco. Florence rose in riot, blood was shed, the blood of Francesco Valori in cold murder. The Convent of San Marco suffered storm; and the friars with their mattoid Prior were cast in prison.

In the interests of justice and of mercy, the Pope's Holiness strove to have their trial held in Rome: but events had roused the Signoria to vindicate the honour of Florence "to satisfy the people who so long had been duped and trained in sacrilege and rebellion." Wherefore, from Rome came Commissioners for the trial of Fra Girolamo Savonarola and his accomplices. Put to the legal torture, he confessed himself charlatan and criminal. He and his lieutenants, Frati Domenico and Silvestro, were found guilty as heretics, schismatics, and rebels against the Holy See, of political fanaticism amounting to high treason and mutiny against his lawful rulers. Handed to the secular judges for sentence, he was condemned, with the two friars, to death by hanging and the burning of their bodies after death. Handed back to the ecclesiastical power the three were degraded from their priesthood, to enable them to undergo the death penalty, avoiding the sacrilege of violence to the persons of those tonsured and anointed. At the very last, by the express commandment of the Lord Alexander P.P. VI there was offered to the condemned a Plenary Indulgence-in-the-article-of-death, with release from all Canonical Censures and Excommunications. Gratefully, thankfully, it was accepted; and the prisoners paid the legal retribution of their crimes.

Had he been an Englishman of the Twentieth Century, instead of a Florentine of the Fifteenth, Fra Girolamo Savonarola would not have been hanged or burned; but censured; suspended, from the exercise of sacerdotal functions, by ecclesiastical authority; and, at last, by medical authority, interned at Broadmoor during the Pleasure of the King's Majesty, as a criminal lunatic.

.   .   .

This year, 1498, was born Don Giovanni Borgia, called "Infans Romanus"; who was said to be a bastard of Cardinal Cesare (detto Borgia) by "a Roman spinster."

This year, also, died the twelve-toed chin-tufted excommunicated little Christian King Charles VIII of France; and was succeeded by his cousin Louis XII, a thin man with a fat neck and lip, and an Ethiopic nose, and exquisite attire, who immediately made two startling claims—for the nullification of his marriage with Madame Jeanne de Valois, and for the confirmation of his claim to the Duchy of Milan. The Lord Alexander P.P. VI always preferred friends to enemies; and, now that Charles VIII was gone to his own place, He gladly welcomed an opportunity of winning the allegiance of France. A commission of jurists went from Rome, who, on the legal facts, declared the marriage between the King and Madame Jeanne to be null and void. A papal dispensation legalized the marriage of the Christian King Louis XII and Queen Anne, his predecessor's widow, whereby her duchy of Bretagne was retained to the crown of France. The claim to the Duchy of Milan was a matter which required consideration.

.   .   .

At the Sixth Consistory of the twelfth of September, 1498, the Lord Alexander P.P. VI named one cardinal, who was

the Lord Georges d'Amboise, Gentleman of the Bedchamber to the Christian Kings Charles VIII and Louis XII; Cardinal-Presbyter of the Title of San Sisto.

.   .   .

At last, the Pope's Holiness consented to allow Cardinal Cesare (detto Borgia) to renounce the scarlet cardinalitial hat and the sapphire cardinalitial ring, for a secular duchy, a royal wife, and a military career; saying that his presence among the clergy was sufficient to prevent reformation.[1]

---

[1] "Una de las mas principales causas que dava, para que el Cardenal de Valencia dexasse el capelo era, porque siendo a quel Cardenal, mientras en la Iglesia estuviesse, era bastante para impedir que no se hiziesse in reformacion."—Zurita, 126.

A marriage was proposed for him with Doña Carlotta de Aragona, Princess of Naples; but rejected by King Don Federigo, who at the same time favoured the marriage which took place between Madonna Lucrezia Borgia and Don Alonso de Aragona, Prince of Bisceglia. The plan of Cardinal Cesare was aided by fresh outbreaks at the pontifical baronage, especially by a new league of Colonna and Orsini on behalf of Cardinal Giuliano della Rovere. Now, no more time was lost. Don Cesare (detto Borgia) renounced his cardinalate in full consistory; and journeyed into France to cultivate the friendship of the Christian King on behalf of the Papacy. New alliances were in the air. King Louis XII saw no reason why he should remain in the ridiculous and paralysing isolation which the braggadocio of his predecessor had won. The Pope's Holiness was by no means secure with Naples whose King Don Federigo, though owing all to Him, was inclined to be obstreperous and to show contempt, and to whose dominions the Catholic King and Queen were reaching. An alliance with the Papacy would suit the plans of France. An alliance with France would be of eminent service to the Papacy, at this moment when Colonna and Orsini were on the war-path, and the Muslim Infidel stirring the East. So, the mission of Don Cesare (detto Borgia) met with great success; a working understanding was arranged by his diplomacy; and the Christian King conferred on him the French Duchy of Valentinois.

It became evident that Milan must cede to France, the new ally of the Lord Alexander P.P. VI; and this signified the final rupture of the alliance of Borgia and Sforza. First, firm friends; next, strong supporters of the House of Borgia; then, indifferent neutrals; later, declared traitors; last, negligible quantities; the conduct of the House of Sforza was influenced by one idea—loyalty to their name. It was the head of the House who was responsible,

Duke Ludovico Maria Sforza-Visconti, a coward, a scoundrel, a traitor, a murderer in intention, the wretch who brought invading Frenchmen into Italy to aid his usurpation of the throne of Milan—to him be all the blame. The Vice-chancellor-Cardinal Ascanio Maria Sforza-Visconti and all the Sforza of Pesaro, Santafiora, Chotignuola, Imola and Forli, followed the head of their House; and, as he led them astray, so he must be decried. Sforza has produced cardinals a many; but never a Pope. Sforza was never nearer to the pontificate than in this reign. Ascanio was more than likely to succeed the Lord Alexander—far more likely than the diabolical plebeian who did succeed. But Sforza followed the head of its House; committing political suicide. Loyalty in any age is rare: under all circumstances it is heroic, admirable.

From the Catholic King and Queen of Spain, Don Hernando and Doña Isabella, came the sometime pontifical captain Don Gonsalvo de Cordoba, charged to scold the Holiness of the Pope because of His new alliance with France. A very old weapon again was refurbished, and Catholic Spain, in fear or envy, menaced a Spanish Pontiff, Who had given her the New World, with Cardinal Giuliano della Rovere's stupid General Council. So, in the shuffling of the cards, misery made strange bed-fellows acquainted.

Then the Orient blazed with sudden war, and the Muslim Infidel began hostilities with Venice. Christendom had lost Lepanto [1]; the Turks were intoxicated with success; and in Rome the Lord Alexander was deep in the scheme of a new Crusade when the year 1498 died.

. . .

Naples looked with sallow eyes on the amicable relations of the Papacy and France. The Christian King Louis XII

[1] But She won a signal and decisive victory there, with the aid of Our Lady of Victory (Νίκη, Poliziano would have said), in 1572.

married Duke Cesare de Valentinois to Madame Charlotte, daughter of Sieur Alain d'Albret and sister of King Jean of Navarre; and then entered into a treaty with the Venetian Senate for the partition of the duchy of Milan. These acts were discomfiting to the Regno, which could only regard the triumph of its enemy and the ruin of its friend as auguries of evil fortune. For Duke Cesare de Valentinois undoubtedly was the enemy of Naples now after the rejection of his suit to Doña Carlotta de Aragona, and in despite of the fact that his mother's daughter, Madonna Lucrezia Borgia, was allied by marriage to the Neapolitan Prince Don Alonso of Bisceglia. The fruit of this last union was a son, born in November, 1499, baptized in the Xystine Chapel by the name Roderico after the August Father of Madonna Lucrezia.

Troubles were brewing for the Sforza. The Vice-chancellor-Cardinal left Rome, and the French invaded his brother's duchy of Milan, driving Duke Ludovico Maria Sforza-Visconti (detto Il Moro) to ignominious flight. Ever ready to take advantage of the weakness of another Power, also ever ready to be jealous of another Power's success, Europe eyed the triumph of France with apprehension and disgust. And when the Lord Alexander P.P. VI shewed pleasure at the fall of Milan, Spain and Portugal in their chagrin sent Orators to annoy His Holiness with invectives against His morals,[1] (as Satan sometimes denounces Sin), and the validity of His election,[2] demanding impossible reforms, and a General Council at the Lateran. These petty incidents met the fate which they

---

[1] "Mores esse profligatos pietatis studium restinctum, flagitiorum licentiam solutam, sanctissimas pretio indignissimis addici—remque esse in extremum poene discrimen adductam."—(Osorius De rebus gestis Emanuelis, Op. I. 595.)

[2] "Italia tutta aviebbe dimostrato lui non esser vero pontifice."— (Marino Sanuto in De Leva, 61.) "Que eran notorias las formas que se tuvieron en se eleccion, y quan graves cosas se intentaron, y quan escandalosas."—Zurita, 159.)

deserved. The Lord Alexander P.P. VI magnificently and magnanimously received the envoys in a public consistory, and made no efforts to prevent them from reciting their lessons. His Holiness invariably treated personalities with good-humoured scorn; and bore the vented spleen of kings as a mere essential inconvenience of His rank, to be brushed away and forgotten with the little muscarial nuisances of a Roman summer.

.   .   .

The year 1499, being the penultimate year of the Fifteenth Century, was occupied as far as the City was concerned with preparations for the Jubilee; that curious ceremony wherewith the Church affords an opportunity to the faithful to cleanse their souls from stain of sin by penitence and pious works. Penitence is an affair entirely personal, to be entreated of between a sinner and his Judge: but the Church, who (according to the Thirty-Nine Articles) "hath power to ordain its rites and ceremonies," prescribes the ceremonial works to be performed. In brief, these works consist in certain visits to certain basilicas of Rome, which must be entered by certain doors, and where certain prayers must be prayed. The Church, being a system, is systematic. In return for these works, always supposing them to be accompanied by the appropriate penitence, She promises, from the infinite treasury of the Merits of our Divine Redeemer remission of the canonical punishment incurred, during his past life, by the sinner now penitent and purposing amendment. This Complaisance on the part of the Church technically is called an Indulgence; and the Jubilee Indulgence is in high esteem and eager acceptation. It is not in any sense a licence to sin; as, by a singularly silly misconception of its name,[1] it has been supposed to

---

[1] Indulgentia=Indulgence, gentleness, complaisance, tenderness, fondness, a remission of punishment or taxation.—(Andrews, Latin-English Lexicon, 1853, p. 789.)

be: but, absolutely, a formal wiping of the slate, a ceremonial enabling of the soul to start anew. The Jubilee begins on Christmas Day with the opening, by the Supreme Pont·ff, of a certain door in the Vatican Basilica, which remains an ingress until the Christmas Day of the century-end; and vast pilgrimages are used to flock into the City at such times. The year 1499 saw erected accommodation for visitors in the Borgo Nuovo, and numerous improvements on the Vatican side of Tiber. Churches were restored and furbished, the Mola of Hadrian strengthened; and the new wing of the Apostolic Palace of the Vatican called the Borgia Tower, which the Lord Alexander P.P. VI had built, was decorated in fresco by the brush of Messer Bernardino Betti (detto Il Pinturicchio).

In his book on the lives of artists which Giovanni Vasari wrote half a century later it is said that Il Pinturicchio painted on a wall of the Borgia Tower a picture of the Blessed Virgin Mary before whom the Borgia Pontiff kneels in adoration. Vasari also says that the painter used, as his model for Deipara, Madonna Giulia Orsini (nata Farnese) who was the Pope's mistress: and this statement is repeated by many, to this day, including the German historian Herr Gregorovius (who pretends to have been guided by documents and by documents alone), as an example of the flagitious profligacy and profanity of the Lord Alexander P.P. VI.

Painters of the Fifteenth Century, in the manner of painters of the Twentieth, took their models as they found them. If the perpetuation of the world's loveliness be no sin,—and on that point there are diversities of human opinion, and one Law,—then the person who is graced with natural beauty incurs, not disgrace, but honour in allowing it to be preserved by painting or by sculpture. Perfect beauty does not seek concealment, but simply admits the world to share its joy, without emotion of vanity or shame, without regard to rank or dignity. Pauline Buonaparte Princess Borghese was the model for Canova's Venus. Bernini modelled his David (in Villa Borghese) from his own γυμνότης, while Cardinal Barberini (afterwards the Lord Urban P.P. VIII) held the mirror. That amiable rake Messer Rafael Sanzio da Urbino painted his baker's daughter as Madonna. Messer Jacopo Sansovino sculptured his Dionusos from a lad called Lippo Fabri, who, from long posing bare, took cold and died of fever; and, in his last delirium, continually leaped from his bed to pose as the god to whom his life was sacrificed. Messer Michelangelo Buonarroti, lost in admiration of his model the son of Messer Francesco Raibolini of Bologna (detto Il Francia), with his naif and customary depreciation of his brother-painters, told the boy that his father made better men by night than by day. Messer Andrea Verrocchio did his slim lean David from one of his alert apprentices. Messer Luca Signorelli painted his own dead son. Messer Rafaele Sanzio himself, times without number, sat for his master Il Pinturicchio. The beautiful Simoneta of Florence was the Venus of Messer Alessandro Filipepi (detto Botticelli); and the sons of Lorenzo and Giuliano de' Medici (two of whom in after years wore the Triregno) did not disdain to sit as models for this master. All the works of art of the Borgian Era, representing saints and sinners, gods and demigods, eudaimones and kakadaimones, all obviously were portraits; the very imperfections, which the century of the Discovery of Man was too eager and too unsophisticated to plane away to fit arbitrary conventions, show this: and volumes might be written of the models of great masters, who let their youth or beauty be set down for all time, and then achieved fame as Rafaele did, or Messer Simone Fiorentini's (detto Donatello) nitid David or superb Saint George, or Messer Andrea del Sarto's wistful Young Saint John.

Wherefore, not only may it be admitted, but defended,

that Madonna Giulia Orsini (nata Farnese), who had come to share with Madonna Lucrezia Borgia the distinction of being the fairest young mother in Rome, sat as model to Il Pinturicchio for the Θεοτόκος of the Borgia Tower.

But, in proof of the ghastly ignorance or devilish malice which has sought to introduce an element of lubricity into this affair, it is necessary that three important facts should not go unconsidered. They are

(α) that the Borgia Tower contained three or four large halls:

(β) that the portrait of Madonna Giulia Orsini (nata Farnese), detta La Bella, in the character of the Blessed Virgin Mary with her Child, is a round picture over the door of the third hall; She is encircled by angels, and there are no other figures in the composition:

(γ) that the portrait of the Lord Alexander P.P. VI is a square picture in the second hall; and the holiness of the Pope is presented in His pontifical habits but bare-headed and without the triregno, devoutly kneeling before the Apparition of our Divine Redeemer Who rises from the tomb.

That is the little matter of the calumny, in support of which the German historian with others of like mind have solved the problem of the squaring of the circle![1]

.   .   .

Now that the French alliance was secure, with the help of the Christian King Louis XII, the Lord Alexander P.P. VI proceeded with the conquest of the Romagna and the reduction of the rebellious vassals of the Holy See. Duke Cesare de Valentinois was named Generalissimo of

[1] De Maricourt.

the pontifical army; and a Papal Bull declared the fiefs of Rimini, Pesaro, Imola, Forli, Camerino, Faenza, etc., to have forfeited their rights until they should have made satisfaction, paying the arrears of annual tribute into the chancery of their paramount lord. The fact was fully realised that it was useless to attempt to pacify "these kakodaimones" with "holy water"; as, as a last resort, after seven years forbearance, force was to be used against Sforza of Pesaro, Sforza-Riario of Imola and Forli, Manfredi of Faenza and the rest. The glowing splendour of the personality of Duke Cesare de Valentinois, without emotion and without remorse, fitted him for his task. He was a perfect egoist, splendidly indifferent to all the world. During his life, his enormous talents, his swift success, his summary acts gained him the reputation of being superhuman, inevitable as Fate. On the eleventh of November 1499, he left Rome with four thousand condottieri and three hundred lancers. His lieutenant and standard-bearer was the same noble and vigorous knight, Don Pietro Gregorio Borgia, of the Veliternian Branch, who had changed clothes with him in 1495, enabling him to cheat the Christian King. On the seventeenth of December, he stormed and captured Imola, whence Madonna Caterina Sforza, widow of Count Girolamo Riario, had fled, refusing obedience or tribute to her suzerain, and anew entrenching herself at Forli, her other fief. She left at Imola such an odious memory of her rule, that in after years the citizens would blush for shame of it, while blessing Duke Cesare de Valentinois, who, as the minister of Divine Justice, made an end.

The encounter between Madonna Caterina and Duke Cesare caused extraordinary exhibitions of vigour and agility on both sides. When a desperate unscrupulous woman struggles with a strong and ruthless man, she will do much damage: but, in the end, she must succumb. Di-

rectly after the fall of Imola, Duke Cesare received letters
from Rome announcing that the Pope's Holiness narrowly
had escaped violent death: for Madonna Caterina, to save
herself and her fiefs, believing that Duke Cesare would be
compelled to relinquish his expedition if the Pope were
dead, had tried to slay the Holy Father by means of venom.
To this end, she had sent two Orators charged with proposed conditions of peace; and also she sent a letter (enclosed in a hollow stick, say some) which would cause the
Supreme Pontiff to fall dead as soon as He should open
it. When the plot was discovered, Tommaso da Forli, a
papal chamberlain who had brought the missive, admitted
his guilt; (under the Question guilt was commonly admitted); and said that he hoped, by the death of the Pope,
to raise the siege of Imola and Forli. This extraordinary
story is recorded by several chroniclers, including Monsignor Hans Burchard the Caerimonarius, the dull and
stupid defamer of the Lord Alexander P.P. VI. The name
of the chamberlain gives rise to curious speculations.
Tommaso da Forli presumably might be a bastard of the
city of Forli of insufficient birth to warrant the adoption
of the appellation of his unknown father or mother; and
who might very well have taken the name of his native city
with the preposition "da" (not "de'," be it noted) as a
surname. Papal chamberlains are nothing more than pontifical flunkeys, and "Thomas from Forli," being a lackey
with access to the Pontifical Person, might have been employed by Madonna Caterina to stab the Pope. That is not
unlikely: but the story of the envenomed letter obviously
is false; and interesting only as shewing the trend of men's
minds in 1499; and as a proof, perhaps, that if, as has been
alleged in the purest ignorance, the envenoming of its foes
was a custom of the House of Borgia, at least one other
Italian court indulged in the same horrible habit upon
occasion.

Madonna Caterina's second recorded act of treachery

took place after she had surrendered the city of Forli to Duke Cesare. She retained possession of the castle, and refused to give it up. As soon as the pontifical artillery began to bombard her fortress on Christmas Day, she flew, from one of the fortalices, a banner bearing the Lion of St. Mark, to make believe that she was leagued with Venice, a republic then at peace with the Holy See. It was a Venetian attached to the staff of Duke Cesare who exposed the ruse, with the affirmation that his Senate had no alliance with Madonna Caterina. The day following, she gave signs of weakening; and requested a parley with her beleaguerer. When Duke Cesare approached, and just was about to put his foot on the draw-bridge over the moat by which the castle was surrounded, suddenly and without warning the machine swung up and in. Madonna Caterina indignantly disclaimed any perfidious intent, and threw all blame on the castellan, Don Giovanni Casale: but all beholders were aware of a deliberate attempt to capture and hideously to kill the Generalissimo, which only had failed through too eager precipitancy. No parley took place; the siege continued; and, in time, this audacious war-wife was compelled to capitulate. Duke Cesare sent her to Rome as a prisoner-of-state, with every chivalrous consideration for her sex as well as for her illustrious birth as daughter of the great Duke Francesco Sforza-Visconti of Milan: and on her arrival in the City she was lodged in the Belvedere Apartment of the Vatican, whence, after a futile attempt at escape, she was transferred to honourable captivity in the Mola of Hadrian.

During the siege of Forli an event occurred, of secondary importance, except as evidence of the mystery surrounding the paternity of Duke Cesare. The Most Worshipful Lord Giovanni Borgia (detto Giuniore) Cardinal-Presbyter of the Title of Santa Maria *in Via Lata* died at Urbino. He was one of the bastards of that beautiful splendid sneak and coward Don Pedro Luis de Lançol y Borgia (Duke of

Spoleto, younger brother of the Lord Alexander P.P. VI, who had been named Prefect of Rome and Castellan of Santangelo by his Uncle, the Lord Calixtus P.P. III, and who died in his flight from Rome in 1458). The said Most Worshipful Lord Cardinal Giovanni Giuniore had been Bishop of Melfi since 1492. In 1496, he was elevated to the Sacred College, and given command of the condottieri which the Lord Alexander P.P. VI was preparing against France; and, when Duke Cesare renounced his scarlet early in 1499, he had ceded to this cardinal his Metropolitan Archbishopric of Valencia. The Lord Giovanni Giuniore had held Legations to Umbria, Bologna, Ravenna and France, and was acting as Legate to Umbria when he died at Urbino. Duke Cesare himself announced this death to the Pope in a letter written from Forli, and dated the sixteenth of January 1500, in these words: "I have news of "the death of Cardinal Borgia, *my brother,* who died at Urbino." Duke Cesare wrote a kind of Latin neither Golden nor Silvern but particular to himself, as also was his Italian and there is no known instance of his using "frater" or "fratello" in the tertiary sense of "cousin." If the dead Cardinal and the Duke were uterine brothers, then Don Pedro Luis was their father; and Duke Cesare was not the son, but the nephew, of the Lord Alexander P.P. VI. The death of the Cardinal, however, has been alleged by some chroniclers to have been caused by venom administered by Duke Cesare. The charge is essentially absurd. There was no motive; for Cardinal and Duke were comrades, *brothers-in-arms,* equally engaged in the reduction of the rebellious Romagna; there could have been no jealousy, for they occupied separate and independent ranks, (of which Duke Cesare had chosen his,) the Cardinal Giovanni Giuniore as Legate being the older man (41), and Duke Cesare the younger (26) as Generalissimo: nor was the Cardinal rich enough to make his death desirable. But, at all events, it was impossible that Duke Cesare should envenom him for the simple reasons that the two were many miles apart during seventeen days before the death, and that no venom of slow action was known to the Fifteenth Century any more than it is to the Twentieth.

. . .

At the Seventh Consistory of the sixteenth (or twentieth) of March 1500, the Lord Alexander P.P. VI named three cardinals, who were

(a) the Lord Don Didaco Hurtado de Mendoza, a Spaniard; Cardinal-Presbyter of the Title of Santa Sabina: (he was afterwards called "The Cardinal of Spain:")

(β) the Lord Amaneus (Amanateus) d'Albret, of Navarre; Cardinal-Deacon of San Niccolo *in Carcere Tulliano:*

(γ) the Lord Don Pedro Luis de Borja, a Pontifical Nephew, brother of the Cardinal of Monreale (Giovanni Seniore); succeeded his deceased cousin Cardinal Giovanni Giuniore as Cardinal-Deacon of Santa Maria in *Via Lata.*

. . .

The Christian King Louis XII, now calling himself the "Second Caesar," was not idle during this year 1500. Duke Ludovico Maria Sforza-Visconti certainly recovered his duchy of Milan; but, after the Triumph given to Duke Cesare de Valentinois in Rome on his return from the Romagna with Madonna Caterina Sforza-Riario as his prisoner-of-war, the prestige of the Papacy was so increased that the French took heart and gained a notable victory at Novara, capturing Duke Ludovico Maria and his brother the Vicechancellor, who then were incarcerated safely in France.

. . .

In July, Don Alonso de Aragona, Prince of Bisceglia, Quadrata, and Salerno, and husband of Madonna Lucrezia Borgia was murdered; and the opinion carefully and carelessly has been cultivated that this was one of the crimes of Duke Cesare de Valentinois and the Lord Alexander P.P. VI.

According to the account of Don Paolo Cappello the Orator of Venice, as given by Herr Gregorovius, Prince Don Alonso, going to the Vatican at eleven o'clock at night on the fifteenth of July, was assaulted on the steps of St. Peter's by masked men armed with poignards, and wounded in the head and arms and thighs. Weak from loss of blood, he dragged himself into the Apostolic Palace, where his wife Madonna Lucrezia swooned at the sight of him. He was carried into one of the rooms; and a cardinal, believing him to be in the article of death, imparted the usual absolution. But his youthful vigour enabled him to progress on the road to recovery, under the nursing of his wife and of his sister-in-law Madonna Sancia, who, with their own hands, prepared his food (they were royal princesses), while the Pope's Holiness provided a body-guard of men-at-arms. No one knew who had wounded the prince: but gossip said that it was the same hand that had slain the Duke of Gandia. Duke Cesare de Valentinois had issued an edict forbidding any one bearing arms to pass between the Mola of Hadrian and the Vatican. Don Paolo Cappello further records that Duke Cesare had said, "I did not wound the prince: but, if I had done so, he had well deserved it." Duke Cesare was not ashamed to visit the invalid; and, in coming away, he had said, "That, which is not done at noon, can be done at sunset." More than a month later, at nine o'clock on the night of the eighteenth of August, Duke Cesare again visited Prince Don Alonso; and, having driven Madonna Sancia and Madonna Lucrezia from the room, he introduced his captain Don Michelotto who strangled the wounded man. After this, Duke Cesare publicly declared that he had killed the Prince of Bisceglia, because the latter had tried to murder him by setting an archer to shoot him silently in the Vatican garden:—so far Don Paolo Cappello.

Monsignor Hans Burchard the Caerimonarius says, that, at eleven o'clock on the night of the fifteenth of July, Prince Don Alonso the husband of Madonna Lucrezia Borgia was found on the steps of St. Peter's, wounded by assassins in the head, the knee, and the right arm. After the assault, the assassins were escorted by forty knights beyond the City-gate called Porta Pertusa. Prince Don Alonso lived near the Vatican in the palace of the Cardinal of Santa Maria *in Portico;* but, owing to the serious nature of his wounds, he was carried into the pontifical palace, and lodged in a room of the Borgia Tower. When King Don Federigo heard of the attempt upon his nephew, he sent Messer Galieno his own leech to cure him. Later the prince was strangled; and the leeches with a certain hunchback servant were put to the Question in the Mola of Hadrian, and afterwards released as innocent.

A chronicle of Pavia of much later date says that Duke Cesare killed Prince Don Alonso at a time when he was in bed with his own wife Madonna Lucrezia.

Before examining the divergences of this evidence, it may as well be said that the original despatches of Don Paolo Cappello the Orator of Venice are not attainable. Many years later, a learned patrician of Venice, Don Marino Sanuto, wrote the History of the Venetian Republic from 1496 to 1533 in fifty-six folio volumes. He cited the state-archives, despatches of orators, etc., and his work is marvellously well done: but, when all is said, the fact remains that the despatches of Don Paolo Cappello, with those of many others, have been edited by a stranger to the writers, and to the circumstances under which they wrote. Monsignor Burchard held an important office at the Vatican. He was German, and inimical to Borgia. On matters connected with his office of Caerimonarius, *i.e.*, the superintendence of public functions, he might speak with some authority: but beyond that he is an inveterate gossip and scandalmonger. In his case, also, it is impossible to know what he really wrote, because the original holograph of his Diarium (with the Diarium of Infessura and other similar works) even now awaits discovery by students of ancient archives.

What charges lie against Duke Cesare de Valentinois? It is Cappello who states that he drove away the women, and caused Prince Don Alonso to be strangled by Don Michelotto. Burchard appears ignorant of these details. It is Cappello who states that Duke Cesare admitted and defended the murder. Of this Burchard says nothing: he relates that the prince was strangled; and, from his mention of the interrogation of the leeches and of the hunchback, it would appear that others beside Duke Cesare were suspected. Cappello says that the prince was poignarded in head, arms, and thighs; Burchard, in head, right arm, and knee. Capello speaks of a guard appointed by the Pope to watch the wounded man. Burchard does not record this. There are discrepancies between the two accounts; some, of reasonable importance: *e.g.*, Burchard's account of the forty knights who escorted the assassins from the City; and of the sending of the royal leech without mentioning any suspicions on the part of King Don Federigo. But nowhere can be found a proved accusation against Duke Cesare de Valentinois, or against the Holiness of the Pope.

From a study of the various statements, (derisable though to some extent they be,) and of known facts, a reasonable enough history of the affair may be compiled, and one which happens to be exculpatory of Borgia.

Don Alonso de Aragona Prince of Bisceglia, Salerno, etc., was a nephew of King Don Federigo of Naples. At the age of nineteen, he married Madonna Lucrezia Borgia, on political grounds to consolidate friendly relations then existing between Papacy and Regno. All accounts agree that this was a genuine love-match as well; and the chronicler Talini says of the prince, "he was the most beautiful youth that I have ever seen in Rome."

A year after the marriage Madonna Lucrezia bore him an heir, Don Roderico; who immediately was provided for with the duchy of Sermoneta. The young Prince and Princess of Bisceglia lived in the palace of the Cardinal of Sante Maria *in Portico* by the Vatican, in order to be near the Pope.

In the year 1500, the relations of Papacy and Regno had undergone a change. The Lord Alexander P.P. VI was now allied with France, the old and still-distrusted enemy of Naples; and King Don Federigo had joined the unmitigable handful of men who were blackmailing the Pope's Holiness with threats of a General Council. The Prince of Bisceglia as a Neapolitan, therefore, would not be persona gratissima to the supporters of Borgia.

When it was desired to reward and exalt a subject, the sovereigns of the Borgian era had the naïve habit of dispossessing one of their enemies, and conferring the vacated fief on their new protégé. In order to enrich Prince Don Alonso with the principality of Salerno, the Majesty of Naples had deprived the noble Neapolitan House of Sanseverini. In order to enrich His grandson the baby Don Roderico with the duchy of Sermoneta, the Holiness of the Pope had despoiled the noble Roman House of Caïetani. And it readily will be understood that Caïetani and Sanseverini were extremely likely to view these losses with anything but resignation.

Regarding the edict of Duke Cesare de Valentinois, that none should go armed betwen the Mola and the Vatican, it must be admitted that this was only a very ordinary precautionary measure. The district named is the immediate precincts of the pontifical palaces of peace and war, which were connected by the fortified gallery-passage, through the Region of Borgo, called Lo Andare; and the bearing of arms within the presence of royalty was, at all times, and in all courts, a capital crime. Duke Cesare as Generalissimo was responsible for the maintenance of order; and he was no laggard in any official capacity. If then, the truth of the stabbing on the steps of St. Peter's and the strangulation in the Borgia Tower be granted, they might be defended as an execution of the death-penalty pre-scribed for a breach of the law, such as the fiery Neapolitan prince is extremely likely to have committed. Royal or pa-trician criminals were frequently done to death in private, by quasi-assassination, to avoid the degradation of the touch of the public carnefex.

Again, granting the said stabbing and strangling, and regarding them as an act of private vengeance on the part of Duke Cesare against the prince; it should be remembered that people had the custom of defending their lives by slaughtering an enemy who set archers to shoot at them in the garden.

But, during the pontificate of the Lord Julius P.P. II (Giuliano della Rovere) the eternal enemy of the House of Borgia, (whose not mean portrait by Messer Rafaele Sanzio da Urbino may be seen at the National Gallery,) the cap-tain Don Michelotto, who is supposed to have strangled the Prince of Bisceglia by order of Duke Cesare, was seized and put to the Question in the usual manner. It was at-tempted to find out, by means of this rigour, the truth about the various crimes which he was said to have committed for his master; and particularly the murder of Prince Don Alonso. But although he was in the hands of a ruthless despot, who legally could have broiled him alive like a forger or could have broken with iron bars every bone of every limb of his body on the Wheel, with none to hinder, Don Michelotto soon was set at liberty as having given no evidence of guilt, either on his own part or of that of Duke

Cesare. It will appear from this fairly convincing test that there is a strong reason for regarding the story of strangulation as a piece of fiction. As a last contribution to the theory, it is suggested that contortions caused by *tetanus,* which might have set in by reason of the poignard wounds, may have simulated, to the ignorant and casual observer, the appearance of strangulation. The bacillus of tetanus is of earth origin, and every one knows the vulgar method of wiping a dagger. Otherwise the strangulation theory may be dismissed.

Of the stabbing on the steps of St. Peter's there is no such room for doubt. The discrepancy between Cappello (edited by Sanuto, understood,) and Burchard, (a copy of him by an unknown hand, also understood,) as to the position of the wounds has no material significance. Head, arms, and thighs, says Cappello; head, right arm, and knee, says Burchard. It is quite clear that the unfortunate youth (he was just of the age of twenty-one years) wore beneath his doublet one of the fashionable mail-shirts of the day, strong enough to turn a tempered blade at closest quarters and yet so fine that it could be hidden in two hands; and which caused him to be wounded anywhere except in his handsome trunk.

The number of wounds and their wide distribution speak of more than one occasion. The frightful loss of blood (the wound in the thigh), the delusions of Fifteenth Century chirurgeons, the elementary condition of the pharmacopœia, the time of year—Sol in Leone—when Rome sizzles in fevers and insanitary stenches, preclude possibility of recovery: and it is only reasonable to conceive that Prince Don Alonso died, after a month's lingering weakness and fever, of the poignard wounds and the attentions of the leeches, unassisted by a problematic noose, or the compression of his windpipe by strong thumbs.

Then who were the masked men with poignards, and who is responsible for them?

In this connection, Duke Cesare de Valentinois has not been named. The Pope's Holiness did not alter His behaviour to him. He found him antipathetic as always: some said He was afraid of him.[1] But He did not cease to use him, to allow him access to His person, to decorate him with titles; and the Lord Alexander P.P. VI was far too magnificently invincible and too conscious of His power, not to have resented the murder of the beloved husband of His charming and favourite daughter. A Pontiff Who could, and did, crush reigning sovereigns at His will, was not likely to fear a mere duke. The clergy treated Duke Cesare, as always, with profound respect. And—Madonna Lucrezia Borgia, until the very end of his life, maintained friendly relations with him; and it was to her that the death of the Prince of Bisceglia brought most grievous trouble. Evidently the people most intimately concerned with Duke Cesare did not look upon him as an assassin: at any rate, the legend of his guilt subsequently emanated, not from them, but from his foes.

There was a total absence of motive on the part of Duke Cesare, unless the theory of legal but private execution, or the theory of justifiable homicide, be maintained. And for want of proof of strangulation, these can be dismissed with deserved contempt.

But—there was a very strong motive for the stabbing present in the Neapolitan House of Sanseverini, and in the Roman House of Caïetani, who had suffered loss of the principality of Salerno, and of the duchy of Sermoneta, in order to the enrichment of Prince Don Alonso of Bisceglia and Salerno and his infant son Duke Roderico of Sermoneta. Is it probable that great barons of the Fifteenth Century, or of any other century, calmly would submit to deprivation of their choicest fiefs, without at least an

[1] "Il Papa ama ed a gran paura del figliuolo duca."—Alberi, Relationi III. iii. 10.

attempt to gain satisfaction of one or another kind? It may be concluded, then, that in all human probability Prince Don Alonso was the victim of a vendetta. His assassination was a private affair. The assassins were professionals in the pay of Sanseverini, or Caïetani, or both together; who, when the deed apparently was done, (here Burchard recording probability is valuable,) were surrounded by forty knights (Sanseverini or Caïetani of course) and escorted out of the City by the nearest gate, Porta Pertusa behind St. Peter's, (the nearest gate to avoid attracting the attention of the bargelli in Borgo or Trastevere), whence, by a short circuit to the south, they would attain the Via Portuense, sixteen miles of which would bring them to Porto on the right bank of Tiber, opposite to the fortress at Ostia on the left bank belonging to Cardinal Giuliano della Rovere.

.   .   .

At the Eighth Consistory of the twenty-eighth of September 1500, the Lord Alexander P.P. VI named ten cardinals, who were,

- (α) the Lord Don Jaime Serra, a Catalan, Vicegerent of Rome, Cardinal-Presbyter of the Title of San Vitale:
- (β) the Lord . . . Bacocz, an Hungarian, Chancellor of Hungary; Cardinal-Presbyter of the Title of San Martino *ai Monti:*
- (γ) the Lord Don Pedro Isualles, a Sicilian; Cardinal-Presbyter of the Title of San Ciriaco *alle Terme Diocleziane:*
- (δ) the Lord Don Francisco de Borja, bastard of the Lord Calixtus P.P. III; who had lived obscurely from his birth in 1441 until now; Cardinal-Presbyter of the Title of Santa Lucia *in Silice* alias *in Orfea:*

(ε) the Lord Don Juan Vera, a Spaniard, Archbishop of Saliterno; Cardinal-Presbyter of the Title of Santa Balbina:

(ζ) the Lord Alois Podachatarios, a noble of Cyprus, the Pontifical Greek Secretary; Cardinal-Presbyter of the Title of Sant' Agata *in Suburra:*

(η) the Lord Giovantonio Trivulzio, a noble of Milan, elevated to oblige the Christian King Louis XII; Cardinal-Presbyter of the Title of Santa Anastasia:

(θ) the Lord Giambattista Ferrari, Bishop of Modena; Cardinal-Presbyter of the Title of San Crisogono:

(κ) the Lord Gianstefano Ferreri, Abbot of San Stefano di Vercello; Cardinal-Presbyter of the Title of San Sergio e San Bacco:

(ι) the Lord Marco Cornaro, brother of Madonna Caterina Cornaro, Queen of Cyprus; Cardinal-Deacon of Santa Maria *in Portico.*

.   .   .

In view of the danger looming in the near East, the Lord Alexander P.P. VI issued a Bull proclaiming a new Crusade; and addressed a Brief in the same sense to the Christian King Louis XII. Venice being in serious and immediate peril received His help in the shape of money and troops. Nevertheless though Modon fell to the Muslim Infidel, even this disaster, giving point to the Pope's exordium, failed to arouse the Christian Princes of Europe from their disgraceful apathy. The Lord Alexander P.P. VI now imposed a graduated crusade tax on the revenues of the Sacred College, each cardinal being mulcted on the value of his benefices. This, though a righteous and elevating ensample, was looked upon with extreme disgust; for, like other men, cardinals are very sensitive in the pouch. Cardinal Raymond Perauld, forgiven for his treachery with

Charles VIII, was named Apostolic Ablegate to Germany charged with authority to reform the abuses, which avarice and ambition on the part of German prelates were causing, to the shame of all right-minded men. But the Elect-Emperor Maximilian—(who, in a picture by Albrecht Durer in the British Museum, modestly is styled *Imperator Cæsar Divus Maximilianus Pius Felix Augustus;* [1] and, in another, on vellum in the same collection, bears, after the imperial titles, the styles of all sovereigns of Europe, including *Rex Angliæ,* in despite of King Henry VII Tudor then happily reigning,)—the Elect-Emperor Maximilian remembered that in 1496 his ill-advised advance into Venetia had been opposed and not received with obsequious adulation; and he now refused to allow the Papal Ablegate to enter his Empire. In such pettiness did the Holy Roman Emperor of the Habsburg House of Austria have continual joy.

This year in Rome was the Holy Year, the last of the Fifteenth Century, the year of Jubilee. The Holy Father extended the privilege to Christendom; and huge pilgrimages of persons of rank and distinction from all Christian countries save Germany and Switzerland flocked to the

---

[1] This title is hopelessly irregular. The *Princeps* of the Holy Roman Empire only becomes *Caesar Romanorum Imperator Semper Augustus mundi totius Dominus universis dominis universis principibus et populis Semper Venerandus* by the herald's proclamation after he has been stripped, anointed, clothed in the consecrated dalmatica, ordained deacon, and crowned with the Iron Crown of Monza and the Gold Diadem of the Empire by the hands of the Supreme Pontiff Himself. The title at present is dormant. If the sovereign is of the Swabian House, precedent demands that he must go to Monza or to Sant' Ambrogio at Milan for the Iron Crown, and to San Giovanni Laterno at Rome for the Gold Diadem. But Imperial coronations, (the sovereign not being of the Swabian House,) at the Pope's pleasure have taken place elsewhere. Caesar Friedrich IV was the last Emperor crowned in Rome. Caesar Francis II was the last to wear the imperial crown. He resigned it in 1806, having taken the title of Emperor of Austria in 1804. Before coronation by the Pope the title of "The Elect-Emperor" is used; and that is all which Maximilian can claim.

Eternal City throughout the year. The pilgrims' alms considerably added to the papal treasury; and, by order of the Lord Alexander P.P. VI, these exclusively were set aside for the pacification of the States of the Church in the Romagna; a magnificent example of the political foresight which secured the temporal possessions of the Holy See during three hundred and seventy years, till 1870. Before the end of the year 1500 the splendour of Duke Cesare de Valentinois was increased by the title of Gonfaloniere of the Holy Roman Church; and, with the ample funds of the Jubilee, he had enlarged his army by the acquisition of several squadrons of French mercenaries, for a new expedition into the rebellious provinces.

During the first year of the Sixteenth Century, A.D. 1501, the Apostolic Ablegate Cardinal Raymond Perauld came to an agreement with the Diet at Nürnberg: and the project of a Crusade was improved by the formation of a new league of the Papacy with Venice and Hungary, (the two countries which lay at the mercy of the Muslim Infidel;) and by some naval successes with the conquest of Santa Maura by Bishop Giacopo da Pesaro.

.   .   .

In the spring, Duke Cesare marched his reinforced army to beleaguer Faenza. There, the citizens had constructed a bastion during the winter at the convent of the Friars Minor-of-the-Observance outside the walls. On the twelfth of April, this defence was taken by the Duke Cesare, who installed a park of artillery to breach the citadel. The brave Faenzesi made sorties from their city for grain and cattle: but the effect of famine soon began to tell. (This account of the siege is Canon Sebastiano di Zaccaria's.) The rich shared their bread and wine with the poor. When money for paying the soldiers failed, the priests and monks gave the sacred vessels. Women took part in the defence, throwing stones from the walls, or strengthening the gabions with earthworks; while the most daring fought, with casque and pike and harquebus, when their men slept. Matrons prayed in the churches. Barefooted boys and girls ran about the streets praying for Divine Assistance for their fathers on the ramparts. On the eighteenth of April, the sixth day of siege, the assault was made. Duke Cesare had advised the neighbouring princes; and Don Alfonso d'Este, heir of Ferrara, with his heraklean brother the athletic young Cardinal Ippolito were come post-haste to see the sight. (It is worth noting that advantage was taken of this visit to plan a marriage between the young widow Madonna Lucrezia Borgia and Don Alfonso d'Este.) The assault lasted from one o'clock in the afternoon till four. The assailants severely suffered from harquebuses, and flaming darts, and showers of stones, with which the beleaguered greeted them, intrepidly fighting on the smoking débris of their walls. Nothing was seen to equal Faenza's valour; but Duke Cesare's condottieri also gave signal proof of bravery. Don Taddeo della Volpe of Imola, on being struck in the eye by an arrow, tore it out and went on fighting, saying that he was fortunate enough to see but half the danger now. Duke Cesare conceived so great an admiration for the courage of his enemies, as to say that, with an army of Faenzesi, he cheerfully would undertake the conquest of all Italy. During seven hours on the twenty-first of April, artillery bombarded the citadel, which now was little more than a heap of ruins. Every night, some of the beleaguered slid over the walls, and escaped into the camp of Duke Cesare, worn by famine and the fatigue of the siege. On the night of the twenty-second, one Bartolomeo Grammante, a dyer, fled from a fortalice where he was on guard and came to the Duke, saying that there was mutiny in Faenza, that ammunition was exhausted, and offering to point out a moment favourable for assault. Incontinently Duke Cesare hanged this traitorous felon near the city-wall, out of respect for the brave Faenzesi and their admirable resistance. Three days later, the end came. The conquerors offered most honourable terms: complete liberty for the Tyrant Don Astorgio Manfredi, and his relations, to go and come at will; the integrity of his property and payment of his debts; confirmation of all rights and privileges for the citizens.

On the twenty-sixth of April, the municipal officers came to the convent of the Observantines where Duke Cesare lodged; and swore between his hands the feudal oath of fidelity to the over-lord, the Holiness of the Pope. At three o'clock in the afternoon, came also Don Astorgio Manfredi with his kin. This unfortunate youth was only of the age of sixteen years, the servant of his own subjects, and an orphan whose father, Don Galeotto Manfredi, had been murdered by his mother, Madonna Francesca Bentivogli. A Venetian chronicler says of him that he was "a sickly lad (*puto mal san*) but beautiful fair and rosy," obviously rotten with struma; and as such he appears in his portrait in the Palazzo Zauli-Naldi of Faenza, wearing an expression of profound melancholy. The young Tyrant and his bastard brother, Don Gianevangelista Manfredi, (who was of the age of fourteen years, and had had a command during the siege,) received so courteous a reception from Duke Cesare that they decided to remain with him. So far, the behaviour of the Generalissimo appears to have been inspired by noble magnanimity.

And here, there is a lacuna. The history of Don Astorgio becomes blank. Research so far has failed to discover any trace of him for months.

Some time after his capitulation, Don Astorgio and his brother were found incarcerated in the Mola of Hadrian, in the royal apartment which Madonna Caterina Sforza-Riario had vacated on going into exile in France: and of this, also, there has been no explanation yet discovered.

It is permissible to suppose that after Duke Cesare generously had granted their unconditional liberty, some imperious political necessity intervened; such as that Don Astorgio and Don Gianevangelista, held as hostages, would guarantee the tranquillity of Faenza, preventing further rebellion. Duke Cesare's apparent breach of faith is not without its parallels in ancient, modern, and contemporary history; a political crime, perhaps necessary, but for which there is neither extenuation nor excuse.

But later still, the story ends in tragedy. The two boys are said to have been killed, and their bodies cast in Tiber. The only two chronicles which have the slightest value are those of Don Antonio Giustiniani the Orator of Venice, who was in Rome; and of Monsignor Hans Burchard the Papal Caerimonarius, who might have been there: though the originals of these chronicles, be it remembered, are yet to seek.

The former wrote to his government,

"*They say* that this night those two young lords of "Faenza with their steward have been slain and thrown "in Tiber.

The latter records in his journal,

"There were found in Tiber, suffocated and dead, the "lord of Faenza, a youth of about the age of eighteen "years, beautiful and well-shaped, with a stone at his "neck; and two youths bound together by the arms, "the one of fifteen and the other of twenty-five years; "and near them a certain woman, and several others.

It is said also that the victims were floating in Tiber in the sight of all.

The affair is the occasion of another of the calumnies which have been cast upon the House of Borgia. Not one word is said by contemporaries implicating Borgia in this crime: yet the modern fiction-monger or quoad-historian who without hesitation did not place it to Borgia's debit would consider himself guilty of dereliction of duty.

The statements of the Venetian and the German, quoted above, will not bear examination in the light of common sense. A rational and unprejudiced observer will have noticed that Giustiniani does not speak of having seen with his own eyes. He is not imparting official information : he reports a mere *on dit*. But Burchard's account is a miracle of Teutonic completeness at all costs, and lack of sense of the ridiculous. He does not say that he has seen the show. He gives no authority for his statements. But he adds, to Don Astorgio and Don Gianevangelista, a youth of twenty-five, a certain woman, and several others ! Is any reliance to be placed on Burchard, uncorroborated and unashamed ? He says that the corpse of Don Astorgio had a stone at his neck, yet he was floating on Tiber in the sight of all ! How can a cadaver float when weighted with a stone ? The density of Tiber is not like that of the Dead Sea or Droitwich Brine Baths. Also, Tiber notoriously is a swift current, far too turbid to permit a crowd of corpses placidly to float in the sight of all. Also, Tiber exclusively was used for drinking and household purposes, and constantly by all Romans, high and low, for swimming : the heraklean Lord Cardinal Prince Ippolito d'Este swam there. Also, the Borgia were pre-eminently clever—cunning, their calumniators say. Then, is it probable that men of any common sense would offer a hecatomb of assassinations to Tiber, and to the sight of all, weighted only by Burchard's single stone ? Finally, how is it that in the history of Faenza, and of the relations of these young lords, there is not a single allusion to the manner of their death ? The learned Padre Leonetti justly contends that the story of the murder is a mere fabrication ; that the scribes, with Burchard and Giustiniani, have seen no floating bodies ; but that they have contented themselves, according to their custom, with fresh vilifications of the Lord Alexander P.P. VI and of Duke Cesare de Valentinois.

Let it be remembered that Don Astorgio Manfredi was "un puto mal san," a sickly or strumous lad. Let it be remembered how extremely easy it is to kill strong boys off, between their fourteenth and their eighteenth year, simply by depriving them of hope and joy. Let the most pathetic history of Don Astorgio Manfredi, of which the barest briefest extract has been given, let his situation, and that of his young brother Don Gianevangelista, be realized with care; and the humanly natural supposition will arise, that these two died natural deaths due to constitutional defects aggravated by hopeless imprisonment in the Mola of Hadrian.

It would be hard, however, if the enemies of Borgia could find nothing worse to say; and the abominable Messer Francesco Guicciardini of Florence, pandar of France, minion of Ghibelline Colonna, does not fail to make use of that curiously common and invariably inconsequent calumny which mediocrity, in all ages, hurls at genius. He writes, "Astorgio was not deprived of life before having first been used, *they say,* to satiate the passions of a certain person." Under the pen of historians who followed Guicciardini, this "certain person" quite naturally has become the Lord Alexander P.P. VI. It is on the authority of this Guicciardini that writers, far from the scene, and long after the deed, have allowed them to assail an old man, a priest, the Head of the Church, with a shameful and execrable accusation. Did Guicciardini make the very difficult examinations of this problematic corpse which medical-law ordains? He was inspired, and very badly, by his hatred. He has not proved the crimes of the Pope. He has only exhibited the fertility of a monstrously unclean and salacious imagination, the dévergondage of a mind stuffed with reminiscences of Tiberius, of Nero, of Elagabalus! (*Réné, Comte de Maricourt.*)

.   .   .

The Lord Alexander P.P. VI had now reached the summit of His magnificent pontificate. With the States of the Church slowly but surely being brought under domination by the splendid gains of Duke Cesare de Valentinois, with the interested support of the Christian King of France and the Catholic King of Spain, (for the latter had the sense to cease from annoying a powerful pontiff), and with His neighbour the Regno under its weak King Don Federigo of no importance, there was nothing that He might not do for the enrichment of the Papacy or the aggrandisement of the House of Borgia. His policy was beginning to take shape. The enormous and magnificent project, which appears to have dictated all His actions, was assuming a concrete form. Difficulties of every kind had beset Him from the beginning; and difficulties, He doubtless knew, would be His constant portion: but by patience, agility of mind, diplomatic skill, singleness of purpose, and His invincible indomitable will, He had beaten down His opponents one by one, or had turned their opposition into support which now enabled Him to act independently and upon His own initiative.

He made short work with the rebellious barons of Rome. He blasted Don Pierfrancesco Colonna with excommunication. He confiscated the fiefs of the Houses of Colonna and Savelli, both of the Ghibelline faction, who had defied Him by secession to Charles VIII and the unmitigable Cardinal Giuliano della Rovere in 1494. He distributed the titles and estates so acquired among members of the House of Borgia.

On the first of September 1501, He issued a Brief legitimating that bastard of Duke Cesare de Valentinois and a Roman spinster, who had been born in 1498, and was known as Infans Romanus; to whom He gave the name Giovanni, after His favourite son the murdered Duke of Gandia, as well as the duchy of Nepi. But, by a second Brief of the same date (in the Archives of Modena) He declares this Don Giovanni Borgia to be the son *not of the aforesaid Duke (Cesare) but of us and the said spinster*.[1]

There exists no explanation of the contradiction in these

[1] "Non de prefato duca sed de Nobis et dicta muliere soluta."

two Briefs. It is, however, certain that no human temptation could induce a Pope to publish such a statement as
that of the second, unless the thing were true; and, in the
case of a Pope as powerful as the Lord Alexander P.P. VI,
there was no superior power which could force Him against
His will. As to one of the Briefs being truth and the other
falsehood, it may be remembered that there is a general
law, a Necessary Proposition, "The lesser is contained in
the greater." The thing was true. The Lord Alexander P.P.
VI, at the age of sixty-seven years, was the father of Don
Giovanni Borgia, whom He created Duke of Nepi in 1501.

The Lord Alexander P.P. VI was a very great man;
guilty of hiding none of his human weakness: and on this
account a Terror to hypocrites of all ensuing ages. Nothing
in the world is so unpleasant, so disconcerting, so utterly
abhorred, as the plain and naked truth.

.   .   .

After the spoliation of the Houses of Colonna and Savelli
—an act which reduced them from that of premier barons
of the Holy See to a position of such insignificance that they
no more appear in the history of this pontificate,—the
Pope's Holiness married Madonna Lucrezia Borgia to Don
Alfonso d'Este, the heir of Duke Ercole of Ferrara. This
was after her year of widowhood. She was now the wife of
royalty, with a near prospect of a throne, worshipped by
the poor for her boundless and sympathetic charity, by the
learned for her intelligence, by her kin for her loving
loyalty, by her husband for her perfect wifehood and
motherhood, by all for her transcendent beauty and her
spotless name. Why it has pleased modern writers and
painters to depict this pearl among women as a "poison-
bearing maenad" a "veneficous bacchante" stained with revolting and unnatural turpitude, is one of those riddles to
which there is no key. If physiognomy be an index to character, the most superficial inspection of the effigy of Ma-

donna Lucrezia Borgia must put her calumniators to endless
shame. In that simple profile, of features clean-cut, delicate,
refined; in those chaste contours so gently rounded, so
sweetly fresh and feminine; in the carriage of that flavian
head well-poised and nobly frank, there can lurk no taint
of decadent degeneracy. In the Ambrosian Library at
Milan, is a long tress of her beautiful yellow hair, shining
and pale; with her scholarly letters to a learned poet and
cardinal the Lord Pietro Bembo, who had dedicated to her
a genial Dialogue on platonics in Italian; an Elegy in Latin,
in praise of her singing and recitation,

> "quicquid agis, quicquid loqueris, delectat: et omnes
> "praecedunt Charites, subsequiturque decor;

with an Epigram on a gold serpent bracelet that she wore,

ARMILLA AUREA LUCRETIAE BORGIAE FERRARIAE DUCIS
IN SERPENTIS EFFIGIEM FORMATA

> "Dypsas cram: sum facta, Tago dum perluor, aurum
> "tortile nympharum manibus decus; at memor dim
> "Eridani, auditaque tua Lucretia forma,
> "Eliadum ne te caperent electra tuarum,
> "gestandum carae fluvius transmisit alumnae.

Another poet of even greater fame, the limpid Ariosto,
praised Madonna Lucrezia as "a second Lucrece, brighter
for her virtues than the star of regal Rome." And even
a modern writer of the eminence of John Addington
Symonds, (who, in his "Renascence" habitually credits
calumnies against Borgia in his text, half-heartedly refut-
ing the same in footnotes,)—even he says, "Were they (the
calumnies) true, or were they a malevolent lie? Physio-
logical speculation will help but little. *Lucrezia shewed all
signs of a clear conscience.*" Precisely. Then it is right
and reasonable to presume that this much-maligned lady
had a clear conscience; and to surcease from shouting
any longer in the ordure which has been cast upon, and

falls from, her fair memory. Let the fact that Herr Gregorovius, brilliant writer, painstaking scholar, German Protestant, fierce and unscrupulous foe of the papacy and of the House of Borgia, has destroyed all accusations against Madonna Lucrezia, silence all suspicion. In his huge work,[1] devoted entirely to her history he has shewn her to be the victim of inventions due to the paid pens of her Father's enemies.

.   .   .

It would be contrary to human nature, had Colonna and Savelli meekly submitted to the confiscation of their fiefs. Armed resistance was out of the question. The heads of those Houses only saved their lives by flight into exile in discontented Germany: but they were not left without one weapon, the last refuge of the unscrupulous. The anonymous libellous pamphlet or epigram lay to their hands.

In the Region of Monti, (the largest district of Rome, including three of the seven hills, Quirinal, Esquiline, Caelian,) which was inhabited by the faction of Colonna, there stood an antique statue of some river-god whom the Romans called Marforio. In the Region of Parione, by Piazza Navona, which was the heart of the mediæval City, near Palazzo Braschi, there stood another antique statue whom the Romans called Pasquino and said that under him the Book of Wisdom for all time was buried. And it was the fashion to pretend that these two statues conversed on current topics, emitting epigrams in the darkness of the night, which were found in writing on their pedestals in the morning. All persons who had an axe to grind at an enemy's expense made use of this convention: and a folio volume would not contain the witty caustic cynical pasquinades (ecce nomen,) which from the Fifteenth to the Twentieth Century have been found at Pasquino and Marforio. This method of spleen-splitting was not neg-

[1] Gregorovius F., *Lucrezia Borgia.*

lected by Colonna and Savelli. Pasquino became loquacious, bitter, oh and smart—but, smart! One epigram may be quoted as a specimen of the railing accusations brought against the Holiness of the Pope by way of reflection on His alleged simoniacal election, at times when He levied taxes or forced loans for the Crusade, or gave no remission of the chancery fees on promotion to fiefs and benefices.

"ALEXANDER SELLS THE KEYS, THE ALTARS, CHRIST.
"HE BOUGHT THEM; AND HE HAS THE RIGHT TO SELL.

But the most virulent of all anonymous attacks, was a pamphlet called *A Letter to Silvio Savelli* which pretended to have come from the Spanish camp at Taranto. It proclaimed to the Elect-Emperor Maximilian and the sovereigns of Europe the crimes which were said to have been committed by the Lord Alexander P.P. VI, Duke Cesare de Valentinois and Madonna Lucrezia Borgia d'Este: perfidy, carnage, rapine, adultery, incest, the heresy of Bulgaria, simony, assassination. Men who have noticed the rabid inconsequence, the grotesque impossibility and filthiness, which characterises certain foreign abuse of England at the present time, will understand the extent to which envious rage will go. Men of the Twenty-fifth Century, who read that degenerate literature, may attach to it an importance as undeserved as that which the Twentieth Century attaches to the *Letter to Silvio Savelli* of the Fifteenth. Humanity, with slight external differences, is identical in all ages. The Borgia were only men and women, boys and girls, when all is said; and the charges made against them are infinitely too monstrously inhuman to be true. Nature terribly would have avenged Herself on such infringements of Her law.

The Lord Alexander P.P. VI read the *Letter to Silvio Savelli*. It is recorded that His Holiness deigned heartily to laugh with His courtiers over the exaggerated absurdity of the satire. As for its coarseness—the Romans always value *simplicitas* and *urbanitas* of speech, *i.e.,* hideous grossness and brutal jest. As for taking offence—well, Consul Caius Julius Caesar laughed at the crabbed little couplet of Caius Valerius Catullus, and invited him to supper; and the Lord Alexander P.P. VI had lived too many years in Italy not to have taken the correct measure of Milanese, Florentines, Venetians, Neapolitans; and He was well able to apportion its just value to extravagance of praise or to extravagance of blame. With His magnificent dignity of temper, He said that in Rome there was liberty of speech: and that He cared nothing for libels against Himself. (Costabili to Duke of Ferrara, 1 Feb. 1502). They amused Him, if they were witty; they pleased Him, if their language shewed distinction: and that was all.

Duke Cesare de Valentinois was not of so gracious a humour. Towards the end of November after the publication of the *Letter to Silvio Savelli,* a certain Messer Girolamo Manciani, a Neapolitan, was taken in the Region of Borgo on a charge of publishing calumnious epigrams against the Duke which proved him to be the author of the famous *Letter.* His right hand and tongue were promptly cut off and out. Two other defamers employed by the Aragonese Dynasty (as Pontano had been, and Sannazar "the Christian Vergil" was) to flout the Borgia underwent a similar mutilation; and when the Orator of Ferrara spoke of them to the Pope, it is said that He answered, "What can We do? The Duke means well; but he does not know how to bear insults. We often have advised him to follow Our example, and to let the mob say what it will: but he answered Us with choler that he intended to give those scribblers a lesson in good manners." The good heart of the Pope spoke there. The Duke was only carrying out the law, by this severity; laws, which it would ill-become the Lawgiver to set aside. Still, the offence being against the person of that Lawgiver, it was open to Him privately to recommend leniency: and that He did. No man could do more.

．　　　．　　　．

Florence, having cast off the despotic rule of the House of Medici, and settled herself as a true republic, was at peace with the Holy See. After the capitulation of Faenza Duke Cesare de Valentinois was created Duke of the Romagna. King Don Federigo of Naples, apprehensive of danger from the alliance of the Papacy and France set abroad the rumour that the Duke intended to conquer Florence and add it to the pontifical state: and, to curry favour with the Holiness of the Pope, he suggested that Tuscany should be erected into a kingdom, with Duke Cesare de Valentinois della Romagna as its crowned king. This attempt to deflect the wave of conquest into North Italy, and away from his own dominions, met with no success. If Duke Cesare ever had entertained the notion of proceeding against Tuscany, he made no efforts whatever in that direction. On the contrary, it was the Regno that was the object of attention. Chance after chance had been given, alliances diplomatic and matrimonial had been made with it: but it continued to be as a thorn in the eye of the papacy, its sovereigns vicious, treacherous, its people dangerous, degenerate. It was cankered to the core; and its time was come. The Lord Alexander P.P. VI signed a treaty with the Christian and Catholic Kings of France and Spain for the division of Naples. The three signatories each had a claim of sorts: the Pope's Holiness as suzerain of certain fiefs and tyrannies, such as Benevento and Tarracina; the Christian King Louis XII as representative of the Angevin dynasty; the Catholic King Don Hernando as legitimate head of the House of Aragon. And incontinently King Don Federigo de Aragona fled into exile, while his kingdom was divided and given to France and Spain.

In 1502 the plans of the Lord Alexander P.P. VI for the defence of Christendom met with success and rebuff. The Elect-Emperor Maximilian sulkily withdrew his prohibition; and Cardinal Raymond Perauld, as Papal Legate, passed through the Empire preaching the Crusade. But Hungary played traitor to the League which she had formed with Venice and the Papacy a year before; and the Majesty of England, King Henry VII Tudor, refused to help. The last perhaps may be explained by the uneasy condition which the realm owed to rebellions fomented by Burgundy for the affliction of the House of Tudor—those of Lambert Simnel in 1487 and Duke Richard Plantagenet of York (vulgarly called Perkyn Werbecke) in 1494-1499.

The movement in the direction of ecclesiastical reform slowly progressed. Germany was still reiterating the cry which, as long ago as the reign of the Lord Calixtus P.P. III, she had raised anent the extortions of the Papal Chancery; and not by any means without some reason. But then, as now, the cry for reform arose from tainted sources. It was not genuine, or sincere; but only a species of blackmail. However the Lord Alexander P.P. VI was willing enough and he gave the idea due consideration, by the advice of Cardinal Francesco de' Piccolhuomini. But, remembering that this Most Illustrious Lord was a nephew of the Lord Pius P.P. II (who, in His earlier years, had assisted at the Council of Basilea); and had the reputation of being a "concilionista," i.e., one whose remedy for ecclesiastical ills is not a Pope, but a Council; the Supreme Pontiff resolved to delay, until that He should see His way more clearly. In a sense the Pope's Holiness deceived Himself; for Cardinal Francesco de' Piccolhuomini (who succeeded Him as the Lord Pius P.P. III) was, as Cæsar's wife was not, "above suspicion." In ordinary matters, when suitable advice is not forthcoming a Pope is liable to hesitate. Of course, in matters of teaching, His position is secure; but, as has been said, in worldly affairs the Pope-well-advised is superior to the Pope-ill-advised. Seeing no present method of securing permanent reform, the Lord Alexander P.P. VI waited. The fruit was not ripe. The psychological moment had not come. It was well to wait; and to let the movement shape itself: for, later, when the hour of reform sounded there arose the majestic Council of Trent. To the Borgia the world greatly owes the Tridentine Decrees—decrees that govern the Church at this day.

.   .   .

In this year 1502, Duke Cesare de Valentinois della Romagna escorted the Lord Alexander P.P. VI to Piombino when he made a state-progress through the conquered states; shewing Him that from that city He could threaten the Republics of Venice, Siena, and Florence, with the tyrannies of Bologna and Ravenna, the last with its interminable feud of the Sforza and the Pasolini dell' Onda.[1] The chief independent states paid tribute to him. By hideous treachery, he captured the duchies of Urbino and Camerino, drove the Duke into exile, proclaimed an amnesty, and observed it against his worst enemies: but he hanged all those who betrayed to him, loving the treachery, hating the traitors.[2] The duchy of Camerino was conferred upon the four-year-old Duke Giovanni Borgia of Nepi and Camerino.

The Christian King Louis XII had a spasm of envy this year, in consequence of Duke Cesare's phenomenal

[1] The present writer once witnessed the reception, in all amity, by the present Sforza, of the present Pasolini dell' Onda, who came peaceably to gain information for his book in praise of Madonna Caterina Sforza-Riario. A singular example of the old order changed and giving place to new.

[2] "Per dar ad intender a tutti che 'l Signor over Signori hanno appiacer "del tradimento, ma non del traditore." Priuli. xxvi. July 1502.

triumphs; and shewed some signs of interrupting the policy
of the Lord Alexander P.P. VI with cries for a General
Council. A model of his, bearing his effigy with the lilies
of France and the legend *Perdam Babylonis Nomen,* made
a great sensation in Rome.[1] But French motives never are
disinterested. The moment another Power wins a success
by expenditure of blood and treasure, that is the time for
pretentious incompetent France, *cane che abbaia non
morde,* to clamour for a share of what she never won,
never could hope to win,—for what, with inconsequent
impertinence, she calls "compensation"! The Holy Roman
Church was not worse off, under the rule of the Lord Alexander P.P. VI, but better off than it had been before: but
the election of His Holiness was always useful as a means
of blackmail. However, Duke Cesare was Generalissimo of
an enormous army. In addition to the four thousand condottieri and three hundred lancers with which he had begun
the campaign, he had enlisted the many thousand mercenaries of the Tyrants whom he had dispossessed, and also
recruited far and wide throughout Italy, where all the
temperamental fighters gladly took service under the most
successful general. And to these he added a foreign bat-
talion of three thousand five hundred fantassini (infantry), pikemen and arbalisters, all Frenchmen, of whose
quality the Christian King was well aware; and, therefore,
sensible enough to refrain himself before a worse thing
happened to him. Indeed, such was his anxiety to give evidence of his desire for peace that he actually offered,—he,
the Christian King of France, the representative of the
Angevin dynasty, offered to resign his claim to the kingdom of Naples in favour of Duke Cesare de Valentinois
della Romagna. He was painfully anxious not to purchase
a General Council at the cost of the conquest of France;
and preferred that a Borgia sovereign, (if such a person-

[1] Costabili to Duke of Ferrara. Rome, xi. Aug. 1502.

age were to be,) should reign in Naples rather than in Paris.

The Romagna immensely was benefited by a strong and decent government where law—martial law, certainly; but law—at last was observed. Duke Cesare's army was the only great Italian army. He, representing the Pope, was absolute in Central Italy, where no Pope had had direct authority for centuries. He was hated; hated by the great baronial Houses which he had ruined, whose heirs he had slain: but he was not even disliked by the people whom he ruled.[1] It was not extraordinary; for the mob always adores the strong bowelless man, the rigid fearless despot, the conquering autocrat who brings peace with security. He took no different measures against rebellious vassals than those taken by his contemporaries, Louis XII of France, Hernando of Spain, Henry VII Tudor of England. He was more precise, more systematic: that is all. All the sovereigns who were his contemporaries congratulated him. The Duke was cruel; almost as cruel as his splendid parallel of the Nineteenth Century; and as fervently disliked and decried: but he was just, with a justice as far above the mawkish humanitarian system of compromise, (which nowadays it is the mode to applaud,) as the sun is above the stars. Through the length and breadth of his dominions he continually went, to oversee the restoration of order, to consolidate his victories. The slightest spark of opposition he relentlessly crushed out. It was a hundred-headed hydra with which he had to deal. As he passed from city to city of his provinces, he left governors in charge of each, bloody men, ruthless giants, equal to the work in hand; for the work was dangerous; and men, whose hearts were triply-cased in hardened bronze, were

[1] "Aveva il duca gittate assai buoni fondamenti alla potenza sua, "avendo tutta la Romagna con il ducato d'Urbino, e guadagnatosi "tutti quei populi, per avere incomminciato a gustare il ben essere "loro." (Machiavelli. Il Principe. Op. i. 35.)

needed, where each man's life was in his own hands until it was in his enemy's. Messer Leonardo da Vinci, that "scientific sceptic," was his engineer in chief and designer of fortifications: and Messer Niccolo Machiavelli said that, of all Princes, he could discover no ensample more blooming and more vigorous than Duke Cesare. The headquarters of the Duke were at Cesena; and that same Messer Niccolo Machiavelli—the only man who ever knew the real Cesare (detto Borgia) naked face to naked face, naked soul to naked soul,—advised the Signoria of Florence that an Orator kept at Cesena would profit the republic more than an Orator at Rome.[1] In his absences from headquarters, Duke Cesare left Messer Ramiro d'Orco there as governor. Cesena was a nest of would-be brigands. Messer Ramiro d'Orco was a governor who made these quail with the steel of his garrison and his own iron will.

It was the winter of 1502. Snow lay deeply round Cesena. In the Citadel the governor was at supper by the hearth, where huge logs blazed and crackled. Halberdiers were standing in attendance; and, on the walls wax torches flamed in their sockets, for the sun was set and the first hour of the night was come. Messer Ramiro d'Orco called for wine; and a page brought a fresh flagon from the buffet. He stumbled among the rushes on the floor in coming, tripped over the feet of a guard; and the falling flagon spilled the wine on the ankle of Messer Ramiro d'Orco. That monster made no more ado. He took the lad by the belt, and slung him into the fire, seizing the nearest halberd and pinning the twitching body to the flaming logs. The hair, in a flash, was gone. The slim legs violently writhed outward, and fell still. Hose and leathern jerkin peeled, and the white flesh hissed and blackened. Then, naught

[1] "Se ne ha contentare costui, e non il Papa, e per questo le cose "che si concludessino del Papa possono bene essere ritrattate da "costui, ma quelle che si concludessino da costui non saranno gia "ritrattate dal Papa." (Dispatch from Cesena xiv. Dec. 1502.)

but small ash showed where a boy had died; and the smell of roasted human flesh mingled with the smell of the meats. Again, Messer Ramiro d'Orco called for wine, unmoved, only inconvenienced. He was the governor of Cesena: he had but punished a clumsy serving-boy.

That is the kind of man who could rule in the Romagna: and it easily will be understood that acting in this way, armed with plenipotentiary authority, Messer Ramiro d'Orco froze his district into a state of comparative tranquillity—a state which gave him the opportunity of looking further afield, and, so it happened, fatally for himself. A very little cruelty of this callosity goes far. Even truculent Cesena grew faint with horror of this fiend.

Duke Cesare acted upon the principle that it is better to be feared than loved—*if one must choose:* but he knew that there is a point beyond which no wise ruler goes: he knew the supreme art of making an end. Murmured rumours of atrocities reached his ears. Sooner or later he would have to bear the odium of the ill-deeds of his deputy. He never shirked responsibility. To shine in the reflected glare of Messer Ramiro d'Orco's evil fame would not suit his purpose. And there were other things.

On the twenty-second of December, when the setting sun cast long blood-red lights across the snow, without warning Duke Cesare galloped into Cesena with an armed escort of lancers. The cowed Cesenesi, turning out of doors to do him reverence, caught bare glimpses of flashing mail and the bull-bannerols of Borgia passing over the drawbridge of the citadel. Presently, from that citadel came Messer Cipriano di Numai, the Duke's secretary, to the house of Messer Domenico d'Ugolini, the treasurer; seeking the governor in the city. Messer Ramiro d'Orco was arrested, and conducted to the presence of his chief.

Surmise that night was rife as to the import of these acts. New vengeance? New taxes? New horror? None could say.

The next morning, letters-patent went to all cities of the Romagna proclaiming that Duke Cesare had arrested his governor Messer Ramiro d'Orco, on the charge of numberless frauds, illegal cruelties, and other crimes. The plaints of the oppressed had grieved the Duke, natural enemy of exaction, avarice, and cruelty, who, having freed the citizens from the ancient terror, wished to impose no new charges on them. The letters-patent concluded, "for the doing of justice to Ourself and to all persons who "have been injured, and for a salutary example to all Our "servants present and future, Messer Ramiro d'Orco will "stand his trial on depositions against him collected.

The trial was not a long one. Legally put to the Torture of the Question, that frightful ruffian admitted the truth of the said depositions; and, chiefly he accused himself of having sold the store of corn belonging to the province, applying the price to his own purposes, to such an extent that Duke Cesare only averted a famine by importing a fresh supply from foreign countries. Lastly, Messer Ramiro d'Orco confessed that he was conspiring with the Orsini to betray to them the city of Cesena; and with Don Vitellozzo Vitelli, Tyrant of Citta di Castello, and Don Oliverotto da Fermo, to pose an arbalister [1] to assassinate Duke Cesare with a bolt from his arbalist.[2] Citizens of Cesena who passed the little square before the citadel, going to the dawn-mass of Christmas-Day, saw a joyful sight—the Justice of the Duke. They saw a glittering axe, fixed in a block upon the snow. They saw on the one side a headless body in rich garments, exposed on a blood-stained mat upon the snow. They saw on the other side the bodiless head of Messer Ramiro d'Orco on a pike.

All chroniclers of the period congratulate Duke Cesare on having delivered his subjects from a tyrannous subaltern as cruel as he was rapacious; and Machiavelli records

[1] Arcuballistarius=cross-bow-man.
[2] Arcuballista=cross-bow.

that His Excellency was pleased to shew that he had the power to make men—and to mar them. Duke Cesare in teaching made use of the sense of sight. He made the peoples of the Romagna see his power, see his justice, see his everpresent indefatigable energy. What wonder then that he was looked upon as superhuman. In the citadel of Cesena a milder governor reigned.

Leaving Cesena on the Festival of St. Stephen, Duke Cesare reached Pesaro on the twenty-eighth of December, where he learned that the conspirators whom Messer Ramiro d'Orco had betrayed, (except the Baglioni of Perugia, and Don Giulio and Don Giovanni Orsini who were in Rome with Cardinal Giambattista Orsini and other prelates of their faction) were at Sinigaglia, which place they were supposed to be besieging on the Duke's behalf; and they sent to him to announce that they had captured the city, but that the governor refused to surrender the citadel save to the Generalissimo in person. Duke Cesare sent avant couriers heralding his arrival with artillery.

At dawn on the Festival of St. Sylvester, the thirty-first of December, he appeared before Sinigaglia. His trusty confidant and captain Don Michelotto led the van with two hundred lancers. Behind these Duke Cesare rode, accompanied by three and a half thousand Italian condottieri and as many foreigners. At the city-gate, Don Michelotto halted his cavalry on the bridge, and the infantry defiled between their ranks, entering the city where the forces of Don Oliverotto da Fermo were paraded. Don Paolo and Don Francesco Orsini, Duke of Gravina, also were present, with Don Vitellozzo Vitelli who wore an ermine mantle and rode a mule like any cardinal. Duke Cesare appeared to be pleased at seeing them and allowed them to kiss his hand in the French style. The atrocious character of these brigands already has been described.

Duke Cesare engaged them in conversation, siding with Don Francesco Orsini and Don Vitellozo Vitelli. When they reached the palace which he was to occupy, the four prepared to take their leave; but he begged them to stay and dine, and to assist him in certain deliberations. As soon as they had crossed the threshold, the Duke's gentlemen made them prisoners.

Messer Niccolo Machiavelli, the official representative of the Signoria of Florence on the staff of Duke Cesare, (a capacity equivalent to that of foreign attaché with an army in the field,) reached Sinigaglia later in the day; and found the city filled with the Ducal mercenaries, who were engaged in stripping the troops of the conspirators and in doing a little pillage of some Venetian merchants. He was going to the palace to get the news, when Duke Cesare rode out, armed cap-à-pie, and said to him, "I have had a chance, and I have taken it; and I have done a service that should cause your Signoria to rejoice." Then he rode away and reduced his turbulent troops to order.

During the night the fate of the conspirators was decided. In deference to their rank, the two Orsini were to be sent to Rome and judged there according to law: meanwhile they were detained at the palace of Sinigaglia under guard. The trial of the others began at once. Put to the Torture of the Question in the usual manner, they soon shewed of what poor stuff they were made. The lily-livered assassin Don Oliverotto da Fermo wept and groaned and reproached Don Vitellozo Vitelli with having led him— innocent lamb as he was—into mischief by inducing him to intrigue against Duke Cesare. On the first day of the new year 1503, at four o'clock in the morning, they were ceremonially strangled in the courtyard of the palace. While Don Vitellozo was struggling with the carnefex, dying by slow degrees, with blackening face and bulging eyes, he screamed continually to Duke Cesare begging hard that he would implore the Lord Alexander P.P. VI to grant him absolution after death and a plenary indulgence, until the red cord (which was his baronial privilege) cut into his gullet, and stilled his swollen tongue.

An example of this kind can leave no doubt in the mind but that, in spite of all to the contrary, the Pontifex Maximus of Rome, simoniacally elected or not, implicitly and explicitly was regarded then as God's Vicegerent, as Earthly Vicar of Christ, by the most flagitious of men. Then what can be thought of the good and clean-living majority?

The bodies were buried in the chapel of the hospice of the Misericordia, the Brotherhood of Pity, one of whose obligations is the care of criminals condemned on the capital charge.

This account of the *colpo-di-stato* of Sinigaglia differs from that to which the world is accustomed. It is said that, when Messer Niccolo Machiavelli returned to Florence, he was induced to make a different statement to the one which he previously had made from personal observation in his first dispatches. According to this second version, there was no conspiracy; and the brigands Vitelli and da Fermo were simply massacred by order of Duke Cesare. It is the execrable Messer Francesco Guicciardini who has prostituted his golden pen to record this so-called version of Machiavelli, which has come to be regarded as veracious history.

"Duke Cesare de Valentinois, acknowledged sovereign of the Romagna, judged his subjects who were guilty of high treason: as chief of the State, he condemned the assassins who sought his life: as generalissimo, he punished treacherous and rebellious subalterns. It is known from other sources, that these two barons were only brigands stained with murders, and that their death was a deliverance for Italy. Without insisting on this point, and if it be said that the procedure of Duke Cesare was odious,—the capture by a ruse and the summary execution,—it may be pointed out that everywhere and in all ages criminals are taken by whatever method may be possible, and that military tribunals have never wasted time in long formalities. There was accusation, trial, and execution, all in regular though rapid form. We well may call the action of Duke Cesare a coup-d'-Etat. He is not more blameworthy than the

Emperor Napoleon III who in 1852 was loudly applauded. Neither is it necessary for his justification to urge the barbarous customs of his age; for we should be forced to remember that, in the Nineteenth Century, our (French) national hero, in a time of peace, caused to be seized on foreign territory, to be carried to Vincennes, and, after the mockery of a trial, to be shot like a dog in the castleditch, an innocent man who was a prince of the blood-royal of France. [Duc d'Enghien?] Yet no man has ever dared to liken the Emperor Napoleon I to a Borgia! (*Réne, Comte de Maricourt.*)

The news reached Rome on the night of the second of January. The blow had been struck with such rapidity as to put complicity of the Lord Alexander beyond the dimensions of time and space.

In the Eternal City, the year had opened with the ceremony called L'Ubbedienza, in which the cardinals renew their vow of fidelity to the Pope, as, formerly, Roman Senators vowed fidelity to the Princeps on each New Year's Day. A cardinal, who would omit this duty except for a valid reason, would cause precisely such a scandal as P. Thrasea Paetus caused to Tacitus by neglecting to swear to Nero. Notwithstanding this renewal of allegiance on the first of January, only three days later the Pope's Holiness found reason to arrest Cardinal Giambattista Orsini, with Archbishop Alviano of Florence, and Don Giacomo Poplicola di Santacroce, Orsini's partisans, being determined once for all to crush that House of incorrigible rebels. This Don Giacomo Poplicola di Santacroce had only himself to blame. His House, the most illustrious of all the sixty conscript families of Rome, had been outlawed in 1482 by the Lord Xystus P.P. IV by reason of the furious feud between Santacroce and Dellavale which had turned the Eternal City for months together into shambles. He should have known better than to put his head in the lion's mouth. Giustiniani, the Orator of Venice, received an account of what had happened from the Pope's Own mobile lips; and embodied the same in a dispatch to his government dated the fourth of January 1503. It appears to be perfectly logical on the part of

the Pope's Holiness, that, in view of the coming trial of
the two Orsini whom Duke Cesare was bringing to Rome,
evidence should be sought among the members of their
faction.

The behaviour of Orsini was impolitic and suspicious to
the last degree. They were under the shadow. Two of their
alleged accomplices had been executed at Sinigaglia. The
cardinal was detained in the Mola of Hadrian. Don Paolo
Orsini and Duke Francesco Orsini of Gravina were prisoners of Duke Cesare. Their circumstances required a
patient policy of inaction pending coming trial, the result
of which they needed not to fear supposing them to be
innocent of conspiracy. On the contrary, they gave clear
evidence of guilt, desperately maintaining an armed rebellion in pontifical territory, ravaging the Viterbo country, and continuing to make leagues with other rebels
whether these were Roman barons or chiefs of independent
banditti.

The Orator of Venice wrote to his government on the
seventeenth of January: "The Pontiff is much disturbed,
and more than ever on his guard. They say that Colonna
and Savelli and all the discontented barons have joined
Orsini. This night there was a panic at the Vatican: no
one knows the cause. The captain of the guard called out
his troops and watched all night under arms."

Prince Gioffredo Borgia of Squillace, now in his twenty-
second year and father of four children, raised a squadron
of condottieri and attacked his August Father's enemies:
but on the night of the twentieth of January, the Orsini
cavalry captured the Bridge of Nomentano where a fortress was; and all the Borgo rose in tumult. Messer Francesco Remolino Bishop of Sorrento, and the Orator of
Siena, left the City for the camp of Duke Cesare carrying
orders that he should leave everything and advance on
Rome, which was in imminent peril. But before the envoys
reached him, on the night of the seventeenth of January,

at Citta di Pieve he suddenly had beheaded Don Paolo Orsini and Duke Francesco Orsini of Gravina, the two prisoners to whom he had promised a legal trial in Rome. The attitude of Orsini perfectly justified Duke Cesare in exercising his rights as sovereign justiciary and breaking his promise. His camp was surrounded by Orsini castles, the two barons undoubtedly were caught in the article of conspiracy; and their summary decapitation became a sudden necessity to intimidate the Orsini conspirators in and about Rome. It was not the custom of the Sixteenth Century to mince matters, from any silly humanitarian motives, by sacrificing thousands of proletariat lives when the fierce slaughter of a brace of notabilities would serve the purpose. The modern accusation, that the Lord Alexander P.P. VI was privy to the execution of these two Orsini, falls to the ground when the dates of His dispatches to Duke Cesare, and of their deaths, are compared.

Cardinal Giambattista Orsini remained a state-prisoner in the Mola of Hadrian, within whose walls he had full liberty. By his own request, his food was sent in daily from his own House; and also he received visits from his relations. There he lived, attended by his own physicians, until the twenty-second of February when he died, and was buried in the church of San Salvatore *in Lauro*. Soon it was said that the Pope's Holiness had envenomed him; and this is a charge which it is utterly difficult to prove.

Giustiniani, the Orator of Venice, who was a friend of the House of Orsini, and always inimical to the Borgia, said without explanation or remark in a dispatch to his government dated the fifteenth of February: "The Lord Cardinal Orsini in prison shows signs of frenzy."

In the dispatch dated the twenty-second of February, he said: "The Lord Cardinal Orsini is reduced to the last extremity, and his physicians say that there is no hope of saving his life."

In the dispatch dated the twenty-third of February, he

said: "I give notice that, yesterday, after the departure of my courier, the Lord Cardinal Orsini died; and this evening, with an honourable escort, he was taken to the church of San Salvatore, and there interred."

Brancatalini, in his Diarium, wrote: "This day XXII February 1503, Cardinal Orsini left the Castle of Santangelo dead, at a half-hour of the night; (5.30-6 P.M.) and Mariano di Stefano with many other Romans accompanied him, and he was borne to San Salvatore *in Lauro.*"

Soderini, Orator of the Signoria of Florence, in a dispatch dated the twenty-third of February 1503 wrote to his government:

"Cardinal Orsini died yesterday: and was buried at the twenty-fourth hour (5-5.30 P.M.) at San Salvatore the church of the House of Orsini; and, by order of the Pope, the body was escorted by his relations, and by the cardinals of the Curia, uncovered and resting on a bier draped with cloth-of-gold, vested in a red chasuble brocaded with golden flowers, on the head was a white mitre, and at the feet were two hats in token of his cardinalitial rank. The monks performed the funeral service; and there were about sixty or seventy lighted torches. May he rest in peace."

Obviously, the Orators of the Powers had no suspicion of venom. Giustiniani gladly would have reported such a rumour had he found himself in a position to do so which would have been consistent with his dignity and duty to the Venetian Senate. When He heard what His enemies were saying, the Lord Alexander P.P. VI took prompt action. On the day after the obsequies He convoked the physicians who had attended the dead Cardinal during his illness and agony; and required them to certify that death was owed to natural causes without any violence due to venom or other means; He made them swear on the Sacrament to the truth of their depositions, which were recorded with the facts of the case in the usual form.

It was customary to consider certain signs as indicating venom; *e.g.,* the spots, the colour, the odour of the corpse. There is no mention made of these. The Pope's Holiness ordered a public funeral, the body was uncovered; and carried openly through Rome. Every one might see it; and, had the Orsini faction discovered any signs which pointed to an unnatural death they surely would have proclaimed their suspicions. The interment on the day after death was, and is, the wholesome Roman custom. The hour, after sunset, was, and is, the hour of burial.

It has been said by modern idealists that the Lord Alexander P.P. VI envenomed Cardinal Orsini in order to inherit his riches. The idea is absurd and ridiculous; for the Orsini would have been the heirs of their dead kinsman. In fact they were. The imputation discredits itself by reason of the gross ignorance on which it is based. It is alleged that the Pope is the heir-at-law of cardinals. He is. But He was not, in the reign of the Lord Alexander P.P. VI. It was the Lord Julius P.P. II (1503-1513) who cupidinously issued the Bull which names the Roman Pontiff heir-at-law of all cardinals, and of all clergy dying in Rome; and this Pope (as Cardinal Giuliano della Rovere) was no friend to Borgia. And this fact ought to dispose of all allegations of cupidinal motive in this, as in other cases.

The Lord Alexander P.P. VI had the Orsini at His mercy. Duke Cesare had executed two chiefs of that House. The Cardinal was secure in the impregnable Mola of Hadrian. If the Pope's Holiness had wished to rid Himself of this one He was quite strong enough to do so, without resort to venom, by a regular execution in public, or in private if preferred, and so defy the odium which inevitably attends the exhibition of venom. But that He had no intention of visiting His prisoners with death, or with anything more than incarceration to keep them out of mischief, may be seen from the fact that a few months later (August 1503) Archbishop Alviano of Florence was released alive and well from the Mola of Hadrian.

As there appears to have been no motive and no necessity for the alleged crime, so also there appears to have been no possibility of its commission. Cardinal Giambattista Orsini was visited daily by his people, and his food was brought to him by them. His physicians also made deposition on oath that his death was not caused by venom.

It is only reasonable to conjecture, then, that being a very old man, *conscius criminis sui* (conspiracy), alarmed by the execution of his accomplices, terrified at his own peril, he succumbed to an entirely natural collapse. The dysentery, which carried him off, goes to support this theory.

.   .   .

The French in the Regno were not prospering; and the favour of the papacy appeared to be leaning towards Spain. The Crusade languished, not for lack of funds (for the Pope's Holiness envoyed a grant of money to Hungary); but because of the want of martial spirit on the part of, and the customary disgraceful dissensions among the Christian Powers. Venice and Hungary threw up the sponge, and came to terms with the Muslim Infidel. The conquest of Eastern Europe and the settlement of the Turks therein was an accomplished fact.

.   .   .

Duke Cesare de Valentinois della Romagna occupied Pesaro. This was the fief of that young Tyrant, Don Giovanni Sforza, whose marriage with Madonna Lucrezia Borgia had been annulled by a canonical impediment. The spoliation of his appanage was a ground of fresh offence. The rupture between the Houses of Borgia and Sforza was irremediable. People spoke of Duke Cesare, now, as the Caesar Augustus of a new Roman Empire, independent, and ruled by the sceptre of a Princeps of the House of Borgia. After the execution of the conspirators at Sinigaglia, the Venetian Chronicler Priuli, who loathed the very

name of Borgia, wrote on the eleventh of January 1503:
"Some wish to make and crown him King of Italy; others
wish to make him Emperor: for he prospers so that no
one dare forbid him anything." [1]

The establishment of a Borgia Dynasty would have
been no treason against the rights of the Papacy. The
rebellious tyrants whom Duke Cesare had overthrown
were unprofitable and even menacing. In their place was
the Duke who brought law, order, and prosperity. Of
course Duke Cesare derived benefit from his victories. The
labourer is worthy of his hire, and even successful English
generals are not begrudged their peerages. Duke Cesare's
duchy of Romagna, his commanding position, his power
to enrich himself by the taxation of his subjects, were a
fair reward for the immense services which he had rendered. The Papacy had now, instead of a lost territory
infested by the scum of European ruffianry refusing to
acknowledge authority or natural law, a vast province inhabited by law-abiding prosperous contented vassals ready
and glad to pay the traditional tribute to their over-lord, in
return for the unwonted safety of their lives and property.
Duke Cesare was in the position of a viceroy. He held
office at the pleasure of the Roman Pontiff. He was persona ingrata to the rulers of the other Italian states, who
were envious of his splendid beauty, of his imperious character, of his extraordinary success, and of his tremendous
potentiality. And they feared this tawny prince who had
the tiger-strength to crush them one and all. Backed by the
spiritual and temporal influence and wealth of the Pontiff,
he could keep his irresistible army of veterans always on
a war-footing, and himself its generalissimo; and so the
Papacy itself acquired, through him, and in him, and for

---

[1] "Alcuni lo volevano far Re d' Italia, e coronarlo, altri lo
volevano fa Imperatore, perche 'l prosperava talmente, che non era
alcuno li bastasse l'animo d'impedirlo in cosa alcuna." (xi. Jan.
1503.)

the first time, a material basis of independence: while, in opposition to the Pope, he could not exist.

There was the policy of the Lord Alexander P.P. VI.

He planned it with deliberation. He spared no pains to put it into effect. He did not want to ruin the Church, because She was the foundation upon which He would build His dynasty. Something of the kind was of absolute and imperious necessity. The Forged Decretals and Donation of Constantine, (which foist had been put forth in a Brief of the Lord Hadrian P.P. I to the Emperor Charlemagne,) "the magic pillars of the spiritual and temporal monarchy of the Popes," severely had been criticized as early as the Twelfth Century. It was left, however, to Messer Lorenzo della Valla mercilessly to denounce them as forgeries in 1440, as already has been shewn here. When the Lord Alexander P.P. VI ascended the pontifical throne fifty-two years later, both Decretals and Donation had been thrown overboard from the Barque of Peter, to lighten the ship: and the Pope had no title-deeds to shew, forged or otherwise, for Peter's Patrimony. Any diplomatist would see that a right, of some kind more inexpugnable than Prescription, was desirable. The Lord Alexander P.P. VI chose Conquest, and the Founding of a Borgia Dynasty. The office of the Church He magnified, that She the better might help the state. He intended that His descendants, members of the House of Borgia, though nominally the vassals should be the suzerains of His Successors: that Borgia should wear the double-crown of Princeps, as well as, and by means of the triple-crown of Pontifex Maximus,—that a dynasty of Borgia should occupy both pontifical and imperial thrones.

There was ruin in the scheme: but not that ruin which vulgarly might be supposed.

It was an intelligent enough policy—of a worldly sort. Only—it was not inspired by religion, nor restrained by morality. When it fell to pieces, the Lord Julius P.P. II was able of its fragments alone to build the Papal States which lasted more than three centuries and a half until 1870.

The power of the House of Borgia was so well founded that the mere death of the Lord Alexander P.P. VI would not have affected it. There was a strong party of Spanish cardinals in the Sacred College, and three of these were of the House of Borgia. The Vicegerent of Rome, the Lord Jaime Serra, Cardinal-Priest of the Title of San Vitale, was a Spaniard also. The Roman barons, Colonna, Orsini, Savelli, Dellavalle were broken; Poplicola di Santacroce outlawed; Sforza-Visconti of Milan, Sforza of Santafiora, Sforza of Chotignuola, Sforza of Pesaro, Sforza-Riario of Imola and Forli, all were exiled. The Roman Cesarini were loyal to Borgia, and had their Cardinal (Giuliano) in the Curia. Spain was friendly, and occupied in the New World. France was friendly, and feeble. Germany was feeble and internally distracted. England was only a fifth-rate power. And the invincible army of Duke Cesare de Valentinois della Romagna was ready to carry into effect its leader's will. But chance, molecules, Providence,—the reader will choose,—disabled Duke Cesare, made him unable to act, or unwilling to act,—the reader again will choose,—at the very moment when his action was imperatively necessary. If, on the death of the Lord Alexander P.P. VI he had had his health, he easily might have done anything, said Machiavelli.[1]

> "The Worldly Hope Men set their Hearts upon
> Turns Ashes—or it prospers; and, anon,
>   Like Snow upon the Desert's dusty Face,
> Lighting a little Hour or two—is gone.[2]

.   .   .

At the Ninth Consistory of the thirtieth (or thirty-first) of May (or June), 1503, the Lord Alexander P.P.

[1] "Se nella morte di Alessandro fusse stato sano, ogni costa gli era facile." (Machievelli, Principe, Op. I. 39.)

[2] Fitzgerald's Rubaiyat of Omar Khaiyam, xvi.

VI named nine cardinals; five of whom were Spaniards, three Italians, and one German. They were:

(α) the Lord Don Juan de Castellar, Bishop of Oleron; Cardinal-Presbyter of the Title of Santa Maria *in Trastevere tit. Calixtus:*

(β) the Lord Don Francisco Remolino, Bishop of Sorrento, a friend of Duke Cesare; Cardinal-Presbyter of the Title of San Giovanni e San Paolo:

(γ) the Lord Don Francisco de Sprata, Bishop of Leon; Cardinal-Presbyter of the Title of San Sergio e San Bacco:

(δ) the Lord Francesco Soderini da Volterra, Canon of the Vatican Basilica; Cardinal-Presbyter of the Title of Santa Susanna *inter Duas Domos:*

(ε) the Lord Niccolo da Flisco, Bishop of Forli, Orator of the Republic of Genoa to the Christian King; Cardinal-Presbyter of the Title of Santa Prisca:

(ζ) the Lord Adriano Castellense di Corneto, Orator of the Lord Innocent P.P. VIII to Britannia Barbara (Scotland); Cardinal-Presbyter of the Title of San Crisogono:

(η) the Lord Melchior Copis, Bishop of Brixen; Cardinal-Presbyter of the Title of San Niccolo *inter Imagines:*

(θ) the Lord Don Jaime Casanova, Apostolic Prothonotary; Cardinal-Presbyter of the Title of San Stefano *in Monte Celio:*

(ι) the Lord Don Francisco Iloris, Apostolic Treasurer, Cardinal-Deacon of Santa Maria Nuova.

Why a learned Catholic historian [1] should go out of his way to call this a simoniacal creation, and his English

---

[1] Pastor L. *History of the Popes,* edited by Fr. Frederick Antrobus of the Oratory.

editor to repeat the calumny, is hard to say. It is bad policy to cry stinking fish, at all times; it is especially silly to do so when the fish are fresh. The Bull *De Simoniaca Electione* directed against Simony was not issued until 1505, in the reign of the Lord Julius P.P. II; and it was not retrospective. In 1503, the Lord Alexander P.P. VI was actually a temporal sovereign, "an Italian Despot with certain sacerdotal additions." The cardinals were the highest degree of His peerage. No doubt they paid for their promotion in the usual way; fees to officials, the crusade-tax on the revenues of their Titles, perhaps even a handsome contribution to the Treasury: but why call this Simony, when it was not Simony *stricte dicte* till two years later? A Red Hat no more can be bought than Strawberry Leaves. A man may use his gold to recommend himself for these head-gears. A man may present £25,000 to the best of all princesses' Hospital Fund, or land worth a quarter of a million to the proletariat; he may "bang a saxpence" in fees to officials for his knighthood, he even may pay pounds sterling in fees to officials for his barony: but he righteously would be enraged if people said that he had bought his knighthood or his barony. The word Simony must be taken as belonging to the Genus *Blessed,* (*e.g.,* Mesopotamia;) or as the bark of a dog who dare not bite. Either it is a mere incantation; or a warwhoop "full of sound and fury signifying nothing." In sober logical earnest, it is inapplicable here.

.   .   .

As the heat of summer increased, the Lord Alexander P.P. VI, now of the age of seventy-two years, used to sit and take the air in the shady gardens of the Vatican, and amuse Himself by watching two little boys at play. They were His bastard and his grandson; Duke Giovanni Borgia of Nepi and Camerino, of the age of five years;

and Duke Roderico of Sermoneta, Madonna Lucrezia's son, of the age of four years.

.   .   .

When the sun entered the constellation of Leo—Sol in Leone, the dog-days—the heat became abnormal; and plague and fevers appeared in Rome.[1] The Orators of the Powers promptly made arrangements to quit the City, for a cool and wholesome villegiatura.

Don Antonio Giustiniani, the Orator of Venice, sent to his Senate a dispatch dated the eleventh of July 1503, in which he wrote: "I went to the palace; and, on entering His apartment, I found our Lord the Pope in His habits reclining on a couch. He received me with good humour, saying that for three days He had been inconvenienced by a slight dysentery, but that He hoped it would be unimportant."

On the next day Giustiniani wrote: "The Pope's Holiness reviewed His troops from a balcony."

On the fourteenth of July, he wrote again: "I went to the palace; and, on entering, I found His Holiness on His throne in the Hall of Pontiffs. He was a little depressed: but looked well."

Messer Francesco Fortucci, the Orator of Florence, sent to his Signoria a dispatch dated the twentieth of July, in which he wrote: "There are many people sick of fevers, and many have died."

On the twenty-second of July, he wrote: "I thank the Signoria for lease of absence, because I myself am un-

---

[1] A comical side-light on this naïve age is given in the Annales Bononiensis, (Muratori xxiii. 890) on the occasion of an outbreak of plague. Penitence, fasting, and flagellation were resorted to. Butchers closed their shops for eight days. And, that sorrow for sin was not confined to respectable people may be gathered from the fact that "meretrices ad concubita nullum admittebant. Ex eis quâdam quae cupiditate lucri adolescentem admiserat, depreheusâ, aliae meretrices ita illius nates nudas corrigiis percusserunt ut sanguinem emitteres."

easy, and almost out of my mind with fright; for so many people are dying of fever, and there is also something like the Pest."

On the evening of the fifth of August, the Lord Alexander P.P. VI rode with Duke Cesare and several prelates to a supper *al fresco* at the villa of the Cardinal of San Crisogono outside the walls. Rome and the surrounding country are particularly unwholesome, though cool, during the hour after sunset. It is said that the Holiness of the Pope was much heated by the exertion of riding there; and that, while He was in this condition, He drank a cup of wine for the sake of coolness. No more hazardous action can be imagined; except on the part of one desiring to court a malarial fever.

Two days later, on the seventh of August, the Orator Giustiniani wrote to his government: "I found the Pope less cheerful and more dull than usual. He said to me, *Sir Orator, all these sick people in Rome, all these daily deaths, make Us fearful, and persuade Us to take more care of Our person.*"

Monsignor Hans Burchard, the Caerimonarius, wrote in his Diarium: "On the twelfth of August, after vespers, between the twenty-first and twenty-second hour, (5-6 P.M.) He (the Pope's Holiness) showed signs of a fever which does not abate."

It should be noted that this is seven days after the garden-supper.

On the thirteenth of August, Giustiniani wrote to his sovereign the Doge of Venice, that the Pope had vomited after eating, and had been feverish all night; that Duke Cesare also was sick: and that no one was admitted to the Vatican. He tells about the supper in the garden of the Cardinal of San Crisogono; and adds: "To-morrow morning I will try to have precise information to send to Your Sublimity."

These dispatches give an excellent idea of some of the

duties of a Sixteenth-Century ambassador, to hang about doors of palaces, to chronicle performances of natural functions, to bribe royal flunkeys and report their gossip in state-dispatches.

On the fourteenth of August, the same Orator wrote that the Pope had been phlebotomized,—"some speak of fourteen, some of sixteen ounces: perhaps it will be true to say ten; and that is an enormous quantity for a man of seventy-three years, which is the age of His Blessedness."

(The Lord Alexander P.P. VI was born in 1431; and was of the age of seventy-two years in 1503.)

"Still the fever does not abate. The Pope has it yet; though less violently than yesterday. To-day the Duke is worse."

The same day, the fourteenth of August, Don Beltrando Costabili, the Orator of Duke Ercole of Ferrara, wrote at some length, no doubt because Madonna Lucrezia Borgia the consort of Ferrara's heir, would expect detailed information when the health of her august and affectionate Father was concerned. He said:

"Yesterday morning, I was informed on good authority that His Holiness has commanded the attendance of the Bishop of Venosa who was sick at home, and of another physician of the City; and that these are not allowed to leave him. I was informed that the Pope had vomitings and fever yesterday; and that they have relieved him of nine ounces of blood. During the day, His Holiness caused some cardinals to play at cards before Him while He rested. I was informed also that last night He slept fairly well. But to-day between the eighteenth and nineteenth hour, (2-3 P.M.) there was a crisis like that of Saturday, of a kind which makes His courtiers uneasy; and every one is unwilling to speak of His condition. I have sought by all means to obtain information: but the more I seek, the less I learn; for the physicians, the chirurgeons, and the apothecaries are not allowed to quit the Presence: from which I conclude that the malady is grave. The Duke of the Romagna also, is very sick with fever, vomitings, and disorder of the stomach. *It is not astonishing that His Holiness, and His Excellency should be ill; for all the courtiers, especially those who are in the palace, are in the same state, by reason of the unwholesome conditions of the air, which, there, they breathe.*"

The last sentence, in italics, is of exceedingly great importance. The operation of venesection did not effect a lysis, as appears from the dispatches of Giustiniani which continue the tale. On the fifteenth of August, he wrote to the Venetian Senate that it was difficult to get positive information: but that the affair was serious; and, that there was likely to be disorder in the City if the Pope died.

On the sixteenth of August, he wrote that the Pope and the Duke continued to be tormented with fevers, and that the Duke's was the more violent. He added that the condition of the Pope must be aggravated by His anxieties and cares, and by the sickness of the Duke.

On the seventeenth of August, Giustiniani wrote again:

"Yesterday I wrote to Your Sublimity by Girolamo Passamonte the courier, who arrived here. To-day I inform you that our Lord the Pope has taken medicine. The fever continually torments Him, not without danger. I am informed by a sure authority that the Bishop of Venosa, chief-physician of His Blessedness and a familiar of the Cardinal Giovantonio di Sangiorgio, (or, perhaps, the Cardinal of San Giorgio *in velum Aureum*, Rafaele Galeotto Sansoni-Riario,) has told his steward that the sickness of the Pope is very dangerous, and that he ought to make the said cardinal hasten hither; which thing has been done."

He adds that the partisans of Duke Cesare, expecting a riot on the death of the Pope, have made secure their property and have taken precautions to prevent ill news from being bruited abroad. This was ordinary political prudence.

On the eighteenth of August, the same Orator wrote,

"Early this morning, our Lord the Pope, knowing of the danger of His sickness, has received His rites; and some cardinals have been admitted into the presence of His Blessedness. The Viaticum was given in secret; for His familiars try to conceal His condition as much as possible. They say, that the Bishop of Venosa, early this morning before the Communion, came from the Pope's Chamber, weeping, and saying to one of his people that the danger was very grave, and complaining with chagrin of the inefficacy of some potions which, yesterday, he had administered. . . . The Duke also is very sick. It has been said to my secretary, *Sir Secretary, this is no time for ceremonies or fine words. Tell the Orator to hasten to inform the Senate of Venice that the Pope* GRAVITER LABORAT. *Also, the same informant said that the Pope cannot live much longer without a miracle."*

On the eighteenth of August, Giustiniani also wrote a second dispatch to the Doge of Venice, in which he said:

"To-day I sent the latest news to Your Sublimity by Lorenzo da Camerino. After he was gone, Messer Scipione, a physician from the palace, came to tell me that yesterday at the sixteenth hour (noon), the Pope, wishing to rise for a certain need, was taken with a fit of choking, and is in evil plight, going from bad to worse; and that in his opinion His Holiness will die to-night:—and, from what he says, I judge the malady to be an apoplexy. Such also is the opinion of this physician so excellent in his art."

The Orator adds that, now, Duke Cesare is neglected; and is preparing secretly to take refuge in the Mola of Hadrian.

Monsignor Burchard makes the following entry in his Diarium, a work of which the original is undiscovered, and copies only accessible to the student. He was perfectly qualified to speak on this subject from personal knowledge; the demise of the Pope being a ceremonial function which he would have to arrange and superintend. He says:

"On Wednesday the eighteenth of August between the twelfth and thirteenth hour (8-9 A.M.) He (the Lord Alexander P.P. VI) confessed Himself to the Lord Bishop Pietro of Culen who said mass in His presence; and, after his Communion, administered the Sacrament of the Eucharist to the Pope, who was seated on His bed; and then finished the mass. Five cardinals were present, d'Oristano, di Cosenza, di Monreale,[1] Casanueva, and di Constantinople, to whom the Pope said that He felt ill. At the hour of vespers the said Bishop of Culen administered the Sacrament of Extreme Unction to Him; and He died in the presence of the datary and the bishop."

[1] Here is a specimen of Mgr. Burchard's or his copyist's gross inaccuracy. He officially was responsible for the conduct of this function. He intimately should have known, and directed, every movement and every gesture of every assistant. And he names, among the cardinals-assistant, the Lord Giovanni Borgia (detto Seniore) Archbishop of Monreale, Cardinal-Presbyter of Santa Susanna, *who had been dead just eighteen days.*

This event took place in the third room of the Borgia Tower occupied by the Library counting from the Library side.

On the nineteenth of August, Giustiniani announced the news to the Senate, and added, "to-day He was carried *de moro*,[1] and shewn to the people; but His corpse was more hideous and monstrous than words can tell, and without human form. For decency, it was kept for some time covered; and before sunset they buried it in the presence of two of the cardinal-deacons attached to the palace."

In reading this dispatch, it must be remembered that Giustiniani hated the Borgia; and that the Lord Alexander P.P. VI was an old man of an obese habit of body, Who had died of a fever in the height of summer, in a most unwholesome quarter of the City, and at a time when antiseptic treatment was unknown.

The Notary of Orvieto, on his return from Rome four days later, publicly described to his municipality all that he had seen of the *novendiali;* and added that he had kissed the feet of His Holiness in St. Peter's:[2] but said nothing of any hideous or monstrous appearance of the corpse.

Soon after death, a rumour was heard to the effect that the Lord Alexander P.P. VI and Duke Cesare de Valentinois della Romagna had died envenomed.

For three months it was only a rumour. A new Pope was elected—Cardinal Francesco de' Piccolhuomini of Siena, who took the name of the Lord Pius P.P. III out of respect to His Uncle, the Lord Pius P.P. II,[3]—and was dead after a two months' reign.

---

[1] *i.e.* in the usual manner, with all the ceremonies required for the obsequies of the pontifical cadaver: not surreptitiously or with maimed rites as some have said.

[2] A dead Pope lies in state in the Chapel of the Trinity in St. Peter's, surrounded by unbleached wax tapers, and with the feet protruded through the screen for the osculations of the faithful.

[3] Enea Silvio Bartolomeo de' Piccolhuomini, 1458-1464.

Then Cardinal Giuliano della Rovere, irreconcilable enemy of Borgia, attained the object of his ambition; and was elected Pope by the name of the Lord Julius P.P. II. And then the rumour took a concrete form.

On the tenth of November it definitely was said that, at the garden-supper of the fifth of August venom had been put into some wine by order of the Lord Alexander P.P. VI; that by a butler's blunder that envenomed wine had been served to the Pope's Holiness and to Duke Cesare: that the former being old had died therefrom; that the latter being young had endured heroic treatment for a cure. Some said that he had been plunged into the ripped-up belly of a live mule or bull amid the steaming palpitating entrails profusely to sweat the venom out of him: others, that he had been dipped in iced-water, and so cured.

Writing several years later, Messer Francesco Guicciardini and Messer Palo Giovio added new details. Guicciardini definitely settled the falsehood in the form in which it generally appears. He gave a list of cardinals, also, and prelates who were to have been envenomed by the Lord Alexander P.P. VI that He might inherit their wealth. Giovio named and described the venom which, he said, the Borgia commonly used. He called it *Cantarella;* [1] and said it was a sugared powder, or a powder under the guise of sugar, which was of a wonderful whiteness, and of a rather pleasant taste. It did not overwhelm the vital forces in the manner of the active venoms by sudden and energetic action: but, by penetrating insensibly the veins, it slowly worked with mortal effect. (Paolo Giovio, Hist. II. 47. VIII. 205.) Is there any toxicological chymist who from this description can give the formula of this extraordinary venom?

The testimony of these two men is tainted. Messer

[1] Qy. A concoction of cantharides? Or was it merely a name, like κανθαρίτης οἰνός? (Plin. 14. 7. 9.)

Francesco Guicciardini who wrote long after the event and solely from hearsay, was a Florentine. Whatever is, and was, of Florence, is cultured, pedantic, artificial, in the highest degree: whatever is, and was, of Rome, is nakedly natural, original, free, and absolute, in the highest degree. It was, and is, a habit of mind in the Florentine to decry Rome and all things Roman. Politically, Messer Francesco Guicciardini was an adherent of the House of Medici; and Medici were naturally the mortal foes of Borgia, seeing that Borgia had acquiesced in and profited by their expulsion from Florence. And he was in the pay of the Roman Colonna, who were Ghibelline by inherited tradition, *i.e.,* upholders of the imperial against the papal prerogative. He was born in 1482; and was of the age of twenty-one years at the death of the Lord Alexander P.P. VI. In 1530, having exhorted the Lord Clement P.P. VII to punish Florence for insults which he (Guicciardini) had received in 1527, he turned traitor against the Medici, writing invectives against them till his death in 1540. He divinely wrote at all times a sonorous and courtly Tuscan, which makes his reader believe that one who could write so exquisitely must needs write truly. Yet he did not hesitate to boast that he had a pen of gold for his friends, and a pen of iron for his foes. Regretfully then it must be said that Messer Francesco Guicciardini does not deserve belief unless his statements can be corroborated.

Touching the matter of the Borgia venom, and especially of the envenoming of the Lord Alexander P.P. VI and Duke Cesare, he is corroborated by Messer Paolo Giovo.

Messer Paolo Giovio was born in 1483, and was of the age of twenty years at the death of the Lord Alexander P.P. VI. He issued no books till twenty-one years later. His first was a quoad-scientific treatise on Roman Fishes (*De Piscibus Romanis*), published in 1524. He was a *dilettante* of a kind. He practised ·amniomancy, or the art of divination by inspection of the membrane, Amnios, in which the unborn child is wrapped—fantastic effort of a seeker after Truth. He was one of those double-faced historians, who wrote one set of memoirs for the highest bidder; (Popes whom they despised, Dukes whom they privately reviled,) and a second set of memoirs for the enemies of the patrons of the first. His Life of the Lord Leo P.P. X (Giovanni de' Medici) is a specimen. Even during his life, he was considered to be a flagrant liar. He used to say, with a dog-like knowledge of his masters the "people" who "desire to be deceived," that the centuries would give his written lies the force of truth. He used an affected and flamboyant rather than a pure style; and was the inferior of Guicciardini. The Lord Clement P.P. VII (Giulio de' Medici), to be rid of his incessant importunity, gave him the bishopric of Nocera; and he died in 1552.

Who, therefore, wishes to believe Messer Francesco Guicciardini uncorroborated, or corroborated by Messer Paolo Giovio, will do so on his own responsibility.

Let it be noted that both Giovio and Guicciardini were Roman Catholics. Their calumnies against the Lord Alexander P.P. VI are their own; and were not invented by dissenters from their creed. The said calumnies very naturally had been adopted by these last as articles of faith; and repeated usque ad nauseam; or resented, with the most unconvincing and inane half-heartedness, by a majority of modern and soi-disant enlightened Roman Catholics, who fear (positively they shew every sign of fear) to credit their own learned clergy of the present day, Leonetti, Velron, Cerri, and Ollivier, to say nothing of the laity, *e.g.,* Comte Réné de Maricourt, who have laboured for justice to the maligned Borgia. Will these astonishingly inconsistent persons prefer to believe the opinion of an atheist, who was incidentally a man of common sense? It is Voltaire who, in speaking of Guicciardini's statement, (that the Lord Alexander P.P. VI was the victim of venom which He had set for his cardinals, that, having killed them, He might take their treasure,) says,

"All the enemies of the Holy See have welcomed this horrible anecdote. I myself do not believe it at all; and my chief reason lies in its extreme improbability. It is evident that the envenoming of a dozen cardinals at supper would have caused the Father and the son[1] to become so execrable, that nothing could have saved them from the fury of the Roman people, and of the whole of Italy. Such a crime never could have been concealed. Even supposing that it had not been avenged by all Italy leagued together, it was directly contrary to the interests of Cesare (detto) Borgia. The Pope was on the verge of the grave. The Borgia faction was powerful enough to elect one of its own creatures: was it likely that the votes of cardinals would be gained by envenoming a dozen of them? I make bold to say to Guicciardini, 'Europe has been deceived by you, and you have been deceived by your feelings. You were the enemy of the Pope; you have followed the advice of your hatred. It is true that He had used vengeance cruel and perfidious, against foes perfidious and cruel as Himself. Hence you conclude that a Pope of the age of seventy-two years could not die a natural death. You maintain, on vague rumour, that an aged sovereign, whose coffers at that time contained more than a million of gold ducats,[2] desired to envenom several cardinals that He might seize their treasures. But were these treasures so important? The treasures of cardinals nearly always were removed by their gentlemen before the Popes could seize them. Why do you think that so prudent a Pope cared to risk the doing of so very infamous a deed for so very small a gain; a deed that could not be done without accomplices; and that sooner or later must have been discovered? May I not trust the official accounts of the Pope's sickness, more than the mere rumours of the mob? That official account declares the Pope to have died of a double-tertian fever. There is not the slightest vestige of proof in favour of the accusation which you have brought against his memory. His son Borgia[3] happened to fall sick at the time when his Father died. That is the sole foundation for the story of the venom.'"

[1] M. de Voltaire speaks of Duke Cesare (detto Borgia) as "the son."

[2] Ducato d'oro=half a guinea with four times its purchasing power. A million of gold ducats would equal £2,000,000 sterling.

[3] M. de Voltaire speaks of Duke Cesare (detto Borgia) as the Pope's son; and of the Pope as Duke Cesare's Father.

THE LEGEND OF THE BORGIA VENOM

ONE of the stock phrases used by biographers and historians of the Fifteenth and Sixteenth Centuries was "he (or she)—died in the odour of sanctity." Another was "he (or she)—died not without suspicion of venom." Both phrases are the merest expression of private opinion, the importance of which depends upon the integrity and knowledge of the user: but in no case do they amount to a dogmatic, final, infallible, or authoritative, decision.

When a person is said to have departed this life in the odour of sanctity, (a purely technical phrase, insusceptible of literal translation,) sooner or later the process of ecclesiastical law is begun for obtaining for the deceased the successive titles, *Venerable Servant of God, the Blessed* —, and *Saint* —. These titles, only being conferred after stringent examinations of quality lasting many years and sometimes many centuries,[1] are taken to prove the pious opinion "died in the odour of sanctity" to have been founded on a verity.

But when a person is said to have died "not without suspicion of venom," it is very rarely that steps are taken, juridically to examine that suspicion with a view to proving it to be founded on fact or falsehood. The world deliberately prefers to believe the worst of man, deliberately prefers suspicion. The expression in the Fifteenth and Sixteenth Centuries was as randomly and as inconsequently

[1] The Venerable Servant of God, King Ælfred the Great of England, has not yet been styled "The Blessed." Sir Thomas More, Lord Chancellor of England under Henry VIII Tudor, only was admitted to the rank of "The Blessed" in 1886, by the Lord Leo P.P. XIII. He now publicly may be invoked by name, and his portraits decorated by a halo.

used as the cry for a General Council, by every one who found occasion to go "against the government"; and it certainly does not command respect by reason of its absurdly frequent repetition. It was the fashion for their enemies to accuse the Borgia of compassing the death of some by venom. It was also the fashion for the Borgia to retort upon their enemies in the same formula. There can be no human doubt that the Borgia and their enemies would have envenomed each the other, had they known how to do so with security and certainty. It was a habit of the Latin Races to see no distinction between venom and steel when the idea was to get rid of a foe. Cold northern nations, the English in particular, always have had a horror of venom, preferring boots, fists, bullet or blade; indeed one of the most hideous penances ordained by English and Post-Reformation law was awarded to criminals who had envenomed the lieges. They were boiled alive. "This year, the XVII March, was boyled in Smithfield one Margaret Davis, a maiden which had poisoned three households that she dwelled in." (Wriothesley's Chronicle, 1542.)

Perhaps to this habit, of regarding the use of venom as so horrible a crime, is due the fascination which those, who are supposed to have attained high eminence in its practice, have for Englishmen. Undoubtedly, Lord Alexander P.P. VI and Duke Cesare de Valentinois della Romagna are regarded as having been artists in venom, possessing knowledge far surpassing that of modern alchymists. They are believed to have envenomed their foes, named and unnamed, by the score; and, at last, to have fallen into the pit that they have digged for others.

Of the cases named, Cardinal Giovanni Borgia (detto Giuniore), the Sultán Djim, and Cardinal Orsini, are the most important. The improbability in the case of the first already has been shown: Duke Cesare and he were friendly; their interests were asymptotic; and they were apart during the seventeen days before the cardinal died. The improbability in the case of the Sultán Djim lies in the fact that the Pope lost 40,000 ducats annually, and the only means of keeping the Turks from Christendom, by his death which was due to natural causes, and took place when he was in the hands of the Christian King Charles VIII at Naples, some weeks after he had left Rome. The improbability in the case of Cardinal Orsini is proved by the tainted source from which the charge emanated; by the publicity of all proceedings before and after his death; and by the sworn testimony of his leeches. Cases of this kind must be considered together; and rejected or accepted together; for rumours do not gain credibility from vociferous repetition: nor does it avail to plead that because advantages accrue from the death of such a one, therefore, the person benefited by the death is likely to have envenomed the deceased. Death is always advantageous to some one living: but in no case named did the Lord Alexander P.P. VI and Duke Cesare reap any gain whatever, but contrariwise loss. As for the statement, that the venom of the Borgia was a slow venom, slow in action, dirigible in absence, it safely may be said that no such venom existed then any more than it does now.

This slow venom is an invention of purveyors of a certain class of fiction, doing vast credit to their imaginative powers, but possessing no tangible existence. These writers of fiction are merchants who must supply their customers with goods upon demand. The Legend of the Borgia Venom is a department of their trade. The public has read it and cried for more according to the sample. The public is pleased to amuse itself. At other times the public has the humour to inform itself; and takes spiritual pastors, and masters, cunning in all learning, in all verities of past and present. From these, the truth is required for mental profit; from the others invention and imagination for mental recreation. The public pays and has the right to to emphasize this fact, and to enrich and illuminate it with a wealth of illustration: but when he comes to speak of Don Michelotto as Duke Cesare's Hangman, and of Sebastian Pinzon as his Poisoner, with the light and easy freedom which one uses in speaking of "the unquestioned things that are"; then one is compelled to conjure up the horrible and fantastic picture of the Generalissimo of the Pontifical Army stalking about the continent of Europe with an official Hangman and an official Poisoner in his entourage. Don Michelotto was a captain of Duke Cesare's condottieri, a valued confidential servant, perhaps, on sudden occasion, as at Sinigaglia, his *executeur des hautes œuvres:* but never a professional Hangman. And Sebastian Pinzon? Is it to be believed that Duke Cesare—for this really is what Herr Burckhardt's amazing statement implies—did so much venenation in the way of business, that it was as necessary to have a Lord High Poisoner attached to his staff as a Groom of the Stola or a Clerk of the Hanaper?[1] The thing is absurd; worthy of comic opera, not of serious history. But the origin of Herr Burckhardt's error shall be traced.

Giustiniani, the Orator of Venice, to whom the Borgia were intensely antipathetic, and who neglected no opportunity of relating rumours detrimental to them, sent to his government a dispatch dated the twentieth of July, 1502, stating, that the Most Illustrious Lord Giambattista Ferrari, Cardinal-Presbyter of the Title of San Crisogono, vulgarly called the Cardinal of Modena, had died; that, in accordance with his testament, his goods and benefices had been distributed; that his archbishopric of Capua had been given to the young and lusty Lord Cardinal-Prince Ippolito d'Este (now of the age of twenty-four years and a person of fashion;) that his bishopric of Modena had been given to his brother; that the greater part of his goods had been

[1] The Clerk of the Hanaper is the domestic in charge of the great gallon goblet called the hanaper.

given to his secretary Messer Sebastiano Pinzoni; that this last bequest was called "the price of blood" for the secretary had envenomed his master, to have his goods; that the Pope had endowed the said secretary with a canonry in Padua, the prefecture of Sant' Agatha in Cremona, a benefice in Rome, another in Mantua valued at five hundred ducats, and had received him *inter familiares.*

Now there is no word in that dispatch which implicates Duke Cesare. We learn that Messer Sebastiano Pinzoni, secretary to the Cardinal of Modena, was said, by rumour, to have envenomed his master in order to profit thereby; and also that the said secretary had been patronised by the Lord Alexander P.P. VI. That is all. It would be unpleasant to think of the Pope's Holiness as the patron of a murderer: yet that would be the obvious conclusion, if the matter ended here. But it does not. There is further record of Messer Sebastiano Pinzoni, which makes it clear that his crime at first was unknown to the Pope; and that on its discovery he was forced to take refuge in flight. It is Monsignor Burchard who records in his Diarium under date Wednesday the twentieth of November, 1504, that the Ruota (the supreme secular tribunal of the Holy Roman Church) delivered sentence against Sebastiano Pinzoni, Apostolic Scribe, who was contumacious and absent, depriving him of all benefices and offices, for that he had slain with venom the Lord Cardinal of Modena his patron who had raised him from the dunghill.[1] Ciacconi says that the Cardinal of Modena was envenomed by Sebastiano Pinzoni, his gentleman-of-the-bedchamber; who, being imprisoned on another charge in the reign of the Lord

---

[1] "Mercurii xx Nov. fuit data sententia in Rota, contra Sebastianum Pinzonum, scriptorum apostolicum, absentem ob contumaciam, privatonis omnium beneficiorum et officiorum" (*interesting to notice that, in the reign of the Lord Julius P.P. II, the eternal enemy of Borgia, a convict on the capital charge was merely ruined, and not sentenced to death;*) "pro quod eo dominum cardinalem Mutinensem patronum suum veneno interemisset, qui eum de stercore eximerat."

Leo P.P. X, when put to the Question, confessed this crime, which he before had denied.

Let it be admitted that Sebastiano Pinzoni envenomed his master, then. But Herr Burckhardt brings no evidence to prove that he was connected with Duke Cesare; nor is it established that he was employed by His Excellency in any capacity, private, or official. But every crime of every criminal in the Borgian Era is attributed to Borgia as a matter of course; and Herr Burckhardt, writing serious history, introduces fiction, and passes off Sebastiano Pinzoni as Duke Cesare's Poisoner!

To turn from the historian to the novelist will afford a little recreation in this quest of the Venom of the Borgia; and, also, the diversion will not be unprofitable: for the novelist is an exceedingly important person by reason that he commands an infinitely wider audience than the historian, and influences, forms, or moulds, an infinitely larger section of opinion. M. Alexandre Dumas in his Crimes Célèbres has much to say about the Borgia. Knowing, as a practised hand, that the best fiction is that which has a substratum of fact and an air of truth, M. Dumas quotes the precious Messer Paolo Giovio and his *Cantarella* which already has been mentioned here. Further, with a wealth of "corroborative detail calculated to give verisimilitude to an otherwise bald and unconvincing narrative," he describes the preparation of a liquid venom which, he says, the Borgia used. A bear was caught and made to swallow a strong dose of arsenic. When this began to take effect, the bear was suspended by his hind-legs head-downward; and incontinent he would fall into convulsions, while from his throat there poured a copious deadly stream of foam, which was collected on a silver plate, bottled in vials hermetically sealed; and this was the liquid Venom of the Borgias.

There were plenty of bears in the Apennines, perhaps even in the Alban Hills within twenty miles of Rome; so the bear is probable enough. Having caught his bear, Duke Cesare would convey him to the Vatican—a large palace truly, but rather too full of people to be desirable as a private venom-factory. On a dark night in a lonely courtyard, the Pope's Holiness and the Duke's Excellency would administer the arsenic to the bear. The method of administration is not described, nor the slinging up of the beast prior to his convulsions, nor the picture of the aged Pontiff skipping round with the silver plate in His solicitude that no drop of the fluid should be lost, nor the solemn bottling of the vials, nor their hermetic sealing with what seal? The Ring of the Fisherman? And M. Dumas carefully omits to say that the nasty mess so secretly and arduously obtained would have been far less venomous than the original dose of arsenic; which, administered neat, without the intervention of an ill-used bear, certainly would have slain: but which would be deprived of most, if not of all, of its venomous potency, by its submission to the digestive processes of M. Dumas' improbable and impossible bear.

.   .   .

Undoubtedly, there were the same venomous substances in and on this earth in the Fifteenth and Sixteenth Centuries, as there are now: some few were known; but many more, and these the most sure and deadly, were not even dreamed of, *e.g.,* strychnine, prussic acid, or the hideous bacilli, accessible as dust to any Twentieth-Century medico who, on the sole condition that he is not instigated by criminal motives, with perfect security to himself can envenom and slay a street, a district, or a city. In the year 1164 Abd-el-Mumin-ben-Ali the Moorish King of Spain chased from his dominions all Jews and Christians who refused the faith of Islam. Among these, to Egypt went the celebrated Moses ben-Maimon. All that was known, he knew; and he knew sixteen venoms; litharge, verdigris, opium, arsenic, spurge or milk-wort, cashew-nut, hemlock, henbane, stramonium or thorn-apple, hemp, mandrake, venomous fungi, plantain, black-nightshade or felon-wort, belladonna, and cantharides. To these, were added in the Borgian Era four centuries later, the tri-sulphite of arsenic, orpiment, antimony, corrosive sublimate, aconite or wolfsbane or monkshood, and perhaps white hellebore, and black or Christmas-Rose; making two and twenty substances known to be venomous.

Undoubtedly, much damage might be done with this arsenal of venoms: but only in the event of the existence of the will to use them, and of the knowledge of the method of their exhibition.

Undoubtedly, there was the will. The fact that Madonna Caterina Sforza Riario (author of a wonderful collection of recipes, domestic and medicinal, a good housewife as well as witch and warrior,) was said to have attempted the envenoming of the Pope's Holiness, as described in Book II, speaks for the fact that venom was feared, and therefore likely to be used. Governments experimented with venoms: for what purpose, who can tell? M. Lamanshy published an interesting document dated 1432, which he found in the Venetian Secret Archives.[1] "Trial has been made, on three porcine animals, of certain venoms, found in the chancery, sent very long ago from Vicenza, which have been proved not to be good."

Undoubtedly, there was the will. Undoubtedly, also, there was not the ability.

.   .   .

Strange and paradoxical though it may seem to be, alchymical knowledge, alchymical art, was in a lower condition during the years succeeding the Renascence of

[1] "Fuit facta proba, in tribus animalibus porcinis, de aliquibus venenis, repertis in cancelleria, missis perantea a Vincencia, qua reperta sunt non esse bona." (Secrets de l'État de Venise, Petersburg, 1884, p. 6.)

Learning, than it had been in the Middle Ages, the so-called Dark Ages, which had gone before. The Dark Ages were the ages of Simples. The Age of the Renascence was the age of Compounds. And, in those compounds, virtue was changed, or lost, by sublimation, by distillation, or annulled by heterogeneous admixture. The following will make this plain.

In the Dark Ages, medicaments were made from single herbs exhibited in the form of draughts, poultices, lotions, or unguents. The old herbaries of Dioskorides, or of Appulejus, were used as text-books; and a few extracts from these will be curious, perhaps valuable, certainly a help to understanding.

(a) The herb Betony or Bishopwort (*Betonica officinalis*) must be gathered in August without the help of iron, the mould shaken from the roots, and dried in the shade. When triturated, two drachms of it, mixed with hot beer or wine or honey, is an antidote to venom, a digestive, a cure for hydrophobia, constipation, toothache, and prevents monstrous nocturnal visitors, or frightful sights and dreams. A lotion, made from the herb seethed in fresh water till two-thirds are evaporated, cures broken-head, epistaxis, fatigue, and rupture; or the leaves may be used as a poultice. (As a matter of fact, Betony is intoxicating, emetic, and purgative.)

(β) The herb Vervain or Ashthroat (*Verbena officinalis*) must be pounded as a poultice for wounds and carbuncles. It is an antidote to all venoms, and dogs may not bark at him who bears it.

(γ) The herb Clovewort (*Ranunculis acris*), wreathed with red thread on the neck during the waning of the April or October moon, cures lunacy.

(δ) The herb Mugwort (*Artemisia dracunculus*), pounded to an unguent with well-boiled olive-oil, will make strained sinews supple. (This is excellent.)

(ε) The herb Ravensleek (*Orchis, Σατύριον*) will cure sore eyes when they are smeared with its juice.

(ζ) The herb Watercress (*Nasturtium officinale*) will with its juice stop hair from falling.

(η) The herb Madder (*Rubia tinctoria*) as a poultice cures sciatica.

(θ) The herb Clover (*Trifolium pratense*) prevents him who carries it from suffering sore jaws.

(ι) The herb Rosemary (*Rosemarinus officinalis*) is good for the teeth.

(κ) The herb Rue (*Ruta graveolens*), eaten green is an antifat; a twig stops nose-bleeding; macerated in vinegar and soused on the brow induces forgetfulness. Recommended for priests who wish to observe their vow of continence.

(λ) The herb Dwarfdwostle or Pennyroyal (*Mentha pulegium*), as unguent, cures sea-sickness; as a salve, or burned as incense, cures fever and bellyache.

(μ) The herb Sage (*Salvia*), as a lotion, cures itch.

(ν) The herb Marjoram (*Origanum vulgare*), steeped in vinegar, cures headache, or may be chewed for a cough.

(ξ) The herb Foxglove (*Digitalis purpurea*), as a poultice, cures sores and pimples, ἕρπης. (Its venomous principle appears to be unknown.)

(ο) The herb Wildthyme or Shepherdspurse (*Thymus campestris*) will remove all inward foulness by the drinking of its ooze.

(π) The herb Violet (*Viola odorata*), made into an unguent with lard or honey, cures wounds.

(ϱ) The herb Wildgourd (*Cucumis colocynthus,*
κολοκύνθος ἀγρία), its inward neshness pounded
in lithe beer without the churnels, will stir the
inward.

Those are Simples, *i.e.,* medicaments derived from single
herbs, easily come-by, within the reach of all; suited to
a simple, but by no means silly, race of men content with
simple things, gifted with faith and sense, and unconcerned
to dive below the surface and explore, or experiment with,
nature's sacrosanct arcana.

.   .   .

The Renascence of Learning, when the works of ancient
writers were rediscovered, devoured, put in practice, filled
men's minds with new ideas, and completely changed
their point of view.

The Most Salubrious Precepts of Medicine, written
by Quintus Serenus Sermonicus in the Third Century;
the Thirty-Seven Books of *Natural History,* by C. Plinius
Secundus (Pliny Senior) which first saw light in A.D. 77;
the eighty-three *Treatises* of Claudius Galenus, (A.D. 130-
200); the thirty-four chapters of the *Animal Medicaments* which Sextus Placitus wrote in the Fourth Century
after the Incarnation; the eight books of Alexandros of
Tralles in Lydia, *On Medicine,* first given to the world in
the Sixth Century;—these were the keys that opened the
door of speculation to the alert and eager men of the Fifteenth Century, already intoxicated by the glorious Discovery of Man.

Weird and wonderful effects were produced by this
flood of knowledge. Weird and wonderful were the new
significances given to natural things, the combinations of
natural objects projected, the doctrines evolved from observation of natural phenomena. The study of nature
became a sacred thing, reserved for the reverent and wise.

Its followers were called magi, or magicians; their pursuit was magic. The magical art was either white or black, for the good or ill of men. Great and holy personages practised white magic: the black was damned by the Church, and the bare suspicion of its practice sufficed to burn. The Lord Alexander P.P. VI distinguished Himself by His severity to the black magi. White magic included the art of healing; divination by cheiromancy, amniomancy, lithomancy, astrology, and also experimented to find out the hidden properties and virtues of all things strange, as well as common. It was a vast field for research; and the men who walked therein were just like boys, eager, sensible, ardent, inexperienced, ready to assume and take for granted.

A most eminent mage was Messer Eurico Cornelio Agrippa. During the pontificate of the Lord Alexander P.P. VI he wrote his learning in a book which he called *The Book of Occult Philosophy*. In the year 1510 he shewed his work to a friend, the celebrated Abbot Trithemius, who was charmed with it, added to it, and advised Messer Eurico to impart it to the elect alone. The advice apparently was taken; for the book was not published till 1531. The mage largely dealt with kabbalistic writing, giving various mysterious alphabets for use in magical recipes. He set forth the sigils planets and planet-signs of certain archangels, patrons of the days of the week, Michael, Gabriel, Samael, Raphael, Sachael, Anael, Cassiel, with their proper perfumes, red wheat, aloes, pepper, mastic, saffron, pepperwort, sulphur. He placed great importance on charms and periapts or amulets.

"St. Thomas Aquinas," he wrote, "that holy Doctor, in his Book *De Fato* saith that even Garments, Buildings, and other artificial Works whatsoever, do receive a certain Qualification from the Stars: and Magicians affirm that, not only by the Mixture and Application of natural Things, but also in Images, Seals, Rings, Glasses, and some other Instruments, being opportunely framed under a certain Constellation, some celestial illustration may be taken, and some wonderful thing may be received."

This being his idea, it is not surprising to find him prescribing for the reduction of an intermittent fever, the following charm of Quintus Serenus Sermonicus to be written on parchment and worn round the neck.

```
a   b   r   a   c   a   d   a   b   r   a
a   b   r   a   c   a   d   a   b   r
a   b   r   a   c   a   d   a   b
a   b   r   a   c   a   d   a
a   b   r   a   c   a   d
a   b   r   a   c   a
a   b   r   a   c
a   b   r   a
a   b   r
a   b
a
```

or, as a protection against evil spirits and dangers of journey, water, enemy, or arms, the beginning and end of the first five verses of Genesis:

צמובח —— בוווד'

written on virgin parchment, or on most pure gold, back and front, with an ink made of the smoke, of incense, or of consecrated wax-tapers, mixed with holy-water. This charm also must be worn round the neck, and its efficacy is conditional upon the belief of the wearer in God the Creator of All.

Men of the Borgian Era knew that the tail or an ibex, dried with its flesh and skin and worn about the person, would ward off magic unless the wearer should consent thereto. This they learned from St. Hildegard's treatise *De Animalibus*. They knew that the herb Heliotrope or Turnsole (*Heliotropion Europaeum*), placed under the pillow of a man who has been robbed, will bring him a vision of the thief and his spoil; and that, when it was set up in a church, unfaithful wives would be unable to go away until it was removed. Their faith in the virtue of gems was very precious; and chiefly derived from the physician Alexandros of Tralles. A cockatrice engraved on green jasper preserved from the Evil Eye. A metal cross tied on the left arm cured epilepsy. A live spider tied in a rag on the same arm cured ague. A metal ring, engraved with the sacred tau **T** (the *"Mark on the Forehead"*), also freed from epilepsy. A ring, set with asshoof, cured ἀδυναμία. A ring, carved with a council of ravens for Apollo, conferred conjugal joy and the gift of clear-seeing. A brownish-yellow jacinth gave sleep. An agate, carved with St. John the Divine, protected from venom. Oriental jasper or heliotrope (blood-stone), engraved with a youth wearing a necklace of herbs, when anointed with marigold juice, conferred invisibility. A copper ring, figured with a lion, a crescent, and a star, and worn on the fourth finger, cured calculus. Amethyst kept the wearer sober, and a papal bull ordained it for episcopal rings. Coral delivered from incubi and succubi. Herakles strangling the lion of Nemea, carved on a honey-coloured sard, cured colic. Carnelian carved with a Hermes Psuchopompos gave cheerfulness and courage. A man might live as long as he liked if he looked at a presentment of St. Christopher (the Christian Herakles) every day.[1] The toad-stone or bufonite (the fossil palatal tooth of the ray-fish *Pycnodus*) which set in a ring was a most potent periapt against black magic. In the University Galleries at Oxford, No. 691, there is a splendid specimen of a double-toad-stone ring; *i.e.*, the stones are set outward on opposite sides of the ring so that the one always touches the closed hand, while the other is free to dismay a magical enemy.

Cheiromancy was expounded by Messer Andrea Corvo

[1] *"Christophori sancti faciem quicunque tuetur
Illa nempe die mala morte non morietur."*

da Carpi, whose deeply religious little treatise adorned with diagrams was published at Venice in 1500.

But the chief of the men of science of the Borgian Era was Messer Giambattista della Porta of Naples. Born in 1445, dying in 1515, he was an exact contemporary of Borgia. What he did not know of natural science, no other man of his epoch knew. His house in Naples was a resort of literary and scientific men of every nation. He established public and private academies of science in all directions, the chief of which were Gli Ozioni of Naples and one called Il Secreti which met in his own house, and to which no mage was admitted unless he had made some new and notable discovery of natural phenomena. This was the academy whose name and air of mystery excited intense ecclesiastical suspicion at Rome, which by hinting at black magic procured the order to close the meetings of the mages.

Messer Giambattista della Porta was a copious writer. He gave to the world a treatise On Physiognomy, in which he judges men's characters by comparing their faces to those of certain beasts; and a diffuse and learned work on cyphers, De Occultis Literium Notis. His great work, however, was The Book of Natural Magic. He says that he began it in 1460, when he barely was of the age of fifteen years;—these were the precocious times when Messer Giovanni de Medici was a Lord Cardinal at thirteen and Prince Gioffredo-Borgia of Squillace a married man and captain of condottieri at fourteen;—and thirty-five years later in 1495, by the help of that lusty young Mæcenas the Lord Cardinal Prince Ippolito d'Este, he published the matured work from which the following recipes are taken.

Very few English people realize the doctrine of Sympathy and Antipathy; or admit that Attraction and Repulsion are Primary Forces. "I do not love thee, Doctor Fell, the reason why I cannot tell," says the Englishman, and worries to find that reason instead of recognising the

Law. "She is simpatica and he is antipaticissimo," says an Italian, stating and admitting a natural law. Messer Giambattista della Porta is very clear on the point of Antipathy, which he illustrates by saying that Vine and Colewort are natural enemies, because Colewort cures drunkenness; that Rue and Hemlock are natural enemies because Hemlock heals blisters raised by Rue: as well as on the point of Sympathy which he illustrates by saying that a wild bull, tethered to a fig-tree, will become tame and gentle; and a dog, laid to a diseased part of a man's body, will absorb the disease.

He says that beasts have knowledge all their own: that ravens use ivy, eagles use maidenhair, herons use carrots, on their nests as natural preservatives against enchantments: that cats eat grass, and pigeons pellitory, for their ailments: that lions with partan agues eat apes, that dim-eyed hawks eat sow-thistle, that serpents rejuvenate on fennel, and that partridges eat leeks to clear their voices.

To prove that he has not gone about the world with eyes closed, he remarks that mice are generated of putrefactions, frogs of rotten dust and rain, red toads of dirt and καταμήνια, and serpents of the hair of horses' manes or of a dead man's back-marrow.

He advises the creation of new animals by cross-breeding; a hunting dog, of a mastiff and a lioness or tigress; a trick dog, of a bitch and an ape; and birds with delicious flesh for gourmets, of a cock and a peahen, or of a cock pheasant and a plain hen. His method of making a bird sociable and friendly is quaint and unique. He says that, before the creature has got its feathers, you must break off its lower beak even to the jaw. Then, having not the wherewithal to peck up food, it must come to its master to be fed.

He advocates the creation of new fruits which sound most daintily, by grafting a mulberry on a chestnut tree, a peach on a nut, a quince on a pear, a citron on an apple, and a cherry on a bay. He advises the making of bread with dates and walnuts; and of wine with quinces.

He will make precious stones—a jacinth by putting lead into an earthen pot, and setting it in a glass-maker's furnace until the lead is vitrified: or an emerald by dissolving silver in aqua-fortis, casting in plates of copper to which the composition will adhere, drying the plates in the sun, setting them in an earthen pot for some days in a glass-maker's furnace.

He says that green and merry dreams may be procured by eating balm, or bugloss, or bows of poplar; and black and melancholy dreams by eating beans, lentils, onions, garlic, leeks.

He will cure toothache with roots of pellitory or of herbane, bruised. For the care of the teeth he recommends a wash made of leaves of mastic, rosemary, sage, and bramble, macerated in Greek wine, (*i.e.,* a strong rich wine grown in dry volcanic soil:) or a tooth-powder made of barley bread-crumbs browned with salt. But his recipe for white and pearly teeth is a master-piece.

"Take three handfuls each of flowers and leaves of sage, nettle, rosemary, mallow, olive, plantain, and rind of walnut roots; two handfuls each of rock-rose (κίστος), horehound, bramble-tops; a pound of flower and half a pound of seed of myrtle; two handfuls of rose buds; two drachms each of sandal-wood, coriander, and citron-pips; three drachms of cinnamon; ten drachms of cypress nuts; five green pine-cones; two drachms each of mastic and Armenian bole or clay. Reduce all these to powder. Infuse them in sharp black wine. Macerate them for three days. Slightly press out the wine. Put them in an alembic and distil them on a gentle fire. Boil the distillation till two ounces of alum is dissolved in it. Keep in a close-stopped vial: and, for use, fill the mouth with the lotion, and rub the teeth with a finger wrapped in fine linen."

An excellent specimen this, of a Compound as distinguished from a Simple; of the sophistication, and of the meticulous personal cleanliness, of people of the Borgian Era.

To cure a man of Envy, says this mage, keep him in the

fresh air, hang carbuncles and jacinths and sapphires on his neck, let him wear a ring made of ass-hoof and smell to hyssop and sweet lilies.

Messer Giambattista Porta's ninth Book teaches how to make women beautiful. There was a fashion which continued the forehead to the middle of the skull; and a depilatory is recommended made of quicklime four ounces, and orpiment two ounces, boiled until a hen's feather dipped into it is bared. This frightful compound must not long remain on the skin; and the burns should be dressed with the gum of aspen-bark (*Populus Tremula*) and oil of roses or of violets. Or, hair may be removed by fomentation with hot water, plucking out with nippers one by one, and anointing the holes with a saturated solution of saltpetre, or with oil of brimstone or vitriol, the process being repeated once a year. Where hair is only thin and downy, the roots of wild hyacinth rubbed on will keep it back.

To dye the hair yellow, (in imitation of Madonna Lucrezia Borgia, whose beautiful yellow hair was much admired,) add enough honey to soften the lees of white wine and keep the hair wet with this all night. Then bruise roots of celandine and greater-clivers-madder, mix them with oil of cummin seed, box-shavings, and saffron; and keep this on the head for four and twenty hours, when it should be washed off with a lye of cabbage-stalks and ashes of rye-straw.

To make the hair grow it should be washed in the liquid that first distils from honey by the fire: or it should be anointed with an unguent made of marsh-mallow bruised in hog's grease, boiled long in wine, added to bruised cummin-seed, mastic, yolk of egg, boiled again, and strained through linen.

To make hair thick and curly, boil maidenhair with smallage seed in wine and oil; or roots of daffydillies, or dwarf-elder, boiled with wine and oil.

Water, in which the bulbous tops of lilies have been

boiled, makes the skin fair: and corrosive sublimate and cerusa (white lead) makes the face white and shining.

For sunburn, white of egg and sugar-candy on the face at night, washed off in barley-water in the morning, is prescribed: and a clear skin is to be had by rubbing with the rind or bruised seeds of melons. It will be obvious that there were "plain" as well as "coloured" women in the Borgian Era; *i.e.,* those who went about their duty (of cultivating their charms) in a wholesome way, and those who used violent and nasty methods.

Messer Giambattista della Porta appears to have used his science and magical art to invent "Some Sports against Women"; which will show what the Borgian Era regarded as permissible practical jokes. He says that, if you wish to discover paint on a face, you must chew saffron before breathing on her, and incontinently she yellows: or you may burn brimstone near her, which will blacken mercury sublimate and cerusa (white-lead): or you may chew cummin or garlic and breathe on her, and her cerusa or quicksilver will decay. But if that you yearn to dye a woman green, you must decoct a chameleon in her bath.

His tenth book deals with interminable and elaborate processes of distillation and sublimation; proving that what was said on a previous page concerning Letters and Art, (viz., that the habit of the time was to think all of the workmanship, and nothing of the material used,) was perfectly true of Fifteenth-Century pharmacy also. These mages sat and boiled their alembics and crucibles; and distilled, and distilled, and sublimed, and sublimed, till the nature of their stuff was lost, or utterly changed, instead of being refined and concentrated as they vainly hoped. They were just like boys, eager, sensible, ardent, inexperienced. They made the inevitable blunders of adventurers. They committed the extravagances of human nature in unwonted circumstances; and the wisdom of the Twentieth Century is the fruit of the fooling of the Fifteenth.

Messer Giambattista della Porta devotes his eleventh book to Perfumes; his twelfth to the making of Greek Fire (from camphor, pitch, spirits and brimstone,) of gunpowder, and of rockets shells and mines; his thirteenth to the tempering of steel.

His fourteenth book contains monstrous and characteristic recipes connected with meats and drinks. If you want to make your guests drunken, mix with their wine the filth of a dog's ear. If you prefer to make them mad-drunk, give them a camel's froth in water. If you want to avoid being overcome of wine, eat leeks and saffron, wear garlands of roses, violets and ivy-berries and carry an amethyst on your person. To keep your boy sober, before he has tasted wine give him the boiled eggs of an owl, to temper his natural heat. If you want delicately to drive unwelcome guests from your table, you may disgust them with the viands in five ways: first, a needle which has sewed dead men's shrouds when stuck under the table will cause all to loathe to eat: secondly, meat secretly peppered with powdered root of wake-robin (*Arum maculatum*) will fetch the skin off their mouths: thirdly, food sprinkled before serving with powdered leaves of cuckoo-pine (—*gen. Arum*) will produce copious salivation: fourthly, knives and napkins rubbed with wildgourd juice (*Cucunis colocynthus, κολοκύνθις ἀγρία*) will give to all they touch a horrible smack: lastly, harp-strings, cut small and strewed on hot meat, will writhe like worms; and so you may rid your table of unwelcome guests.

If you would bone a pigeon, draw, and soak in vinegar for four-and-twenty hours; then pull out the bones, wash well, fill with herbs and spices and roast or boil it. To make tender a tough capon, boil it before roasting. But, if you desire to give your friends much joy, entertain them to a goose cooked alive. In the courtyard, pluck your goose except her head and neck, and cover her with lard and suet. Build a ring of faggots round her; not too narrow, lest she evade the roasting, nor too wide lest the smoke choke her, or the fire burn her. Inside the ring of faggots, on the ground occupied by your plucked and larded goose, place several pots of water mixed with salt and bearwort. Light the faggots slowly. When the goose begins to roast she will walk about; but she cannot escape; and you have her wings. When she grows weary and very hot, she quenches her thirst with the medicated water, and cools her heart and her inward parts. You continually must moisten her head and her heart with a sponge at the end of a cane. At last, you will see her run incontinently up and down; and presently stumble. Then she is empty, and there is no more moisture in her heart. Wherefore you may take her away, and set her on the table to your guests: she will cry when you pull off her pieces; and you almost may eat her before she has died.

The fifteenth and last book of Natural Magic treats of various modes of conducting secret correspondence by invisible inks, writing on eggs or naked backs of drugged couriers, counterfeit seals and writing, messages by pigeon or by arrows.

Those are the things of which a sober learned and most eminent physician of the Fifteenth Century seriously has written, and called Natural Magic. He shews the innocent ingenuous mind of a child rampant among new toys.

.   .   .

Having shown something of this mage's knowledge, it may be said, now, that, scattered about his Book of Natural Magic, carelessly and incidentally, there are allusions to certain venoms. He says:

I. that ἐξάμβλωσις may be procured by exhibiting the wine that Pliny calls Phthorium (Φθόριος) (Plin. 4, 16, 19, § 110), made from the grapes of a vine on which hellebore, wildgourd, and scamony have been grafted:

II. that *Mandrakes* (Μανδραγόρας, *Mandragora* (*Atropa Officinalis*) growing by a vine, will make its grapes hypnotic:

III. that one drachm of belladonna (—*gen. Atropa*) or stramonium (thorn-apple, *Datura stramonium*) in water, (which they will infect without taste or smell,) "will make men mad without any hurt, so that it is a most pleasant spectacle to behold such mad whimsies and visions. It is very pleasant to behold. Pray make trial," he lightly says. But he adds that one ounce of these drugs will make a man sleep four days:

IV. that one drachm of Nightshade rind (*Solanum nigrum*) in wine will give sleep; a little more, madness; a large dose, death:

V. that Hemlock (*Conium maculatum*) in wine will cause death:

VI. that the drachm dose of belladonna, bruised in wine, is good for driving away unwelcome guests.

It will be noticed that three of these six prescriptions contemplate death.

Messer Giambattista della Porta emphatically states that no single venom will kill all living creatures; "for what is venomous to one may serve for the preservation of another, which comes not by reason of the quality but of the distinct nature." He gives a lengthy list of substances with the animals to which they are fatal, *e.g.,* wolfebane kills wolves; henbane, hens; daffydillies, mice; black hellebore, oxen; white hellebore, pigeons; ivy, bats; comfrey, eagles; pondweed, urchins; mustard-seed, larks; vine-juice, cranes; willow, tom-tits; pomegranate-churnels, falcons, vultures, sea-gulls, blackbirds; and nux vomica, dogs. In regard to the last, it should be understood that the Fifteenth Century called fox-glove (*Digitalis purpurea*) nux vomica; and had not succeeded in extracting the vegetable alkaloid Strychnine, in its modern insolated form, from the Javanese Στρύχνος nux vomica, of which it is the active principle.

To complete the exposition of this typical Fifteenth-Century man of science, his chief Antidote to Venom is appended here.

"Take three pounds of old oil and two handfuls of St. John's Wort, (Balm of the Warrior's Wound, *hypericum.*) Macerate for two months in the sun. Strain off the old flowers, and add two ounces of fresh. Boil in Balneo Mariae (a bain-marie) for six hours. Put in a close-stopped bottle and keep in the sun for fifteen days. During July, add three ounces of St. John's Wort seed which gently has been stamped and steeped in two glasses of white wine for three days. Add also two drachms each of gentian, tormentil, dittany, zedoary, and carline, (all of which must have been gathered in August,) sandal-wood and long-aristolochie. Gently boil for six hours in Balneo Mariae. Strain in a press. Add to the expression one ounce each of saffron, myrrh, aloes, spikenard, and rhubarb, all bruised. Boil for a day in Balneo Mariae. Add two ounces each of treacle and mirthdate. Boil for six hours in Balneo Mariae. And set it in the sun for forty days.

"In plague, or suspicion of venom, anoint the stomach, wrists, and heart; and drink three drops in wine. It will work wonders," says Messer Giambattista della Porta.

.   .   .

The pharmacy of the Renascence, to quote the confession of the charlatan Cagliostro, consisted *in herbs and words,* "in verbis et in herbis."

The practice of medicine during the Borgian Era appears to have been entirely empirical. Physicians experimented on the vile body of their patient, trusting to luck, or chance, or faith, to work a cure. In contracts it was expressly stated that physicians must have the reputation of being *fortunate* (felix). Chirugeons were totally unaware of the circulation of the blood. So much stress here is laid upon the art and craft and mystery of medicine and its exponents, because from these, and from these alone, the knowledge and use of venoms could be obtained; and, if the blind can lead the blind without both falling into the same ditch, then there might be some foundation in fact for the legend of the Borgia Venom. But while physicians and chirugeons and apothecaries solemnly bought three little boys for a ducat each, drew off their blood and sublimed it into a potion to save the life of a senile pontiff; or did such monkey-tricks as Messer Juan de Vigo did to the Lord Julius P.P. II a few years later, all with quite convincing evidence of gravity and good faith, one must conclude that these mages acted according to the very best of their knowledge and belief; but that, in quantity as well as quality, their belief was vastly superior to their knowledge. Nardaeus says [1]

"The famous chirugeon Juan de Vigo, perceiving that an ulcer of the Lord Julius P.P. II became every day more stubborn, and that the Pope persisted in refusing all manner of remedies, hit upon a new method of cure: for he boiled together, in a brass kettle, for three hours, old rags cut in pieces, crumbs of fine bread, plantain, and a fomentation of arsenic sublimed in rose-water; after which, drying them, and applying them by way of powder to the wound (to which he had sworn that he would apply no more plaisters,) he cured the Pope in a very short time, to the admiration of all concerned."

Infantile as was the condition of medical science in regard to life, it was not one jot more robust in its observations of death. The cases of the suspicious demises of two cardinals, not during the reign of the Lord Alexander P.P. VI, but a few years later, will illustrate this.

In 1508, during the reign of the eternal enemy of Borgia the Lord Julius P.P. II, a nephew of His Holiness died, the Lord Galeotto Franciotto della Rovere, Cardinal-Presbyter of the Title of San Pietro *ad Vincula*. And, says Mgr. Paris de Grassis (Burchard's inimical successor as Caerimonarius,[2] "I saw on his face and on his body such "spots as seemed to be the effect of a dose of venom; and "all the others formed the same opinion."

[1] in Pentade Quaest. Iatrophilologicarum, p. 122. Ed. Geneva 1647, quoting Juan de Vigo, Lib. II, Chirug. Tract. II, 5.
[2] Mgr. Paris de Grassis *On Mgr. Hans Burchard* is fine indeed!

After autopsy, the chirugeons found no venom, but "certain bloody spots: wherefore they judged him to have died "of a superfluity of blood; and, if he had been phlebot-"omized, he would have had no harm."

The second case is that of the Lord Christopher Bainbridge, Cardinal-Presbyter of the Title of Santa Prassede, and Orator of King Henry VII Tudor at the Court of the Lord Leo P.P. X. He died in Rome, in 1514; and, says Mgr. Paris de Grassis the Caerimonarius, "when his death "was ascribed to venom (—*this surely ought to prove that the suspicion was habitual, and no more appropriate to the Borgia than to any other family of this period,*—) "by "command of the Pope he was eviscerated, and it was "found that his heart was diseased on the right side."

Now this Cardinal Bainbridge, whose death obviously was due to organic disease, has come down to posterity as a victim of venom; while Cardinal Dellarovere, whose *salma* presented far more suspicious, in fact distinctly suspicious, symptoms, is reputed to have died a natural death!

Of all the wonderful and subtle recipes for venoms which are believed to have been possessed by European potentates about this time, only one now is accessible: but it is dated 1540, exactly thirty-seven years after the Lord Alexander P.P. VI died of his double-tertian fever. It is a Venetian recipe, and comes from the Secret Archives of the Council of Ten.[1] Arsenic, antimony, orpiment, and aconite, are to be subjected to a long long process of preparation, similar to those wondrous stews in which Messer Giambattista della Porta, in company with every other respectable mage, had his continual joy; and, when all is done, the ignorant inventor of this horrible venom says that he cannot guarantee its success. Why? The dose of any single one of those four venomous ingredients alone would have been fatal. Why should their combination bring uncertainty? For the simple reason that the boiling

[1] Lamansky. Secrets de l'Etat de Venise. Petersburg. 1884.

and the sun-baking, the sublimation and the distillation, which so prolongedly was practised, set up chemical change, reaction, decomposition, destroyed the virtue or the nature, and effectually altered or annulled the venomous properties originally possessed by the subject of so much empiricism. As simples, they certainly would have been veneficous. As compounds, they might have caused grave inconvenience. But, heterogeneously compounded with alien matter, boiled to disintegration for weeks and months together, their effect surely could not be predicted. They might have been dangerous; or they might not: there is no knowing.

.　　.　　.

There is no defined charge against the House of Borgia of having compassed their enemies' deaths by means of venomous rings. The vulgar conception of a venomous ring is not unconnected with a needle-point, (or point,) projecting from the bezel, along which a minute drop of deadly venom can be made to flow; and which pierces the hand that grasps it, inducing syncope and death. Or, another kind conceals a small box in the bezel, containing a tiny capsule of glass wherein venom innocuously lurks, until the glass is broken on the lips.

At the Victoria and Albert Museum of South Kensington, and at the University Galleries of Oxford, there are very splendid collections of rings. Neither collection contains a ring having the legendary needle-point, (or point :) but each collection has a ring which may have been a proximate occasion of the vulgar belief.

N° 916 at South Kensington is a massive ring of brass, $1\frac{7}{16}$ inches in diameter; and has an octagonal bezel externally armed with a quincunx of spikes. It belongs to the Eighteenth Century, and is of the kind worn by Bavarian peasant-lads on the right middle finger at the present day.

N° 385 at Oxford is an Italian ring of the Fourteenth

Century, of gold *niello,* very beautiful. The bezel projects, and ends in the revolving rowel of a Fiery spur.

Both of these rings are weapons, intended hideously to scratch and tear an adversary's face. There is no hollow in them that might harbour venom; and they are in no sense venomous rings according to the popular specification: but they are rings,—means of violence of another species—; and, (men being what they are,) these rings may have formed the germ of the tradition.

However, at Oxford and South Kensington, there were rings labelled *Poison Rings,* at the close of the Nineteenth Century.

N° 479 in the Fortnum Collection at Oxford, is an Italian ring of the Sixteenth Century, of gold, and having a tiny χερούβ carved in cameo projecting from the high gold bezel. This bezel is hollow, pierced by two pinholes. Its capacity is under an eighth of a cubic inch. The hollow bezel may have been used to contain perfume, introduced through the pinholes: but it is more reasonable to conjecture that the hollow is due to a desire to economise the precious metal.

N° 533 in the same collection, is a German ring of the Seventeenth Century, of gold, and having a large rough pearl set *in,* not on, its bezel. Minute examination with microscope and probe proves that there is absolutely no room in this ring for any venom whatever; and that neither this, nor the foregoing, deserves the designation *"Poison Ring,"* which, however, discreetly is queried on the actual official labels. Apparently, the said labels purely are a concession to the unreasoning vulgar, who expect as a right to find at least a specimen of venomous rings in every respectable museum.

At South Kensington there is a massive ring of iron, plated and damascened with gold. It is Italian, of the Seventeenth Century, $11\frac{1}{12}$ of an inch in diameter. Its octagonal bezel is a tiny box having a hinged lid. This

might have held a relic. There is no ground for supposing
that it ever concealed venom.

Of these three so-called Poison Rings, the South Kensington specimen, and N° 533 at Oxford, belong to a period
at least a hundred years after the demise of the Lord
Alexander P.P. VI and Duke Cesare (detto Borgia). Only
N° 479 in the Fortnum Collection, by any exercise of
imagination, can be planted in the Borgia Era. It is
labelled *"Sixteenth Century"*; and the Lord Alexander
P.P. VI reigned in Rome, as God's Vicegerent, during the
first two years, seven months, seventeen days, of that century. There is no earthly cause to connect His Holiness
with that ring: but for the purpose of the argument, let it
be granted that N° 479 with its cameo χεϱούβ belonged
to the Borgia Pontiff, that the hollow bezel was used as a
receptacle for venom, and not for perfume. What then?

If the venom were a powder, the Pope's Holiness would
have to poke it in with a pin, and close the two tiny holes
with wax. Then, when the time came for envenoming the
usual cardinal, He assiduously would pick out the wax, and,
by violent jerks and shaking, induce the venom to present
itself for application. If the venom were a liquid, (M.
Dumas' bear-juice for example,) the same process of
waxing up and pin-picking would be necessary.

But there was no venom known to the Borgia, or to
any other man or woman of that era, which would kill, with
as small a dose as would go in that ring. The venoms of
the Fifteenth Century were administered (when they were
administered) by the drachm, or by the ounce—not by the
grain. The recipes have been displayed here. To harbour
a fatal dose of the known venoms, such as Messer Giambattista della Porta describes, a monstrous and vast ring
would be needed, more gigantic than those bronze-gilt *anuli*
used as credentials by the pontifical couriers of the Lord
Pius P.P. II (1458-1464). N°s 665 and 666 in the South
Kensington Collection, two and three-eighths, and two

inches, respectively, in diameter. The processes of brewing and stewing, so dear to the mages, without any doubt were a direct disposition of Providence for the security of human life; for they effectually withdrew the sting from venomous substances, and made it perfectly impossible for would-be murderers (and they were more than many) to kill, except accidentally, or with enormous doses and the disadvantages coincident thereto.

No doubt the Twentieth Century still has a little to learn. No doubt that wisdom would wait upon research among the mountains of documents stored in the archives of the Italian patriciate and baronage, Colonna, (not Orsini, whose papers were destroyed by fire in 1702) Savelli, Poplicola di Santacroce, Sforza-Cesarini, Carafa, Caïetani, Piccolhuomini, Borgia of Milan and Velletri, etc. No doubt in the Vatican Secret Archives (the Lord Alexander P.P. VI left one hundred and thirteen volumes in large folio of His acts.) infinite fields of information are white for harvest. There is nothing to prevent the reaping, but the lack of reapers. No doors are shut. No secrets are reserved. "The Popes have need of nothing except the truth."

Meanwhile, this only can be said:

The empirical methods of the Borgian Era preclude the possibility of anything approaching artistic venenation.

Not one of the definite accusations against the Borgia have been proved. On the contrary they are shown to lack valid foundation.

There is no authentic evidence regarding the Venom that the Borgia are said to have employed.

In fact, there was no Venom of the Borgia.

.   .   .

.   .   .

PONTIFEX MAXIMUS ALEXANDER VI ET PRINCEPS

In reviewing the Pontificate of the Lord Alexander P.P. VI notice must be taken of the fashion which represents Him as having been in continual fear of deposition on account of the simony by which He is alleged to have bought the papal power. It already has been shewn that no law existed, which made simony an annulment of election to ecclesiastical benefices, until the reign of the Lord Julius P.P. II. It remains to be considered whether the distribution of offices, with which the Lord Alexander P.P. VI signalized his election, in any case would give colour to the charge of simony.

The Conclave for the election of a Pope begins with the Mass of the Holy Spirit chaunted in the Chapel of St. Gregory. Afterwards, the cardinals go in procession, singing *Veni Creator Spiritus,* to take possession of the cells which they will have to occupy. These cells are erected in a hall of the Vatican, communicating with the Xystine Chapel. They are mere frameworks of wood hung with fringed curtains of baize, green in the cases of cardinals who are creatures of previous pontiffs; violet in the cases of cardinals who are creatures of the pontiff just deceased. On the front of each cell is a curtained doorway over which the armorials of the occupant are shewn, surmounted by a little swinging window. Each cardinal has a bed, a table, and a chair. His attendants support life in discomfort as best they may. Three hours after avemmaria, all doors and windows communicating with the outer world are walled up. Guards on the outside watch every avenue of access, under command of the Hereditary Marshal of the Church, now Prince Chigi, then Prince Savelli. To every cardinal are allowed two conclavists for his attendants, a chaplain and an esquire. A cardinal-prince, or one aged and infirm, may add a third. In addition to the cardinals and the conclavists, there are enclosed a sacristan with his subsacristans, a secretary with his undersecretaries, five masters of ceremonies, a confessor, two physicians, a chirugeon, two barbers, an apothecary, with their respective boys, a mason, a carpenter, and servants for menial work. Great care is taken that none of these lay-persons should be agents of the orators of the secular powers; and they are made to swear a stringent oath of secrecy. As a matter of fact, they are not allowed to know anything of the proceedings in the Xystine Chapel. Meals are served at stated hours, through a revolving cupboard (ruota) in the outer wall, supervised by cardinals-inspectors. Flagons are of bare glass, lumps of bread or meat are cut open, that no messages from the outer world may pass in by these means. Nor may any single thing pass out. Urgent private letters written in the Conclave are subject to cardinals-censors. Cardinals, who have need, may speak to visitors, but in presence of witnesses; and all communication must be open, and in a language that all can understand. These interviews take place at a window, the cardinal being on the inside, his visitor on the outside: but the conclavists and others are forbidden to approach the window on any pretext whatever.

In the Xystine Chapel, at the moment of the election, the cardinals alone are ocular and auricular witnesses of what takes place. Certainly all proceedings are recorded in the Acts of the Conclave. But the original acts of the Conclave that elected the Lord Alexander P.P. VI are not forthcoming: they very likely were lost in the Sack of Rome in 1527, when the Catholic Catalans and Lutheran Goths of the Elect-Emperor Don Carlos V gambled in the gutters for nuns and for the wives and daughters of Roman citizens. This then is the situation. All accounts of the Conclave of 1492, including the dispatches of Orators to their respective governments, are based on hearsay, or popular rumor. Historians have no other material; for there is none.

The cry of simony always is raised at every election of a Pope. It is only an exemplification of the law that Attraction and Repulsion are Primary Forces. That the Lord Alexander P.P. VI on His election did strip Himself of His new palace, and of His multitudinous benefices, cannot be denied. Why need it be denied? It always is done; for a cardinal who is elected Pope has no more need of these things: he leaves them with his scarlet and ermine cappamagna when He is endued with the plain white frock of Christ's Vicar. The giving away of His cast-off goods and offices cannot be twisted into an act of simony, unless there is a distinct stipulation that they are given and taken as the price of a vote. And no such distinct stipulation is extant. It is difficult to see why cardinals should be considered likely to be guilty of such degeneration. As a class of men they stand high: they generally are possessed of illustrious birth; they generally are possessed of such enormous wealth as to place them beyond the range of pecuniary temptation; and invariably they are men of merit, the fine flower of their profession. As far as mundane honours go, they have tasted all the glory that the world can offer, except one glory. No layman may kneel on the same bench with a cardinal, unless he be a reigning sovereign. No layman may make a fourth in a carriage containing three cardinals, not even a reigning sovereign. Their rank places them far above peers or princes. They are not eligible for the Athenæum Club, but nothing that the world can offer will improve their position except the Papacy; yet they are suspected, as a class, of intrigues and cabals of the basest kind, mere financial operations; and rarely, very rarely, is there any ground for the suspicion, the prize for which they are said to struggle generally being beneath their notice, the petty advantage which they are thought to desire being unworthy even of their contempt; for cardinals are tired men, tired of splendour, tired of the earthly things; and they are not invariably vile.

When, therefore, the absurd people who wish to prove simoniacal the election of the Lord Alexander P.P. VI, or the stupid craven Catholics who fatuously think to conciliate by joining rabidly in the hue and cry against a Pope, can show a definite declaration from one or more of the cardinals-assistant of the Conclave of 1492, couched in some such terms as there, *"I acknowledge and confess that, seduced by the dignities and the money that he offered me,* (or, *intimated by the menaces of Cardinal Rodrigo de Lançol y Borja,) I allowed myself to be corrupted; and, against my will and better knowledge, I sold my vote to this unworthy cardinal:* or, *I declare that I have resisted all his promises, threats, and flatteries, and firmly have refused to sell my vote to Cardinal Rodrigo de Lançol y Borja:* then and only then, can this silly or malicious calumny be said to have any foundation in fact.[1]

One thing is perfectly certain. The Lord Alexander P.P. VI, Who really was the last man in the world *à S' encanailler,* never behaved as though He had gained the Triregno by illegitimate means. Not when all Europe yelped around His footstool did He blench or quail or shew a sign of fear. The heathen raged; and the people imagined a vain thing. The kings of the earth set themselves; and the rulers took counsel together. The Monarchs of Naples nagged; the Catholic King and Queen denounced; the Christian Kings minced, grimaced, and gibbered; Caesar Semper Augustus protested; Cardinal Guiliano della Rovere raved and nursed sedition; the barons of Rome revolted; the dukes and tyrants and republics of Italy took up arms; the dominions of the Pope's Holiness were

[1] Cf. Maricourt.

invaded; the eternal City suffered violence; the sacro-sanctity of the pontifical person was in imminent danger: but the invincible Lord Alexander P.P. VI magnificently retired into the Mola of Hadrian, the only spot in all Christendom where His rule remained; and held His Own, inflexibly, implacably, with an enormous dignity impossible in one who was a mere usurper, a venal simoniac. So much is sure. The demeanour of the Lord Alexander P.P. VI in direst straits, was the demeanour of a man who had no doubt regarding his own integrity.

.   .   .

The so-called scandals of His private life are shewn to have been based upon the malice or the idle gossip of His enemies. He sat in "the fierce light that beats upon a throne." He was the father of a family. He was not the first or the last Pope Who has been the father of a family. His immediate predecessor, the Lord Innocent P.P. VIII, admitted the paternity of seven children. A successor, the Lord Paul P.P. III, also used Himself in a similar manner: nor are these all. If this be vicious, it was only vicious in the Lord Alexander P.P. VI because He was the Lord Alexander P.P. VI; for in other men the same thing was, and is, tolerated, accepted, applauded. A patrician or a plebeian may steal a horse: but a Pope may not look over the wall. *Ille crucem sceleris pretium tulit, hic diadema.*[1] However, as a father, He exhibited an illustrious example of paternal virtue. He was kind, loving, affectionate to his children; solicitous and self-sacrificing for their welfare and advancement. That He employed His spiritual power, to build up the temporalities of His family, was a temptation, to avoid which He would need to have been more than human. It was the custom of the time. It was an imperious necessity of the situation.

.   .   .

[1] Decii Junii Juvenalis, Satura xiii.

The murders and venenations of which He has been accused, in company with Duke Cesare, fail of proof; and indeed His guiltlessness as instigator, principal or accomplice, appears in every case to be beyond question.

The murder of Don Juan Francisco de Lançol y Borja, Duke of Gandia, remains a mystery: but what evidence there is distinctly points to a vendetta of Orsini directed against the Pope through His Captain-General.

The murder of the Prince of Bisceglia is referable rather to a vendetta of Sanseverini and Caïetani, than to the Pope or Duke Cesare (detto Borgia).

The deaths of Don Astorgio and Don Gianevangelista Manfredi are susceptible of the Venetian Orator's explanation, *puto mal san;* there positively is nothing to connect the Pope or the Duke with them.

The death of the Sultán Djim was due to natural causes, while he was in the hands of the Christian King; and the Pope's Holiness was a pecuniary loser (to the extent of about £80,000 a year) by his death.

The death of Cardinal Orsini was due to natural causes, according to the sworn testimony of physicians provided by the House of Orsini.

Fra Girolamo Savonarola O.P. was executed on a capital charge by due process of law; and the Pope was an unwilling agent for the administration of that law.

(The crime of Fra Girolamo really was that of intriguing with a foreign power with which his country was at war. General Booth committing treachery with Mr. Kruger, or Mr. Ira D. Sankey with the Son of Heaven Kwang Su, would be Twentieth-Century parallels of Savonarola and Charles VIII.)

Cardinal Giovanni Borgia (detto Giuinore) died a natural death.

Messer Ramiro d'Orco, Don Vitellozzo Vitelli, and Don Oliverotto da Fermo had a legal trial by court-martial, and paid the legal penalty of crime.

Don Paolo and Duke Francesco Orsini of Gravina suffered merited death, due to the exigencies of civil war in which they and their House were the aggressors.

There remain two other violent deaths to be accounted for, which were not of sufficient importance to treat of in the history of this pontificate, the case of Calderone Perotto, and that of Messer Francesco Trocces.

It is said by Don Paolo Capello, the Orator of Venice, in his Diarium, (or rather in that edition of the said Diarium which was prepared forty years later by Don Marino Sanuto,) that Calderon Perotto was a Spanish lad of eighteen years, one of the Pontifical pages; and that he was stabbed by Duke Cesare (detto Borgia) at the Pope's feet. The fact is related without comment or explanation. It would not be safe to attach much importance to the statement, because Don Paolo Capello's original document is not forthcoming and Don Marino Sanuto's version of what he wrote is the only version accessible. But the alleged murder of the page Perotto is not, like other calumnies, a posthumous invention; for it is mentioned in the atrocious *Letter to Silvio Savelli* described on an earlier page. The Pope is not, and was not blamed. The murder, if it were a murder at all, is attributed to Duke Cesare (detto Borgia); and it was not an unusual thing for a lord to slay a servant in the Borgian Era. That was common enough; but to do it in the presence of the Holiness of the Pope certainly was sacrilege; and this last circumstance makes it probable that the whole story is a pure invention; for the guilt of sacrilege lightly was not incurred even by the most bloody and abandoned villains: and Duke Cesare was not of that species.

The other death, that of Messer Francesco Trocces is more probable, and mentioned in several dispatches of Orators. He was a papal chamberlain (confidential flunkey of the cloak and sword,—minor situation dear to *petits maîtres* of the English and Keltic bourgeoisie now;) and was employed as governmental courier. The Republic of Venice was playing fast and loose with the Lord Alexander P.P. VI, disliking to see Duke Cesare's amazing success in the Romagna; and its Orator, Don Antonio Giustiniani carried on relations of a doubtful kind with Messer Francesco Trocces, in the usual manner of ambassadors who find that they can buy state-secrets from a "crapule." Suddenly, Messer Francesco fled from Rome to Civita Vecchia. He had been complaining to the Venetians about Duke Cesare; and all his treachery had come to light. The Duke's steel claws were far-reaching. The traitor was captured there and brought to Rome, strangled, and his body hanged on Tor Savelli as an example to others of his kind. Legally speaking he was executed for the crime of high treason; and the formal exposure of his corpse gives the lie to the idea of clandestine assassination. The practice of secret trials and summary executions is odious to the Twentieth Century: but, in the Fifteenth and Sixteenth, not only all civilized governments, but even barons who had power of life and death over their retainers, used these means as a matter of course; and that alone should be sufficient to exonerate the Borgia from blame.

It has been said of the Lord Alexander P.P. VI that He habitually envenomed his cardinals, that He might have their goods. The following story is given not in this connection, by Mr. F. Marion Crawford, and is here inserted on account of its frequent significance. At the corner of the Via Lata in the Corso of Rome, is the Palazzo Doria Pamphili, a typical Roman palace of the Borgian Era, two-thirds the size of the Vatican Basilica, and able to accommodate a thousand inhabitants. It was built by Cardinal Santorio (?), who bought the site from the Chapter of Santa Maria *Maggiore,* and expended thousands of gold ducats in the erection of a House Beautiful. All through

the reigns of the Lord Alexander P.P. VI and the Lord
Pius P.P. III, he remained in unmolested possession: but
during the pontificate of the Lord Julius P.P. II (Giuliano
della Rovere) the Pope's Holiness said to him that his
palace was "more suitable for a secular duke than for a
prince of the Church"; and forced him to make Him a free
gift of it for His Own nephew Don Francesco della
Rovere, whom He had created Duke of Urbino. The unfortunate Cardinal Santorio died soon after of a broken
heart. It was not Borgia who caused *his* death, in order to
have his palace: but Borgia's eternal enemy.

.   .   .

As a secular sovereign, no contemporary of His even
deserves to be named in comparison with the Lord Alexander P.P. VI. His reign broke the back of the turbulent
ambitious selfish baronage which had ravaged the papal
states for centuries. He was an independent Pope; willing
to enter into alliances, it is true, so long as they served His
purpose: but just as willing to throw over His allies and
stand alone upon occasion. If His interests leaned more
in one direction than another, it may be taken that He was a
Sforza+Cesarini Pope, rather than a creature of Colonna
or Orisin as the custom was. His political policy entirely
was directed to the substitution of peace and order with
security of life and property, instead of the anarchy and
desolation which He saw on His accession. He fully lived
up to His official title of RULER OF THE WORLD; and the
sovereigns of Europe at all times found Him sternly rigorously just, amenable neither to fear nor flattery. He was
an admirable FATHER OF PRINCES AND OF KINGS. Notwithstanding all that weakly has been said to the contrary,
the Holy Roman Church and Christendom owe a vast
debt of gratitude to Him. He found feebleness and war and
tumult at His coming: at His going He left behind Him

differences removed, rebellions quelled, and a tradition of consolidated strength. He was the Fosterer of Justice and of Peace. He was a great and wise Princeps.

. . .

As Pontifex Maximus, EARTHLY VICAR OF JESUS CHRIST OUR SAVIOUR, He merits reverent admiration. His habits and tastes were of the simplest kind, in an age of singular luxury. He was temperate in His diet; and the Orators of the Powers commented with disgust upon the fact that He never had more than one dish upon His table. He slept but little. His amusements occupied a mere fraction of His time: but, during recreation, He unbent His awful dignity, and enjoyed Himself with the frank abandon of a school-boy. He was a patron of painters: but men of letters incontinently drove their pens against Him; for the Lord Alexander P.P. VI was confronted by the problem of dealing with a new enemy to Christ's flock and to civilization—He had to regulate the printing-press in the interest of morals; and, as a duty of His office, He ordained the censorship of printed books, He inaugurated the "Imprimatur," He "muzzled the printer's devil."

Yet He was a gentle and kindly-affectioned Shepherd. In 1492, the Jews were expelled from Spain. He entertained them in security in Rome. In 1494, He was horrified by news of the diabolical atrocities of the Grand Inquisitor of Spain; and though He Himself was a Spaniard, He appointed four assessors with equal power, to restrain the excesses of Torquemada. The Spanish Inquisition never had the countenance of Rome, but Her bitterest opposition. The wanton ingenious cruelty of that infamous Tribunal was due to the fiendish strain of African black blood which tinges and defiles the bluest blood of Spain; and was committed in explicit defiance of the commands of God's Vicegerent. It is true that He gave America to Spain, and

Africa to Portugal.[1] The Bulls of Donation show that He considered it to be the Pope's duty to teach the Gospel to all nations, and to compel the observance of natural laws. He believed that, before the heathen could hear the Gospel, or observe those laws, it was necessary to make them subjects of a Christian Power. He knew that conquest makes more converts in one day, than preaching in three hundred years. He took as abruptly practical and business-like a view of things as though He had been fortunate enough to have been born an Englishman. And He acted upon the extremely scriptural principle that civil rights and civil authorities lawfully cannot obstruct the propagation of the Faith. None knew better than He that the Treasure was in an earthen vessel[2]: but, as chief bishop of the Church far above all principality and power and might and dominion,[3] He spoke, exhorted, and rebuked, with an authority. Let no man despise Him.[4] There was no other representative of Christianity; there was no other, in all the world, who even claimed to be the representative of Christianity, at that time. The Lord Alexander P.P. VI, magnificent and invincible, was the only one. Let no man despise Him.

As Pastor, He was merciful; as Judge, severe and just. His laws against witchcraft and Black Magic were of the most stringent kind. He used the means which every other sovereign in Europe also used. "East of Suez, some hold, the direct control of Providence ceases; Man being there handed over to the power of the Gods and Devils of Asia—" the most observant of modern English writers says. Men who have lived in the Far East, where Christian

---

[1] Have these Bulls been rescinded? If not, it is possible that they form the ground of the dull and bitter and radical animosity of Spain and Portugal to Anglo-Saxondom of the present day. In the light of these Bulls, England and America are usurpers and excommunicate!

[2] Ep. II to Cor. ii. 7.

[3] Ep. to Eph. i. 21.

[4] Ep. to St. Titus ii. 15.

influence is very feeble, will recognize the singular correctness of Mr. Rudyard Kipling's theory. Men, also, who at first hand have studied modern recrudescences of devil worship, modern flirtations with kakodaimoniacal agencies, the Luciferianism of modern France, will not mutter with patronizing superiority of superstitions and old wives' fables; but perfectly well will know that hideous abnormity with which the Pope's Holiness had to deal. Only the wilfully ignorant deny the actuality of diabolic manifestations, called witchcraft and Black Magic in the vulgar tongue. The ostrich who buries her head in sand is like to these. By the side of high civilization there always runs the impulse to savagery, the weird and radical decadence which wanders on dark paths. Hellas and Rome pried into the mysteries of Isis; Christendom entertains Turlupins, Rosicrucians, Indian gumnosophists, and Mahatmas; the Borgian Era played with the Roaring Lion; the Victorian Era with Sathanas and his sorrows. "Perhaps," "after all," "audi alteram partem",—hesitation, compromise, want of defined principle, lack of courageous singleness of mind,—amounting to Emasculation—is the mental note of the Twentieth Century. The Fifteenth had not a tithe of the knowledge now possessed: but it was awfully convinced, strong, and decisive, within its limitations. Then, there was no place for the palterer—except against the wall.

Other malefactors felt the flail which, like Osiris; He wielded equally with the crook. Notaries of the Pontifical Briefs debauched by the undisciplined rule of previous Popes, had become corrupt. In the absence of restraint they habitually forged briefs nominating to benefices, not only in Italy, but in all Christian countries. The ambition of German clergy created the demand. The flagitious notaries managed the supply. They sold their forged briefs privately to whoso would pay the price, and they pocketed the proceeds of this nefarious traffic. In 1497, the Lord Alexander P.P. VI found them out. Some promptly were broiled on Campo di Fiori, the nineteenth of October; one, the Lord Archbishop of Cosenza, and three secretaries, deprived of their benefices and degraded from their clerical estate, solemnly were immured alive in the Mola of Hadrian. These miserable criminals lived some years in their solitary cells, as the custom was, literally feeding on the bread of tears and the water of affliction until they died. (*Burchard, Diarium.*) One has heard fables of nuns immured. Here is a fairly genuine case of an immured archbishop. Immuration is the same punishment which the Twentieth Century metes out in countries where capital punishment has been abolished:—solitary confinement;— nothing more. The archbishopric of Cosenza was conferred on Cardinal Francisco de Borja, bastard of the Lord Calixtus P.P. III.

The assiduous attention to the duties of His office which the Lord Alexander P.P. VI exhibited is perfectly astounding; and pregnant with indubitable signification.

He reformed the monasteries of Austria, and the secular clergy of Portugal. He confirmed the Rule of the Religion of Friars Minim, founded by San Francisco da Paola. He approved the Rule of the Third Order of Friars Minor, founded by San Francesco d'Assisi. He permitted Madame Jean de Valois to found her Religion. In 1499, He confirmed the Rule of the Jesnats of San Girolamo, a congregation of laymen leading a religious communal life under the Rule of St. Aurelius Augustine, nursing the sick, and distilling aquavita, (as Carthusians distil Chartreuse, yellow and green, now.) He founded and confirmed in Rome the Order of Military Knights of St. George, for the defence of Christendom against the Muslim Infidel. He granted privileges to the College at Windsor: (Chapter of St. George, or King Henry VI Plantagenet's Foundation at Eton?) He approved the Order of Praying Knights of St. Michael in France. He reformed the Order of Military

Knights of Christ in Portugal. He canonized no saints. His personal piety was simple, diligent, and real. He greatly revered the Deipara, the Blessed Virgin Mary. In her honour, He ordained the bell which rings at sunset, sunrise, and noon, for the *Angelus Domini* in memory of The Incarnation. On His death-bed, He said, "We always "have had, and have, a singular affection for the Most "Holy Virgin."

In the Secret Archives of the Vatican, (merely a technical term, for they are open to all the world,) His original acts are preserved; the veritable Briefs and Bulls which He laboured to utter during His reign. They are bound in one hundred and thirteen large-folio volumes, each tome containing about ten thousand separate documents.[1] To understand what kind of thing is a Papal Bull or Brief, the Epistles of St. Peter, which are easily accessible, may be mentioned as the best examples extant :—earnest disquisitions, simple or scholarly, dealing authoritatively with subjects the most vital. The Lord Alexander P.P. VI is responsible for more than a million of these; and He only reigned eleven years.

The days and nights appreciably were not longer then than now. WHERE, THEN, DID THE LORD ALEXANDER P.P. VI FIND THE TIME TO ACCOMPLISH THE MULTIFARIOUS TURPITUDES WITH WHICH HE HAS BEEN CHARGED?

He was the father of bastards. He was not the first or last,—plebeian, patrician, potentate, or pontiff.

He was inflexible to foes. Was ever peace assured except by a stern martinet?

The Lord Alexander P.P. VI was a very great Prince, a very faithful Pastor, a very human Man.

By members of that Church, at least, which He so ably ruled, He should be regarded as above and beyond criti-

[1] Réné, Comte de Maricourt, who quotes M. L'Abbé Morel in *L'Univers.*

cism (so-called), amenable to no judge, ecclesiastical, or secular.[1] For the rest—the dwellers in glass houses . . .

.   .   .

.   .   .

[1] When it becomes a question of blaming a priest or a Pope, the principle of proportion demands that the lesser should bear. Two modern Roman Catholics have presumed with "unctuous rectitude" to scold the Holiness of the Pope as follows:

"From a Catholic point of view, it is impossible to blame Alexander too severely."—(History of the Popes. Pastor + Antrobus. VI. 139.)

This inhuman pronouncement is saved by the "a." Comment is needless: but there is another "Catholic point of view."

SPARKS THAT DIE

*"A fire, that is kindled, begins with smoke and hissing, while it
lays hold on the faggots; bursts into a roaring blaze, with
raging tongues of flame, devouring all in reach, spangled with
sparks that die."*

On the death of the Lord Alexander P.P. VI, Duke Cesare
de Valentinois della Romagna was the most potent personage in Italy. Several of his veteran legions under Don
Michelotto held the Eternal City. Usually, during the No-
vendiati after a Pope's demise, armed bands of Colonna
and Orsini pervaded the streets, to intimidate the Conclave
with their war-cries *Column—Column—, Bear—Bear—*.
In August and September 1503, the baronial partizans
were dumb; and all Rome shouted *Duca—Duca—Duca—*
for Duke Cesare. He might have done anything that he
pleased.

Now, if Duke Cesare were the ambitious ruthless
impious despot and villain which a fashion has painted him,
he must also have been a fool; in that he did not force the
Sacred College to raise another Borgia to Peter's Throne.
There were three Borgia cardinals ready to his hand, all
quiet and malleable and inoffensive, and two of them aged
men; viz.,

> (*a*) The Lord Luis Juan de Mila y Borja, Cardinal-
> Prior-Presbyter of the Title of Santi Quattro
> Coronati and Bishop of Lerida; first cousin and
> contemporary of the Lord Alexander P.P. VI:
>
> (*β*) the Lord Francisco de Borja, Cardinal-Presby-
> ter of the Title of San Nereo e Sant' Achilleo,
> Archbishop of Cosenza; bastard of the Lord
> Calixtus P.P. III:

(γ) the Lord Pedro Luis de Borja y Lançol, Cardinal-Deacon of Santa Maria in Via Lata; son of the late Pope's sister Doña Juana de Borja by her marriage with her cousin Don Guillelmo de Lançol.

The last was a young man, a contemporary of Duke Cesare himself, and appears to have been of a modest and retiring disposition. Whether his youth would have taken fire at being crowned with the Triregno, is an open question. He was not elected, and is numbered with the sparks that die. The Cardinal de Mila had resided nearly half a century at his bishopric in Spain; and was completely out of touch with his Italian relatives, as well as with the Sacred College.

But Cardinal Francisco de Borja seems to have been an ideal nominee for the purpose of Duke Cesare. He owed his rank to the Lord Alexander P.P. VI. He was of the age of sixty-two years, a gentle old gentleman of placid nature, of sweet and lovable habits, easily plastic. If he had been elected Pope by the influence of Duke Cesare, the consolidation of the Borja Dynasty would have been an accomplished fact. Theoretically, it matters not a jot who may be the Pope, Caius or Balbus, Peter or Paul. If there be any basis for the claims of the Holy Roman Church, Her mission goes on till the world's end, as well and as inevitably when Borgia, as when Pecci, reigns; as well and as inevitably under Boys of the age of twelve and eighteen years, like the Lord Benedict P.P. IX and the Lord John P.P. XII, as under Saints, like the Lord St. Sylvester P.P. and the Lord St. Fabian P.P.; as well and as inevitably under a Jew, like the Lord St. Peter P.P. as under an Englishman like the Lord Hadrian P.P. IV. The personality of God's Vicegerent is of no consequence whatever to the purity of the Faith, or to the triumph of the Holy Roman Church. These things being so, it is hard to understand why Duke Cesare did not menace with his unconquerable army the Sacred College, or assassinate samples of the cardinals who should decline to vote at his direction; until, by ultimate intimidation, he should have secured the election of his candidate. If he had been the godless wretch that his enemies designated, he would have achieved some such *colpo di stato* as this.

But, in the *rôle* of an unconscionable villain, Duke Cesare was a failure—an accented failure. Contrariwise, he comported himself as exemplarily as any good and pious Catholic. Most likely his fever, or the murderous remedies of his physicians, was responsible for this. There is no doubt but that the scheme for a Borgia Dynasty had been adumbrated; and that this was the psychological moment for giving it concrete expression: but the death of the Lord Alexander P.P. VI, and Duke Cesare's own illness came with sobering effect to him; and his course of action may be translated thus—that he resolved not to usurp the prerogative of the Supreme Disposer of events. For a villain, the resolve was weak: but it was what was to be expected of a splendid man of sense.

Duke Cesare knew that he held his riches, his supremacy, his titles of Duke of Romagna, Gonfalonier of the Holy Roman Church, and Castellan of Santangelo, solely at the pleasure of the Pope; yet he made no effort to secure the election of a Pope who would confirm his possession of them. There is still in existence a ring of his, (they call it a "Poison-Ring"—but of that much has been said—) which bears the splendid motto

FAYS CEQUE DOYS AVIEN QUE POURRA
Do thy duty, come what may.

That principle informed his action now. Duke Cesare did his duty.

He renewed his feudal oath of allegiance in the presence of the Sacred College. He formally recognized the supremacy, during the interregnum, of the Cardinal-Dean and the Cardinal-Chamberlain. He divested himself of the semblance and reality of power, by relinquishing the Mola of Hadrian (which impregnable fortress he held as Castellan of Santangelo, and whence he could have overawed both the Vatican and Rome). Further, finding that the mere presence of his army in the City was considered disrespectful to the Conclave, he retired it to his province of the Romagna; and he himself withdrew to France to his duchy of Valentinois.

So the Conclave of 1503 met in absolute freedom; and elected, as Successor of St. Peter, Ruler of the World, Father of Princes and of Kings, and Earthly Vicar of Jesus Christ our Saviour, the Lord Francesco de' Piccolhuomini, Cardinal Archdeacon of Sant' Eustachio, Archbishop of Siena, who deigned to be called the Lord Pius P.P. III, in memory of His august uncle, the Lord Pius P.P. II [1] Who had reigned from 1458 to 1464.

Then momentous events came thick and fast. The new Pope, on His coronation in St. Peter's, graciously permitted Duke Cesare to return to Rome. Such a mighty and splendid vassal as he was naturally inspired fear and distrust among the clergy. Such a trenchant weapon as he possessed in his unconquerable veteran army was described as a danger to the papacy. It is always very hard to make the clergy understand that a laic can be as sentimental and conscientious and self-sacrificing as a clerk. The word was put about that, seeing the Romagna to have been reduced to order, the necessity for Duke Cesare's army had ceased to be. Naturally, the clergy could not be expected to understand the necessity for an "army of occupation." The first rumour speedily grew into the statement that Duke Cesare's army was to be disbanded.

Colonna and Orsini heard, in their ugly exile, in their battered fortresses. Like the chained woves on the Capitol who know when rust makes thin their fetters, they lifted

[1] Enea Silvio Bartolomeo de' Piccolhuomini.

up their horrid heads and waited till the ultimate link should part. If Duke Cesare's army were disbanded, thousands of condottieri would be at large, brigands ready to take service under a new chief, under any banner. Why not under the banners of the Column and the Bear? Colonna and Orsini in alliance, reinforced by those same unconquerable mercenaries, might recover their old position, and once more become the strong right and left hands of a feeble Pope of their own; and then the days of the hated Borgia would be numbered. Colonna and Orsini, like their antipodes righteousness and peace, forgot their ancient feud and each kissed other. Duke Cesare indeed was in evil case.

And then, suddenly, after a pontificate of six and twenty days, the Lord Pius P.P. III died.

This moment was the opportunity of the psychic epileptic, the Lord Cardinal-Bishop Giuliano della Rovere, eternal enemy of the House of Borgia. He had emerged from the exile, which his innumerable treasons and malfeasances had merited, in time for the election of the Lord Pius P.P. III during Whose short reign he had employed himself to his own advantage. He had no friends. He gained the loathing of all with whom he had to do. The Sacred College to a man was inimical to him. He was not wealthy. He was thoroughly plebeian, he had no learning, no diplomatic skill, no charm. And there, on the other hand, was the splendid Duke Cesare, feared; yes: but admired also; and his unconquerable army was within call. A second time the election appeared likely to depend on him.

Cardinal Giuliano della Rovere was a desperate man. The only advantage that he possessed was, that at this time when all the other cardinals were in a state of nervous perturbation at the unusual occurrence of the deaths of two Popes in three months, he alone preserved his equanimity. He alone knew what he wanted. His colleagues in the Conclave were mentally collapsed: they showed signs of a liability to come under the influence of, to take advice, to take even direction from any one who would tell them what they wanted; and chiefly from him who was the one strong man of Italy, the man with the veteran army, Duke Cesare de Valentinois della Romagna (detto Borgia). The strongest laic is no match for an unscrupulous clerk when it comes to wits. Cardinal Giuliano della Rovere saw that he could gain the Sacred College, by gaining Duke Cesare. He concentrated all his crude rough desperate will on the one point.

.   .   .

The historian Varillas, who writes as a violent upholder of the Papacy, relates an extraordinary story; which, if true, is a veritable solution of mysteries; which, in short, is so strange, that it very likely is not fiction, historical or otherwise, but the blind and naked Truth, emerging from her well unabashed, luciferous, and, natuarlly, unwelcome.

He says that Duke Cesare proposed to the Second Conclave of 1503 to elect a cardinal whom he should name: that Cardinal Giuliano della Rovere, becoming aware of this, endeavoured to attract Duke Cesare's influence to himself: that to this end the said Cardinal privately announced to the said Duke that he was his father after the manner of men, further alleging this to have been the cause of his (the said cardinal's) enmity against the Lord Alexander P.P. VI deceased: that the said Cardinal asked the said Duke to assist him, his father, to gain the papal throne, promising, in return for such assistance, after his coronation with the Triregno, publicly to acknowledge the said Duke as his son, to confirm him in possession of his duchies and his conquests, and to retain him in all the offices which he then held: that the said Duke believed the said Cardinal, and by withdrawing from opposition, and by exerting full influence in a filial manner, he had compassed the election of the said Cardinal Giuliano della Rovere: that after his election the said Cardinal had belied all his promises, deprived the said Duke, of Umbria, and the Romagna, and all the fiefs which he had won, and of all the situations which he enjoyed, and finally had harassed, despoiled, and exiguously persecuted, all who bore the name of, or were connected with, The Borgia.

This is an extremely probable tale. Certainly a part of it is true, and perhaps the whole.

The identity of the father of Duke Cesare (detto Borgia) is involved in mystery.

The Brief of the Lord Xystus P.P. IV[1] dated the first of October 1480, which dispenses Messer Cesare from the necessity of proving his legitimacy, calls him "son of a cardinal bishop and a married woman," *de episcopo cardinali genitus et coniugata.*

The Brief of the Same, dated the sixteenth of August 1482, which makes Cardinal Rodrigo de Lançol y Borja administrator of Messer Cesare's estate, calls the boy "son of a cardinal bishop and a married woman," *de episcopo cardinali genitus et coniugata.*

The name of this "cardinal bishop" is not given in either Brief.

Most of the scribblers, diarists, chroniclers, orators, speak of Don Cesare, Cardinal Cesare, and Duke Cesare, as the son of Cardinal Rodrigo de Lançol y Borja (the Lord Alexander P.P. VI). Some, like Peter Martyr and Fioramondo Brugnolo call him "nephew of a brother of our Lord the Pope." In his autograph letter to the Pope, dated the sixteenth of January 1500, he himself speaks of Cardinal Giovanni Borgia (detto Giuniore), (who was the son of Don Pedro Luis de Lançol y Borja, own brother of the Lord Alexander P.P. VI) as "my brother."

In no official document is he named as the son of Cardinal Rodrigo de Lançol y Borja (the Lord Alexander P.P. VI) : but the Venetian Senate, in conferring on him the

[1] Secret Archives of the duchess of Ossuna and Infantado.

patriciate of that Republic in 1500, styled him "nephew of Pope Alexander."

The Lord Alexander P.P. VI never called him "son": but, in an autograph Brief of recommendation addressed to the Christian King Louis XII, He introduced Duke Cesare as His "heart."

Duke Cesare's subscription of a letter, which he wrote to the Pope on the twenty-eighth of January 1503, at the time of the Orsini revolt, is very curious. He signed himself "The most humble servant and most faithful handiwork of Your Holiness." *Vestrae Sanctitatis humillimus servus et devotissima factura*. As cardinal he might, and did, call himself the Pope's "creature," *creatura:* that is the form. A son, however, is not "handiwork" in any sense of the word: but a duke, who is made by his sovereign's signature of his patent, precisely is.

The authorities, who call Duke Cesare "nephew," may be dismissed. Popes, like other human beings, generally have nephews *stricte dicte vel late*.

His own appellation of Cardinal Giovanni Giuniore is susceptible of the meaning "comrade."

And "factura" will bear reference to his duchy, gonfalonierate, castellanship, etc.

Who then was the father of Duke Cesare?

Madonna Giovanna de' Catanei (wife of Don Giorgio della Croce, and, after his death, of Don Carlo Canale,) was certainly his mother. Two official inscriptions bear witness to this. The first, which was published by Signor Gnoli in the *Nuova Antologia* of the first of February 1881, refers to a house on Campo di Fiori which she left as an endowment for anniversary masses for the repose of the souls of herself and her two husbands named. The deed is the work of Messer Andrea Caroso, Notary Public, and is dated the fifteenth of January 1517. In it she is called "Vanoza Catanea *madre del Duca Borge*." The second is her epitaph on her tomb in Santa Maria del

Popolo (Forcella. Iscrizioni delle chiese di Roma I. 335) shewing her natural pride at finding herself the mother of two dukes, a prince duke, and a sovereign duchess.

"Faustiae Cathanae, *Caesare Valentiae,* Johannae Candiae,
Jufredo Scylatii, et Lucretia Ferrariae ducib. filiis nobili
Probitate insigni religioni eximia pari et aetate et
Prudentiae optime de xenodochio Lateranen. Meritae
Hieronimus Picus fidei commis. procur. ex test(amento) pos(uit).
Vix(it)ann. LXXVI m. IV d. XIII. Objit anno M.D.XVIII.
XXVI Nov."

In the absence of anything more authoritative than the foregoing, the story of Varillas remains the most probable solution of the mystery. The Lord Alexander P.P. VI never named, never treated, Duke Cesare as His son; never shewed for him the paternal love and affection which He shewed for his bastards, Don Pedro Luis, Madonna Girolama, Duke Juan Francisco, Duchess Lucrezia, Prince Gioffredo, Madonna Laura, Duke Giovanni. Yet Duke Cesare was splendid and superb; his abilities were immense, and pre-eminently useful to the Pope. And the Pope used him on all occasions as His most serviceable subject, rewarding him with lavish generosity for the service which he rendered. Between the Duke and his Sovereign Patron, there was a certain privileged and familiar confidence: but never intimate relationship, or filial or paternal love.

The status of Cardinal Giuliano della Rovere; his furious, blind, instinctive, and eternal hatred of the Lord Alexander P.P. VI and of every one connected with Him, is susceptible of an extremely human explanation. It bears the strongest possible resemblance to that very singular and very distinguishable passion of revengeful jealous rage which consumes the vulgar man in regard to a superior (in rank, breeding, or physique,) who shall have supplanted him in the favours of a lady.

Cardinal Rodrigo and Cardinal Giuliano, both were cardinals and bishops at the time of the birth of Duke Cesare. Cardinal Rodrigo had wealth, illustrious ancestry, incomparable charm of manner, a sumptuous aspect. He was magnificent and invincible. Cardinal Giuliano as a boy had peddled onions in a boat between Arbisola and Genoa, he had no money except the revenues of a few benefices, he was of a saturnine habit of mind, repulsive to his fellow creatures. His portraits, as cardinal on his medal by Sperandio, as Pope by II Caradosso (Ambrogio Foppa), shew him as a hatefully ugly man with satyr-brows, sunken and bleared eyes, fierce but haggard mien, and the animal appetites hugely predominant in the lips, the back of the head, and the curious little muscles which obliquely tend downward right and left in the region of the root of the nose. In the age of the Discovery of Man, Cardinal Giuliano della Rovere's physique did not qualify him to gain, or retain, the fidelity of any woman whom, inevitably, he would hunger to possess.

Nothing is known against the character of Madonna Giovanna de' Catanei except that she was the mistress, first of Cardinal Giuliano della Rovere, second of Cardinal Rodrigo de Lançol y Borja. A woman who indulges in systematic adultery *and sacrilege* is liable to be as false to her lovers, as she is to her husband and her God, at least until she has repented of her crimes and sins, giving proof of her repentance by surceasing from those same to lead a godly righteous and sober life, as Madonna Giovanna did during the whole reign of the Lord Alexander P.P. VI, and especially in, and after, 1508, when she was converted, together with Madonna Fiametta, a leman of Duke Cesare's, by hearing Frat' Egidio da Viterbo preach the Lent in Rome. But history and rumour agree in this, that with the exception of these two separate intrigues lasting from 1473 to 1481 Madonna Giovanna de' Catanei was "alioquin proba mulier" as even the rascally Paulo Giovio says, (Vita Gonsalvi 212)—otherwise, an honest woman.

It is humanly probable that Duke Casare was the son of Cardinal Giuliano della Rovere by Madonna Giovanna de' Catanei. He was born in 1474, "son of a cardinal bishop and a married woman." The following year, 1475, the lady bore to Cardinal Rodrigo de Lançol y Borja, Don Juan Francisco; in 1478, Madonna Lucrezia; in 1481, Don Gioffredo. It is as humanly natural that, after the birth of Duke Cesare, Cardinal Rodrigo should win the mother from Cardinal Giuliano; as that in 1492 he should win the Triregno from him in full conclave. The two prelates were antipathetic from heel to crown. There was bound to be rivalry between them. The loss of the papal throne in 1492 would have embittered Cardinal Guiliano della Rovere: but, by itself, hardly could have imparted that virulent vicious smack to his revenge that made him agonize, during twenty years, to dispossess and grind to powder the House of Borgia. The introduction of the feminine element provides a key to the enigma of that pettiness.

The narration of Varillas, therefore, deserves consideration as a contribution to the solving of the mysteries of the unquenchable hatred of Dellarovere for Borgia, and of Duke Cesare's relations with the Lord Alexander P.P. VI.

Whatever the truth may be, it is circumstantially evident that to Duke Cesare de Valentinois della Romagna, his advocacy or neutrality, his influence exercised or his abstention from opposition, Cardinal Giuliano della Rovere owed his election in the Conclave of November 1503. He chose to be called the Lord Julius P.P. II.; and He instantly set about the ruin of the House of Borgia.

.   .   .

The three Borgia cardinals naturally did not vote for Cardinal Giuliano della Rovere. Cardinal Luis Juan de Mila y Borja did not deign to attend the Conclave: but remained at his bishopric of Lerida in Spain. Cardinal Pedro Luis de Lançol y Borja, immediately after the election, passed into voluntary exile in the Regno without speaking to the Pope. Cardinal Francisco de Borja followed the custom of his House in regard to the voting: but he remained in Rome; and no doubt hoped with his charming innocent good nature that the Lord Julius P.P. would be satisfied, would be appeased, now that the world had nothing more to give Him. The Cardinal was bitterly disappointed.

From Madonna Lucrezia's little boy, Duke Roderico, His Holiness seized the duchy of Sermoneta; and restored it to the Caïetani from whom it originally had been taken, and who hold it still. (The present Duke of Sermoneta also has the superb sword of state which Maestro Ercole, the master-sword-smith of his age, had made to carry before Duke Cesare (detto Borgia) when he officiated as Cardinal Ablegate at the coronation of King Don Federigo of Naples in 1497. It is a miracle of damascening and design, a lesson to Twentieth-Century makers of decorative swords who heap glories on hilt and scabbard, and leave the blade to be hidden. Of this sword of Duke Cesare's the blade is the soul. The sheath of plain embossed leather is in the Victoria and Albert Museum.)

Then, the Lord Julius P.P. II demanded of Duke Cesare the renunciation of his duchy of the Romagna. That province was a fief of the Holy See; and it was competent for the Holiness of the Pope to deal with it at His pleasure: but, seeing that to Duke Cesare's splendid services, the Papacy practically owed the peace, the possession, the heftiness of the Romagna, heretofore a hell of turbulent bandits, brigands and assassins who defied their Overlord to collect His revenues,—the demand of the Lord Julius P.P. II at least was discouraging.

Duke Cesare, while willing to take the oath of allegiance of a feudal vassal to the Prince, refused to relinquish the fortresses of the Romagna which by conquest he had won, and garrisoned with his veteran army, now disbanded by the Judas wiles of Cardinal Giuliano della Rovere, and re-enlisted under alien banners.

Whether the Lord Julius P.P. II had made, or had not made, promises before His election, He was now *de iure* and *de facto* Ruler of the World, and absolutely despotic. He arrested Duke Cesare in Rome; and imprisoned him as a rebel in the Borgia Tower. The utter and vacuous helplessness of the Duke is in striking contrast to the masterful energy of all his previous life. Some enormous mental shock might produce such degeneration; the hideous treachery of Cardinal Giuliano della Rovere as related by Varillas, for example. Duke Cesare behaved, in his misfortune, like a son staggered, struck breathless and speechless by a revelation of a father's iniquity. A Bull of Deprivation despoiled him of all fiefs and dignities held from the Holy See, and confiscated all his personal property. He literally was stripped naked. In 1504, he escaped from Rome to Ostia in disguise, and thence to Naples. Here he might have found a pied à terre; and, with the splendour of his past achievements, have won an opportunity of recovering his lost estates by war: but the Lord Julius P.P. II, conscious of the danger to His peace that such an aggrieved and notable personality would be, had intrigued with the Catholic King; and, on Duke Cesare's arrival in the Regno, he was re-arrested, and shipped to a new prison in the castle of Medina del Campo in Spain.

.　　　.　　　.

The marriage of Madonna Lucrezia Borgia with Don Alfonso d'Este was a most happy one. The sweet young bride had made herself beloved by all Ferrara, from her husband's father Duke Ercole to the meanest of his subjects, by her beauty, her goodness, and her wonderfully able versatility, three indispensable qualities in the wife of the heir to the throne. Attired in "a mulberry satin gown embroidered with gold fish-bones, each two fingers broad,"

with the lace-flounce worth thirty thousand ducats (say
£60,000) which, according to Giovanni Lucido, was in her
wedding-chest, she would amuse herself in the ducal palace
by witnessing performances of the *Casina* or the *Miles
Gloriosus,* comedies of Plautus. Sometimes, (as Sanuto,
the Venetian Orator at Ferrara, informed his government,) she would remain all day in her apartments, writing
letters, and having her head washed: or she would sit for
hours and listen to the violin-music of her adept young
husband. On the Maundy Thursday of the first year of her
marriage, she publicly washed the feet of one hundred and
sixty poor men. Her observance of religious duties was as
notable as the spirit of genuine piety which pervades her
many letters still extant.

On hearing of Duke Cesare's *disgrazia,* Madonna Lucrezia earnestly wrote to the Marquess of Mantua, and
to her friend, sister-in-law, and confidante, the Marchioness Isabella, begging them to use the influence of their
House of Gonzaga with the Lord Julius P.P. II to procure
his freedom. The times were out of joint for Este personally to interfere; for Madonna Lucrezia was stricken
down with the effects of an ἄμβλωσις, and the old Duke
Ercole was breathing his last sigh.

On the nineteenth of January 1505, the Lord Julius
P.P. II issued His notorious Bull against Simony; striking
a new blow at the House of Borgia, by the aspersion cast
upon the memory of the Lord Alexander P.P. VI.

Duke Alfonso d'Este and his Duchess Lucrezia ascended the throne of their duchy in due course; and negotiations with the Holiness of the Pope, for the enfran-
chisement of Duke Cesare, might have been, and would
have been instituted: but, early in the spring of the year
Ferrara was threatened by famine, and the hands of the
young sovereigns were entirely occupied. Had Duke
Cesare been own brother to the Duchess Lucrezia, perhaps
more urgent steps would have been taken; but she never

seems to have regarded him otherwise than as a half-brother, who was her Father's most useful servant, and her mother's shame. Duke Alfonso proceeded to Venice to buy food stuffs in view of the famine, for the patriarchal rule obtained in Ferrara; and left the Duchess Lucrezia as Regent of his state. Her lovely womanly character may be seen in an edict which she issued for the protection of Jews, who were attacked and pillaged by Christians rioting for food; and in the sweet indignant letter, abounding in mis-spelt words (as do all good and distinguished women's letters,) and enjoining the Podesta (mayor) to be energetic about securing to the Jews protection of their lives and property equally with the Christians.

When Duke Alfonso returned, after some months' absence during which the Duchess sent him periodical and frequent accounts of her regency, addressed "To the Most Illustrious and Most Excellent Lord, My Most Honourable Lord and Consort, These, with speed—speed—speed—" the summer brought plague on the heels of famine. The visitation was most severe. The unselfish exertions of the Duke and Duchess were noble and untiring. The health of the Duchess Lucrezia suffered; and before the year was over she gave birth to a dead child.

In 1506, Duke Cesare de Valentinois escaped from his Spanish prison, and made his way into the neighbouring realm of Navarre, where the King Jean d'Albret was brother to his wife Madame Charlotte d'Albret, Duchess of Valentinois. The events of the last three years had not broken his splendid spirit. All his triumphs, all the results of his strenuous energy and talent had been nullified for him. At the age of thirty-three years he was despoiled of his life's work, and was a ruined man. The Romagna for ever was gone from him. His French duchy seems to have been of small account. Still, he was not crushed, he had the courage to begin again to carve out a career in a new

Julius P.P. II. Perugia was the seat of the Baglioni. Twenty years before, in 1487, there had been an outbreak of the feud of Baglioni and Oddi, months of continual rioting, the gutters running blood, the city like a slaughter-house; until Oddi was driven away, and Baglioni turned the place into a fortress and the churches into barracks. In 1491, in another outbreak, Baglioni hanged a hundred and thirty conspirators from the windows of the Palazzo Communale in a single day; and, (with the quick reversion from carnage to piety which is a characteristic of the age,) incontinently erected five and thirty altars in the public square, and caused continuous masses to be said and pro-cessions to be performed, to purify the city and to procure repose for the souls of the slain. Duke Cesare made a marked impression on these brigands, who learned to give him little trouble: but, when he was dispossessed and his long sword sealed in its scabbard, Baglioni took the bit between their teeth and reared, refused tribute to their sovereign Over-lord, and broke out in rebellion in the customary manner. The Lord Julius P.P. II promptly raised an army which He led in person; and reduced Perugia. Without precautions for His safety, trusting to the moral effect of His presence for the inviolability of His sacrosanct person, He adventured Himself in the heart of the rebel city, and beat Don Giampaolo Baglioni to his knees. In a man of sensibility this hardihood would indi-cate a very dare-devil: in the case of the Supreme Pontiff a distinction must be made between courage and mere plebeian callousness. Messer Niccolo Machiavelli sneered at this miserable Don Giampaolo Baglioni, because he lacked the boldness to strangle his unwelcome visitor, the Lord Julius P.P. II, and so crown his life of crime with a signal act of "Magnanimità"! Certainly a man would need some boldness to strangle the Pope, the Ruler of the World, the Father of Princes and of Kings, the Earthly Vicar of Jesus Christ our Saviour! Certainly, a man who as the Apollo of the Belvedere, when first it was discovered at Porto d'Anzio (Antium). It is true that He bought in 1506, for six hundred gold crowns (?) the Laocoon, (which Messer Michelangelo Buonarroti saw unearthed in the Baths of Titus,) to the supreme disgust of his "art-adviser" who declared that the two sons of the Thymbraian priest were not boys, but little men. It is true that He bought the Ariadne (which He called Cleopatra), the Torso of Herakles, and the Commodus, unearthed on Campo di Fiori, and now in the Vatican. He did these things because they were modish things to do in 1506. One gained more κῦδος in the pose of a Sixteenth-Century Maecenas, than as Successor of the Galilean Fisherman. The plebeian pontiff of the Sixteenth Century was ashamed of His plebeian predecessor of the First. The times were changed, he argued, as the faithful vainly argue to excuse prelatical vagaries now. He preferred competition with "men of the world" to the cure of souls. He was quite unable to appreciate intellect. He was congenitally incapable of appreciating the delicacy, or the validity, of Letters. The plebeian chiefly is touched by way of the sense of sight; and the Lord Julius P.P. II understood naked statues, things which He could see: wherefore He bought Apollo and Laocoon and the rest. There is not the slightest credit due to Him for discrimination in His purchases, or for a deliberate choice of what was beautiful. Men happened to dig up those marbles in Roman territory just then. Any one could see them to be beyond the ordinary. Any one could see them to be antiques. It was the fashion to buy antiques; and the Terrible Pontiff bought —bought as retired grocers buy, who buy their libraries by the cwt. Also, He had Messer Michelangelo Buonarroti at His ankle, with whose advice it would have been difficult for a sardonic goat to commit an artistic blunder. They were a pair, those two, the artist and the pontiff, *uomini terribili,* terrible men, both. Messer Michelangelo had been educated at the expense of Lorenzo de' Medici in the Palazzo Medici of Florence and the Villa Medici of Fiesole. There, at the suggestion of Canon Angelo Ambrogini (detto Poliziano), he had sculptured his Battle of Herakles with the Centaurs, while listening to Fra Girolamo Savonarola and Messer Giovanni Pico della Mirandola surnamed the Phoenix of Genius (*Fenice degli iugegni.*) Could any man but Poliziano have suggested a more admirable subject for Michelangelo than this of weird muscular gigantic energy? In 1500, in the reign of the Lord Alexander P.P. VI, he had carved his lily-pure Pietà of the Vatican Basilica, the most divinely pure presentment of God's Maiden Mother, of the $M\eta\tau\varrho o\pi\acute{a}\varrho\vartheta\varepsilon\nu o\varsigma$, save those of Alessandro Filipepi (detto Botticelli) since Byzantine art had faded. Now, he was in Rome, "art adviser" to the Terrible Pontiff, eating his own heart in inactivity, burning and yearning to work with his own hands, with all the passionate excruciating torture suffered by every artist who may not put his talent "out to the exchangers." It was the lust of creation in Michelangelo that made him terrible to his fellow men. His incivilities to his colleagues are proverbial. "Goffo nell' arte" he flung with contemptuous scorn to Messer Pietro di Cristoforo Vanucci of città della Pieve (detto Perugino) who had a picture-shop at Florence, and bought estates with the proceeds of his smooth and stony saints and seraphs, stencilled by his pupils on the canvases, and touched by himself in his workshop or picture-factory at Perugia, at the very time when Oddi and Baglioni each were tearing the other's throats to tatters outside his door. Then in 1508 the Lord Julius P.P. II ordered Messer Michelangelo to paint the ceiling of the Xystine Chapel. The gods on high Olympos never allow a man to do the thing that he wants to do: they are jealous lest man should create a god. Messer Michelangelo wanted to practise sculpture; wherefore he was told to paint a ceiling. "I'm not a painter!" (Nè io pittore!) he roared to the Terrible Pontiff, who fulminated and thundered in reply. They both were terrible men; and they unrestrainedly spoke with perfect frankness as between man and man, using no set form whatever.

The Terrible Pontiff, like all clerical patrons, was an infernal nuisance to the Terrible Painter, who well-nigh killed himself by years of ceaseless toil, lying on his back upon a scaffold in the filthy air that hangs about a ceiling. He would have no assistant save a boy or two. He lived, and ate, and slept on the scene of his labour. Many times the Terrible Pontiff came to see what was being done; and every time the Terrible Painter instructed Him in the art and mystery of anathema, and drove Him away. At last the Lord Julius P.P. II threatened to have Messer Michelangelo flung down, and the scaffold pulled about his ears: but this was when the work was done. The Terrible Painter had the scaffold removed, and invited his patron to view the sumptuous ceiling. The Terrible Pontiff came; and saw; and suggested that the scaffold should be re-erected so that the work might be touched up with—ultramarine and gold-leaf!

．　　　．　　　．

In Ferrara, the year 1506 was marked by one of those tragical expositions of naked human passion which afflict humanity in every age. Madonna Angela de Borja y Lançol, a cousin of the Duchess Lucrezia—being the daughter of the Lord Alexander P.P. VI's sister, Doña Juana, by her marriage with Don Giullelmo de Lançol, and sister to Cardinal Juan de Borja y Lançol (detto Giovanni Seniore), Archbishop of Monreale, and Cardinal Pedro Luis de Borja y Lançol,—was a maid-of-honour attached to the suite of the Duchess of Ferrara. She was very beautiful, and is called in the chronicle "a most elegant damsel"— *damigella elegantissima.* Two younger brothers of Duke Alfonso, the athletic Cardinal Ippolito d'Este, and Don

Giulio d'Este (bastard of the old Duke Ercole) fell in love with her. Madonna Angela favoured the Bastard Giulio whose lovely eyes she unreservedly admired—consequently, as the manner was, his rival Cardinal hired four professionals to put out those eyes. Naif unpaltering straightforwardness of the Sixteenth Century! The operation failed of execution, for the Bastard Giulio, being forewarned, escaped with his eyes unharmed. But such conduct does not make for the peace of a state, brawling royalties affording disedification to the mob. The laws of Ferrara, paternal in character, ordained a scale of penances graduated to the rank of culprits: for example, a working man, who obscenely swore, would pay a fine; a swearing burgess paid a double fine and a swearing noble was mulcted of a triple fine. Therefore Duke Alfonso put the ban on his brother, the Lord Cardinal Ippolito, who retired to Rome to nurse his discontent and plan his next move against the Bastard Giulio. Madonna Angela, who was no more to be blamed than any other girl whose charms have inflamed a lusty pair of rivals to desperation, married the third, Don Alessandro Pio Estense di Savoja, Count of Sassuolo. The bandit [1] Cardinal Ippolito had not long to wait in exile. If he had been the Master of Fate, he could not have devised a neater or completer vengeance than that which came to him. It is one thing to attempt to blind a bastard brother who is a royal prince. It is another thing to compass the death of a brother who is a reigning sovereign. The robust young Cardinal was equal to the first: but above the second.

Duke Alfonso's brothers, Don Ferdinando d'Este and the Bastard Giulio, engaged in a conspiracy to assassinate him. News of the plot reached Cardinal Ippolito in Rome. He promptly warned Duke Alfonso of his danger. Finding themselves discovered, the conspirators fled. Don Ferdinando was caught: but the Bastard Giulio, good at escapes, took refuge in sanctuary with his brother-in-law the Mar-

[1] One *bandito,* under sentence, or ban, of exile.

quess of Mantua, who replied to Duke Alfonso's demand for extradition that, if evidence of guilt were shown, the criminal should be delivered up to justice. Evidence was shown, in the shape of the full confession of Don Ferdinando; and the Bastard Giulio passed into his sovereign brother's hands. Brought to the common block in the square of Ferrara, the two detected traitors were allowed to suffer all the pangs of the approach of death: but, at the last moment, Duke Alfonso in his mercy granted a reprieve, commuting their penance to life-imprisonment.

.   .   .

Early in 1507, died Duke Cesare de Valentinois (detto Borgia), a mean inglorious death for one who had been in life so mighty a man. While commanding a small squadron on behalf of the King of Navarre, he was killed in a petty skirmish by the castle of Viana. His corpse was quietly interred in the cathedral of Pampeluna, which, by a curious coincidence, had been the first piece of ecclesiastical preferment conferred on him by the Lord Alexander P.P. VI. So ended a phenomenal personality in which superb and tawny beauty of physique, prodigious force of character, fierce all-conquering energy, swift unerring almost-feline agility of action, and transcendent splendour of achievement, were blasted and nullified and marred, humanly speaking, by one single delicacy of respectful conscientious self-sacrifice and supreme confidence in clerical honour. His beautiful elegy by Ercole Strozzi,

"Ille diu, qui dum caelestibus auris
Visitur, implet onus laudis, caelumque meretur"

is too well-known to be quoted at length. He left three children,

(a) Madame Eloise de Valentinois; who married, first, the Sieur Louis de la Tremouille, second, the Sieur Philippe de Bourbon, Comte de Busset, whose direct descendants flourish in France at the present day:

(β) Don Girolamo de Valentinois; who, by marriage with Madonna Isabella Carpi patrician of Ferrara, had issue Madonna Lucrezia de Valentinois married, in 1562, to Don Bartolomeo Oroboni patrician of Ferrara, who died in 1565.

(γ) a bastard Madonna Camilla Lucrezia; (evidently the offspring of an intrigue carried on when Duke Cesare was in Ferrara in 1500-1 arranging the marriage of Madonna Lucrezia Borgia to the heir of Duke Ercole d'Este;) born of Duke Cesare and a married woman in Ferrara; according to the deed of legitimation,[1] dated 1509, where Madonna Camilla Lucrezia is said to be "of the age of more than seven years": she became Abbess of San Bernardino in Ferrara, in 1545; and died in 1573.

The Duchess Lucrezia Borgia d'Este was deeply grieved by the death of Duke Cesare her half-brother. There is a very touching letter written by her friend and sister-in-law, the Marchioness Isabella Gonzaga of Mantua, to Duke Alfonso who at that time was in Rome. It is dated the eighteenth of April 1507; and describes how that the Duchess of Ferrara, on receiving the sad news, immediately

[1] Observe the chivalrous gentleness of the Borgian Era in regard to women, compared with the bald mercilessness of modern parochial and civil Registers. In these deeds of legitimation, the woman is never named, and not always the man. The weaker party is never punished by eternal gibbeting, by eternal record of her shame by name. She is always permitted to hide under the veil of *coniugata,* or *soluta,* "a married woman" or "a spinster." Still, the Twentieth Century is humane to the wolf's brother and the hyæna's cousin; and nourishes a Society for the Prevention of Cruelty to Animals: and perhaps that balances the Fifteenth and Sixteenth Centuries' humanity and chivalry to sex.

went to the church of the monastery of Corpus Domini and remained during two days and nights, praying for the repose of the soul of Duke Cesare de Valentinois. A simple act; and precisely what any good Christian woman would do in similar circumstances.

.   .   .

A year later, on the fourth of April 1508, at the Castle of Ferrara to the immense joy of all, *formosus puer est formoso natus Aprili,* says Benedetto Lampridii in his Carmina Inedita, the Duchess Lucrezia bore to Duke Alfonso a son and heir, who was baptized by the name Ercole.

During this year, a league of the Powers was formed under the Elect-Emperor Maximilian directed against Venice; and Duke Alfonso, whose dominions marched with those of that Republic, threw in his lot with its foes. While he was engaging the Venetians on the Romagna frontier, the Duchess Lucrezia ruled as Regent in Ferrara. She administered government of the state with the same sweet womanly thoroughness as she shewed in the administration of the government of her domestic affairs. History is rich in records relating to this lovely lady. She superintended the household matters of her palaces with a minute attention to detail which, to the modern middle-classes, would appear amazing in a Sovereign Duchess. To set a fashion of rare liberal-mindedness she appointed the Jewess Mazzolino to the care of her extensive wardrobe, and Messer Ludovico as her physician. Her régime was of the simple patriarchal type of the old Duke Ercole, who, on the occasion of an outbreak of plague in 1500, issued an Edict which said that "Duke Ercole d'Este, for good reasons to him known, *and because it always is well to be on good terms with God,*" ordained religious processions every day throughout Ferrara. A second quaint Edict of the same fatherly potentate, (which incidentally speaks for the meticulously cleanly personal habits of the Borgian Era, so strenuously maintained on a previous page of this book,) proclaims that "inasmuch as bakers are known to knead "their dough with feet that, frequently, are unclean, such "practices must not continue except on penalty of fine or "imprisonment: but the dough must be worked with clean "hands *and nails*."

Evildoers, all the same, had a shocking time. Mario Equicola gives exact particulars of a certain Madonna Laura (name suppressed) who, being caught in adultery, was immured alive; that is to say, she was publicly confined in a cell a few feet square, with a little window, outside the episcopal palace, near the entrance on the right of the high altar of the cathedral of Ferrara. Perjurers went about after their conviction with their tongues securely nailed to little logs of wood. The accounts for the nails and logs exist. Duchess Lucrezia's sumptuary laws were unsuccessful. The sex of the legislator prevented her from manufacturing laws to regulate fashion, which could be put into practical effect. That was perfectly natural; nor does the failure in any way reflect upon the excellence of the intentions of her ducal highness. She ordained that no woman should wear a gown whose value was higher than the sum of fifteen ducats (say £30), nor jewellery worth more than fifty ducats (say £100). She furnished a specification of the gems which might be worn, and of the fabrics of which gowns might be made. Also, she precisely specified the quantity of material that might be used, and the cut and fashion that was to be adopted. Further, in order to secure the observation of these laws, she ordained a box, having a slit in its lid like a modern letter-box, to be placed in the cathedral by the holy-water-stoup; so that fathers, husbands, or lovers, who found themselves outraged by the length or the rotundity of the skirts, or the bulk of the sleeves, or the violence of the style of their women-folk,— and the cost of the same,—secretly might drop in denunciations while in the act of taking holy water; the said denunciations afterwards to be attended-to in a legal manner by the justiciary. Delightfully solemn and futile effort of a charming woman. Well, it failed; not on account of the female peacocks of Ferrara, but by reason of the very skewbald harlequins whose propriety and purses it had aimed to benefit. How many denunciations secretly were dropped into Duchess Lucrezia's precious box, how many scandalized fathers, husbands, and lovers, sneaked about their daughters, wives and lemans, is not known. Only one thing is known,—there was not a justiciar in all the duchy of Ferrara, married or unmarried, who dared even to allude to, much less to act upon, the said denunciations, and enforce the law.

On the twenty-fifth of August 1509, the Duchess Lucrezia gave birth to a second son, Don Ippolito d'Este, named after his uncle the heraklean Cardinal; and who, in after years, became Archbishop and Cardinal of Milan.

All through 1508 and 1509 the war went on. In December of the latter year, a powerful Venetian fleet advanced to the mouth of the Po, devastating the country on both banks, and invading the duchy of Ferrara with frightful atrocities. Duke Alfonso, hurrying to meet the foe, won a glorious victory at Policella: but the war dragged on till 1512, keeping him in camp, away from his capital, which almost exclusively was governed by the Duchess Lucrezia (she bore Don Alessandro d'Este in 1511), assisted by Cardinal Ippolito d'Este, now no longer a bandit, but completely in the confidence and favour of his sovereign brother.

.   .   .

On the fifth of February 1510 died the noble and strenuous knight Don Pietro Gregorio Borgia of the Junior Branch. He had been high in honour with Duke Cesare de Valentinois della Romagna since he saved him from the clutches of the Christian King Charles VIII in 1495; and had served him as mounted scale-armoured arbalister, lieutenant, and standard-bearer. On the fall of the Duke, he returned to his allegiance to the Regno now ruled by the Catholic King Don Hernando. He was Viceroy of the province of the Abruzzi when he died, and was buried in the Church of San Clemente at Velletri, his native city.[1] His fine epitaph[2] runs:

"HIC REQUIESCIT NOB. ET STRENUUS EQUES DOM. PETRUS BORGIA, CATAPHRACTOR. LOCUM-TENENS, AC SIGNIFER CESARIS BORGIAE ISPANI VALENTINI DUCIS, QUI OBJIT AN. DNI. MDX. D. QV. MEN. FEB."

.   .   .

The year 1511 is remarkable for a wildly frenetic insurrection on the part of the gentle old Cardinal Francisco de Borja, which cost that Most Worshipful Lord his rank and his life. There is a limit to human endurance. In some men it is wide; in others narrow: but human nature subjected to unnatural suppression and restraint, sooner or later desperately will struggle to burst its bonds. This principle has never been understood by the clergy. It is one of the disabilities under which they labour in dealing with men. History teems with examples of amiable, would-be obedient, and respectful characters, tried beyond their strength by inconsiderate ignorant oppressive injustice on the part of churchmen, and transformed into savagely bitter and appallingly destructive suicides. There is no better example than Cardinal Francisco de Borja.

He was of the age of seventy years. Though his illustrious House had been predominant in Christendom during more than fifty of those years, he had never sought to benefit by the fact that his father was the Lord Calixtus P.P. III, nor to intrude himself among the mighty who

---

[1] Theuli. Bonaventura Abp. Teatro Istorico di Velletri, II. 5.

[2] Vit. Synop. Stef. Borgiae S.R.E. Card. Ampliss. (Peter Paul of St. Bartholomew, discalced Carmelite. Rome, 1805, I. 2.)

were his blood-relations. Not till he was on the verge of his sixtieth year did he become a personage; and then his august cousin, the Lord Alexander P.P. VI, in admiration of his enchanting disposition, dignified him with the scarlet hat and the rank of Cardinal-Presbyter of the Title of Santa Lucia *in Silice, (Atti Consistoriali)*. Later, he proceeded to the Title of Santa Cecelia, *(Ciacconi* and *Moroni)*; thence again to the Title of San Nereo e Sant' Achilleo *(Atti Consistoriali)*; and last to the Title of San Clemente. He also was Treasurer of the Holy See, Bishop of Teano, and Archbishop of Cosenza.

Seeing the exacerbating measures which the Terrible Pontiff, the Lord Julius P.P. II was using against the House of Borgia, and especially the spoliation of the two little boys Duke Roderico and Duke Giovanni, this very sympathetic old cardinal had the indiscretion to put his frank opinion of the Pope's Holiness into certain letters which he wrote to the Orator of Ferrara at the Court of Rome. This opinion could not fail to be unfavourable and the reverse of complimentary. No doubt the Orator was in direct communication with his sovereign, Duke Alfonso d'Este, whom he would keep advised of the trend of sentiments and of events in Rome. These letters came, by means which it would be improper to describe, into the anointed hands of God's Vicegerent. His Holiness read them; and vehemently enraged himself against the Duke Alfonso d'Este of Ferrara, and upon Cardinal Francisco de Borja, whom he incontinently flung into prison with every species of indignity. The Sacred College, tremorous for its own security if such treatment of a Purpled One should pass without remonstrance, exerted its influence on the Holiness of the Pope, and procured the ungracious liberation of Cardinal Francisco de Borja.

But the ill was done. The milk of human kindness effectually had been soured; the placid amiable old gentleman had been changed into a violent malcontent breathing threatenings and slaughter, and whose fiery Spanish blood at last was boiling over. Two other cardinals joined in his savage revolt, the Lord Bernardino Lopez de Caravajal Cardinal-Bishop of Sabina, and the Lord Guillaume de Briçonnet Cardinal-Bishop of Praeneste (Palestrina). These three decamped from Rome to Pisa, where, a fourth, the Lord Réné de Prie Cardinal-Presbyter of the Title of Santa Sabina, having joined them, they constituted themselves as a General Council; and dared to cite the Lord Julius P.P. II to shew cause before them why He should not be declared a Pseudopontiff, and deposed from Peter's Throne, by reason of the irregularity of His election due to Simony and other crimes:—an excellent example of the sauce for the goose being served to the gander.

Melpomene is own sister to Thalia; and never has a ghastlier tragedy been more comically played. This self-styled Council of Pisa laboured under the disadvantage of being radically schismatic. Only the Roman Pontiff can summon, or confirm the decrees of, a General Council. The acts of the Schismatic Council of Pisa, therefore, were hopelessly and irretrievably invalid. The very impossibility of the whole affair is proof conclusive that these four well-intentioned, well-living pathetic old men had been tried beyond their strength, beyond all patience, goaded by insult and by gross injustice into frenzy. Their conduct was simply frenetic.

The Lord Julius P.P. II replied to Cardinal Francisco de Borja with short incisive action. By His supreme authority He issued a Bull of Deposition from the cardinalate; and denounced him to all Christendom as an heresiarch and schismatic with whom none might have to do. A Bull (Bulla Monitorii Apostolici) was issued on the twenty-eighth of July 1511 *"cotra tres reverendissimos cardinales . . . . ut redeāt ad obedietâ S.d.n. ne Schisma in eccl. in sancta dei oriet."* This was followed by a second *"Bulla intimatiois Generalis Concilii apud Lateranum per S.d.n. Juliu Papâ II edita,"* directed, with the scrupulous politeness of a cleric about to crush, against *"dilectu filiu nostru Franciscu Tituli Sancti Clementis pbyterum Cardinalem";* who *"in seipsis armis assumptis et pro sacerdotalibus vestis Thorace* [1] *indutis et gladiis armati Papã se cotulerãt."* Printed contemporary copies of these two Bulls are in the British Museum; and bound with them, but, strange to say, uncatalogued (A.D. 1900)—(strange, because of the unique perfection of everything at the British Museum)— is the momentous Brief announcing the issue of the Bull of Deposition. Its title is *"Breve Julii Secudi Pont. Max. ad reges, duces, et principes christianos, etc. "Julius Papa II"* addresses Himself to

"Our well-beloved son in Christ			Maximilian, Elect-Emperor, Always August;
"	"	"	Louis (XII), of the French, the Most Christian King;
"	"	"	Hernando, of Aragon and the Two Sicilies, the Catholic King;
"	"	"	Emanuele, of Portugal, the Illustrious King;
"	"	"	Henry (VII), of England, the Illustrious King; [2]
"	"	"	James (V), of the Scots, the Illustrious King;
"	"	"	Wladislaf, of Hungary and Bohemia, the Illustrious King;
"	"	"	Jean and Katherine, King and Queen of Navarre;

[1] It appears to be a little inconsistent of a Pope, Who wished Messer Rafaele Sanzio to paint Him with a sword and not a book in His hand, to object to a Cardinal in a Breast-plate: *for the sword is the weapon of offence; but the Breast-plate, of defence merely.* But many terms in this Bull are simply "corroborative detail calculated to lend an air of verisimilitude to an otherwise bald and unconvincing narrative"—simply words, "full of sound and fury, signifying nothing."

[2] The Twentieth Century may be shocked to notice that, in the Sixteenth, England ranked as the fifth Power in Europe, *after Portugal.*

"Our well-beloved son in Christ	Sigismund, King of Poland;
" " "	John, King of Denmark;
" " "	Carlo, Duke of Savoja;
" " "	Lionardo Lauredano, Doge of Venice;"

and proclaims that "this day, in Public Consistory, We have deprived" of all things ecclesiastical, and of the cardinalitial hat, (*galero cardinalatus*), Bernardino Cardinal-Bishop of Sabina, Guillaume Cardinal Bishop of Praeneste (Palestrina), Francisco Cardinal-Presbyter of the title of San Nereo e Sant' Achilleo (a clerical error for his Title, as given above in the Bull, was San Clemente), and Réné de Prie Cardinal-Presbyter of the Title of Santa Sabina, that they no longer may be considered Cardinals, nor called Cardinals, by word or by writing. The Brief is *Dated at Rome at St. Peters, and given Under the Fisherman's Ring, the twenty-fourth of October* 1511 *and the eighth year of Our Pontificate*. This summary is appended here as an example of form.

Death had hurled his dart before the Terrible Pontiff. Cardinal Francisco de Borja died of an apoplexy at Pisa, before the sentence of his disgrace and deposition reached him there.

The student of history, who seeks a field wherein few yet have walked, will be well advised to investigate the life of this gentle and quiet cardinal, who departed in the tragic blaze of madness and revolt.

.   .   .

In 1512 death relieved the Lord Julius P.P. II of two more of the Borgia whom He loathed: for there died in his Neapolitan exile the Most Worshipful Lord Pedro Luis de Lançol y Borja, Cardinal-Deacon of Santa Maria *in Via Lata,* Arch-presbyter of the Liberian Basilica (Santa Maria Maggiore), Abbot of San Simpliciano at Milan, and Arch-bishop of Valencia in Spain. Having heard a rumour of the death of the Supreme Pontiff, he was on the verge of returning to Rome for the Conclave; but he was killed by falling from his mule at Naples, where he is buried in the church of San Piercelestino without any memorial.

This year also died Don Roderico de Aragona e Borgia, at the age of thirteen years, the son of Madonna Lucrezia by her first legitimate marriage with Don Alonso de Aragona Prince of Bisceglia. He had been despoiled of his duchy of Sermoneta in favour of Caïetani by the Lord Julius P.P. II; and his existence as a step-son was embarrassing in Ferrara, except to his mother, who most sincerely mourned him.

The Duchess Lucrezia was to suffer much this year. The Lord Julius P.P. II put the ban of Greater Excommunication upon her beloved husband Duke Alfonso. As the consort of a Borgia—a Borgia universally adored, a sovereign Borgia, a Borgia of unblemished character,— the Duke of Ferrara naturally was intensely antipathetic to the Holiness of the Pope. If that were not enough, the facts remained that Duke Alfonso was the friend of France, (as the Supreme Pontiff's predecessor also had been); and, he was cognizant of Cardinal Francisco's disesteem for the Lord Julius P.P. II. Naturally the Pope's Holiness found the Duke's Excellency most annoying. The awful import of Excommunication barely can be realized at the present time. People idly wonder why the excommunicated take their case so seriously— why they do not turn to find amusement, or satisfaction, in another channel,—why they persist in lying prone in the mire where the fulmination struck them. And, indeed, in modern times the formal sentence rarely is promulgated, and only against personages of distinction, like the German Dr. Döllinger, or the Sabaudo King Vittoremanuele II di Savoja, whose very circumstances provided them with the means to allay the temporal irritation of the blow. There are excommunications *"gerendae* sententiae" and

"latae sententiae." In the former, excommunication **is**
threatened for some act: but the offender must have sentence passed upon him. In the latter, the offender is excommunicate the moment he performs the act forbidden,
("ipso facto"). This however operates only "in foro
interno," and in the Eyes of God. To make it effectual
"in foro *externo"* it is necessary that the guilt be proved
and be declared to be so by some "competent judge." Excommunication *latae sententiae* appears not to have been
uncommon in the Victorian Era. A Leading Case occurred
in December 1882, when it was enforced against a Scots
clergyman on the strength of the following letter :—

"ROME, 6 December 1882.

"MY DEAR LORD ARCHBISHOP (of Saint Andrews and Edinburgh),
—I have just received a message from the Cardinal-Prefect (of
Propaganda, Cardāl Simeoni,) to tell your Grace 'che il noto
sacerdote il quale voleva citare i Vescovi incorrerebbe senza dubbio
la censura al primo atto efficace che ponesse, ossia all' atto della
citazione, come *cogens Ecclesiasticum ad tribunal laicum.* Se fosse
ancora in tempo sarebbe bene che l'Arcivescovo ne avvertisse il
Sacerdote per distoglierlo da tale atto.'

"Yours very respectfully,
"F. A. CAMPBELL,
"(then Rector of the Scots College of Rome.)"

The censure was Excommunicatio latae sententiae speciali
modo reservatae Romano Pontifici. Bulla *Apostolicae
Sedis. VII.*[1] Seldom does a case of Excommunication
terminate in a perridiculous collapse, as this one did,
when the Cardinal-Prefect denied having sent the quoted
message. Seldom, on the whole, is Excommunication *latae
sententiae* made effectual by proof of guilt and declaration
of proof of guilt by a competent judge. The effect can be
produced in another and far more exitial way. Simple
secret instructions, or even hints, can be given by bishops

[1] See *Menghini. (C. Canon)* Opinion . . . upon the Question
whether . . . John Carmont D.D. incurred the Major Excommunication, etc. *J. Anderson and Son. Courier and Herald Offices,
Dumfries. 1886:* and leading article in *Scotsman,* May 11th, 1886.

to clergy, or adverse opinions can be expressed by one clerk to another, suggesting that it would be well (that it would tend ad majorem Dei gloriam, some say,) to obstruct the worldly welfare of such and such an one, to refuse him his rites and sacraments, or at least to offer the last upon such conditions as the "proper pride" in human nature will disdain to accept. This mode is purely devilish. It is capable of abuse by unworthy clerks for personal ends. It admits of no defence, of no appeal, of no redress, by the very reason of its intangibility. It constricts a man in phantom folds. It blanches him with venomous breath. The world, ever ready to pity some obscene dog who manifests his pain, here sees nothing save one bruised and broken; desperately digladiant, struggling with some invisible (and therefore incredible) foe. The civilized world goes in terror of the invisible; goes by "on the other side." Excommunication of any kind is a fearsome thing for him to whom the Faith once delivered to the saints is the only prize worth having. To the man who, in defect of spiritual advice, is convinced of his own integrity, to whom the sacraments are as "odorifera panacea," [1] to whom the sacraments are the only means which keep him from Despair, their deprivation, by the revenge of a personal enemy, of an offended vanity abasing spiritual powers to satiate secular ambition, signifies that, for the excommunicate, the light goes out of life, love is eradicated from the heart, confidence in man is killed, hope is banished from death. Sympathy he may have from aliens, if he can humiliate himself to expose his grievous wounds: but he may have it only at a price which in honour he cannot pay—the price of insincerity to his convictions—the price of apostasy. The dire Ban of excommunication, formal or informal, drives a man wild; turns his hand against every man, and every man's hand against him; he is savage; he is a Bandit, actually and literally. Sometimes

[1] (Verg. Aen. XII. 419.)

he becomes criminal. Ostracism practised is a school for
scoundrels. Far more merciful—divinely merciful, not
humanly—it would be to slay outright the body; than to
doom a soul to live a solivagous life of torture—the torture
of Hopelessness. That is why Excommunication is so horrible in this present age of works. That is why it was so
trenchant a weapon in the ages of faith. It was, and is,
perfectly impossible to be resisted by one who is, and was,
sincerely faithful. Often enough, an excommunicate sovereign would try resistance; for sovereigns are stronger
than ordinary plebeians in the matter of resources. Then,
when an interval for consideration had elapsed, the second
blow of the Flail would fall—Interdict: his demesne would
be made to suffer loss of the means of grace, the sacraments, which were denied to him. His subjects generally
rose, resentful and revolting. There was no reason why
they should be afflicted, when submission of their sovereign
to God's Vicegerent would suffice for their enfranchise-
ment. But sometimes Interdict also failed. The third blow
came. Subjects were absolved from their oath of allegiance
to the excommunicate; his throne was declared vacant;
kings and princes of Christendom were invited to invade
his realm, to take his crown and sceptre, to expel him a
homeless friendless connudate outcast in a world that
shunned him like a pestilence, like the horrid leprous scab
of creeping things which his blasted human body inevitably
would become. Then, suppliant, submissive, he crawled to
his Canossa; as the late Duke of Lauenberg crawled to the
Lord Leo P.P. XIII the other day; as Caesar Fridericus
Ahenobarbus Semper Augustus abjectly crawled to, and
waited at, the gates of the huge Englishman, Nicholas
Breakespeare, the Lord Hadrian P.P. IV, who ruled the
world eight hundred years ago, "Not for thee, but for
Peter," that indignant Emperor muttered, perforce doing
groom's service for Peter's Successor, holding the stirrup
of the pontifical palfrey. "For Us, *and* for Peter," the

superb English Pope retorted, as He bent Caesar to His unconquerable will. Arrogant? Arrogant—of any miserable mortal man who did not believe himself to be, who had not been officially crowned and saluted, and to whom every emperor and king and prince of Christendom, every Christian sovereign and subject of Europe, had not sworn allegiance as, "Ruler of the World, Father of Princes and of Kings, Earthly Vicar of Jesus Christ our Saviour."

When the action of the human mind is inspired by the principle endeavoured here to be set down, the inexpugnable face of Excommunication, (magnified by the assent to its validity of the excommunicated one,) perhaps, may be realized. Duke Alfonso d'Este could not hope to stand where Caesar Semper Augustus fell. Naturally, he went in desperate and horrid fear. He knew that he had not deserved to be gibbeted as a Bandit before the world: but he knew also that, before the Holiness of the Pope, he, a sovereign-regnant, was crushable as a worm. He lost no time in omitting to seek release from the hideous ban.

Early in 1513, he chose the poet Messer Ludovico Ariosto, with his beautiful Greek profile and noble intellect, secretary and laureate of Cardinal Ippolito; and named him as his Orator to open negotiations with the Pope.

The Lord Julius P.P. II was perfectly implacable. He had not pardoned the indiscreet criticisms of Cardinal Francisco de Borja, who had passed beyond His power. It was the complete ruin of Borgia that alone would slake His passionate thirst for vengeance;—and a Borgia was Duchess of Ferrara. He did not intend kindness to the consort of that Duchess: and He resolved to begin, in a clerical manner, with intimidation. Accordingly, He admitted Messer Ludovico Ariosto to an audience; and immediately ordered him to quit the Vatican by the door before he should be thrown from the window. After this reception of a proffered olive-branch, the Pope's Holiness coolly awaited Duke Alfonso's next move.

Don Fabrizio Colonna flourished in the favour of the Lord Julius P.P. II; and he, also, was under many vital obligations to the Duke of Ferrara. He, in his turn, tried the role of peacemaker between pontiff and sovereign; and so far succeeded, that the Holy Father farcically permitted the Duke to come to Rome, assured of a favourable reception, to plead his cause and to arrange the terms of his submission.

He came. He saw the Ruler of the World. He was conquered. The Terrible Pontiff named the sole conditions on which He would consent to remit the ban of excommunication. Nothing could be more enormously radical and sweeping. They were, abdication of his sovereignty over the city and whole duchy of Ferrara, with absolute renunciation for himself and his heirs for ever of all rights therein, in favour of the Holy See; also, his retirement to voluntary life-long exile at the little city of Asti in the province of Lombardy. Death and obliteration of the Borgia, not by vulgar assassination but by constitutional withdrawal of the means to live, was the aim of the Terrible Pontiff; wherefore He would strip naked Duke Alfonso, as aforetime He had stripped naked Duke Cesare.

Duke Alfonso d'Este refused to purchase release from excommunication on these disgraceful terms. The Lord Julius P.P. II let him have hints which gave to understand that the said terms might be mitigated. By various subterfuges he was detained in Rome.

The army of the Terrible Pontiff stealthily was advancing on Ferrara.

There was only a woman there.

Duke Alfonso chanced to hear of the pontifical stratagem. On the instant, he made his plans for quitting Rome. But he found that he was in a prison. The Terrible Pontiff held him; and would not let him go. The Lord Alexander P.P. VI may not have been a Saint: but He never dirtied His honour like this.

This treachery of the Holiness of the Pope disgusted the Ghibellinism of Don Fabrizio Colonna. This was not what he had contemplated, when he persuaded Duke Alfonso to adventure his right hand in the jaws of the Wolf of Rome. Considering himself to be responsible, his own honour at stake, he played a counter-stratagem upon the Lord Julius P.P. II. By his aid, the Duke broke prison; and, under his protection, in his fortress of Marino fifteen miles from Rome, a safe asylum was provided. Duke Alfonso desired to hasten to defend his duchy now menaced by the Pope: and all Colonna acclaimed his resolution. Don Prospero Colonna undertook to bring him there where he would be. Travelling by night through hostile territory, environed by ever-present dangers, at length disguised as Don Prospero's cook, the royal and ducal Bandit reached Ferrara.

In the city there was joy. In the duchy there was confidence restored. In the heart of the Duchess Lucrezia there was gratitude for the safety of her much-loved lord. Ferrara was fresh from four years successful war: an excessively dangerous enemy to assault, now that her leader led her. The pontifical army executed a second strategic movement at the double—to the rear.

And, before the year 1513 was three months old, the Terrible Pontiff, the Lord Julius P.P. II, (Who, according to Monsignor Paris de Grassis, successor to Burchard as Papal Caerimonarius, suffered from the French Disease,) died at Rome, raving in His last delirium "Frenchmen, begone from Italy! Begone from Italy, Alphonso d'Este!"

Dreadful end of a curious revengeful disappointed plebeian who was Ruler of the World! The monstrous Moses of Michelangelo, in San Pietro *ad Vincula,* marks His ambitious unfinished tomb.

.   .   .

The Most Illustrious Lord Giovanni de' Medici, Cardinal-Deacon of Santa Maria *in Domnica,* was the son of

Lorenzo de' Medici of Florence, born the eleventh of December 1475. His mother was Madonna Clarice Orsini, one of the sweetest and best of good mothers. Her husband said that his own mother chose her for him,

"Tolsi donna . . . ovvero mi fu data.

When Don Giovanni was of the age of seven years (the age of reason, technically), the Christian King named him Abbot of Fonte Dolce, on the nineteenth of May 1483, in which preferment the Lord Sixtus P.P. IV. confirmed him twelve days later by Brief dated the thirty-first of May 1843. On the first of June he received the ecclesiastical tonsure, when episcopal hands wielded scissors to cut the child-clerk's hair in five places—on the front, the back, the right, the left, and the crown, of the head—while bishop and boy recited the pslam verse:

"The Lord is the portion—	"*Dominus pars*—
"Of mine inheritence—	"*Haereditatis meae*—
"And of my cup—	"*Et calicis mei*—
"Thou are He Who shall re- store—	"*Tu es Qui restitues*—
"Mine inheritance to me—	"*Haereditatem meam mihi*—

and finally the bishop endued him with the fair white linen surplice, (super pellicem) the official vesture of his clerical estate. The symbolism of this mystery seems to be that the clerk enlists himself in the regular army of the Church Militant, sacrificing an actual piece of his person as a pledge of his fidelity, and receiving as handsel, so to speak, his uniform. From this date the child was called in his family Messer Giovanni, (Mr. John). On the first of March 1484, he was named Abbot of Passignano. He grew up a good and manly boy, fond of nice things, grave, quietly merry, and a perfect gentleman. On the third of March 1489, his father's friend the Lord Innocent P.P. VIII created him Cardinal-Deacon of Santa Maria *in Domnica;* but, as he was only of the age of thirteen years, the creation was reserved *in petto,* while he continued his studies under Canon Angelo Ambrogini (detto Poliziano) ; who, in 1492 wrote to the Pope about his pupil,

"This youth is so formed by nature and education that, being in-"ferior to none in genius, he yields not to his equals in industry, "nor to his teachers in learning, nor to old men in gravity of de-"meanour. He naturally is honest and ingenuous, and he has been "so strictly bred that never from his mouth there comes a lewd, or "even a light, expression. Though he be so young, his judgment is "so secure that even the old respect him as a father. He sucked piety "and religion with his mother's milk, preparing himself for his "sacred office even from his cradle. (Ep. v. Lib. VIII)

In the Public Consistory of the twenty-second of March 1492, he was admitted to the Sacred College, receiving the scarlet hat and the cardinalitial sapphire-ring, (whose value was six hundred zecchini d'oro—say, £1200) ; and he was of the age of sixteen years, three months, eleven days.

During his cardinalate his most delightful trait was the loving kindness which he showed to his young cousin Giulio, (Botticelli's most precious model), the bastard of Don Giuliano de' Medici, by Madonna Antonia Gorini of Florence, and who ended his life as the Lord Clement P.P. VII. Cardinal Giovanni got him ennobled as a Knight of St. John of Jerusalem of Malta, and Prior of Capua; and gave him an honourable position in his household as confidential counsellor ; and, indeed, it was to Don Giulio, attending him as esquire in the Conclave of March 1513, that Cardinal Giovanni generously said, when the result of the squittino (scrutiny) was made known, "Come Giulio, let us enjoy the Papacy, since God hath given it to Us:" and he immediately raised His cousin to the purple, giving him His Own vacated rank of Cardinal-Deacon of Santa Maria *in Domnica*.[1]

[1] These two charming personages used a most beautiful hand-writing, neat, clear, well-mannered, decisive; as may be seen in the private Brief of the Lord Leo P.P. X, *placet et ita motu proprio mandamus;* and in the letter of Cardinal Giulio de' Medici, dated April 1516; which are preserved in the British Museum 23.721.

Cardinal Giovanni, like all the Medici, was congenitally myopic. In all presentments of him, there is the slight forward bend or set of the neck which marks the short-sighted man. Messer Paolo Giovio says that he surveyed the world through a concave crystal, and that this affected his skill as a sportsman. Messer Rafaele Sanzio's portrait of him and his cousin shows him with this concave crystal spy-glass in his hand. No doubt his physical incomplete-ness wonderfully aided in developing his enchanting taste and temperament; for it is well known that the best artist is the man who does not see all.[1]

The crowd, waiting outside the Conclave of 1513 for the annunciation of the new Pope, were confronted by a door-way builded of the fragments of other buildings. Some of the stones bore portions of mutilated inscriptions; and the crowd amused itself by piecing these together. But there was one large stone above the lintel, whose inscription baffled explanation. It bore the letters

M. C. C. C. C. X. L.

and presumably had come from some edifice dated 1440. Presently, the door was flung open; and the scarlet Cardi-nal-Archdeacon proclaimed, "I announce to you great joy. We have for a Pope the Lord Giovanni de' Medici, Cardi-nal-Deacon of Santa Maria *in Domnica,* who wills to be called Leo the Tenth." And in the doorway stood the white figure of the new Successor of St. Peter, of the age of thirty-eight years. His head straining a little forward, peering through His half-closed bright eyes, lifting His hand in Apostolic Benediction. Instantly a wag in the kneeling crowd explained the cryptic inscription *Multi Cacci Cardinales Creaverunt Caecum X (decimum) Leonem;* "Many short-sighted cardinals created a short-

[1] Whistler counts his myopia as his chief talent.

sighted one Leo the Tenth." This is a specimen of wit in the year 1513, bright, quick, direct, pungent, and finished.

. . .

The election of the Lord Leo P.P. X was an immense relief to the Duke and Duchess of Ferrara. It meant deliverance from unscrupulous persecution; for the Pope's Holiness now was patrician, and at least a gentleman, though no enemy to the House of Borgia. So Ferrara and Borgia went in peace. The duchy had been at war for nearly six years, almost without cessation; her resources were quite exhausted; her exchequer was empty. So keen was the distress, that, in order not to add to his people's burden by pressing for his revenues, Duke Alfonso pawned his plate, and Duchess Lucrezia her jewels which were of enormous value. These were redeemed three years later: and it is to the inventory, made when they were pawned, that modern knowledge of their extraordinary rarity and worth is due.

. . .

On the thirteenth of September, 1513, was born in Rome, of Don Tarquinio Poplicola di Santacroce and Madonna Ersilia his wife, the Noble Don Prospero Poplicola di Santacroce, afterwards Cardinal-Presbyter of the Title of San Girolamo *degli Schiavoni* and Nuncio, who introduced Tobacco into Italy and gave it the name *Erba Santacroce,* Holycross Herb.

. . .

The life of the Duchess Lucrezia, during the next few years, was a life of calm after storm, *post tot naufragias tuta.* She won fresh fame by her goodness to young girls, whom she provided with dowries, to tempt them to keep continency by marrying well. Delightfully practical age, which went directly to the point of attempting no maudlin half-measures, "so sweetly mawkish and so smoothly dull"! The ideal of the professional philanthropist, then, was to make virtue easy, and vice difficult. The ideal of the professional philanthropist, now, is to make virtue horribly vulgar and vice an imperious necessity. The Duchess Lucrezia had observed that the lack of money is the root of all evil; and, at that root she struck.

Charming descriptions are extant of the evenings which this egregious lady spent in conversation with poets and scholars, listening to music, and working on the lovely embroidery for which she was so celebrated. On the third of July, 1515, she presented her lord with a daughter. The same year she was grieved by the death of her friend, the great printer, Messer Aldo Manuzio. That cool-headed, shrewd, and very learned Venetian, the hereditary enemy of Ferrara, has left laudations of the Duchess Lucrezia which are sincere and unsurpassable. It is not singular that the great and good among her intimate contemporaries should be those who praise her; and that her defamers should be professional squibbers, notoriously base and venal. The following year, the eleventh of July, 1516, she suffered the loss of her little son who was of the age of five years. Is the touching letter, by which she conveyed the news to her confidante and sister-in-law, the Marchioness Isabella Gonzaga of Mantua, the letter of a wicked woman or of a good? She says,

"—the Most Illustrious Don Alessandro, my youngest son, after "a long and painful illness, in which remedies were of no avail, "was seized by a cruel dysentery. Yesterday, at the fourth hour of "the night, (say, midnight,) the poor little man (*poverino*) yielded "his blessed soul into the hands of our Lord God, leaving me much "afflicted and full of sorrow; as Your Excellency, being a woman "and a tender mother yourself, may easily believe.[1]

On the Festival of All Saints, she bore another son to Duke Alfonso, who was baptized by the name Francesco.

.   .   .

[1] Belriguardo. xi Jul. 1516.

On the twenty-sixth of November, 1517, there died in Rome Madonna Giovanna de' Catanei, the mother of the Duchess Lucrezia; and was buried in Santa Maria *del Popolo* by the Flaminian Gate. Nine of her letters to her daughter, and rather crabbed letters too, are preserved in the Archives of Modena. They are subscribed, *"La felice ed infelice madre;* which seems precisely to describe her condition. She was a happy mother; happy in the gorgeous loveliness of her children, happy in their good fortune, happy in being the mother of two dukes, a prince-duke, and a sovereign duchess: but unhappy, in that human law made their father not her husband. Another letter of hers, dated from Rome the fifteenth of December, 1515, and signed "Perpetua Oratrice Vanozza," has been the means of causing some uncertainty as to her real name. The following is suggested as an explanation.

"Vanozza," of course, is a familiar abbreviation of "Giovanozza", which is equivalent to "Big Jenny". Italians are deliciously disrespectfully inoffensive in their use of universal and personal nicknames; which are taken conferred without the least aggrievance. "Perpetua Oratrice" [1] is not a name at all: but a quasi-official style.

In England at the present day, one frequently is startled by the receipt of a letter, from some fervent member of that devout female sex (for which Holy Church, knowing needs, diurnally prays), bearing as signature the names of the writer, with the addition "E de M." If one has not yet seen the lions, (as the Fifteenth Century said of a novice,) one looks for the university degree, knightly order, municipal or parochial rank, of which those letters are the sign. But, when one knows them to stand for "Enfant de Marie," one remembers that a pious sodality, of

---

[1] Oratrice (oratrix) is a rare word=but perfectly classical; and its use shews that the Renascence of Learning had done something to improve ecclesiastical Latin, and, by consequence, Italian also.

French origin and called "The Children of Mary," is an excessively and universally fashionable one among females; and doubts are at an end.

It is probable that there was some such pious association for females of the Borgian Era. Madonna Giovanna always was a respectable well-living character: but we know that she found salvation, was converted, became *dévote,* in 1508, when she sat under Frat' Egidio da Viterbo preaching a course of Lent sermons in Rome.

It is suggested, then, that at once she began "to make her soul," to prepare to meet her God, for she was well on in years; and that she became a member of some Confraternity of Perpetual Prayer, resembling those of the present day whose members divide among themselves the duty of praying the clock round, so that an unending stream of supplication shall flow toward the Throne of Grace. It is suggested, that, being a human woman, cherishing no objection to a little perfectly legitimate advertisement of virtue (like the ladies of the "E de M" description), Madonna Giovanna de' Catanei formed the habit of signing her private letters "The Perpetual Suppliant, Big Jenny."

Her epitaph has been given on p. 294.

.   .   .

There are two documents of this year, 1517, which go to prove that, at this time, there existed no idea of concealing the parentage of Don Giovanni Borgia the sometime Duke of Nepi and Camerino. The boy appears to have made his home with his sister, the Duchess Lucrezia; for both documents are issued under her protection and authority. She was nineteen years older than her brother, who now was of the age of twenty-one years; and her notable good-nature, as well as her royal estate, make it natural enough that she should be more mother than sister to her august Father's youngest son.

The first brief (they both are quoted in Cittadella,) is dated "sub die I° Nov., 1517"; and names the Bishop of Adria as Don Giovanni's agent in some pecuniary transaction, he being less than twenty-five, and more than eighteen years old. It begins, "Ferrariae in palatio habi-"tationis Ill^{mi} . . . Ill^{mus} Dominus Joannes Borgia, *frater* "Ill^{mae} Dominae Lucretiae Borgiae Ducissae Ferrariae, "minor annis vigintiquinque, maior tamen decem "octo,——."

The second brief is addressed to Messer Filippo Strozzi; and claims, from the consuls of Pesaro, the baggage which the young noble had lost after his shipwreck in sight of that city! It is dated the second of December, 1517; and begins, "Mandatum Ill^{mae} Dominae Ducissae Ferrariae "in palatio Ducali . . . Illma Domina Lucretia Borgia Es-"tensis . . . suo nomine, et nomine ac Tanquam coniuncta "persona Ill^{mi} Domini Joannis Borgiae *eius frater*——.

Little or nothing further has been discovered regarding the life of this youth. His history, with that of his brother Prince Gioffredo Borgia of Squillace, waits to reward research in the archives of Naples, Nepi, Camerino and Ferrara. Reluctantly, they must be left here among the *Sparks That Die*.

.   .   .

The following announcement closes the second epoch of the House of Borgia. It is dated the twenty-first day of June, 1519; and was sent by flying posts to his nephew, the Marquess Federigo Gonzaga of Mantua: "It hath "pleased the Lord God to take unto Himself the soul of "the Illustrious Duchess, my much-beloved Consort. "(Signed) Alfonsus Dux Feraria.

The "Illustrious Duchess" Lucrezia Borgia was buried

in her favourite church at the monastery of Corpus Domini, by side of her husband's mother the Duchess Leonor de Aragona, deeply and sincerely mourned by her children, and her husband Duke Alfonso d'Este, and, indeed, by all Ferrara duchy crowding round her bier. She was only in the forty-second year of her age.

May she rest in the fragrant peace of her good deeds.

.   .   .

BOOK THE THIRD
THE BRILLIANT LIGHT [1]

"A fire that is kindled, begins with smoke and hissing, while it
"lays hold on the faggots; bursts into a roaring blaze, with
"raging tongues of flame, devouring all in reach, spangled
"with sparks that die; settles into the steady genial glare, the
"brilliant light, that men call fire;"

THE Borgia, who have gone before, present no difficulty to the Twentieth Century. When once their formula has been learned, they are found to be men of like passions with ourselves. They were born—they struggled through life with an amazing amount of dignity and success—they died. For a reason which has yet to be explained, the human race has made them serve for hell-myths, for prodigies of turpitude, for symbols wherewith to express ultimate and abysmal crime.

"The slave of his own appetites, in bondage to conventional laws,
"his spirit emasculated by the indulgences, or corroded by the cares
"of life, hardly daring to act, to think, or to speak, for himself;
"man,—gregarious man,—worships the world in which he lives,
"adopts its maxims, and treads its beaten paths. To rouse him from
"his lethargy, and to give a new current to his thoughts, heroes
"appear from time to time on the verge of his horizon; and hero-
"worship, Pagan or Christian, withdraws him for a while from

[1] Authorities for this sketch of Saint Francisco de Borja, General of Jesuits, and sometimes Duke of Gandia, etc.

1. Ribadaneira. Life.
2. Cardinal Alvaro Cienfuegos. La heroica vida, etc. del grande San Francisco de Borja. Madrid 1717.
3. Monumenta Historica Societatis Jesu. Madrid 1894-5.
4. Sir James Stephen. Essays in Ecclesiastical Biography.
5. A. M. Clarke. St. Francis Borgia. Lond. 1872 etc.
The last was prepared under the auspices of the late Fr. John Morris, S.J.; and is useful in giving the modern English Jesuit point of view.

"still baser idolatry. To contemplate the motives and the career of
"such men may teach much that well deserves the knowing: but
"nothing more clearly than this—that no one can have shrines
"erected to his memory in the hearts of men of different generations,
"unless his own heart was an altar, on which the daily sacrifices,
"of fervent devotion and magnanimous self denial, were offered to
"the only true Object of human worship.[1]

The wheel of time makes one unerring revolution; and
lo, a saint,—a Borgia Saint.

To write of Saint Francisco de Borja, so that he may
be known of men, is more than difficult. Each man knows
another, not by his strength but by his weaknesses, not as
surpassing but as lacking such and such of the Ideal; for
weakness makes men kin. And Saint Francisco de Borja
gave no sign of human weakness, little or no sign of human nature, after he had reached his manhood. He has
been called "a magnified non-natural man"; and that is the
only point of view from which he can be observed. He
lived entirely on the supernatural plane: the world, to
him, was nothing but an enemy with whom he would have
neither art nor part: he was in it, but not of it: his ways
were not men's ways, nor his thoughts men's thoughts: he
rightly cannot be liked, or disliked, hated, or loved, admired or even judged. He must be taken as he was, com-
parable to none, the exact antipodes of his strenuous august
invincible magnificent ancestors for there are "diversities
of gifts," in opposition to all human ideals, a "magnified
non-natural man." His note is brilliantly personal. He was
utterly and absolutely selfishly solicitous about his own
salvation. He made that the unique object of his life; and,
to that end, he deliberately chose renunciation, hardship,
ignominy, utter and extreme. His singular devotion, to
the task of living according to his light, is a phenomenon
of an intensity beyond the natural, environing him with
an aura as of one aloof, as of one alien among men, and,
therefore, altogether antipathetic to men.

[1] Sir James Stephen. Essays in Ecclesiastical Biography. i. 29.

He was the great-grandson of the Lord Alexander P.P. VI, Whose bastard Don Juan Francisco de Borja, Duke of Gandia in Spain, Prince of Teano and Tricarico, Count of Chiaramonte, Lauria, and Cerignola, Constable of Naples, and General of the Pontifical Army, had married Doña Maria de Aragona, a princess of the royal House of Aragon. After the mysterious murder of her husband at Rome in 1497, the Duchess Doña Maria married Don Enriquez de Luna, uncle and Master of the Household to the Viceroy Don Hernando of Castile, and Grand Commander of Leon, who soon left her widowed the second time. She lived at Baeza in Granada, and devoted herself to her two children, Doña Isabella, and Don Juan II de Borja, who succeeded his murdered father as Duke of Gandia and the rest. When her son married, she retired to the monastery of Poor Clares (the Second Order of the Religion of San Francesco d'Assisi) at Gandia, where she took the vows of a nun, and became Suor Maria Gabriella till her death in 1537. Her daughter, Doña Isabella, who was betrothed to the Duke of Segorbe, obtained the necessary dispensations, broke before marriage from her affianced husband; and followed the Duchess of Gandia her beloved mother to the Poor Clares, where she also took the vows as Suor Francisca de Jesus.

Don Juan II married, first, Dona Francisca de Castro y Pinos; secondly, Doña Juana de Aragona, bastard of Archbishop Don Alonso de Aragona of Saragossa nephew of the Catholic King Don Hernando of Spain.[1] Fourteen children were the offspring of these marriages;

Don Francisco, the Saint:
Don Alonso, Abbot of Valdigna:
Don Enrico, Cardinal-Deacon of San Nereo e Sant' Achilleo:

[1] A second bastard of Archbishop Don Alonso de Aragona, also called Doña Juana, married Don Felipe of Austria, and became the mother of the Emperor Carlos.

Doña Luisa, married Don Martino de Aragona y Gurrea, Duke of
    Villahermosa:
Don Rodrigo, Cardinal-Deacon of San Niccolo *in Carcere Tulliano:*
    "while still a youth" (Ciacconi)
Don Pedro Luis, Viceroy of Cataluna:
Don Tommaso, Archbishop of Saragossa, (in succession to Arch-
    bishop Don Juan de Aragona bastard of Archbishop Don
    Alonso,) and Viceroy of Aragon:
Don Felipe, Knight of Montesa and Governor of Oran:
Don Diego, died young:
*Doña Juana, First Abbess of the Royal Monastery of Discalced
    Carmelites at Madrid. She died in the Odour of Sanctity:*
Doña Leonor, married Don Juan de Gurrea:
Doña Magdalena, married Don Hernando de Proxita, Count of
    Almenara:
Doña Margarita, married*Don Fadrique de Portugal y Cordo:

Doña Isabella, followed her grandmother Doña Maria (Suor Maria
Gabriella), and her aunt Doña Isabella (Suor Francisca de Jesus)
to the Poor Clares of Gandia, of which monastery she became Abbess.

That is a very characteristic family of a Grandee and
Hijo de algo (son of something) of Spain. Leaving the
heir out of the question, the eight sons divide between
them two cardinalates, an archbishopric, an abbacy, two
viceroyalties, and a governorship; while, of the six daughters, two enter religion and become abbesses, and four
marry grandees and semi-royalty of Spain. It is worth
noting too, that shame on account of their origin, or their
ancestors' supposed misbehaviour, has not yet made its
appearance. Alonso was the name of many royal bastards
of the House of Aragon, as well as of the Lord Calixtus
P.P. III. Rodrigo was the name of the Lord Alexander
P.P. VI, who also began his public career in the Cardinal-
Diaconate of San Niccolo *in Carcere Tuliano,* and Whose
eldest bastard (ob. 1481) was called Pedro Luis. All these
names were repeated here in the third and fourth generation; and the eldest son of Don Juan II, bore the second
name of his murdered grandfather, Francisco.

The Terrible Pontiff, the Lord Julius P.P. II **was**

reigning in Rome, when Don Francisco de Borja was born in 1510 at the ducal palace of Gandia in Spain.

The Terrible Pontiff was only a terrible memory ten years later, and the Lord Leo P.P. X was trying hard to "enjoy the Papacy," in Rome when riots arose in Gandia, the ducal palace was sacked, and Don Juan II, with his family, was forced to flee for life. Don Francisco, then a gracious boy of ten, was sent to his uncle Archbishop Don Juan de Aragona at Saragossa,[1] who supplied him with a house and retinue suited to his condition, and masters who taught him music, fencing, and Latin grammar; for he was to be bred as became the heir to the duchy of Gandia, and the future head of the Spanish Branch of the House of Borja.

In January, 1522, died the Lord Leo P.P. X; and the Lord Hadrian P.P. VI, a ship-carpenter's son out of Utrecht in Flanders, was elected Pope, called the Laocoon a pagan idol, walled-up the Belvedere statue-gallery of the Vatican; and died. To Him, in 1523, succeeded Cardinal Giulio de' Medici, cousin and life-friend of the Lord Leo P.P. X, who ascended Peter's Throne under the title of the Lord Clement P.P. VII. Great changes were taking place in Europe. By marriage, conquest, inheritance, or lapse, the Holy Roman Empire had passed into the hands of Spain. The Elect-Emperor Carlos V, though he ceremonially had not been crowned with the Iron Crown or the Double Golden Diadem, ruled in Spain, Naples and Southern Italy, Germany, Austria, and part of France. King Henry VIII Tudor, the Defender of the Faith, was becoming a power in England. The Christian King of France was his rival: but the Continent of Europe mainly was the Elect-Emperor's, and wholly, perhaps, the Roman Pontiff's.

---

[1] Anciently Salduba, colonized by Caius Julius Caesar Octavianus Augustus B.C. 27, who called it Caesaraugasta; afterwards corrupted into Saragossa.

At the age of fourteen years, Don Francisco de Borja went to Tor de Sillas as page of honour to the Infanta Doña Catalina, the Elect-Emperor's sister, who was about to be married to King Don Juan III of Portugal.

When the marriage took place in 1525, Don Francisco did not accompany his royal mistress to her new kingdom; because his father, who had for him a higher ambition, had commanded his return to Saragossa to study rhetoric and philosophy under his uncle, the Archbishop Don Juan. Here he remained until he passed his seventeenth year; and in 1528 he entered the Court of the Elect-Emperor Carlos V, where his robust physical beauty, his courteous manner, and his brilliant ability gained for him a notable reception.

Humanly speaking, this acceptance of service under such a potentate is most astonishing in a youth of the gracious piety of Don Francisco. The Elect-Emperor was hot and reeking from the commission of what must have seemed to be a perfectly appalling crime—the ghastly Sack of Rome of 1527, the fierce beleaguerment of God's Vice-gerent the Lord Clement P.P. VII in the Mola of Hadrian, carnage, pillage, rape, rapine, sacred monastic enclosures violated, virginity deflowered, nuns and the wives and daughters of Roman citizens gambled for and ravished in the public streets by the Elect-Emperor's unpaid army of drunken Lutheran Goths and Catholic Catalans. It was to the Court of this monarch that Don Francisco de Borja brought the gracious flower of his maiden manlihood.

Amid voluptuous surroundings, he found that it was better to marry than to burn; and, in 1529, being then of the age of nineteen years, he led in marriage the Noble Doña Leonor of Portugal. The Elect-Emperor, to mark imperial approval, perhaps, also, from the generous benevolence of a man who himself is about to receive— (he had come to terms with the Lord Clement P.P. VII, and was hoping for the Dual Coronation,)—created Don Francisco Marquess of Lombay.

The relations between Pope and Elect-Emperor were after this fashion. Both were exhausted: both were desirous of peace. Peace, then, was signed, and a perpetual alliance, on the twentieth of June, 1527. The Elect-Emperor had gained territory from Venice, and detached Genoa from France; the Pope's Holiness had promised to invest him with crown of Naples, (which his predecessor the Catholic King Don Hernando of Spain had stolen from the bastard Aragon dynasty in 1501); and formally to crown him as Holy Roman Emperor. The Lord Clement P.P. VII had gained a strong ally, who guaranteed to subdue rebellious Florence for the pontifical nephew Duke Alessandro de' Medici, to consolidate the alliance by marrying the Bastard Doña Margarita of Austria to the said pontifical nephew; and to procure the restoration of pontifical authority in Emilia, Ravenna, and Cervia. They had been hideous enemies, these two; and the Elect-Emperor had behaved abominably. Even now, he refused to go to Monza or to Sant' Ambrogio at Milan for the Iron Crown, or to the Lateran Basilica of Rome for the Golden Imperial Diadem, as by precedent he would have been compelled to do, had he belonged to the House of Swabia. But he was a Spaniard, arrogant, cruel, unscrupulous, and infamously powerful; and he insolently told the Pope's Holiness that he had not the habit of running after crowns, for, instead, they came to him.

If the coronation of the Successor of St. Peter be a remarkable function, the coronation according to the Roman Rite of the Successor of Caius Julius Caesar Octavianus Augustus is but one degree less sumptuous. It would be worth the while of any man of the Twentieth Century to exchange lives with William of Hohenzollern, for the sake of the opening which lies before him. In the case of Carlos V, all ceremonies duly were observed. The Lord Clement P.P. VII came to Bologna, a neutral city, for the coronation, and the Elect-Emperor met Him there.

On the twenty-second of February, 1530, in the Chapel of the Apostolic Palace, the Iron Crown [1] was set upon the imperial head. Two days later, in the Cathedral of San Petronio, curtains were drawn around the imperial canopy forming a pavilion wherein the Elect-Emperor stripped naked for the anointing with holy oil and chrism. He was ordained deacon, vested in the sacred imperial dalmatica, endued with orb and sword and sceptre offered by reigning sovereigns, God's Vicegerent crowned him with the high closed Double Crown of Empire and heralds proclaimed him

Caesar

Romanorum Imperator Semper Augustus Mundi Totius Dominus Universis Dominis Universis Principibus et Populis Semper Venerandus.

These things having been done, Pope and Emperor appeared in the cathedral porch. There, Caesar Carlos V, vested in full imperial insignia, held the Pontiff stirrup as He mounted, and led His palfrey several paces, as a public act of homage and allegiance to Him by Whose Sanction Kings Do Reign. Then, he mounted his own charger, and rode by the Lord Clement P.P. VII's side through the city of Bologna making knights, as the way is, when the Pontiff left him.

It is probable enough that the Marquess Don Francisco de Borja witnessed, and assisted at, this superb ceremony. He was attached to the personal suite of Caesar Carlos V: but there is another circumstance that implies that, in some way or another, most presumably in the flesh, he was brought into contact with the Pope's Holiness about this

---

[1] A plain gold band, studded with uncut gems, round whose inner rim runs one of the Nails that nailed our Divine Redeemer to the Cross of Calvary hammered into a flat band to press the brows of him who wears the Iron Crown. It may be seen enshrined in the Treasury of the Cathedral at Monza.

time. It is that a little later, the Supreme Pontiff conferred an extraordinary favour on his illustrious House,
consisting of Five Privileges granted to Duke Juan II of
Gandia, his heirs and descendants of both sexes, and whom-
soever they might marry, IN CONSIDERATION OF THE SIG-
NAL SERVICES RENDERED TO THE HOLY SEE BY THE HOUSE
OF BORGIA. This unmistakably distinct statement shews
that calumnies and lampoons of Messer Francesco Guicciardini had made no ill impression on the Lord Clement
P.P. VII, who actually had met that writer when he was
the guest of the *bas bleu* Madonna Veronica Gambara during the coronation festivities at Bologna. The fable of
Borgia iniquity is a plant of later growth. In 1531 the
House was considered to have rendered signal services, de-
serving recognition, *for a perpetual memorial.* Hence the
granting of the Five Privileges which follow here.

I

"To any confessor whom they may select,[1] powers to absolve them
"from the gravest ecclesiastical censures and penalties: to commute
"the obligation of fasting to almsgiving: once a year to absolve
"them in cases usually reserved to the Holy See; or from any oath
"or vow but those generally excepted.

II

"Special indulgences for the hour of Death, and for visits to a
"church, or an altar: also, for every mass offered *by* a scion of the
"House (he being in priest's orders), or *for* any scion of the House,
"indulgences equal to those which might be gained at the altars of
"San Sebastiano, San Lorenzo, Santa Pudentiana, and Santa Maria
"*de Panis* in Rome.

[1] In Catholic countries one is bound to use the clergy of one's
own parish.

III

"Permission to use *Lacticinia* (all food made of milk and eggs) and meat,[1] on fast days throughout the year: this permission to extend to guests and servants of the family. Permission to take luncheon at midday, and dinner at night. Permission to receive the sacraments within prohibited times.[2] Permission to be buried on any day in the year, Easter alone excepted.

IV

"Priests who are scions of the House of Borgia may anticipate or postpone their recitation of the Breviary Offices without observing the fixed hours, reciting the whole office at once, or dividing it at their pleasure.

V

"To female scions of the House of Borgia, or connections by marriage, liberty once a month to enter the enclosure of nuns,[3] taking with them four others to converse with the nuns, and to eat with them, provided only that they do not remain for the night." (*La heroica vida, etc., del grande San Francisco de Borja,* by Cardinal *Alvaro Cienfuegos. Madrid,* 1717. I. iii. 3, 4.

The marriage of the Marquess Don Francisco, and the Marchioness Dona Leonor, of Lombay, resulted in the birth of eight children, who were,

Don Carlos, the heir:
Don Juan, Count of Ficalho; Viceroy of Portugal; Ambassador of King Don Felipe III.; Author of *Empresas Morales* (1581): Married to Doña Lorenza Oñaz de Loyola, heiress of Don Beltrano, Señor de Loyola:
Don Alvaro, Marquess of Alcaguizes; Ambassador of King Don Felipe III to the Holy See:
Don Hernando, Knight of the Order of Calatrava:
Don Alonso, Chamberlain to the Empress Maria:

[1] Milk and meat were forbidden during Lent, and on every Saturday throughout the year.

[2] *e.g.,* one might marry in Lent or Advent.

[3] To enable the Borgia ladies sometimes to see their relations in the Monastery of Poor Clares, whose Rule is one of the strictest.

Doña Isabella, married Don Francisco de Sandoval y Rojas,
    Marquess of Denia, Count of Lerina: (from this marriage
    descends the ducal house of Lerina:)
Doña Juana, married Don Juan Enriquez de Almanas, Marquess
    of Alcanices:
Doña Dorotea, nun at the monastery of Poor Clares in Gandia.

Six years the Marquess Don Francisco spent in the
duties of a husband, father, and courtier. In 1536 he
accompanied Caesar Carlos V on a futile vainglorious expedition into Provence. Harassed by the French commander
Montmorency, his vast preparations all nullified, his troops
wasted by disease and discredited by disaster, half his
army *hors de combat* by reason of famine and plague, two
months of inglorious campaigning sufficed for Caesar
Carlos V. The French raised the peasantry against him;
his retreat became a rout; and only a shattered fragment
of his once-magnificent army reached the gates of Milan.
Burning to retrieve his shame in the eyes of Europe, he
launched a second vast expedition against Algiers; only to
encounter a second ignominious disaster. Such were the
Marquess Don Francisco de Borja's experiences of war.

In 1537, died in the monastery of Poor Clares at Gandia,
the Suor Maria Gabriella (Doña Maria de Aragona y
Luna) widow of the murdered Duke of Gandia (bastard
of the Lord Alexander P.P. VI), and grandmother of the
Marquess Don Francisco. The same year, also, death
claimed his brother Don Rodrigo, who had enjoyed the
Cardinal Diaconate of San Niccola *in Carcere Tulliano* only
one year.

In 1539 an event occurred which fundamentally affected
the Marquess Don Francisco. He and his wife the Marchioness Doña Leonor, were lord- and lady-in-waiting to
Caesar's wife, the Empress Doña Isabella. While Caesar
was at Toledo trying to wring a grant of money from the
Cortes of Castile, a sudden illness took the Empress, and
she died. The Marquess and Marchioness of Lombay were

entrusted with the duty of bringing the imperial corpse for burial to Elvira. There, was performed the ceremony of verification. Before the opened coffin, the Marquess Don Francisco was required to swear before the magistracy, that its contents were the mortal relics of the Empress Isabella. Corruption had set in, completely ravaging the dead: the face was like no human face and totally unrecognizable. The Marquess Don Francisco swore, not from recognition, but from knowledge that the coffin had never left his care. But a permanent impression scathed and branded him. He saw Death the Inevitable, the Horrible. Life at its highest and best, such as he himself enjoyed, offered no equivalent to, no consolation for, the end which none escape. He resolved to qualify for life eternal.

Perhaps the most prominent note in the Spanish character is singlemindedness. It can pursue a single aim with a concentration of energy, with a fulness and pertinacity of unwavering will which is simply astounding. Is it kind and noble: the kind nobility of Don Quixote de la Mancha exemplifies Spanish ideal. Is it cruel: the ruthless remorseless impersonal cruelty of Torquemada make worlds to wince. Is it pious: it achieves complete disagreeable detachment of soul from every earthly sentiment, possession, hope, desire. Is it impious: a Spaniard will ravish an abbess of eighty, the corpse of a virginal novice, the statue of Truth. Is it gay: no lark in the sun on the morning of Easter is gayer. Is it gloomy: black moonless night, unstarred, brooding on pools obscure, shadowed by funeral pines, is not more fathomless than the deep depth of gloom veiling sad Spanish eyes. The sight of the dead Empress Isabella drew that veil across the joy of living, for the Marquess Don Francisco. He resolved to abjure the world: he prayed that God would shew the way, and break the bonds that bound him there. He was of the age of nine and twenty years.

When he returned to Toledo, Caesar named him Viceroy of Cataluna and Knight of the Order of Sant' Jago. Entering with zeal on his new duties, he swept away the brigands who made travelling dangerous and obstructed commerce in his province. He found justice hard to come by; and the judges corrupt and venal. He reformed them all. Hospitals for sick and needy, schools and colleges for the education of the young, sprang up under his viceregal rule. A Sixteenth Century Viceroy was responsible, not to press or parliament or self-styled philanthropists; but to one earthly power alone—the Caesar. So long as his province regularly paid its tribute, and gave no trouble to the imperial exchequer, the Viceroy had absolute freedom. He was a despot in all but name. On this account, a Viceroy who laboured for his people's welfare was something of a novelty. The piety of the Marquess Don Francisco grew intenser; he changed his habit; going to Holy Communion once a week instead of once a month. He was trying to detach himself from the world—that despotic Viceroy.

Presently, there came a new kind of religious man, neither monk, nor friar, nor secular priest (to speak strictly), but a priest, one Padre Aretino Aroaz, "of the company of Jesus," he said; and he preached before the Viceroy at Barcelona. From him, the Marquess Don Francisco heard the marvellous history of the marvellous man, the Señor Don Iñigo Lopez de Recalde, of the House of Loyola; who born in 1491, the year before the Borgia Lord Alexander P.P. VI began to rule Christendom from Rome, had followed a career of arms; taken a serious incapacitating wound in 1521; became converted; gone on a pilgrimage to Nuestra Señora, the $M\eta\tau\varrho o\pi\acute{a}\varrho\theta\varepsilon\nu o\varsigma$, of Montserrat, in 1522; lived ten months in an hermitage at Manresa; studied theology in that same city of Barcelona; testified everywhere to his faith in Christ; been imprisoned by the Spanish Inquisition for heresy—six weeks at Alcala, three weeks at Salamanca; studied theology again in Paris from 1528 to 1532; received Holy Order as a priest;

founded a Religion of military priest-knights of Christ; gained the sanction and benison of Christ's Vicar, the Lord Paul P.P. III, for his "Company of Jesus"; [1] and given to the world a book of Spiritual Exercises for the training of the soul in counsels of perfection. All this was of extreme interest and significance to the Marquess Don Francisco. To know more, he entertained a correspondence with this Padre Iñigo de Loyola in Rome.

This same year 1539, the Viceroy's brother Don Enrico had news that the Lord Paul P.P. III deigned to raise him to the Sacred College, as Cardinal-Deacon of San Nereo e Sant' Achilleo, the Title of which previously had been held by Cardinal Francisco de Borja, bastard of the Lord Calixtus P.P. III who died excommunicate in 1511. Setting out for Rome to receive the cardinalitial insignia, Don Enrico reached Viterbo, where he suddenly died in September 1540. His epitaph in the Vatican Basilica shews that no shame was known at this date on account of descent from the invincible Lord Alexander P.P. VI.

"Henricus . Gente . Borgia . natione . Hispanus .
Patria . Valentinus . Alexander . VI. . Pronepos .
Ducis . Gandiae . F . dum . in . maxima . spe . assurgeret .
Immatura . morte . heu . nimium . raptus . est .
Spiritus . in . caelo . corpus . hic . quiescit."

There were now no cardinals of the House of Borgia. In 1543, died the Duke Don Juan II. de Borja, father of the Viceroy Marquess of Lombay, who now succeeded to the Duchy of Gandia, the principalities of Teano and Tricarico, the counties of Chiaramonte, Lauria, and Cerignola. Having obtained Caesar's leave to resign the Viceroyalty of Cataluna, Duke Don Francisco de Borja returned to court, where he was appointed Master of the Household of the Infanta Doña Maria de Portugal. This princess was betrothed to the Infante Don Felipe, son of Caesar Carlos V; and it appeared that worldly ties were

[1] The Bull *Regimini* was not finally sealed till xxvii Sept. 1540.

not to be untied, but tightened for the Duke of Gandia. But
the Portuguese Infanta died before marriage, her household was dispersed; and Duke Don Francisco retired to
his duchy, where he began to make plans for a new college
for the Company of Jesus (which perfectly had charmed
him), and for a new monastery of Dominican nuns in
whom his Duchess Doña Leonor was interested.

.   .   .

The year 1546, in a most signal manner marked the
Duke of Gandia's progress along the road of detachment
from the world.

The Duchess was sick. The Duke was praying for her
recovery. The FIGURE on the Crucifix spoke to him.

What follows here rests on sworn testimony at the subsequent process of canonization, later to be described; a
formal legal process that, from its scope and stringency,
demands as much consideration as the Report of a Royal
Commission, or, better still, a Decision of the Judicial
Committee of the Privy Council, in modern England.

The FIGURE on the Crucifix spoke: " — oyo una voz
sensible, carinosa e distinta, que Christo articulaba desde
aquella estatua muerta." [1]

IT said: "Si tu quieres que te dexe à la Duquesa mas
tempo in esta vida, yo lo dexo en tu mano; pero te aviso
que à ti no te conviene esto." *If thou askest Me to leave
the Duchess longer in this life, I will do so; but I warn thee
that this will not be profitable to thee.*[1]

The Duke of Gandia repeated this to his confessor. He
also told him his reply, which was as follows:

"What is this, O my God? Dost Thou indeed commit to a weak
and trembling hand like mine, a Power which belongs to Thy Divine
Omnipotence? What art Thou, O my Only Good? And what am I,
that Thou should'st desire to do my will; when I was sent into the

[1] *La heroica vida, etc., del grande San Francisco de Borja, by
Cardinal Alvaro Cienfuegos.* Madrid, 1717, III. i. 115.

world for the purpose of doing Thine Alone, and of obeying, not only Every Command, but Every Inspiration of my Rightful Master? What Immeasurable Goodness is This, that, in order to shew favour to a creature, Thou should'st be willing to abrogate Thy Supreme Prerogative as his Creator! Since it is my wish to belong, not to myself, but altogether to Thee, I desire that, not my will, but Thine, should be done. Leave nothing O Lord to the decision of Francisco de Borja. Remember how often his feelings have blinded him and led him astray. Surely I cannot do less in return for Thine Infinite Condescension and Gracious Generosity, than to offer to Thee the lives of my wife and children as well as mine own, and everything, in fact, that I possess in the world. From Thine Hand I have received all: to Thee do I return all: earnestly entreating Thee to dispose of all according to Thy Good Pleasure."

The Duchess died.

It is unnecessary to engage in a disquisition anent the Speaking Crucifix. It is conceivable that He, Who made the ass of Balaam speak, could also make a statue speak. It already has been said that this history deals with matters which, as far as little human knowledge goes—and that is not far—, are out of the course of nature. The affair most rigorously has been investigated, and admitted, by a competent tribunal, whose verdict must be taken as going as near the path of truth as it is possible for a human tribunal to go. Therefore, the item of the Speaking Crucifix, with other items of supernatural manifestation, will be related as they occur, without attempts to explain them away, or to fit them with an adequate apology. If it be granted that they be possible, they at once become extremely probable. The length and elaboration of the Duke of Gandia's reply are considered, by some, as proving it to have been composed after the event, and with due consideration. This conclusion is quite worthy of notice, because it is open to serious and practical objection. The few men, and the many women, who habitually pray to God and to His saints, who are in direct frank frequent and habitual communication with the other world, will be perfectly well aware of the

spontaneous ease with which ideas automatically sort themselves, the formal phrases of the special language automatically flow, from the lips of those whose life is one continual prayer. To these the Duke of Gandia's utterance
presents no difficulty : they recognize a foreign tongue with
which they chance to be acquainted. Also, it is quite permissible to understand those words as not having been
uttered actually, but as clothing the sentiments of the mind
of the Duke of Gandia.

Viewing the affair from a human stand-point, ordinary
men will regard Duke Don Francisco's conduct as abhor-
rent, as heartless, as utterly brutal. It was. Granting the
circumstances, he deliberately sacrificed the life of his
wife. But his conduct was purely superhuman, purely supernatural. He was one of the many Roman Catholics of
the Sixteenth Century—the Twentieth is less prolific—
who really and truly believed *In The Life Of The World
To Come*. His actions prove it. He knew that every man
inevitably must submit to the hideous ordeal of surrender-
ing to God's enemy, Death, as the price of entrance to
eternity. He judged that, the sooner this ordeal was over,
the better it would be. Therefore, confident in the merits
of his Saviour and his wife's, the chance of translation
being offered, he incontinently accepted on her behalf. It
was the act of a truly Christian, of a cruelly unworldly
man. "He wished to be rid of his wife!"

He did wish. Is it wrong to accept the joy of heaven
for one loved, suffering here on earth? "But his wish was
selfish!"

His wish was selfish. The Duke of Gandia gained by
the death of his wife. He gained liberty to tear the flesh
of his gracious body with thongs and scourges. He gained
liberty to abdicate his duchy, his marquessate, his two
principalities, his three counties ; to strip himself of every
farthing of his enormous wealth ; to forsake his home, his
children, his palaces, and his power ; to starve on foul bread

and fouler water; to wear odiously ugly clothes; to do menial service for his natural inferiors; to wheel manure in barrows; worst of all, to herd with vulgar men; to make himself disliked and scorned and hated, literally——: if it be selfish to desire these things, then the Duke of Gandia was a selfish man. "It is impossible to admire him!"

People who say these silly things make the mistake, commit the injustice, are guilty of the absurd inconsistency, of judging the Duke of Gandia by comparing him to their own ideal. He must be regarded as he was; not as he might have been if he had imitated the ideal of some Twentieth-Century plumber, haberdasher, or journalist. It is not necessary to admire him. He never courted admiration; nor imitation either. What he did was personal between himself and his God. He acted up to his lights He obeyed the voice of his conscience. He took for his ideal, that of San Francesco d'Assisi,

NUDUS NUDUM CHRISTUM SEQUENS,

He had the right. The affair was his. And his deeds can be related only: for, to use them to teach a lesson or to point a moral would be like a vain beating of the air. Lessons in this department of knowledge are given by no human instructor; and they are given solely to the hearts of willing learners.

The first hindrance was removed.

A few days after the death of the Duchess, Père Pierre Lefevre of the Company of Jesus arrived at Gandia, by previous arrangement, to lay the foundation stone of the college which the Duke was building for the Jesuits. He brought with him the Book of Spiritual Exercises written by the General Padre Iñigo de Loyola. The Duke of Gandia took advantage of his presence to perform these Spiritual Exercises, consisting of prayers, pious meditations, and rigorous and systematic searchings of the heart.

Feeling profited by this experience, he wrote to the Lord Paul P.P. III, begging Him to pronounce Apostolic Approval of the book. In course of post, (which the Sixteenth Century carried on by means of private couriers,) that is to say in the course of a few months, he received from the Holiness of the Pope a Brief of Recommendation. The Bull of Approval was issued on the thirty-first of July 1548.

This Brief caused him to resolve to join the Company of Jesus; and he wrote his resolution to the General without delay. When the death of his Duchess made him free to renounce the world, he seriously had thought of becoming a Friar Minor. His name Francisco gave him San Francisco d'Assisi, the founder of the Religion of Friars Minor, as his patron-saint: the abject poverty, the singular contempt of the world, the awful austerities of the Franciscans admirably agreed with his habit of mind. He consulted his resident chaplain who himself was a Friar Minor. To this friar, there came a vision of Madonna Mary saying, "Tell the Duke to enter the Company of my Son." To Duke Don Francisco, also, a statue of Madonna Mary spoke the same words. Hence his final resolution.

Padra Ribadaneira of the Company of Jesus, who, afterwards was his confessor, and who wrote the life of the Duke of Gandia and swore before five tribunals of the truth of every word that he had written, says (xv. 238) that, for the next seven days, Duke Don Francisco was afflicted with an apparition of a sumptuous mitre always floating above his head. He had much fear. He knew that, when a person of his quality relinquished a brilliant secular career, an equally brilliant ecclesiastical one lay open to him. This was the very last thing that he desired. He swore to God that, unless the apparition left him, and he should be allowed to practise poverty during his whole life yet to come, he would refuse to don the clerical habit: for he felt the prospect of dignity to be a danger. Then the apparition left him: How exceedingly natural is this example of unconscious cerebration. It would have been strange indeed if the Duke's crushed and bruised humanity had not asserted itself in phantasmal apparitions.

The singular reply of the General of the Company of Jesus shall be given in full. Its curious worldly care for the worldly welfare of worldly people, its wonderful depth of spirituality for him who is spiritually minded, its complete grip of the subject, its polite piety, its discreet judgment, its personal humility, its impersonal dignity, its authoritative decision, its quaint gravity of form, stamp it as the work of a great and powerful mind. Padre Iñigo de Loyola wrote as follows:

"MOST NOBLE LORD:—

"It gave me great delight to hear of the resolution with which God in His Infinite Goodness has inspired you. Since we, who are on earth, are unable to render Him sufficient thanks for the favour which He has been pleased to show to our humble Company, in calling you to join it, I humbly beseech the angels and the saints who are now enjoying His Presence in heaven to supply our deficiency in this respect. I trust that Divine Providence will cause this decision of yours to be the means of effecting much good, not only in regard to your own soul, but to the souls of many others who may be led to follow your example. As for us who are already members of the Company, we shall strive to serve with increased devotion the Gracious Father, who has given us so skilled a labourer to aid in the work of cultivating the tender vine, which He has been pleased to entrust to my care, although I am in every respect unworthy of the office. In the name of the Lord, I therefore receive you at once as our brother, and shall henceforth regard you as such. Most truly can I promise to feel for you, now, and always, an affection proportioned to the large-hearted generosity with which you desire to enter the House of God, there to serve Him more perfectly.

"With reference to your enquiries as to the time and manner of your entrance into the Company, I have laid the matter before God in prayer. It is my opinion that this change must be made with much caution and deliberation, in order that you may not leave any of your immediate duties unfulfilled; otherwise it may not prove to be A.M.D.G. (Ad Maiorem Dei Gloriam—*To The Greater Glory Of God;* the motto of the Company of Jhesus.) You had better keep the affair a secret at present; at least as far as it is possible to do, striving meanwhile so to arrange things as to be free as soon as you can, and at liberty to carry out the plan you so ardently desire to execute for the love of our Lord.

"In order to make myself more plainly understood, I may as well say that, as your daughters are of a marriageable age, I think you ought to endeavour to see them suitably settled. It would be well if you were also to choose a suitable wife for your eldest son, the Marquess of Lombay. In regard to your other sons, it would be better not to leave them dependent upon their elder brother: but to assign to each a suitable and sufficient income of his own; allowing them meanwhile to pursue their university career. It is reasonably to be hoped that, if they fulfill, as I trust and believe they will, the promise of their youth, the Emperor will extend to them the favour he has always shown to you; and will bestow upon them, when the right time comes, appointments in keeping with their rank. You must also try and push on the various buildings you have begun; for I think it desirable that they should all be completed, before the great change you are contemplating is generally made known.

"Meanwhile, you cannot do better, since you are already a proficient in most branches of human learning, than apply yourself to the study of Theology. It is my wish that you should do this with much care and pains; for I should like you to take a doctor's degree in the University of Gandia.

"I cannot conclude without inculcating upon you to take every possible precaution in order to prevent this astonishing piece of news from being prematurely divulged. I feel that I need add no more on this head.

"I shall hope to hear frequently from you; and I will try to give you all the advice and assistance you may need. In the meantime, I shall beseech our Lord to grant you all graces and blessings, in ever-increasing abundance.

That truly is an extraordinary letter. The two men had never met. Only a few letters at long intervals had passed between them; yet there is not the slightest doubt or misunderstanding. The humble priest, readily but not avidly, calmly but not arrogantly accepts the role of mentor to the brilliant duke. He is very glad to get a duke—who will have done with dukedom: but he will allow no looking back when once the hand is put to the plough. The severance must be absolute and irrevocable; and, to this end, Padre Iñigo de Loyola gives an exhibition of plain and practical common sense expressed in terms of courteous and definite command, *It is my wish—I think you ought——*

So during the next four years the Duke of Gandia laboured to carry out the orders of his ecclesiastical superior, removing the only hindrances that bound him to the world. His late wife's sister Doña Juana de Meneses acted as mother to his children. In 1548, he married his heir the Marquess Don Carlos of Lombay, at the age of eighteen years, to Doña Magdalene de Centellas y Cardona, Countess of Oliva. In 1549, he married his daughter Doña Isabella to Don Francisco de Sandoval y Rojas, Marquess of Denia and Count of Lerina. He finished the buildings of the Dominican monastery at Gandia, and of the Jesuit College which is richly endowed with houses for poor scholars, and for children of the Maranas or Jews on condition of baptism. He also obtained charters from the Lord Paul P.P. III and from Caesar Carlos V. raising this college to the rank of an university.

At last, in 1550, he left his duchy of Gandia and journeyed toward Rome, escorted by a retinue of thirty servants, and his second son Don Juan de Borgia of the age of seventeen years. He had to pay the penalty of his extraordinary notoriety. On his passage through Ferrara, the reigning Duke (who himself came of Borgia stock) met him with fêtes and processions. At Florence, Duke Cosmo de' Medici accorded a state-reception. He was going to renounce the world; and the world made a triumphal progress of his going. His desire to slink into the lowest place won him attention verging on adoration. His chagrin was undisguised. He envoyed an avant-courier to ask his superior's leave to enter Rome by night avoiding publicity. Padre Iñigo de Loyola peremptorily refused: for the Duke of Gandia was too good an object-lesson to be thrown away. His entrance into the Eternal City, whose citizens even in 1550 revered the memory of Borgia, was like that of a king who comes into his kingdom. The Lord Paul

P.P. III sent ambassadors to welcome him, and to offer lodging in the Apostolic Palace of the Vatican: but the Duke of Gandia hurried to the Jesuit College; doing obeisance at the feet of the General and Founder of the Company of Jesus. So these two unique personalities first met, whom now men call Saint Ignatius of Loyola, Saint Francis of Borgia.

Padre Iñigo de Loyola immensely admired the Duke of Gandia. This last, whose gracius and brilliant figure caused him to be compared to Apollo and gained for him the nickname The Modern Narcissus, already was known to fame as a ruler and orator born. He was the master of enormous wealth and influence; and his only ambition in life was to strip himself of these and abnegate his will at the command of another. During his sojourn in Rome, he lavished his revenues on the foundation of the Roman College. The honourable title of Founder was offered to him by his own General: but he begged to be excused; and the title afterwards was accepted by the Lord Gregory P.P. XIII, Who named the college The Pontifical Gregorian University of Rome. Meanwhile, he sent a courier to Augsburg, where Caesar Carlos V was, with a letter in which he asked his sovereign's leave to resign all his titles and estates. While he was waiting for the reply, his General obliged him to fulfil all the duties of his ducal rank; whereby he was brought into intimate relations with the Holiness of the Pope and the Curial Cardinals. Even in this august assemblage he won regard. The Pope and the cardinals became so fond of him, that they disliked the notion of allowing so brilliant a man to bury himself in the severe Religion of Padre Iñigo de Loyola. It was a waste of talent, they said: and the Supreme Pontiff proposed instantly to name him cardinal, like his dead brothers Don Rodrigo and Don Enrico.

It did appear to be a waste of talent. But that was a personal account which the Duke of Gandia would have to settle with his Judge. In these specimens of abnormal humanity, interference invariably is fatal, owing to natural forces. It always is the safest and wisest plan, not to hinder, but to help a sane well-meaning man, who is aware of his responsibilities, to do the thing which he wants to do. For human nature is capable of amazing outbreak, violence, and divarication, where it is not free.

After four months in Rome, suddenly, and with no leave-taking, the Duke of Gandia fled to Spain. The prospect of a scarlet hat had become too real, too terrifying. Of course there is not the slightest danger that a man may be made cardinal against his expressed desire. The cardinalate is not an infectious disease like the plague, or scarlet fever; nor is it a sacrament, like baptism, which leaves an ineradicable mark upon the soul. It conceivably is possible that only brutal rudeness and incivility will suffice for its avoidance:—but they will suffice. And it can always be renounced, rare though renunciations be. The Duke of Gandia was a very gracious lord, in full possession of all his faculties, utterly uninfluenced; and, no doubt, he wished to avoid an occasion when his conscience would direct him to be ungracious or uncivil to the benevolence of the Holiness of the Pope. In his flight, he first went to the castle of Loyola, where his General had been born, to thank Heaven for the nativity of that marvellous man: then, onward again, a few miles to the little town of Oñata in Guipuscoa, where there was a house of the Company of Jesus. The Lord Paul P.P. III died in Rome this year 1550: and was succeeded by the Lord Julius P.P. III.

The Duke of Gandia received a Brief from Caesar Carlos V, dated the twelfth of February 1551, giving permission, to divest himself of rank and to renounce the world, with very much regret at losing the allegiance of his most brilliant subject, and solely because Caesar felt that to refuse would be opposition to the Divine Will. He made the formal act of renunciation before a notary at Oñate;

bestowing his duchy, his principalities, and his counties on his heir, the Marquess Don Carlos of Lombay; distributing his estates and wealth among his children. He laid aside his sword, which, according to the fashion of the courtiers of Caesar Carlos V, he rode cock-horse, (so to speak,) as it hung between his legs. He had his hair cut short, and the tonsure shaved on his head. He changed his ducal robes for the shabby ill-fitting black habit of a Jesuit. On Whit Saturday he was ordained priest; and the Duke of Gandia disappeared in Padre Francisco de Borja. In his after life, he never would allow of any allusion to his former style, except when he chanced to hear of the refusal by the Company of Jesus to admit a would-be but unsuitable novice, when he would say, "Now I thank God from the bottom of my heart for having made me a duke; for assuredly there was nothing else about me which could have induced the superiors to accept me": an opinion which shews that Padre Francisco's extremely poor opinion of himself betrayed him into exaggeration—a little human touch which brings him nearer to human understanding.

He said his first mass privately in the chapel of the castle of Loyola, on the first of August 1551, the Festival of St. Peter's Chains; and gave Holy Communion to his second son, Don Juan de Borja, who, having found it hard to leave his father, was losing his young heart to Doña Lorenza Oñaz de Loyola, heiress of the Señor Don Beltrano de Loyola.

Padre Francisco's second mass was a public function. All the people round about persisted in nicknaming him "Lo Santo Duque," *The Holy Duke.* The Lord Julius P.P. III granted a plenary indulgence to all who should assist at this mass, on the usual conditions of confession and communion. To satisfy the multitude the mass was to be said in the city of Vergara: but no church would hold the crowd, and the altar was erected in a field by the hermitage of Santa Ana. It began at nine o'clock in the morning of the fifteenth of November 1551, and continued till three in the afternoon, so overwhelming was the number of communicants. (The ordinary mass lasts half an hour.) The sermon was preached by Padre Francisco in the courtly Castilian dialect: but it is recorded that people of all provinces understood him, even those whose native tongue was Basque. A certain Don Juan de Moschera publicly cursed him; to whom Padre Francisco instantly went, begging pardon for being worth a cursing.

He set up as a hermit in a wooden cell near the Jesuit House at Oñate; and gained fame as a preacher, especially (strange to say) among the learned clergy. Men who take pleasure in approving of others, newcomers, of the same trade, are very rare: but for the clergy to approve of a preacher is rarer. He wrote a manual of Advice to Preachers, which had an unusual vogue. He was very fond of the breviary hymn *Vexilla Regis prodeunt,* (The Royal Banners forward go;) and repeated with delight of soul the stanza,

> *"Arbor decora et fulgida,*
> *Ornata regis purpura:*
> *Electo digno stipite,*
> *Tam Sancta Membra tangere.*

"O Tree of glory, Tree most fair, ordained those Holy limbs to bear;
How bright in purple robe It stood, the purple of a Saviour's Blood."

("Hymns Ancient and Modern.")

He worked miracles. A lady had two splinters of wood; the one was unnotable, the other was a Relique of the True Cross: but which was the Relique was not known. Padre Francisco, to decide, broke them both; from one, Blood dropped upon a piece of paper. An Infanta of Spain put him to a similar test: but in this case the relique was said to be a piece of the skin of St. Bartholomew Apostle (he was flayed alive), with another. Padre Fran-

cisco tore both skins; and again blood dropped from one
on linen. The blood-stained paper and the blood-stained
linen, with both reliques, are in the monastery of Poor
Clares at Madrid. Multitudes came to see the quondam
duke as hermit: they said that they saw a radiant nimbus
lighting the pallor of his brow; and to prevent Padre
Francisco from becoming puffed up, (an excessively unnecessary precaution, one would think,) his superior at
Oñate, Padre Ochiva, set him to hard menial labour, to
dig, saw, carry stones, chop wood, light fires, help in the
kitchen, and wheel barrows of manure. The General, to
whom every detail was reported, sent Padre Francisco to
preach in Portgual, where the Company of Jesus was little
known; and his mission met with great results. With himself he was most severe. All physical beauty was gone
from his once gracious body, macerated in ceaseless austerities. He took the habit of signing his letters *Francisco
Pecador,* "Francis the Sinner": but his sapient General
promptly stopped that practice, saying that Singularity was
not the seed of Sanctity. All letters which came to him
addressed to The Duke of Gandia, he returned, inscribed
Not for me, Francisco S.J.

The Lord Julius P.P. III issued a Brief, offering him a
scarlet hat. He sent a firm refusal in reply. It has been
said that he feared to accept the cardinalate, lest he should
be elected Pope at the next Conclave. The statement is
absurd; because

> (*a*) in theory, the election of the Successor of St.
> Peter is the work of the Holy Spirit; and *ubi
> Spiritus ibi libertas,* where the Spirit is there is
> liberty: not cardinals alone, but humble priests
> as well, or newly tonsured clerks, or any Chris-
> tian male, is eligible:—there is no such absurd
> thing as a restriction on the Right of the Divin-
> ity to choose his Vicar; and Padre Francisco,

He was the first to establish the Jesuit Noviciates: and the Noviciate at Simancas was his favourite. Here are his methods of dealing with novices. A certain novice of noble birth and breeding, but pious all the same, found it intolerable that he should have to wait upon himself with no menial to truss his points, or brush his clothes, or sweep his floor to serve him. Padre Francisco heard his complaint; and, having there another novice, who in the world had been a valet, he ordered him on his obedience to serve his noble brother. The thing was done; and in a little while, the noble novice sensibly took shame at his own singularity, as might have been expected; and dispensed with further service. Another noble novice found his narrow cell and his hebdomadal shirt altogether insupportable. Padre Francisco promptly furnished him with a large room, and a clean shirt every day; and, presently, he grew to hate his privileges, renounced them, and assimilated himself with the rest. Padre Francisco at least believed what already has been said here, viz., that the wise man does not hinder, but helps the sane well-meaning man who is aware of his responsibilities, to do the thing that he desires to do: for, if that thing be undesirable, the doer quickly will find it out, and so convince himself; while the thing undone, the wish unsatisfied, causes the unconvinced to hanker after, to struggle for, and to revolt. Once when Padre Francisco was visiting the College of Sant' Andrea of Valladolid, the resources were at an end; and there was neither food nor money in the house. Natheless, he ordered the bell to be rung as usual for supper though the board was bare; and, in the nick of time, there came to the outer door an old grey-headed man with a huge lovely boy, strangers in the city, who brought baskets of meat and bread and fish and eggs and wine, and a purse of money: whom the pious have called St. Andrew and an Angel.

The year 1555 saw three Popes; the Lord Julius P.P. III, Who died and was succeeded by the Lord Marcellus

P.P. II, Who died and was succeeded by the Lord Paul P.P. IV.

In 1556, Padre Iñigo de Loyola died; and Padre Francisco instantly began to invoke his departed chief,—*Holy Ignatius of Loyola, pray to the Lord our God for me;*— while Pade Jago Laynez was elected General of the Company of Jesus.

In 1558, also died the Holy Roman Emperor Carlos V, who long had given himself to religion. On his death-bed, Imperial Caesar cried for "santo Padre Francisco de Borja" to assist him in his agony. But the Jesuit was unable to arrive except in time to preach the funeral oration. Caesar had shown to the priest the unparalleled respect and honour of naming him executor of his will; an office which the unworldliness of Padre Francisco impelled him to decline. The royal and imperial family, conscious of the κύδος which they would gain by his acceptance, appealed against his decision. The Princess-Regent also invoked the General, who issued a command upon obedience; which Padre Francisco perforce obeyed, carried out the provisions of the will of Caesar Carlos V, taking as little as possible of his own share, to avoid offence. Of course, all he had would go to the funds of his order, his vow of poverty debarring him from personal possessions.

In 1559, he was in Portugal once more, sick of an intermittent fever at Evora. The people of this country, natural enemies of Spain and Spaniards, so loved Padre Francisco that they said he must be a Portuguese. During his sickness, he wiled the weary waiting and cheered his soul by setting music to the anthem *Regina caeli laetare* ("Rejoice, O Queen of Heaven"), and the hundred and seventy-six verses of Psalm cxviii, Vulgate Version, *Beati Immaculati,* (Psalm cxix, Authorized Version, "Blessed are the undefiled in the way.") This year, his sister Doña Juana de Borja y Aragona (Suor Juana de la Cruz,) died In The Odour of Sanctity. She was the first Abbess of the Royal

Monastery of Sandalled (Discalced) Carmelites in Madrid. This year 1559, died the Lord Paul P.P. IV and the Lord Pius P.P. IV succeeded Him. In 1560, Padre Francisco calmed the terrified population of Oporto during a total eclipse of the sun, spontaneously preaching an impassioned sermon on the eclipse, of mortal sin, which veils man's soul from the Sun of Righteousness. Then, again, sickness laid him low; neuralgia, paralysis, ulcers. The vile body was resisting the strain which he made it bear.

Restored to health in 1561, he was summoned to Rome and named Vicar-General of the Company of Jesus. Let it never be forgotten that, while the Borgia Pontiffs paved the way for, Padre Francisco de Borja governed the Jesuits throughout the world while the General Padre Jago de Laynez was present at the Œcumenical of Trent. The connection betwen the House of Borgia and the Tridentine Decrees is of enormous significance. Here, at last, was the General Council for the Reformation of the Holy Roman Church, summoned and legally constituted by lawful authority. For years, self-seeking malcontents, ecclesiastical and royal, had howled for it. Now, it was come: but the German schism was an accomplished fact. The cry had gone through Christendom that Rome was effete, corrupt, on the verge of decay and dissolution. And lo, She arose in Her strength, and cut away the parasitic ulcers that long had blurred with open wounds Her contours; refurbished spiritual arms long rusted; set Her house in order; and was ready again, like a giant refreshed, for Her interminable affray. The Barque of Peter went into dock. The Garden of Souls was weeded. The Council of Trent reformed the Holy Roman Church: and a Borgia, as General's deputy, was ruling the Company of Jesus in all the world.

During four years, Padre Francisco was Vicar-General in Rome. He preached often in the Spanish church of San Giuseppe on Via del Monserrato. The Religion of

Padre Iñigo de Loyola endured one of its numerous phases of attack. In this world, things being as they are, to such an institution a liability to disesteem is inevitable. Persecutors and calumniators arose; and Padre Francisco showed a talent for successful defence. Having completely crushed himself, he could bring to his cause an amount of irresistible force of which the ordinary man, distracted by the whimsy interests of this and that, is altogether unaware.

His behaviour, in one of those cases with which the Holy Roman Church occasionally shocks the world, is quite remarkable. His son Don Alvaro de Borja, who was about the age of twenty-seven years, and Ambassador of Spain in Rome, desired to marry Doña Laniparte de Almansa y Borja, daughter of his own sister Doña Juana, and of the age of about fourteen years. Padre Francisco refused to countenance a marriage between his granddaughter and his son, between uncle and niece: refused to ask the Pope's Holiness for the necessary dispensation. Whereupon, Don Alvaro approached the Lord Pius P.P. IV directly, in his capacity of ambassador, and obtained the dispensation; while the Pope scolded Padre Francisco for his conduct in the matter.

In 1565 Padre Jago Laynez died. Deliberately shutting their ears to his appeals, the Jesuits elected Padre Francisco de Borja Prepositor-General of the Company of Jesus on the second of July. With the single exception of the Roman Pontiff, he now was the most powerful ruler in Christendom, general of an army unrivalled in discipline, utterly reliable, because voluntarily enlisted and morally ruled. Yet he gave no sign of pride or pleasure. He was a perfect Jesuit, humanely sensitive, completely self-distrustful. He said "It is evident that our Lord has condescended to assume the government of this Company since He sees fit to use so deplorably unworthy an instrument." What words could express more sincerely abject and unworldly humility than those?

Aut pati aut mori was his motto. As General, he relaxed not one of the stern rigorous austerities with which he kept under his body and brought it into subjection. Every passion and appetite of his human nature he deliberately killed. He slept little. He ate little. He had freed himself from every earthly love.

What he might have been!

What he was!

A brilliant and gracious duke, master of territories and boundless wealth, father of a noble family allied with the bluest blood of Spain, honoured by his sovereign, reverenced by his equals, loved by his kin, adored by his dependents.

A sinister shadow of a man, racked with continual pain, deliberately apart from all his kind, feared, disliked, distrusted, alone, suffering,—alone.

Every day he systematically meditated during five hours on superhuman things. Every morning and every night, he subjected his conscience to rigorous examination, and confessed even every impulse to evil thought. He prayed without ceasing. Once, when travelling in Spain with Padre Bustamente, the two slept side by side on the bare floor of a loft, because there was no room for them in the inn. Padre Bustamente, being asthmatic, spat all night long, unknowingly, on the face of his companion, who never moved. In the morning light, he was horrified to see what he had done: but Padre Francisco consoled him, saying that in all the world no more suitable place could have been found. He had been very urgent with his sister Doña Juana, Abbess of the Poor Clares at Gandia, that she should persevere in penance and mortification till her life's end. Has there ever been a case of a consistent Roman Catholic who has committed suicide from religious melancholomania? Rarely; if ever: for the Church, wisely recognising that peculiar temperament, has provided a system where voluntary mortification has its places, its rules, and may be practised by whoever will.

Padre Francisco had the gifts of intuition and of clear-seeing, which generally are found developed respectively in women and brute beasts. He knew when a house was about to fall some time before it fell. He knew, on seeing a courier from his eldest son, that an heir was born to the Duke Don Carlos of Gandia. The courier did not relish this intuition, thinking that he deserved reward for his good news: of which disgust, also, Padre Francisco was aware; and gave reward. *The greater the detachment from the world, over worldly things the greater power is gained.* People who saw Padre Francisco during his generalship, saw rays of mysterious light playing round his head. The phenomenon of the electric aura now is well-known; and the camera will show it on occasion. Often, in his trances of prayer, he was seen floating above the ground.

In 1566 the Lord Pius P.P. IV died; and, succeeding Him, the Lord Pius P.P. V. stopped his coronation procession at the Jesuit House in Rome, that He might pay His respects to the holy General. In 1569 Padre Francisco again was stricken with fever. Recovering, he made a pilgrimage to the Holy House of Nazareth, which angels carried over the sea from Palestine and set down at Loreto by Ancona. In 1571 the Pope's Holiness sent an embassage to France and Spain and Portugal, to rouse the sovereigns of Christendom against the Muslim Infidel. The ambassadors were the Papal Nephew, the Lord Michele Bonello, son of Madonna Gardina the Pope's sister, born at Boschi near Alessandria, who at his august Uncle's first creation in 1566 had been named Cardinal-Presbyter of the Title of Santa Maria *sopra Minerva* with the cognomen Alessandrino; and Padre Francisco de Borgia, Prepositor-General of the Company of Jesus. The two left Rome in

1571. In Barcelona, they settled a long-standing dispute between the government and the cathedral chapter; for Padre Francisco was ever a peacemaker. In the province of Cataluna, which was not unmindful of him who had been its viceroy, the ambassadors were received with the highest honour.

The record of this journey, through the scenes of his youthful glory, is one of the most pathetic things in human history. This sinister emaciated phantom shabbily robed in thread-bare black, whose thin lips bit perpetual pain; this great and narrow spirit with eyes tardy and grave, furtively, drowsily, reluctantly, regarding earthly things, having seen the heavenly; this mendicant, whose companion was a prince of the church sumptuous in ermine and vermilion,—he was no stranger in Cataluna, where aforetime as marquess, duke, and imperial viceroy he had exercised despotic and sovereign rule. Now he thought no place low enough, foul enough, for his deserts. He was in, but not of, the world.

At Valencia, his children and his grandchildren knelt to kiss his way-worn feet. They prayed him to visit his duchy of Gandia. He refused. He was no longer of the world.

He preached for the last time in the cathedral of Valencia—Valencia the shrine of the House of Borgia. Here, a century and a half earlier, Canon Alonso de Borja had been raised to the bishopric. The Bishop of Valencia became cardinal. The Cardinal of Valencia became the strenuous Lord Calixtus P.P. III. From Xativa by Valencia sprang Don Rodrigo de Lançol y Borja, Bishop of Valencia, Cardinal of Valencia, the magnificent invincible Lord Alexander P.P. VI. That splendid Don Cesare (detto Borgia) also was Bishop of Valencia and Cardinal, before he renounced the purple for the French duchy of Valentinois. Three huge personalities had borne the name that now was represented by this obscure wan figure whose voice, whose magic pleading fading voice, thrilled in the aisles of Valencia's fane. Here, in Valencia, the fire was kindled; hence, from Valencia, blazed the all-devouring flame; here, in Valencia, the cresset glowed with steady brilliant light, so shining before men that they might see good works, and glorify the Father which is in heaven. Padre Francisco de Borja preached for the last time in the cathedral of Valencia.

In France, the ambassadors met with no success. That miserable country was in the throes of the Huguenot Rebellion; and the Queen-Dowager, Madame Caterina de' Medici, ruled the maniac King. After travelling through France in the winter, gaining converts and confirming the churches, but failing in the object of their journey, the ambassadors reached Turin; and became guests of the Duke of Savoy. Padre Francisco, utterly worn out with exertion and anxiety, his vital forces being on the verge of exhaustion, fell ill on the second of February, Candlemas Day 1572. The exigencies of courtly etiquette bored him to distraction; and he hurried on. Low Sunday found him in Ferrara. Here, having concluded his ambassadorial duties, the last remains of his strength departed. His nephew, the Duke of Ferrara, gave him a royal escort, and a royal litter, as he was too weak to ride, and sent him onward to Rome. During this last journey, it was noticed that, though he lay still, more like a corpse than a man, his characteristic gesture of command remained with him to the very end.

He attained the Flaminian Gate of Rome on the twenty-eighth of September. All the Company of Jesus were there to receive their dying General. He was carried to the Jesuit House, and the last Sacraments of Unction and Viaticum fortified his soul.

On the Festival of St. Michael Archangel, he lay a-dying. The next day his speech departed. His last words, the last words of the sometime gracious and brilliant duke,

the last words of the Jesuit General, were the words of a
simple little Christian child, "I long for Jesus."

He had done with the Latin of the Church. He had
gone back to his mother-tongue, "A Jesus quiero."

On the first of October 1572, he died of a decline, being
of the age of two and sixty years.

.   .   .

Instantly, the pious opinion was entertained that Padre
Francisco de Borja had died in The Odour of Sanctity.

It was found impossible to undress the corpse. Among
others, his brother Don Tommaso de Borja, the Viceroy of
Aragon, made an attempt to perform the last duties, but all
without success. This same Don Tommaso, who afterwards
became Archbishop of Saragossa, wrote a detailed history
of this phenomenon which he calls miraculous. Various
explanations are given of the sudden and complete *rigor
mortis,* which, however, are mystical, not practical ones. It
is said that modesty prevented the disrobing, or that it was
intended to hide the scars of long-practised austerities, or
that the greatest reverence was due to the body which had
been the temple of the Holy Spirit.

His family, and all who in his life had known him,
looked upon Padre Francisco de Borja as a saint : as such,
they privately venerated his fragrant memory, and invoked
the aid of his intercession. No public honours were accorded, for his right to these had not yet been made clear :
but it was alleged that these private invocations produced
marvellous results. Two shall be named. The physicians
attending the Duchess of Uzeda in child-bed found themselves unable to effect delivery owing to congenital mal-
formation. After the invocation of the dead Jesuit, instant
safe and painless delivery took place with perfect health
to mother and child. Queen Doña Margarita, wife of King
Don Felipe III of Spain, endured puerperal fever. The
invocation of Padre Francisco brought a cure. Then, and

with these credentials, the Company of Jesus formally peti-
tioned the Papal Nuncio in Spain, Monsignor Decio Carafa
afterwards Cardinal, to order an enquiry into the virtues
and miracles of the Servant of God, their departed General.
Five tribunals were found at Valencia, Madrid, Barcelona,
Saragossa, and Recanati; multitudes of witnesses were
examined and cross-examined. Padre Ribadaneira, confessor of the deceased, confirmed on oath his book on the
life of Padre Francisco de Borja. From this book, many of
the foregoing facts are taken. In 1615, after thirty-seven
years' labour, the proceedings of the five tribunals in
writing were sent to Rome, where Spain's ambassador presented them to the Lord Paul P.P. V with recommending
letters from King Don Felipe III, the Grandees and Hidal-
gos of Spain, archbishops and bishops, cathedral chapters,
municipalities, and universities.

The Supreme Pontiff was pleased to refer the matter to
the Sacred Congregation of Rites, the Roman tribunal
competent to deal with such a case. Before this court, all
evidence was verified; and a decree was issued attesting
the orthodoxy of the teaching of the Venerable Servant of
God, his sanctity of life, and the authenticity of the alleged
miracles, satisfactorily to have been proved; and granted
permission to proceed to Beatification. The Lord Paul
P.P. V confirmed this decree; and named three Apostolic
Commissioners to carry on the cause in Spain. The proceedings of a Royal Commission are so well understood,
that it merely is necessary to say that the business of an
Apostolic Commission is to search for information, to
hear and weigh evidence, and to compile a report on
a given subject.

Meanwhile, the claims of Spain to possess the remains
of her renowned son were recognized; and on the twenty-
third of February 1617, the body of the Venerable Francisco de Borja, (except an arm retained at the Gesù in

Rome,) was translated to the chapel of the Jesuit House
in Madrid.

In 1623, the eight years' labours of the Aspostolic Commission were concluded; and brought to the usual scrutiny
in Rome. Later, the verdict was given to the effect that the
sanctity and miracles of the Venerable Francisco de Borja
fully had been established; and that, therefore, he was
worthy of Beatification: which decision duly was confirmed by the Lord Gregory P.P. XV.

Thirty-one years later, on the thirty-first of August,
1654, a decree in accord with this decision was issued by
the Sacred Congregation of Rites, and ratified by the Lord
Urban P.P. VIII,[1] Who, on the twenty-fourth of November, published the Bull of Beatification with the Office and
Mass in honour of the Blessed Francisco de Borja for the
Universal Church.

Another seventeen years of public prayers and legal
action passed; and on the eleventh of April 1671, the Lord
Clement P.P. XI solemnly canonized Saint Francisco de
Borja, adding to the Roman Martyrology, which is the
official roll of sanctitude, the three lines, in which the Holy
Roman Catholic Church delivers Her authoritative judgment, and of which the following is a literal translation:
*"Sixth day of the Ides of October. This day, at Rome, is
kept the festival of Saint Francisco of Borja, Repositor-
General of the Company of Jesus, memorable, having abdicated secular things and refused dignities of the Church, by
asperity of life, the gift of prayer.*

In 1680, the reliques of the saint were translated to the
gorgeous church in Madrid which the Duke of Lerma built
A.M.D.G. To the Greater Glory of God, and of his ancestor St. Francisco de Borja. So, a century after his death,
a Borgia was numbered with the Saints.

---

[1] This Pontiff once was asked to give an opinion as to who had
been the greatest Popes. He answered, St. Peter, St. Sylvester,
Alexander VI and Ourself.

Rational human judgment may be glad to stand aside before the sober judgment of the Church, so far removed from bias, from ecstatic extravagance, so calmly judicially personal. She has divined all, and is reticent. She has settled his key. She has struck his note, and is sufficient. She has shewn him in an *Ideal Content*. He "left all"; and for that She honours him: and She has Scriptural Warrant.

"An accomplished courtier, a clever diplomatist, a brilliant and gracious viceroy, a perfect religious.

"A masterful imperious character—in breaking his own will he broke himself.

"A magnified non-natural man.

"Saint Francisco de Borja—Memorable—By asperity of life—By the gift of prayer.

"Memorable.

*   *   *

*   *   *

ASHES

*"A fire, that is kindled, begins with smoke and hissing,
while it lays hold on the faggots; bursts into a roaring
blaze, with raging tongues of flame, devouring all in
reach, spangled with sparks that die; settles into the
steady genial glare, the brilliant light, that men call
fire: burns away to slowly-expiring ashes;—*

FROM the birthday of the Life eternal of St. Francisco de
Borja, the Spanish Branch of the House in his direct
descendants increased and multiplied; intermarried with
the grandest names in Spain; and decreased in importance,
until its extinction in the penultimate decade of the last
century. Four only, of these, need be mentioned here.

Don Gaspard de Borja was a great-grandson of the
Saint, and son of Duke Don Francisco de Gandia by his
wife Doña Juan de Velasco Tovar. He studied at the Com-
plutensian University, becoming a Laureate in Theology
and Dean of the University. He was the first Grandee of
Spain to occupy the Chair of Professor and Public Lec-
turer. At the instance of the Catholic King, he obtained a
Canonry at the Metropolitan Cathedral of Toledo; and here
he began to nourish the enormous ambition of becoming
the third Pope of the House of Borgia.[1]

On the seventeenth of August, 1611, he was named
Cardinal-Presbyter of the Title of Santa Croce *in Gerusa-*

[1] "Card. Zappata ajebat frustra Card. Gasparem Borgia mores
"componere et a natura recedere, ut Pontificatum assequatur. Quan-
"doquidem a multis annis Spiritus Sanctus non spiret in Hispania,
"Cubebat nihilominus fidem adhibere inani, et fatuae predictioni
"bovem tertio murgiturum. Quod assentatores interpretabantur ut
"post Calixtum III et Alexandrum VI, ipse tertius Pontifex renun-
"tiantur, et famiglia Borgia, bovem in scuto ferens." (*Arnidenio, in
"Vite m. s.s. de' Cardinali*)

lemme, being then a youth; "invenis," says Ciacconi; twenty-two years of age, says the exact and uniquely well-informed Moroni. On the fifteenth of May, 1630, he was raised to the Cardinal-Bishopric of Albano, and named Archbishop of Seville. In Rome, he was on the Sacred Congregation of the Holy Office, and ambassador of the Catholic King to the Holy See. In the Kingdom of Naples, he was Viceroy. He bought, (Mr. Henry Harland wittily says that one may buy such things,) the additional title of "Father of the Poor," by distributing annually in charity ten thousand crowns; and he exchanged his archbishop of Seville for that of Toledo. In 1641, he held a diocesan synod over which his Vicar-General presided as his proxy, and governed his archdiocese, while he was cultivating his ambition in Rome. He was an unwilling assistant at the two Conclaves, which elected the Lord Gregory P.P. XV and the Lord Urban P.P. VIII. And in November, 1645, while England was in the throes of the Great Rebellion, he died at Madrid, after fifty-six years of life, and thirty-four of cardinalate, a disappointed man, and was buried in the metropolitan cathedral of Toledo.

.   .   .

Don Francisco de Borja, great-great-grandson of the Saint, son of Duke Don Carlos de Gandia by his wife Doña Maria Ponce de Leon, was born on the twenty-seventh of March, 1659. He was a man of singular and extraordinary piety and learning, Archdeacon of Calatrava and Canon of Toledo. By his proved fidelity he gained the favour of the Catholic King Don Carlos II, who made him Councillor of Aragon. From Rome, he received the bishopric of Calagurita; and (on the fourteenth of November 1699, according to Moroni, or on the twenty-first of June 1700, according to Guarnacci,) the scarlet hat of the cardinalate and the archbishopric of Burgos. He died on

the fourth of April 1702, undistinguishable from other
ecclesiastics of his rank.

.   .   .

Don Carlos de Borja was brother to the foregoing. Born
at Gandia his family's fief on the thirtieth of April 1653
(Moroni), or 1663 (Guarnacci,) he studied theology at
the college of Sant' Ildefonso, and succeeded his brother as
Archdeacon of Calatrava and Canon of Toledo. On the
death of Archbishop Don Pedro de Portocarrero, the Lord
Clement P.P. XI named him Archbishop of Tyre and
Trebizond *in partibus infidelium;* a see held at the present
moment by an Englishman who is the ornament of the
"Black" drawing-rooms of Rome. From Tyre and Trebizond, Archbishop Don Carlos de Borja rose to the Patri-
archate of the Indies, continuing to reside in Spain where
he shewed piety and zeal as chaplain and almoner to the
Catholic King Don Felipe V. On the thirtieth of September, 1720, he was raised to the Sacred College; and in his
capacity of cardinal, hurried to Rome for the Conclave of
1721. There, he found already elected and crowned, the
Lord Innocent P.P. XIII, who named him Cardinal-
Presbyter of the Title of Santa Pudenziana, and placed him
on the Sacred Congregations of The Index of Prohibited
Books, of Indulgences, of Signaturae Gratiae. He died at
the Royal Villa of Sant' Ildefonso near Madrid on the
eighth of August, 1733, and honourably was buried there.
He has left nothing of his personality, save a physically
effete but beautiful gentle generous shadowy visage, in
his portrait painted by Procaccini, and engraved by Rossi
in Guarnacci II. 357-8.

.   .   .

So the Senior Branch, in the line of the direct descendants of the murdered Duke of Gandia, bastard of the Lord
Alexander P.P. VI, withered in sumptuous obscurity ; heap-

ing up secular titles and estates by marriage, heaping up ecclesiastical dignity and preferment by the enchantment of the Borja name added to personal merit, until its final extinction only eighteen years ago. The names and titles of the last of the Spanish Borja, here recorded, will shew what that House had accumulated in a bare four hundred years—three principalities, seven duchies, ten marquessates, sixteen counties, and one viscounty, besides knightly orders and decorations.

His name was

> Don Mariano Tellez-Giron y Beaufort Spontin Pimentel de Quiñones Fernandes de Velasco y Herrera Diego Lopez de Zuñiga Perez de Guzman Sotomayor Mendoza Maza Ladron de Lizana Carroz y Arborea Borja y Centelles Ponce de Leon Benavides Enriquez Toledo Salm-Salm Hurtado de Mendoza y Orozco Silva Gomez de Sandoval y Rojas Pimentel y Osorio Luna Guzman Mendoza Aragon de la Cerda Enriquez Haro y Guzman.

His titles were

> Prince of Squillace,[1] Eboli, Melito;
> Duke of Osuna, Infantado, Benevente, Plasencia, Béjar, Gandia, Arcos de la Frontera, Medina de Rioseco y Lerma:

[1] It would be very interesting to know how and when this title passed from the line of Prince Gioffredo Borgia into the line of his elder brother Don Juan Francisco de Borja the murdered Duke of Gandia; for Prince Gioffredo, married at fourteen, certainly originated a notable branch of Borgia, which, in the Seventeenth Century intermarried with the Orsini Duke of Gravina. It is most unusual for a title *to turn back,* as it were, and vest itself in another branch. And what has become of the principalities of Teano and Tricarico, and the counties of Chiaramonte, Lauria, and Cerignola which were held by the murdered Duke of Gandia, his son Don Juan II, and the son of the last St. Francisco de Borja?

Marquess of Tavara, Santillana, Algecilla, Argüesco, Gibraleon, Zahara, Lombay, Peñafiel, Almenara y Cea;

Count of Benevente, Plasencia, Béjar, Gandia, Arcos de la Frontera, Medina de Rioseco y Lerma, Real de Manzanares, La Oliva, Belaleazar, Ureña, Casares, Melgar, Baiten, Mayorga y Fontenar;

Viscount of La Puebla de Alcocer.

He was Ten Times Grandee of Spain of the First Class, Knight of the Orders of Calatrava, of St. John of Jerusalem, of the Golden Fleece, Knight Grand Cross and Collar of the Orders of Carlos V, of St. Hermenegild, of St. Alexandra Newski, of the Christ of Portugal, of the Crown of Bavaria, of the Legion of Honour, etc., etc., etc.

He died without issue on the second of June 1882.[1]

[1] All from *El Blason de España,* by Don Augusto de Burgos, III. i. 85-95.

BOOK THE FOURTH

A FLICKER FROM THE EMBERS

A fire, that is kindled, begins with smoke and hissing, while it lays hold on the faggots; bursts into a roaring blaze, with raging tongues of flame, devouring all in reach, spangled with sparks that die; settles into the steady genial glare, the brilliant light, that men call fire: burns away to slowly-expiring ashes; save where smouldering embers flicker, and nurse the glow,—

WHILE St. Francisco de Borja was his contemporary in the Spanish Branch, Don Pietro Borgia, (the great-grandson of that Don Pietrogorio Borjia who was the Trusty familiar of Duke Cesare de Valentinois della Romagna and Viceroy of the Abruzzi,) was living in Velletri on the frontier of the Regno, the little Volsican city where his family had been settled since Don Niccolo Borgia was its Regent in 1417. He married Madonna Filomena—*gentildonna molto pia,* is the sweet breath of her, which Archbishop Bonaventura Theuli has preserved for us,[1]—and had three children:

(*a*) The youngest son, Don Polidoro Borgia, died in his youth, the year before St. Francisco de Borgia died General of Jesuits in Rome. His epitaph, in the porch of Santa Maria del Trivito at Velletri, is as follows:

> D. O. M.
> POLIDORO BOR-
> -GIAE INVENI VIR-
> -TUTIBUS ET
> MORIB. ORNAT-
> ISS. FILUMENA

[1] Theuli. *Teatro Istorico di Velletri.* Velletri, 1644, III. 304.

MATER HECTOR
I.V.D. ET HORAT-
IUS BORGIA FR.
B.P . VIX . A . XXII
OB. . A . M.D . LXXJ
DIE XII
OCTOB.[1]

(β) The second son, Don Orazio Borgia, became commander of a squadron of Pontifical Cavalry; and fell gloriously fighting in the Crusade of Hungary, 1597.[2]

(γ) The eldest son, Don Ettore di Pietro Borgia, married Madonna Porzia Landi, who bore him two sons:—The younger, Don Alessandro Borgia became Dean of the Cathedral-chapter of his native city. The elder, Don Camillo Borgia, became Governor of Velletri, married the Noble Madonna Constantia Gallinella, and died in 1645. His epitaph,[3] in the chapel of the Visitation of the Παρθενομητηρ (the patron-saint of the Veliternian Borgia) in the cathedral of San Clemente at Velletri, is as follows:

D. T. V.
CAMILIO BORGIAE NOBILI
VELITERNO
HECTORIS I.C. ET D. PORTIAE LANDAE
FILIO NON MINUS CELEBRI
AVORUM TOGA ET ARMIS INSIGNIUM
CLARITUDINE ILLUSTRI
IN PATRIAE REGIMINE
CONSULI JUDICI ET RECTORI
VIGILANTISSIMO
VITAE CANDORE MORUM SUAVITATE
UBIQ. CLARO OMNIBUS CHARO
ANNO AET. SUAE LV ET MEN. IV
EXTINCTO
DIE XXVI. SEPT. A PARTU VIRGINIS

[1] Theuli, III. 335.
[2] Ricchi, 251.
[3] Theuli, III. 312-3.

M. DC. XLV
ALEXANDER I.V.D. ET HUIUS CATHED.
CANONICORUM DECANUS FRATER
HECTOR I.V.D. EX NOBILI CONSTANTIA
GALLINELLA FILIUS
EXTREMUM AMORIS
MONUMENTUM
MŒSTISS . POSUERE [1]

Don Camillo Borgia left three sons:

- (α) The youngest, Don Giampaolo Borgia, was a canon of Velletri:
- (β) The second, Don Ettore Borgia, was a celebrated Jurisprudent, who held governorships of pontifical cities, and was auditor-general and familiar of Prince Savelli, the Hereditary Marshal of the Holy Roman Church:
- (γ) The eldest, the Noble Don Clemente Erminio Borgia, Roman Patrician, and Governor of Velletri, who married Madonna Cecilia Carboni, by whom he had seven children at the least.

Five of these children of Don Clemente Erminio Borgia have been traced.

They were:

- (α) Madonna Angela Caterina Borgia, who became a nun in a convent of Santa Lucia *in Silice* at Rome, and who died In The Odour Of Sanctity:
- (β) Don Fabrizio Borgia, born 1689, studied ten years with his uncle Canon Giampaolo Borgia, became Bishop of Ferentino in 1729, and died in 1754:

[1] While it indubitably is Christian, this epitaph shews that the modern sophistication, which has destroyed belief in the world to come, already had made its appearance in Italy. Death here is no longer regarded with the calm dignity perceivable in earlier epitaphs, (that of his lineal ancestor Don Pietrogorio Borgia, for example), but as a Horror and an End.

(γ) Don Cesare Borgia, was a Knight Commander of the Order of St. John of Jerusalem of Malta in 1703: [1]

(δ) Don Alessandro Borgia, born 1682, studied with his brother Don Fabrizio under their uncle Canon Giampaolo; won the laurel wreath of the Archgymnasium of Sapienza at Rome; in 1706, was attached to the Secret Nunciature of Monsignor Bussi at Cologne; [2] in 1716, became Bishop of Nocera, and in 1723, Prince-Archbishop of Fermo. [In *Museum Mazzuchelliana* (Tom. II. Tab. CXCIV, p. 382-3) there is an engraving of a medal of this prince-archbishop, which was struck to commemorate the consecration by him of his nephew, (the son of one of his sisters whose name remains to be discovered,) Don Pierpaolo Leonardi, as Prince-Bishop of Ascoli. The obverse of the medal shews three bishops sitting and one kneeling, with the legend A. Borgia Archiep. et Princeps Fermanus P. Paulum Leonardum Ep. et Prin. Ascu-

[1] The Order of Malta, or of St. John of Jerusalem, was founded by Don Gerardo di Martiquez di Provenza, warden of the Hospital of St. John Baptist for Pilgrims, in 1098. The Hospitallers were dedicated to the service of the poor; and wore a black habit, with an eight-pointed Maltese Cross, in white, on the breast. They took vows of poverty, chastity and obedience. The Regular Foundation was delayed till 1104 when Baldwin I was king in Jerusalem. The Rule was that of St. Aurelius Augustine; and the Order was finally confirmed by the Bull of the Lord Paschal P.P. II in 1113. Its Constitution admitted of Knights of Honour and Brothers of Devotion; the former swore to defend the Faith against all enemies, the latter to minister to pilgrims and afflicted. There were two badges, a cross of six points in gold enamelled white, and a crowned cross of eight points of the same, worn on a black riband. The Order had a Priory in London before the Reformation—St. John of Jerusalem in Clerkenwell—whose original gate and crypt may yet be seen. The present soi-disant Order which occupies this Priory has yet to shew authority for its existence.

[2] P. E. Cav. Visconti in Tipaldo.

LAN. INUNGIT. The reverse shews the θεοτόκος in Assumption blessing two churches, with the legend UTRIUSQUE ECCLESIAE PATRONA FIRMI ET ASCULI A.D. M.D.CCLV.] Prince-Archbishop Alessandro Borgia died in 1764.

(ε) the heir Don Stefano Camillo Borgia, of the Supreme Magistracy, who married Madonna Maddalena Gagliardi, and had issue,

(α) Cavaliere Giampaolo Borgia, general in the Pontifical Army:

(β) The Noble Don Stefano Borgia, in whom the embers of the House of Borgia flickered a hundred years ago.

. . .

Don Stefano Borgia was born at Velletri on the third of December, 1731. His early education was conducted in that little Volscian city where his House had been established certainly since 1417, and probably since the Document of Donation of the Lord Lucius P.P. III, 1181–1185. (*Ricchi.*) Later, he went to his uncle the Prince-Archbishop Alessandro Borgia of Fermo, with whom he lived, and under whom he studied, till the latter's death in 1756. The nature of this education can be judged from Don Stefano's after-life in which he cut so noble a figure as ecclesiastic, diplomatist, ruler, scholar, archæologist, man of letters, and Christian gentleman.

At the age of nineteen years, he had written a learned little treatise on the monument of the Lord John P.P. XVI; and a Short History of the ancient city of Tadino in Umbria, with an exact account of the latest researches among its ruins, two octavo volumes published in Rome 1750-1: so that when he arrived in the Eternal City after his uncle's death, he found himself appreciated not only for his illustrious name, but also for the crescent ability of which he had given evidence. Three years later, in 1759,

he was named Governor of the city and duchy of Benevento, the pontifical fief formerly occupied by another
Borgia, the murdered Duke of Gandia. Here he wrote his
Historical Memorials of the Pontifical City of Benevento
from the Eighth to the Eighteenth Century, in three
quarto volumes published in Rome, 1763-9. In 1764 he
was secretary to the Sacred Congregation On Indulgences.
In 1765, at the age of thirty-four years, his hands were
anointed and he received the order of priesthood. In
1770 he was named Secretary *a secretis* to the Sacred Congregation of the Propagation of the Faith. (v. title-page
of his *De Cruce*.)

His career was now well-begun; and he had time to
pursue his favourite occupations of letters and archæology.
Writing under his initials S. B., he published in 1773 his
discovery of a Venetian Kalendar of the Eleventh Century
from a vellum MS., and a Koptic and Latin Fragment of
the Acts of St. Koluthus. In 1774, he published an edition
of the Lord Pius P.P. II's (Enea Silvio) work, *Against
the Turks*. In 1775 the Signor Abbate Stefano Borgia
addressed to the Etruscan Academies of Cortona and
Florence, a duodecimo Philological Dissertation on an
antique gem-intaglio, "la pregiabile vetusta agata—la bella
e rara gemma—Gemma Borgiana—"; which the celebrated
and learned antiquary Martinello, in a letter to Padre
Ignazio della Croce a sandalled Augustinian, calls *most
scholarly and precious*. In 1776 he produced a work in
quarto on the Shrine of St. Peter in the Vatican Basilica.
In 1779 he published a folio on the curious Cross of the
Vatican which is venerated on Good Friday, with the
Syriac Rite of Salutation of the Cross, all most learnedly
set forth and illustrated with notes and commentaries.

He did not forget his House, or his native city of Velletri: for he established there the Borgia Museum of Antiquities, which chiefly was famous for the Mexican Codex
of his presentation, lately found worthy to be produced

in facsimile in Rome with a splendour and importance unapproachable by English publishers.

In 1780, he brought out his quarto on the Ancient Cross of Velletri, "a cross-full of reliques conserved in the cathedral with much decency." (*Theuli II,* 158.) It is a curious and luscious work, which relates the history of the Cross, a fine gold piece encrusted with large single pearls (unionibus) and other gems, from the middle of the Thirteenth Century, when it was given to the Veliternian Cathedral of St. Clement by the Lord Alexander P.P. IV, who, before His election was known as the Lord Rainaldo de' Conti di Segni,[1] Cardinal-Bishop of Ostia and Velletri.[2] The year 1788 saw the issue of a new quarto from his gifted pen, being a Short History of the Temporal Dominion of the Apostolic See in the Two Sicilies; which went into a second edition the following year.

But at this point, the year of the French Revolution, the fortunes of the Abbate Stefano Borgia took a signal turn opening limitless possibilities. The Lord Pius P.P. VI named him Cardinal-Presbyter of the Title of San Clemente, in the Consistory of the thirtieth of March, 1789; and promoted him from the secretariate of Propaganda to the Prefectures of the Sacred Congregation of Index and of the Pontifical Gregorian University of Rome.

The cardinalitial scarlet is the proper setting for this noble personage. The Most Eminent Lord Stefano Cardinal Borgia becomes at once a type of the huge and sumptuous princes of the church, to whom letters and the fine arts lend their glamour. "Quest' Amplissimo Porporato," as his friend and biographer the sandalled Carmelite Fra Pietro Paolino da San Bartolomeo calls him, had the two marks whereby the perfect gentleman and

---

[1] The Sforza-Cesarini, who in the Fifteenth Century intermarried with the Borgia, enjoy the Duchy of Segni at the present day.

[2] Coronelli, Bibl. Univ. II. 870.

scholar universally may be known. He had a pretty taste
for letters, a habit of acquiring rare books and manuscripts; and was himself a writer of extreme distinction.
He had also a passion for collecting beautiful and singular
things, especially engraved gems. The magic of carven
precious stones enchanted him, as camei and intaglii ever
have enchanted men of delicate and powerful mental
mould. The times in which he lived were not convenient
for the cultivation of these exquisite tastes: but it is in no
case desirable that they should be cultivated. They lead
nowhere, neither to heaven, nor to hell. Essentially they
have no relation to the work of life, or death; and it is not
well that they should usurp attention—for there are greater
things. But the possession of these tastes is an imperative
necessity to him who would do those greater things; for
they bring, as nought else brings, the habit of discrimination, of selection, of appreciation; they refine and temper
and grace the steel with which the greater deeds of life,
and death, are done: and, so, their only end is served;
while he who has them in the nature of him, not laboriously
acquired but congenitally possessed, is the better man, the
more capable man, the more enduring, skilful, potent, and
triumphant man, and, correlatively, the happier man.
Cardinal Stefano Borgia, then, having this gentle generous
love for books and precious stones, most naturally became
one of the most distinguished ecclesiastics of his age.

In 1791, he published as a supplement to his Short
History, a learned quarto in Defence of the Temporal
Dominion of the Apostolic See in the Two Sicilies. To
this, he added, in 1793, a treatise on two Koptic saints,
Koluthus and Panesnice, whose original Acts were in his
possession. But it chiefly was as Cardinal of the Curia, as
Protector of Religious, as Ruler and Governor, as Pro-
prefect of Propaganda (to which he was appointed in
1798,) that he manifested his ability and sterling worth.
When the armies of Revolutionary France invaded Italy,

engaging in those extravagant monstrosities of turpitude which habitually disgrace the French toward the close of every century, His Eminence allowed nothing of war or tumult to disturb the serene and strenuous performance of his multifarious offices. In those horrid times, when another or lesser man would have been paralysed, he retired with superb dignity from Rome to Padua, whence he continued to administer and govern not his own estates only, but all the foreign dioceses and missions throughout the world which were subject to Propaganda. And it was here in Padua that he quietly found time to do a beautiful and noble deed, by which alone, had he done nothing else, he would have prepared for himself a more illustrious name.

At this time, the College of Cardinals contained a certain August Personage, an Englishman of paramount importance.

When, in the Revolution of 1688, King James II Stewart had been driven from his kingdom of England by the Prince of Orange, His Majesty took refuge in France. His son Prince James, vulgarly called the Old Pretender, unsuccessfully warred for his rights in 1715; and, on the death of his father, assumed in exile his birthright with the style, James III D.G. of Great Britain, France and Ireland King F.D. King James III had two sons,—observe the admirable insouciant carriage of head on their medals as boys. The elder, Prince Charles Edward, as Prince of Wales, vulgarly called the Young Pretender, advanced his father's claim to the crown of England by force of arms in 1745. The result was the Massacre of Culloden Moor. The younger, Prince Henry Benedict, he Duke of York, was a priest. Hunted from France by Hanoverian diplomacy King James III found refuge in Rome, where, at length, he died; the Prince of Wales succeeding him as King Charles III. Prince Henry Benedict meanwhile rose in ecclesiastical rank through the Cardinal-Bishopric of

Ostia and Velletri (Cardinal Borgia's city), to the Cardinal-Bishopric of Tusculum and the Vicechancellorship of the Holy Roman Church. His medal, by Filippo Cropanesi, dated 1766, shows his royal Stewart profile, still with the admirable high carriage of head, and the legend

HENRICUS M.D. EP. TUSC. CARD. DUX. EBOR S.R.E.V. CANC.

In 1788, his brother, King Charles III, died at Rome; and was buried with his father in the crypt of the Vatican Basilica. As he left no legitimate heirs, his rights in the Majesty of England devolved upon Cardinal Henry Benedict Stewart, who was known as His Royal Highness the Cardinal Duke of York. This Personage combined with transcendent beauty and truly royal demeanour, rare and solid virtue and the exreme of good sense. Nothing could have been more perfectly kingly than his easy and ready realization of his situation. He was aware, as well of his hereditary rights, as of the fact that his subjects, having settled down under an usurping dynasty, had disowned and would disown his claims on their allegiance. He had seen war in his path. He had no insatiable craving for a crown. He arrived at a decision absolutely luminously wise. That the rights of his dynasty should suffer no diminution, by renunciation on his part, he made a technical assertion, of his sovereignty, proclaiming his accession in such a way that the usurpation of his throne by the Elector of Hanover, (vulgarly called George III) should be undisturbed, *except by England's Will*. He caused a medal to be struck, bearing on the obverse His Majesty's effigy in a cardinal's habit with zucchetto and the pectoral-cross of his episcopate,—the kingly head is drooping now—; with the legend:

HENRY THE NINTH, OF GREAT BRITAIN, FRANCE AND IRELAND, KING DEFENDER OF THE FAITH, CARDINAL-BISHOP OF TUSCULUM.

The reverse shows a design of Faith, at whose feet are the cardinalitial hat and kingly crown, and who turns from the Lion to the Cross; with the legend:

NOT BY THE DESIRES OF MEN BUT BY THE WILL OF GOD.

At the same time was struck a touch-piece, for distribution among the few loyal English who had not bowed the knee to Hanoverian Baal, and for curing those afflicted with struma or *king's evil;* an occult power which died with this last Stewart. The obverse bears a design of a frigate with the legend:

HENRY THE NINTH, OF GREAT BRITAIN, FRANCE AND IRELAND, KING, BY THE GRACE OF GOD, DEFENDER OF THE FAITH, CARDINAL-BISHOP OF TUSCULUM.

The reverse shows St. Michael Archangel overcoming the Dragon, with the legend:

TO GOD ALONE BE GLORY.

And that was all,—an enduring record, carven in perennial bronze, that the King's Majesty had come to the inheritance of his ancestors. He believed in his Divine Right, the right implied in his existence, his existence by the Sanction of Him by Whom kings do reign; and he simply affirmed his Right, waiting for his people to recognize him as their lawful sovereign, to do their part as he had done his. Could anything be more superbly, more contemptuously kingly than this distinction of the parts of sovereign and subject? Cardinal-King Henry IX was happy in his lot, for he had a goodly heritage,—in the Holy Roman Church. Had His Majesty desired, the Supreme Pontiff could have released him from his ecclesiastical estate and obligations by a stroke of the pontifical pen, to enable him to prosecute his indubitable right. But he did not so desire. He had chosen the better part—peace—and the happiness of the subjects who were his, but who never would own him as their liege lord and sovereign. No more splendid and disinterested example of self-sacrifice exists in human history than the spectacle of this King of England who scorned to seek to compel unwilling homage. It was indeed the act of a king.

After the technical assumption of sovereignty, His Majesty made no further claim.[1] He did not hesitate to use his regal style on monuments which he erected in his Sub-Urban Diocese, or in similar places: but he was content to be called the Cardinal-Duke of York, as before, though all the world knew him as he really was, and invariably accorded the respect due to him as a prince of the church. There was, however, one notorious exception. The chivalrous nation of France, which formerly had revenged itself on the Lord Alexander P.P. VI by attacking Madonna Giovanna de' Catanei and Madonna Giulia Orsini nata Farnese, was just as ready now to srike at the old and helpless; and it is to the shameful atrocities of France that England owes the noble action of a Borgia in regard to the last of the Royal House of Stewart.

It has been said that Cardinal Stefano Borgia was at Padua in the autumn of 1799 while the regicidal armies of the French Consulate were earning infamy by ravaging the pontifical states. From Padua His Eminence indited a private letter, dated the fourteenth of September, 1799, addresssed to an English baronet, one Sir John Coxe Hippisley, at Grosvenor Street, London, which will tell a tale. The Cardinal wrote as follows, in beautiful Italian with the incorrect spelling of a gentleman born:

[1] By his last will and testament, Cardinal King Henry IX bequeathed his rights in the English Crown to the descendants of Anna Maria d'Orleans, (daughter of Henrietta Stewart, and niece of King Charles I,) who married Duke Vittoramadeo of Savoja; from whom descends—not the Bavarian Princess of the Order of the White Rose, but—King Vittoremanuele III of Italy.

"The friendship with which you honoured me in Rome encourages
"me to lay before you a case worthy of your most mature reflection:
"which is, that, among the other cardinals who have taken refuge
"in Padua, here is also the Cardinal-Duke; and it is greatly afflict-
"ing to me to see so great a Personage, the last descendant of his
"Royal House, reduced to such distressed circumstances, having
"been barbarously stripped by the French of all his property" (dai
"Francesi barbaramente spogliato di tutto;) "and, if they deprived
"him not of life also, it was through the mercy of the Almighty,
"Who protected him in his flight both by sea and land, the miseries
"of which, nevertheless, greatly injured his health, at the advanced
"age of seventy-five; and produced a very grievous sore in one of
"his legs.

"Those who are well-informed of this most worthy Cardinal's
"affairs, have assured me that, since his flight, having left behind
"him his rich and magnificent valuables, which were all sacked and
"plundered both at Rome and Frascati, he has been supported by
"the silver-plate which he had taken with him, and of which he
"began to dispose at Messina; and, I understand, that in order to
"supply his wants during a few months in Venice, he has sold all
"that remained.

"Of the jewels [1] that he possessed, very few remain, as the most
"valuable had been sacrificed in the well-known contributions
"(forced levies would be a juster word than the gentle Cardinal's
"meek contributions) "to the French our destructive plunderers;
"and, with respect to his income, having suffered the loss of forty-
"eight thousand Roman crowns annually by the French Revolution,
"the remainder was lost also by the fall of Rome; namely, the
"yearly sum of ten thousand crowns assigned to him by the Apostolic
"Chamber, and also his particular funds in the Roman Bank.

"The only income which he has left is that of his benefices in
"Spain,[2] which amount to fourteen thousand crowns: but this, as
"it is only payable in paper at present, is greatly reduced by the
"disadvantage of exchange; and even that has remained unpaid for
"more than a year, owing, perhaps, to the interrupted communication
"with that kingdom.

"But here it is necessary that I should add that the Cardinal is
"heavily burdened with the annual sum of four thousand crowns
"for the dowry of the Countess of Albany his sister-in-law; three
"thousand crowns for the mother [1] of his deceased niece; nor
"fifteen hundred for divers annuities of his father and brother: nor

[1] A ring belonging to Cardinal King Henry IX, containing minia-
tures of his father and mother, King James III and Queen Clementina, has found its way into the Fortnum Collection at the Oxford
University Galleries.

[2] "Benefices in Spain," the possession of which is alleged as a
crime in the Lord Alexander P.P. VI, appear to be common enough.

"has he credit to supply the means of acquainting these obligations.

"This picture, nevertheless, which I present to your friendship,
"may well excite the compassion of every one who will reflect
"upon the high birth, the elevated dignity, and the advanced age of
"the Personage whose situation I now sketch in the plain language
"of truth, without resorting to the aid of eloquence. I will only
"entreat you to communicate it to those distinguished persons who
"have influence with your government; persuaded as I am that
"English Magnanimity [2] (*la Magnanimitá Inglese*) will not suffer
"an Illustrious Personage of the same nation to perish in misery.

"But here I pause, not wishing to offend your national delicacy,
"which delights to act from its own generous disposition, rather
"than from the impulse and urgency of others.[3]

"We have here (Padua) not only the Cardinal-Duke, but other
"cardinals, namely, the two Doria, Caprara, and Livizzani; and
"perhaps very soon they will all be here, as it is probable that the
"Conclave will be held in this place; for it has pleased God to
"deliver from all His labours the so eminently unfortunate Lord
"Pius P.P. VI, Who cherished for you the most tender affection,
"and Who was pleased when He was in the Carthusian convent
"(*Certosa*) at Florence to invest me with the charge of the Propre-
"fecture of the Congregation of the Propagation of the Faith.

"My paper fails me, but I shall never fail of being

"Your true friend and servitor (*servitore*)

"STEFANO, CARDINAL BORGIA."

That letter was written in September, 1799. It is not
clear by what route Cardinal Borgia's courier carried it
to England, nor how long was occupied by the journey.
It manifestly is probable that the frightful disorders in
France closed the short road through that country; and the
short road in time of peace was not traversed in less than

---

[1] Miss Clementina Walkinshaw, Countess Alberstorf, the mistress
of King Charles III.

[2] The word *magnanimitá* had undergone a change of meaning
since the Sixteenth Century, when Messor Niccolo Machiavelli
sneered that the Baglioni of Perugia shewed no *magnanimitá*, because they did not garrote the Lord Julius P.P. II, their guest.

[3] Could any hint be more obscurely obvious, more insinuatory of
compliment? Cardinal Borgia's little trick of leaving the initiative (!) to John Bull is a master-stroke of Latin diplomacy, whose
strength is, now, and ever, in the pulling of wires.

three weeks. An English lady [1] who married Don Lorenzo Sforza-Cesarini Duca di Segni, etc., (they were the grandparents of the present Duke Lorenzo,) made the journey with post-horses in the autumn of 1837; and described it in detail to the present writer a few years ago, incidentally mentioning that, between London and Rome, it was necessary to pass in and out of the Pontifical States no less than five times, with the usual custom-house inconveniences. What then would the journey have been in 1799, when France, internally distracted, was inimical to all and sundry, especially to England and England's friends! Further the journey from Vienna to Venice occupied a fortnight, as may be seen from the dates of succeeding letters on a later page. These considerations are necessary to explain the fact that three months elapsed before Cardinal Borgia was able to acknowledge Sir John Coxe Hippisley's reply; for, during those three months, the journey—the long journey—had to be made twice over by the courier, going and returning; which would leave little time for action beween.

It is curious to think that these events occurred only a hundred years ago; and that this intimate view of the private and secret history of the last royal Stewart, and the

---

[1] From the ANNUAL REGISTER, 1837, p. 147. *"xvii Sept. 1837. At the private chapel of the rt. rev. the bishop Griffiths, (Vicar-Apostolic of the London District) Caroline Shirley, only daughter of Robert Sewallis Shirley, Viscount Tamworth, to Don Lorenzo Sforza, Duca Sforza, only son of the late Don Francisco Sforza, Duca Sforza, of Rome."*

(There is a slight inaccuracy in this notice. Duke Lorenzo should be described as *only surviving son* of Don Francisco, not as *only son;* for Don Francisco's elder son, Don Salvatore, died xix May 1832; and Don Francisco's daughter Donna Anna, wife to Don Marino Torlonia, egregiously failed, before the Tribunal of the Ruota, to dispossess her younger brother the aforesaid Don Lorenzo, the legitimate son, born on the night between xvii and xviii of March 1807, to the aforesaid Don Francisco Sforza-Cesarini, by his wife the Duchess Geltruda de' Conti. This hideous law-suit was the excitement of all Rome at the time.)

last illustrious Borgia, should have been suffered to remain obscure. Had there been any disgraceful element in the transaction, concealment could be understood: but contrariwise, the very greatest credit is reflected upon all concerned, on Borgia, on Stewart, on Englishmen, and—to give the devil his due—on the Elector Hanover, vulgarly called George III. The indiscretions, the human weaknesses of the earlier Borgia are the things by which they are remembered:

> "The evil, that men do, lives after them;
> The good is oft interred with their bones."

Here, then, is a good deed of a Borgia, which incontinently shall be translated from its inadequate sepulchre, ostended for the veneration of the faithful, and enshrined anew more worthily. Upon receiving Cardinal Borgia's enchanting letter, Sir John Coxe Hippisley sent to his Eminence a draft for £500, begging him to offer this to the August Personage, "for the exigencies of the moment"; and promising to air the matter in a proper quarter.

The meticulous precautions which invariably are taken to secure the freedom of the Conclave for the election of a Pope, already have been described here. On the death of the Lord Pius P.P. VI alluded to in Cardinal Borgia's letter, when Rome was in the hands of the French and all Italy distracted by foreign occupation, the Sacred College made its way by slow degrees and amid infinite peril to Venice, where it assembled in the convent on the Island of San Giorgio, and enclosed itself in Conclave with all formality. This means, among other things, that no cardinals were allowed to receive or to send out letters, unless these were subjected to a rigorous examination by the Cardinal-Censors; the object of which is to prevent the voting from being influenced by secular and external Powers or considerations.

On the fourth of January, 1800, the said Cardinal-

Censors on the Island of San Giorgio permitted the egress of a letter from Cardinal Borgia to Sir John Coxe Hippisley, acknowledging the receipt of the £500, speaking of the gratitude and satisfaction of the August Personage at knowing what was being done on his behalf. "I find myself shut up here in Conclave for the election of a new pontiff, (says Cardinal Borgia,) with thirty-four cardinals, who, when they heard of the English generosity to their Illustrious Colleague," [1]—and he describes the many kindly complimentary and genuinely admiring sentiments which these Italian Cardinals, in common with Italians of all epochs and of all ranks (excepting cardinals of the Nineteenth Century) [2] always felt and feel for England and the English. The letter is subscribed in the politely respectful third person,

> "Suo servitore cordialissinio ed Amico
> "S. Card. Borgia."

On the twenty-sixth of February 1800 a second letter was allowed to pass out of the Conclave from Cardinal Borgia to Sir John; a short note, in fact, which said that an English gentleman [3] had just been permitted to enter the Conclave, being the bearer of "a very polite letter from Lord Minto" to the August Personage. This "very polite letter" is given in its original form, as well for its own sake, as for an example of the French of English diplomacy a hundred years ago. It is addressed to the Cardinal-Duke of York.

---

[1] "Io qui mi trovo racchiuso in conclave per l'elezione del nuovo pontifice con trenta quatro Cardli, i quali avendo saputa la generositá Inglese verso dell' Illustro loro Collega."

[2] It is too early yet to speak about the twentieth.

[3] It was Mr. Oakley, heir of Sir Charles Oakley Bart., who was entrusted with this confidential and very delicate mission.

"De Vienna, 9 *Feb.* 1800.

"Monseigneur,

"J'ai reçu les Ordres de Sa Majesté le Roi de la Grande Bretagne
"de faire remettre à Votre Eminence la somme de deux mille livres
"Sterling, et d'assurer V.E. qu'en acceptant cette marque de l'interêt
"et de l'estime de S.M. elle lui fera un sensible plaisir. Il m'est en
"même tems ordonné de faire part à V.E. des intentions de SM. de
"lui transmettre une pareille somme de £2000 Sterling au mois de
"Juillet si les circonstances demeuraient telles que V.E. continuât à
"la desirer.

"J'ai donc l'honneure de la prevenir que la somme de £2000 Stg.
"est déposée à la maison de Messieurs Coutts et Cie., Banquiers à
"Londres à la disposition de Votre Eminence. En executant les
"Ordres du Roi mon Maitre, V.E. me rendra la justice de croire
"que je suis infiniment sensible à l'honneur d'être l'organe des senti-
"ments nobles et touchants, qui ont dicté a S.M. la démarche dont
"elle a daigné me charger, et qui lui ont été inspirés d'un coté par
"ses propres vertus, et de l'autre tant par les qualités éminentes de
"la Personne Auguste, qui en est l'object, que par son désir de
"reparer partout où il est possible, les desastres dans lesquels de
"fleau Universel de nos jours a paru vouloir entrainer par préfér-
"ence tout ce qui est le plus digne de Vénération et de Respect.

"Je prie V.E. d'agreer les assurances de mes hommages respec-
"tueux et de la Vénération profonde avec laquelle

"J'ai l'honneur d'être

"De Votre Eminence

"Le très humble et très obeissant Serviteur

"Minto

"*Env. Ex. et Min. Plen. de S.M.B.*
"*à la Cour de Vienne.*

Stripped of polite verbiage this letter conveyed to Cardinal King Henry IX the offer of an annuity of £4,000 for so
long as he might please to need it. It is ungracious to say
with some Scots that, after all, the Elector of Hanover
only offered to the Majesty of England a calf of his own
cow. The situation was fraught with difficulty. The essen-
tials and the accidentals of his birth combined to make
Cardinal Henry Benedict Stewart the only rightful King of
England. He could not help that; any more than any man
can help being the son of his father and mother, born in
lawful wedlock; and King-ship, being of Divine origin,
can only be conferred or transferred or confirmed by the
Divinity acting through His Earthy Vicegerent, the Roman

Pontiff. With these principles to guide him, and the circumstances being as they were, Cardinal Henry grandly decided to be king only in name. His mere existence, however, made the tenure of the occupant of the English Throne to some extent uncertain: for an alien dynasty can never feel entirely comfortable while any of the dispossessed remain. The old order had changed, and had given place to new: but the New could not know that the Old would accept—would condescend to accept—help in its private necessity. It was a most delicate position. On the other hand, it was out of the question that the King's Majesty should make known to Englishmen his desperate plight, for Cardinal Henry was every inch a King. But the good heart and clever pen of Cardinal Stefano Borgia solved that difficulty, by invoking on grounds of private friendship the intervention of Sir John Coxe Hippisley.

The method of relief, when relief was seen to be required, was a task for the wits of diplomacy. When the English choose to change their sovereign dynasties, they at least should secure their nation against the disgrace of seeing, perishing in indigence, one who truly could say *My grandfather formerly wore the Crown, touched for the king's evil on the steps of St. Winifred's Well, and reigned as King in England*. The spectacle of the blind beggar of Constantinople, crying "Date obolum Belisario" is shameful enough for one continent, and can be spared the disgrace of repetition. A pension on the Civil List would have met the needs of the case: but it would have had many disadvantages. It would necessitate publicity; it would have been most disagreeable to the gentle pride of the August Personage whose life and character commanded nothing but respect.

At the present day, one is accustomed to hear members of a certain class of Scot, desirous of shining at least in a reflected light, boasting that their forbears were "out in the '15" or "out in the '45." One does not so often hear an

Englishman congratulating himself on his descent from heroes who endured confiscation, attainder, in the self-same cause—but in 1688. The English resist aggression at the outset; they are used to, are glad to, make sacrifices for, not bargains of, their sovereigns; and, needing no reflected light, they are not good boasters. There is no doubt that a great deal of Scots' flesh was given in 1715 and in 1745 for the House of Stewart. There is no doubt that some Scots' gold was offered on the same account. But one has not heard that the loyal Scots—loyal, as they say, to the Stewarts,—ever attempted to minister to the necessities of their liege Lord, the Cardinal King Henry the Ninth. Ethics, derived from Master John Knox, whose iconoclastic ardour stopped at the "saxpence" and made it the idolatrous object of supreme worship of dulia and hyperdulia and latria, no doubt mitigated the sentiment of loyalty in regard to a king who happened to be a prelatical papist. A national fund, a fund raised by the adherents of the Stewarts, to provide a yearly income for their exiled sovereign, would have been graceful and acceptable. It is the duty of a people to maintain its monarch; and it is not beneath the dignity of monarchy to accept such maintenance offered in loyalty. Peter's Pence is nothing but a fund of yearly offerings instituted by King Ælfred the Great of England for the maintenance of the Sovereign Pontiff. In the case of Cardinal King Henry the Ninth, however, no such guaranteed annuity was forthcoming from the nation of which no inconsiderable part admitted his right to rule. Loyalty to the Stewarts—practical living loyalty—was confined to individuals, few in number; and it became necessary to seek another method of solving the difficulty.

Private munificence, towards the King *de jure,* on the part of—let it be said, for Cardinal Henry himself said it, and none had more right to decide than he—on the part of the King *de facto,* King George the Third, the official representative of the English nation, was the only possible method, which was likely to be agreeable or acceptable. Therefore, an annuity of £4,000 was offered, not from the Civil List, not from the Nation, but from the Privy Purse, from King George to Cardinal Henry—from one English Gentleman to another. The delicate tact and straightforwardness with which the Envoy Extraordinary and Minister Plenipotentiary of His Britannic Majesty at the Court of Vienna made the offer; the complimentary terms of his letter to the "August Personage;" his guarded denunciation of the French robbers of the Cardinal as "the Universal Plague of our time which "seems to design the destruction of all that is most worthy "of Veneration and Respect;" his proffered homage;—all these qualities egregiously deserved Cardinal Stefano Borgia's epithet "very polite," and made the proposal one which honourably and gratefully could be accepted. At least the Cardinal-Duke of York was pleased to think so, as the two letters following here will shew. It may be observed that they are written in incoherent and peculiar English. Let it be remembered that they were written by a very old gentleman, under circumstance of extreme agitation; in a language of appalling difficulty which, though his native tongue, was altogether strange to him; for he had not lived in England, and, in his life-long exile, he used nothing but Latin with his clergy or Italian with his friends.

He wrote from the Conclave on the Island of San Giorgio on the twenty-sixth of February, 1800; and the letters are sealed with the Royal Arms of England and France surmounted with the Cardinalitial Hat instead of the Crown.

(I. To Lord Minto.)

"With the arrival of Mr. Oakley who has been this morning with "Me, I have received by his discourse, and much more by your

"letters, so many Tokens of your regard, singular consideration, and
"attention for My Person, that oblige Me to abandon all sort of
"ceremony, and to begin abruptly to assure you My dear lord, that
"your letters have been most acceptable to Me in all shapes and
"regards. I did not in the least doubt of the noble way of thinking of
"your generous and beneficent Sovereign; but I did not expect to see
"in writing so many and so obliging expressions that well calculated
"by the Persons who receive them and understand their force, im-
"pressed in their minds a lively sense of tenderness and gratitude
"which, I own to you, obliges me more than the generosity spon-
"taneously imparted.

"I am in reality at a loss to express in writing all the sentiments
"of My Heart, and for that reason leave it entirely to the interest
"you take in all that regards My Person to make known in an
"energetical and convenient manner all I fain would say to express
"My thankfulness which may easily be by you comprehended after
"having perused the contents of this letter.

"I am much obliged to you to have indicated to Me the way I
"may write unto Coutts the Court Banker, and shall follow your
"friendly insinuations. In the meantime I am very desirous that you
"should be convinced of My sentiments of sincere esteem and
"friendship with which My dear lord with all My heart I embrace
"you.

"HENRY CARDINAL."

(II. To Sir John Coxe Hippisley.)

"Your letters fully convince me of the cordial interest you take
"in all that regards My Person, and am happy to acknowledge that
"principally I owe to your friendly efforts, and to them of your
"friends, the succour generously granted to relieve the extreme
"necessities into which I have been driven by the present dismal
"circumstances. I cannot sufficiently express how sensible I am to
"your good heart: and write these few lines in the first place to
"contest to you these My most sincere and grateful sentiments and
"then to inform you by means of Mr. Oakley an English Gent^n
"arrived here last week, I have received a letter from Lord Minto
"from Vienna, advising Me that he had orders from his Court to
"remit to Me the sum of £2000 Sterling, and that in the month of
"July I may again draw, if I desire it, for another equal sum. The
"letter is written in so extremely obliging and genteel a manner,
"and with expressions of singular regard and consideration for Me,
"that, I assure you, excited in Me most particular and lively senti-
"ments, not only of satisfaction for the delicacy with which the
"affair has been managed, but also of gratitude for the generosity
"with which has been provided for my necessity.

"I have answered Lord Minto's letter, and gave it saturday last to

"Mr. Oakley who was to send it by that evening's post" (the am-
"bassadorial courier) "to Vienna, and have written in a manner that
"I hope will be to his lordship's satisfaction. I own to you that the
"succour granted to Me could not be more timely, for, without it,
"it would have been impossible for Me to subsist on account of the
"absolutely irreparable loss of all My income, the very funds being
"also destroyed; so that I would otherwise have been reduced during
"the short remainder of My life to languish in misery and indigence.
"I would not loose a moment's time to apprize you of all this, and
"am very certain that your experimented good heart will find proper
"means to make known in an energical and proper manner, these
"sentiments of My grateful acknowledgment.
"Your best of friends,

"HENRY CARDINAL.

Of the remaining history of H.R.H. The Cardinal-Duke
of York it is not necessary to speak here. He died in 1807,
and was honourably buried in the Vatican Basilica with
his father and his brother, in a tomb which bears their
names and styles, James III, Charles III, Henry IX, last
of the Royal House of Stewart, three kings "who paid
three crowns for a mass," who sacrificed the crowns of
Great Britain, France, and Ireland, rather than their religious convictions. May they rest in peace.[1]

.   .   .

[1] It should be said that loyalty to the Stewarts, as it has been here
entreated of, implies no shadow of disloyalty to the present Royal
House of England. The law of Prescriptive Right by itself would
be sufficient to require the most dutiful allegiance on the part of
all the subjects of Her Most Sacred Majesty the late Queen-
Empress. But it may be said further, that, as far as Roman Catholics
are concerned, the most ingeniously scrupulous conscience can have
no possible doubt about its obligation, since the Lord Leo P.P. XIII
accorded that formal Recognition of the late Queen's Majesty as
Queen by the presence of an Apostolic Ablegate at the Jubilee of
1887. In the course of this book the immense importance which
sovereigns of the Borgian Era attached to this Recognition has been
shewn. They were ready to fight for it, knowing that without it they
could not hope to stand. In the present instance it was not even
asked for; and its spontaneous granting by the Roman Pontiff
should emphasize the fact that, what formerly might have been a
matter for discussion, is now an imperative religious duty, namely,
undeviating loyalty to the Royal and Imperial Dynasty of Queen
Victoria.

The action of Cardinal Stefano Borgia which just has been described, was not the only evidence of nobility of soul that he exhibited during the long Conclave of 1799–1800. He did, or rather he did not do, another deed; the neglect of which suffices to win him high renown.

It already has been manifested here, that the tide of human ambition runs at its highest in the Conclave for the election of a Pope. At different periods of history, the papacy has been regarded as an appanage of the empire, or of the great Italian baronies, Crescenzi, Colonna, Orsini, Savelli, Medici. The House of Borgia, not without reason of a kind, desired to rank with these; and cardinals of that House complacently expected election. There already had been two Borgia Popes, the strenuous Lord Calixtus P.P. III. and the invincible Lord Alexander P.P. VI. The great-grandson of St. Francisco de Borja, Cardinal Don Gaspero, publicly hoped to be the third, and was disappointed. Now, in the last year of the Eighteenth Century, was enclosed in another Conclave another Borgia Cardinal, the noble Cardinal Stefano, and it confidently was expected that he would emerge therefrom not Stefano, but PETER, crowned with the Triregno, the pontifical diadem made of feathers of white peacocks encircled with three crowns of gold.

Humanly speaking his chance of election was not chance but certainty. He was admitted on all hands to be *facile Princeps* of the Sacred College. His learning, his dominant power, his simple piety, his universally sympathetic personality, assured him of an unanimous majority, had he chosen to enter the ranks of the cardinals-competitors, that is to say of the cardinals who were eligible and also willing.

When a man is aware of his own ability to do certain legitimate and beneficent deeds, the world is wont to call him fool as well as knave when he neglects to seek the situation, the opportunity, for exercising his peculiar talent.

In this matter, the world is not ill-advised. Then, if an ecclesiastic is convinced that, in a certain position of authority, he can do God-service, why should he be deterred from seeking that position by craven terror of the inevitable scowls, rodomontades, and lampoons of envious incompetent venal mediocrity? The Lord Pius P.P. II was not afraid. He knew His own powers. He was convinced of the purity of His intentions; and, as Cardinal Enea Silvio Bartolomeo de' Piccolhuomini, he met the schemes of Cardinal Guillaume d'Estoutville in the Conclave of 1458 with counter-schemes, and accomplished His Own elevation to the pontifical throne. There is another and more intimate example, nearer home, and no later than the last century: the example of a provost of a metropolitan cathedral chapter, who knew his power, who knew the lawfully designated successor of the archbishop to be unfitted for the responsibilities of office, who kept an agent at the Vatican to urge his candidature when the see was vacant, until the Lord Pius P.P. IX, declaring it to be *un colpo-di-stato di Domeniddio,* transformed the convert-provost into Westminster's Archbishop. It cannot be alleged that Cardinal Henry Edward Manning became inglorious by giving practical evidence of his contempt for the ridiculous and wicked doctrine which is preached by vicious degenerates, that *the Almighty intends much of His Good Work to be wasted.* It cannot be alleged that Cardinal Manning was actuated by personal arrogance, or by desire for personal aggrandisement. His whole life of saint-like self-sacrifice, of intensest humility, of ascetic mortification, of ceaseless toil for the spiritual and temporal welfare of all men without distinction of creed, has proved the contrary. By the same token, on this score, there would have been no stain on the noble character of Cardinal Stefano Borgia had he desired to exert himself to compass his own election to the Throne of Peter.

But he did not so desire. Indeed, he shewed himself

unwilling to be elected; and the Sacred College made choice of the next Most Eminent Lord, the Benedictine Cardinal Gregorio Luigi Barnabo Chiaramonte, whose accession was proclaimed under the name of the Lord Pius P.P. VII. So Christendom still lacks the third Borgia Pontiff,—a lack unlikely soon to be made good; seeing that, since Cardinal Stefano, no Borgia wears the scarlet hat; yet by no means irremediable, seeing that the House of Borgia is living, and not dead.

Little remains to be written of the last pre-eminent Borgia. On the death of Cardinal Gerdil, Cardinal Stefano was promoted from the Proprefecture to the Prefecture of Propaganda Fide.

In 1804, while attending the debile Lord Pius P.P. VII to Paris, (whither His Holiness had been summoned for the coronation as emperor of the Corsican upstart Consul Napoleon Buonaparte, Cardinal Stefano Borgia died, at the age of seventy-three years, on the Festival of St. Clement the twenty-third of November, at Lyons, and was buried there in the cathedral. It is worth noting that he had been baptized in the cathedral of St. Clement at Velletri in December 1731; that he derived his cardinalitial Title from the church of St. Clement in Rome; and that on the Festival of St. Clement 1804, he died. His friend, Fra Pietro Paolino da San Bartolomeo, a sandalled Carmelite, wrote his biography. The celebrated Cancellieri composed his elegy, which has been republished by Bodoni. The Borgia Museum of Antiquities which he established in Velletri, and whose elaborate catalogue is the work of his uncle Don Filippaurelio Visconti, in chief part is in the Royal Museum of Naples; the College of Propaganda has the lesser part, and also his splendid library.

.   .   .

The House of Borgia continues to flourish in the descendants of Cardinal Stefano's brother, the CAVALIERE

GIAMPAOLO BORGIA OF VELLETRI, a general in the pontifical army; who married the representative of two of the most important houses of the Romagna, often mentioned in these pages as having been subdued by the splendid Duke Cesare (detto Borgia) di Valentinois della Romagna, in the campaigns of 1499 and 1501-2,—the Countess Alcmena [1] Baglioni-Malatesta of Perugia. Eighteen children were the issue of this marriage. The names of five have been recovered at the date of writing, viz., the eldest, Cavaliere Camillo; Don Clemente; Don Alessandro; Don Cesare; and the youngest Don Francesco.

> (a) THE CAVALIERE CAMILLO BORGIA, born 1777, was Adjutant-General and Field-Marshal under King Joachim Murat of Naples; Aulic-Counselor and Chargé d'affaires of the King of Denmark in Rome; Knight of the Legion of Honour,[2] and of the Order of the Two Sicilies.[3] Distinguished in arms by his military talent, he was not less renowned in the kingdom of Letters. After his retirement from the army, he travelled much in Northern Africa to study Lain antiquities. At least one of his works has achieved fame —the *Plantisfero Borgiano*. He married Mdlle. Adelaide Quaison, (who died in 1865); and he died in 1817, leaving issue

[1] 'Αλκμήνη. It is curious to note the survival of Greek names in the ancient families of Etruria.

[2] The Legion of Honour is a French Order founded during the Consulate of Napoleon Buonaparte, 20 Fiorile, An. x: ratified by the Christian King Louis XVIII on VI July, 1814. It is governed by a Grand Master who is the Emperor, King, or President of France according to the fashion. It contains five classes. The Knights and Officers wear silver crosses. The Commanders, Grand Officers and Grand Crosses wear the decoration in gold. The motto is HONNEUR ET PATRIE. (*Tettoni e Saladini. Teatro Araldico.*)

[3] The Order of the Two Sicilies were founded by Joseph Buonaparte, XXIV Feb. 1808, to recompense loyalty, courage, and long service. (*Tettoni e Saladini. Teatro Araldico.*)

Don ETTORE BORGIA, born at Velletri in 1802, a Roman Patrician, Knight of Honour and Devotion of the Order of St. John of Jerusalem of Malta, Knight-Commander of the Order of St. Gregory the Great, Gonfalonier of Velletri, National Representative of Velletri in the Roman Parliament of 1848, and Provisional Governour of Velletri in 1871. He departed this life, in 1892, at Melazzo in Sicily, being of the age of ninety years; and his death without issue extinguished the Veliternian Branch of the House of Borgia.

(β) Don CLEMENTE BORGIA OF ROME, who married Donna Luisa Calderoni, and died in 1852, leaving issue,

(α) Don Adriano, who died unmarried:

(β) Don Tito, who died unmarried:

(γ) Don Costantino, a prelate, (author of *De Cathedra Romana Sancti Petri Principus Apostolorum Oratio,* etc. a quarto published at Rome in 1845;) died unmarried in 1878:

(δ) Don AUGUSTO, a prelate, born 1820. His death, on the second of September 1900, without issue, extinguished the Roman Branch of the House of Borgia.

(γ) Don ALESSANDRO BORGIA, born 1788, Balì of the Order of St. John of Jerusalem of Malta, died 1872.

[1] The Order of St. Gregory the Great was founded by the Lord Gregory P.P. XVI for Merit, Civil and Military, I Sept. 1831. There are four classes, viz. First, and Second Grand Cross, Commanders, and Knights. The obverse of the octagonal silver medal bears an eight-pointed cross in red enamel, with a shield in pretence shewing an effigy of the Lord St. Gregory P.P. I the Great (the Pope who sent St. Augustine to convert the English, A.D. 596) The reverse bears the legend, PRO DEO ET PRINCIPE GREGORIUS XVI P.M. ANNO I. (*Tettoni e Saladini. Teatro Araldico.*)

(δ) Don Cesare Borgia, was a Knight-Commander of the Order of St. John of Jerusalem of Malta; and followed the profession of a man of letters in Ferrara, (the city of which his kinswoman, Madonna Lucrezia, formerly had been the sovereign duchess,) until his death in 1861.

(Here should be inserted the names of thirteen children of the Cavaliere Giampaolo Borgia and his wife the Countess Alcmena Baglioni-Malatesta of Perugia, which, at present are not accessible. The eighteenth and youngest son of the said Cavaliere Giampaolo was,)

(ε) The Noble Francesco Borgia, born 1794; Knight of Honour and Devotion, and Hereditary Commandant of the Order of St. John of Jerusalem of Malta; Knight of the Order of the Lily of France [1]; Knight of the Order of the two Sicilies; Patrician of Rome: who married the Noble Luigia Ferrari di Cremona, Dowager-Countess Cassera (died 1855); and established the House of Borgia in Milan on his marriage with a Milanese lady in 1822. He died in 1861 leaving issue,

(a) The Noble Alcmena, married to the Marquess Paolo Litta-Modignani of Milan:

(β) The Noble Cesare Borgia, *(the present Head of the Illustrious House of Borgia)*; Knight of Honour and Devotion

[1] On the second of April 1814, M. le Comte d'Artois permitted the National Guard of Paris to wear a silver Fleurdelys suspended from a white watered riband, in recognition of service. On the twenty-sixth of April, a Star was substituted for the Fleurdelys, and a blue border added to the white riband. The Decoration was called the Order of the Lily of France, and all *decorés* made to swear an oath of fidelity to God, and of obedience to the King. (*Tettoni e Saladini. Teatro Araldico.*)

and Hereditary Commandant of the
Order of St. John of Jerusalem of
Malta; Patrician of Rome, (which patriciate gives its holder the right to the
title of Count;) born at Milan on the
twenty-seventh of January 1830; married in 1856 Donna Clementina Taran-
tola (who died in 1884) and has issue,

(a) DON FRANCESCO BORGIA, born in
1863; married in 1885 the Marchioness Eugenia Litta-Modignani
di Menzago e Vinago, Patrician of
Milan; and has issue,

(α) DON CESARE BORGIA, born
1886:

(β) DON ALESSANDRO BORGIA,
born 1898:

AD MULTOS ANNOS

.   •   •

"A fire, that is kindled, begins with smoke and hissing,
"while it lays hold on the faggots; bursts into a roaring
"blaze, with raging tongues of flame, devouring all in
"reach, spangled with sparks that die; settles into the
"steady genial glare, the brilliant light, that men call fire;
"burns away to slowly-expiring ashes; save where smoul-
"dering embers flicker, and nurse the glow, until propitious
"breezes blow it into life again."